EDENSZERO

10

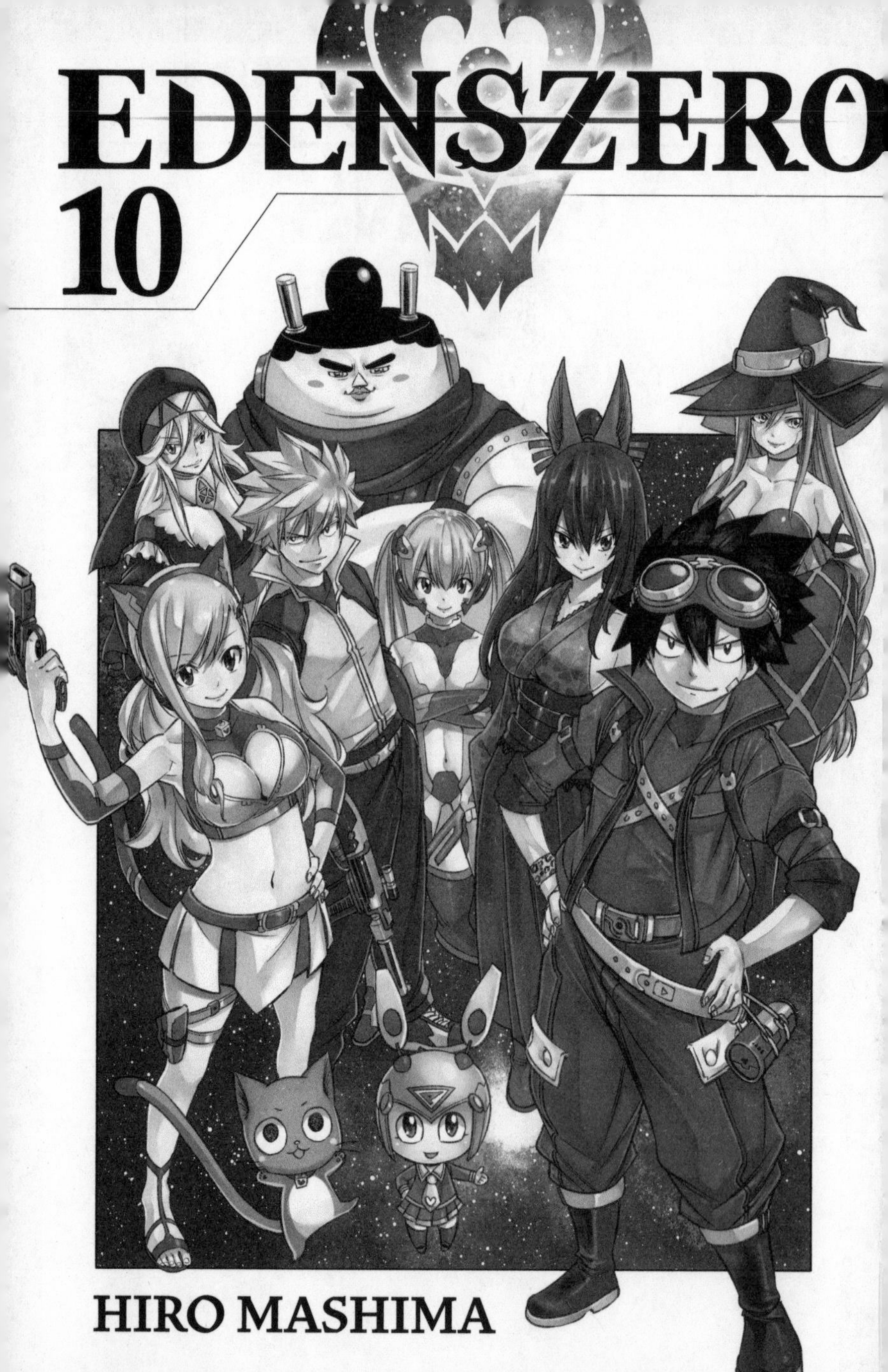

HIRO MASHIMA

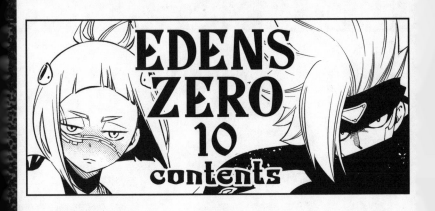

EDENS ZERO 10
contents

EDENSZERO

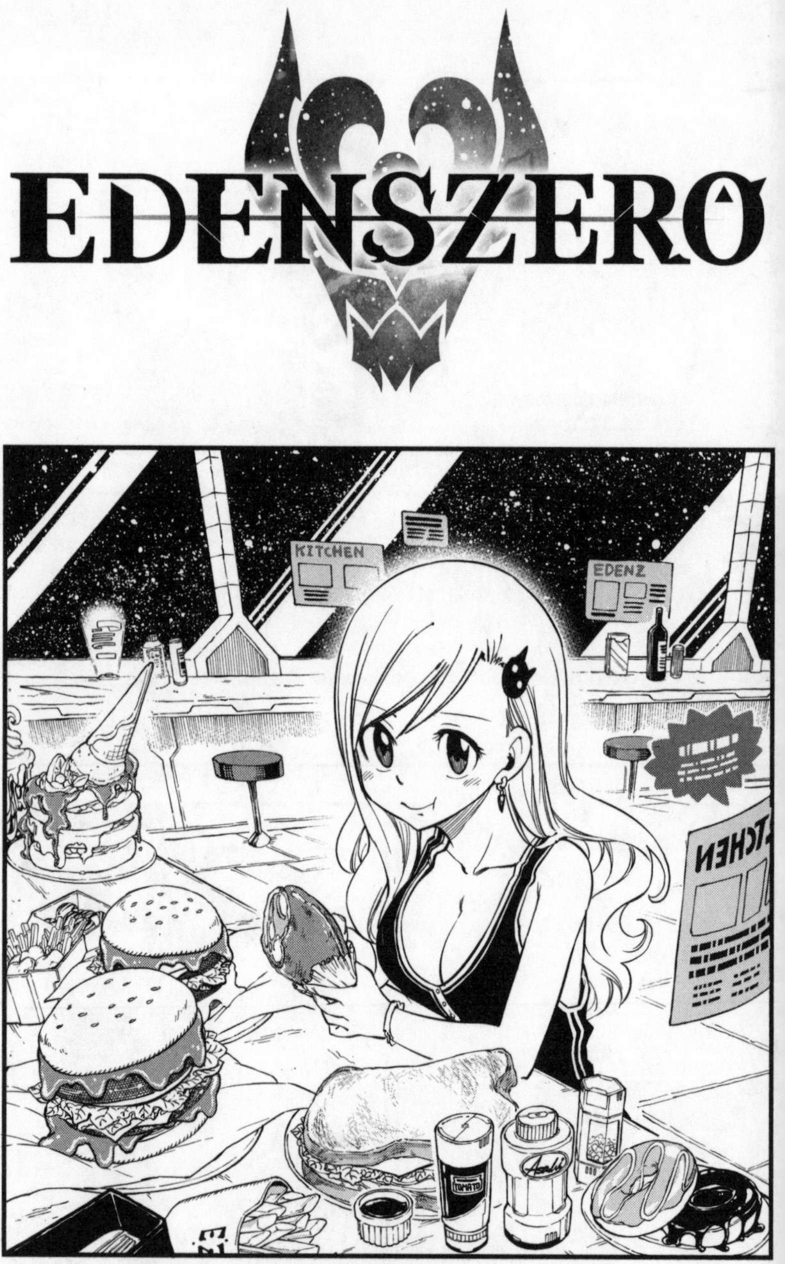
KITCHEN
EDENZ
TOMATO

CHAPTER 78: NO.29

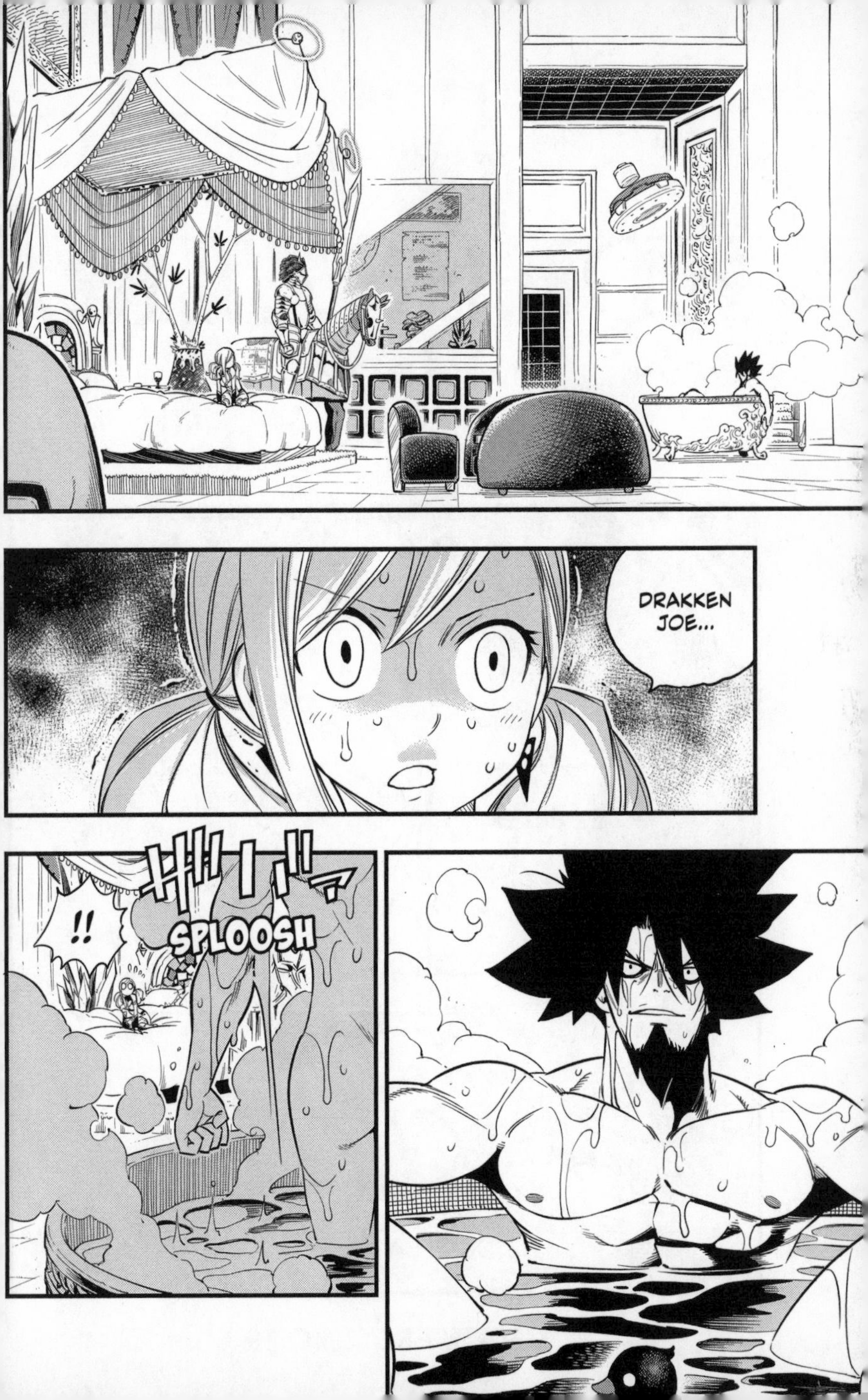
DRAKKEN JOE...
!!
SPLOOSH

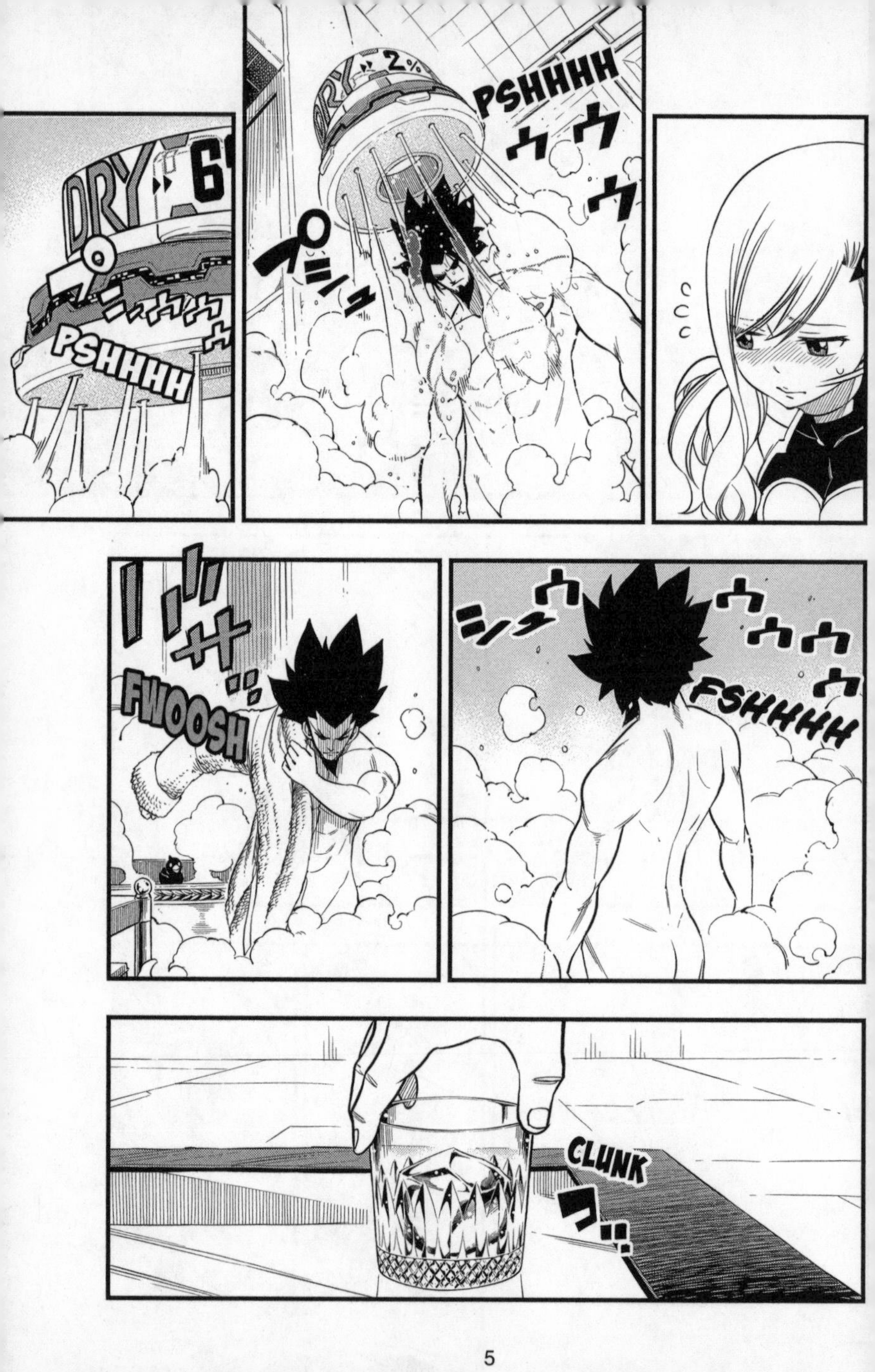
DRY 2%
PSHHHH
DRY
PSHHHH
FSHHHH
FWOOSH
CLUNK

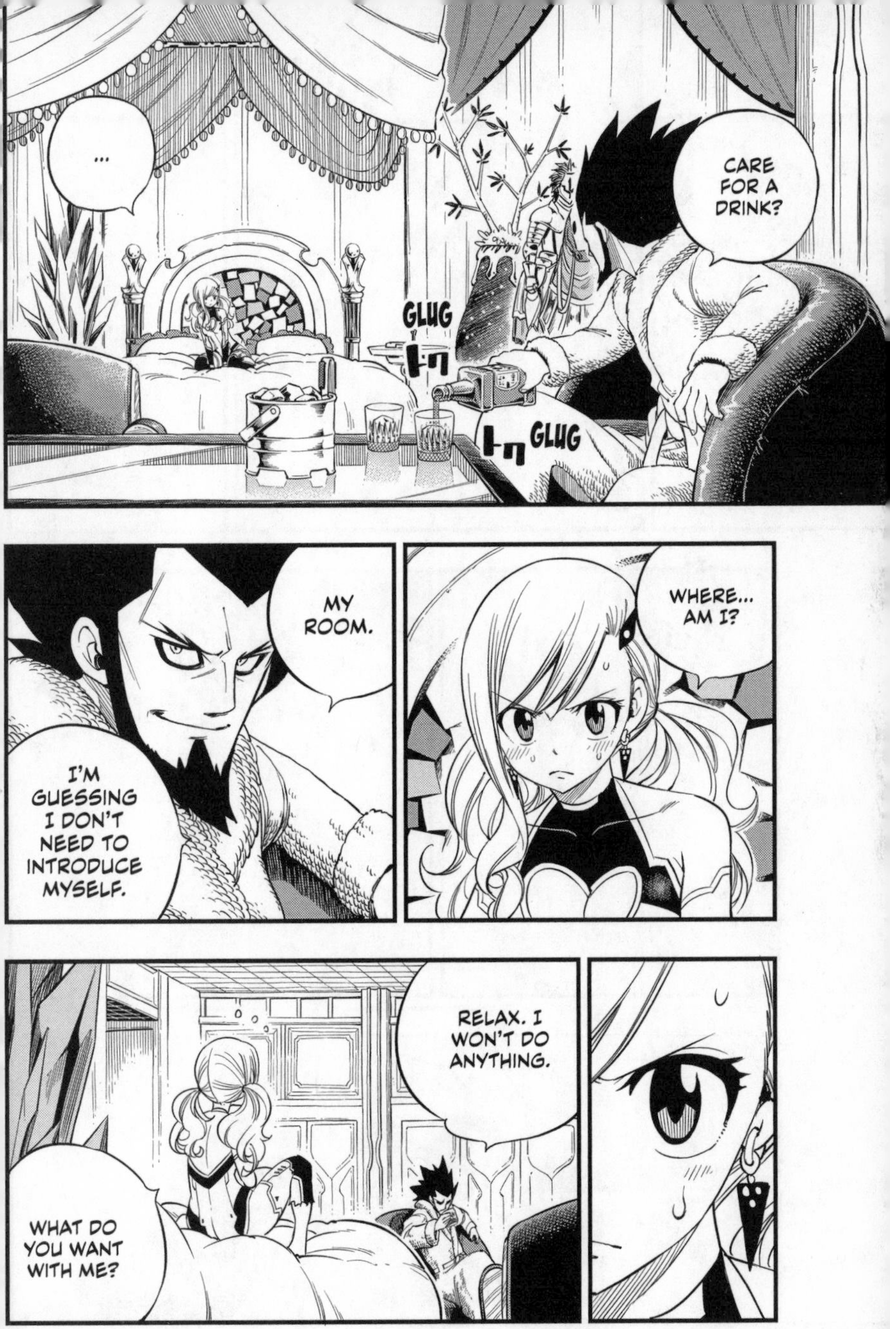
CARE FOR A DRINK?
...
GLUG
トク
トク GLUG
WHERE... AM I?
MY ROOM.
I'M GUESSING I DON'T NEED TO INTRODUCE MYSELF.
RELAX. I WON'T DO ANYTHING.
WHAT DO YOU WANT WITH ME?

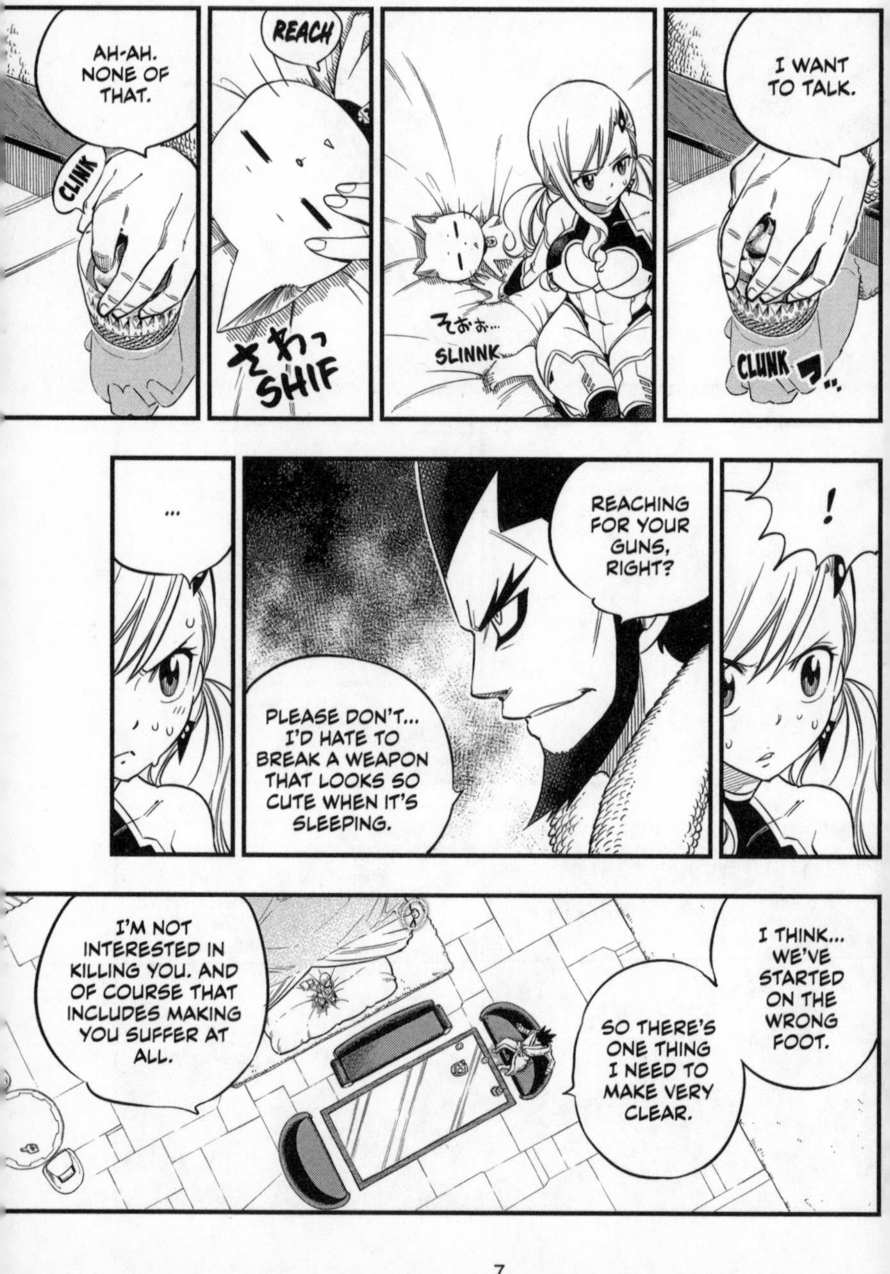
I WANT TO TALK.
CLUNK
そぉぉ…
SLINNK
REACH
さわっ
SHIF
AH-AH. NONE OF THAT.
CLINK
!
REACHING FOR YOUR GUNS, RIGHT?
PLEASE DON'T... I'D HATE TO BREAK A WEAPON THAT LOOKS SO CUTE WHEN IT'S SLEEPING.
...
I THINK... WE'VE STARTED ON THE WRONG FOOT.
SO THERE'S ONE THING I NEED TO MAKE VERY CLEAR.
I'M NOT INTERESTED IN KILLING YOU. AND OF COURSE THAT INCLUDES MAKING YOU SUFFER AT ALL.

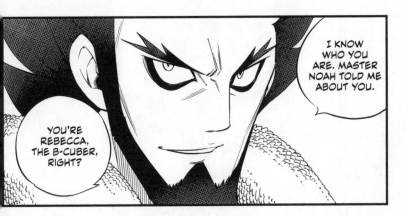

I KNOW WHO YOU ARE. MASTER NOAH TOLD ME ABOUT YOU.
YOU'RE REBECCA, THE B-CUBER, RIGHT?
MASTER NOAH SOLD US OUT...
YEAH, YOU SHOULDN'T TRUST GUYS LIKE HIM.
WHY ARE YOU AFTER THE *EDENS ZERO*?
BECAUSE THERE'S ***SOMETHING VERY PRECIOUS*** ON THAT SHIP.
EDENS

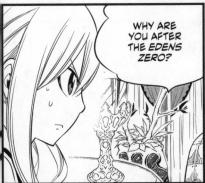

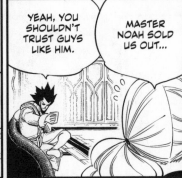

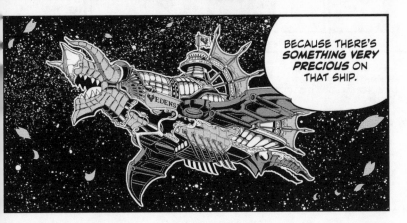

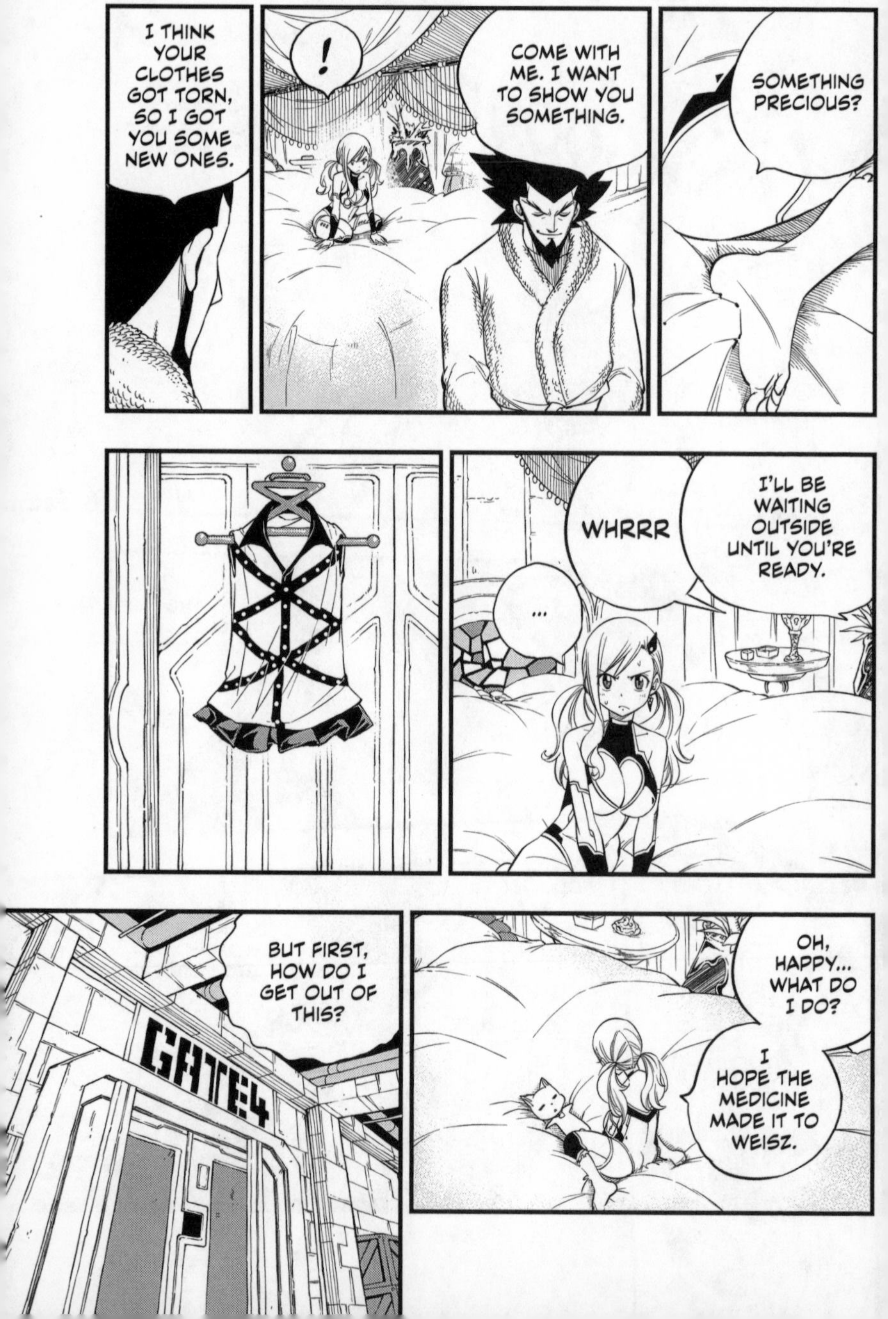
SOMETHING PRECIOUS?
COME WITH ME. I WANT TO SHOW YOU SOMETHING.
!
I THINK YOUR CLOTHES GOT TORN, SO I GOT YOU SOME NEW ONES.
I'LL BE WAITING OUTSIDE UNTIL YOU'RE READY.
WHRRR
...
OH, HAPPY... WHAT DO I DO?
I HOPE THE MEDICINE MADE IT TO WEISZ.
BUT FIRST, HOW DO I GET OUT OF THIS?
GATE 4

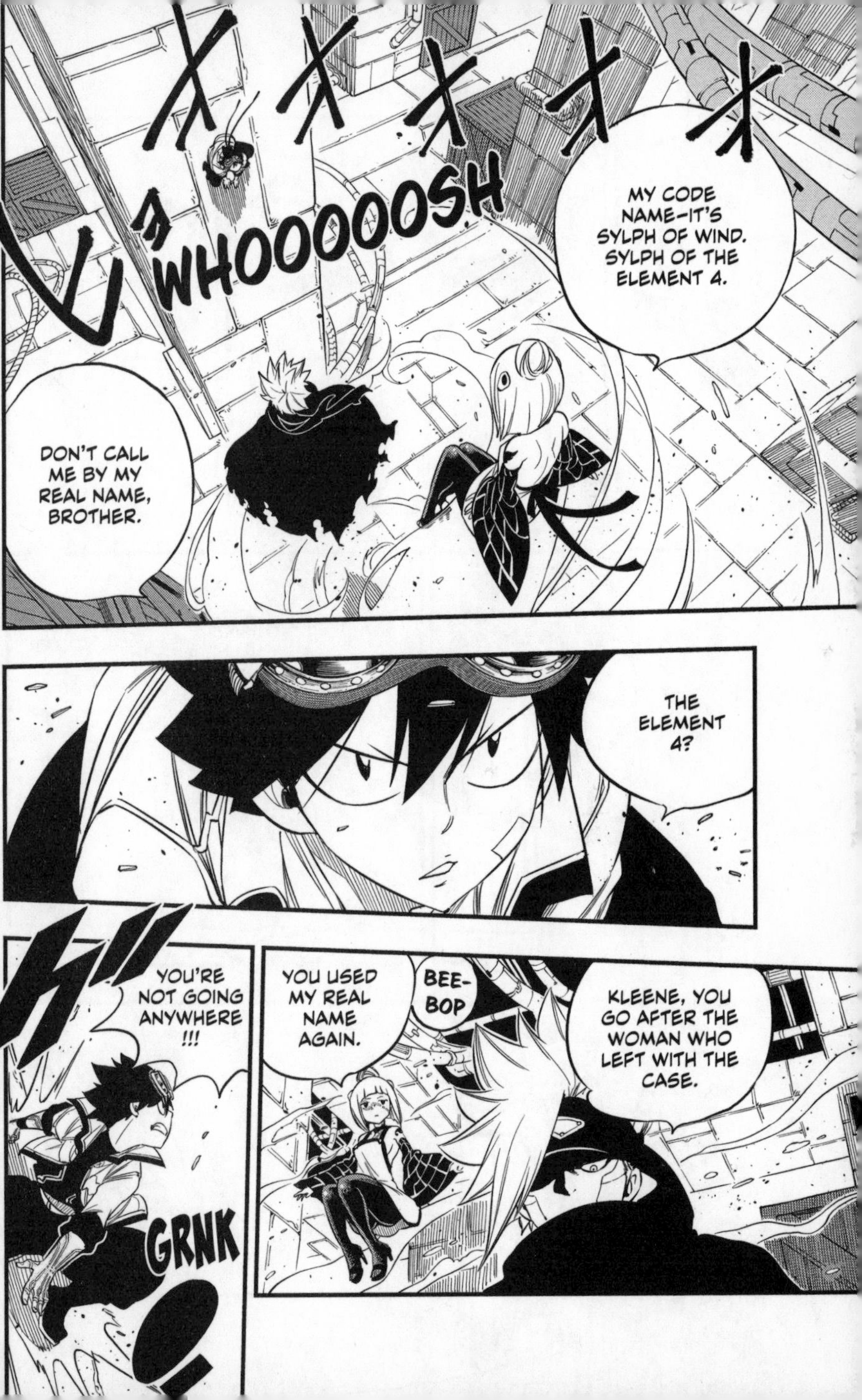
WHOOOOOOSH
MY CODE NAME—IT'S SYLPH OF WIND. SYLPH OF THE ELEMENT 4.
DON'T CALL ME BY MY REAL NAME, BROTHER.
THE ELEMENT 4?
KLEENE, YOU GO AFTER THE WOMAN WHO LEFT WITH THE CASE.
BEE-BOP
YOU USED MY REAL NAME AGAIN.
YOU'RE NOT GOING ANYWHERE!!!
GRNK

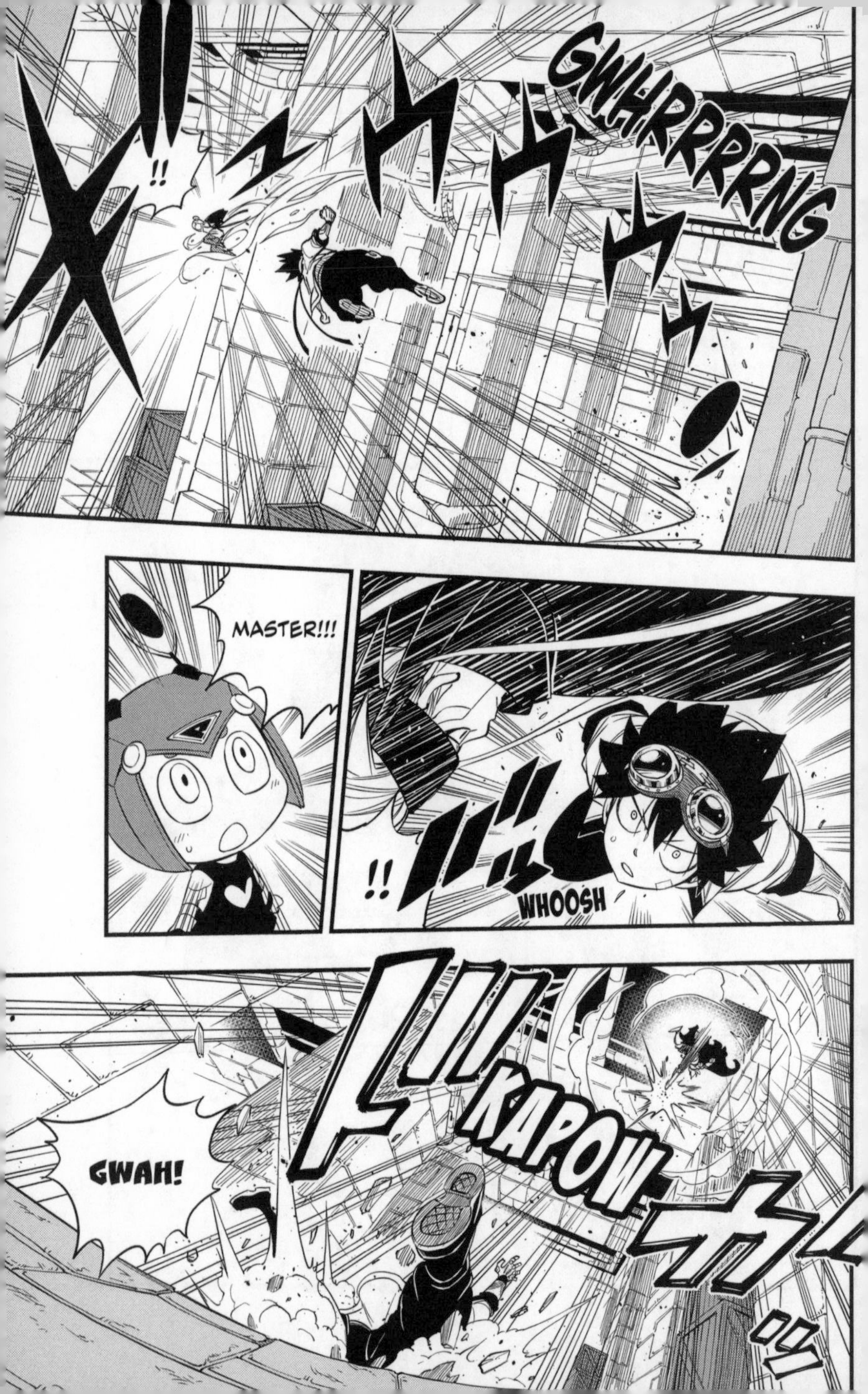

GWHRRRRNG
!!
!!
WHOOSH
MASTER!!!
KAPOW
GWAH!

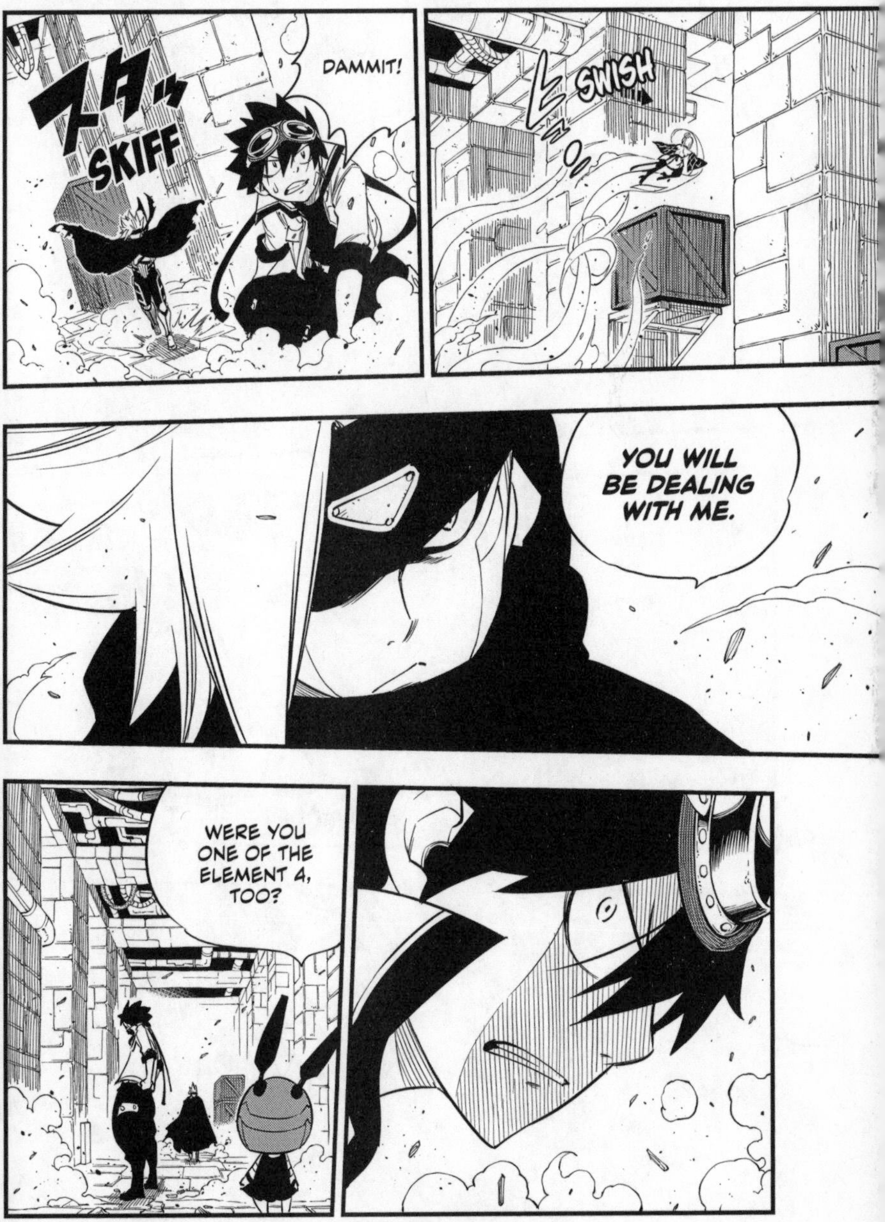
SWISH
スタッ
SKIFF
DAMMIT!
YOU WILL BE DEALING WITH ME.
WERE YOU ONE OF THE ELEMENT 4, TOO?

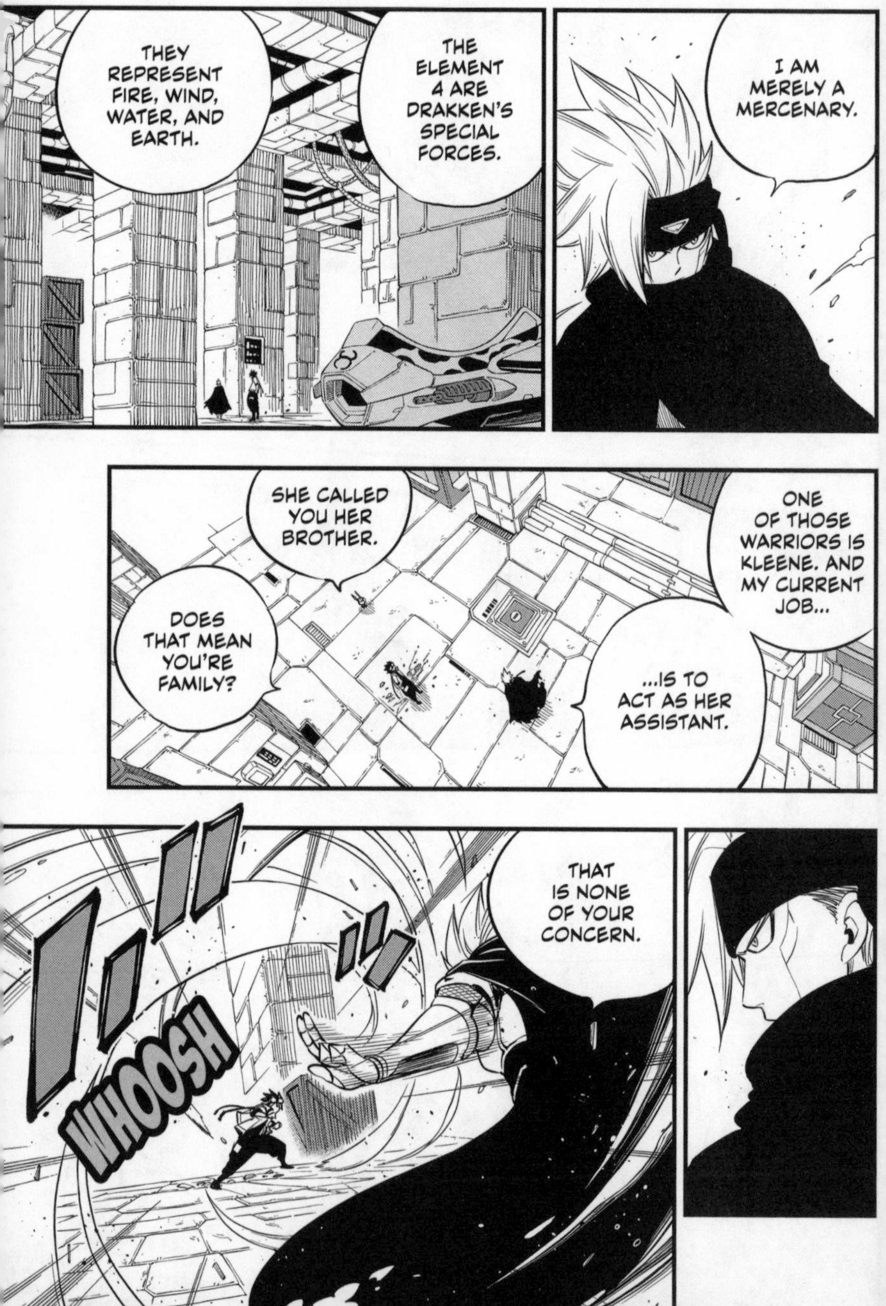
I AM MERELY A MERCENARY.
THE ELEMENT 4 ARE DRAKKEN'S SPECIAL FORCES.
THEY REPRESENT FIRE, WIND, WATER, AND EARTH.
ONE OF THOSE WARRIORS IS KLEENE. AND MY CURRENT JOB...
...IS TO ACT AS HER ASSISTANT.
SHE CALLED YOU HER BROTHER.
DOES THAT MEAN YOU'RE FAMILY?
THAT IS NONE OF YOUR CONCERN.
WHOOSH

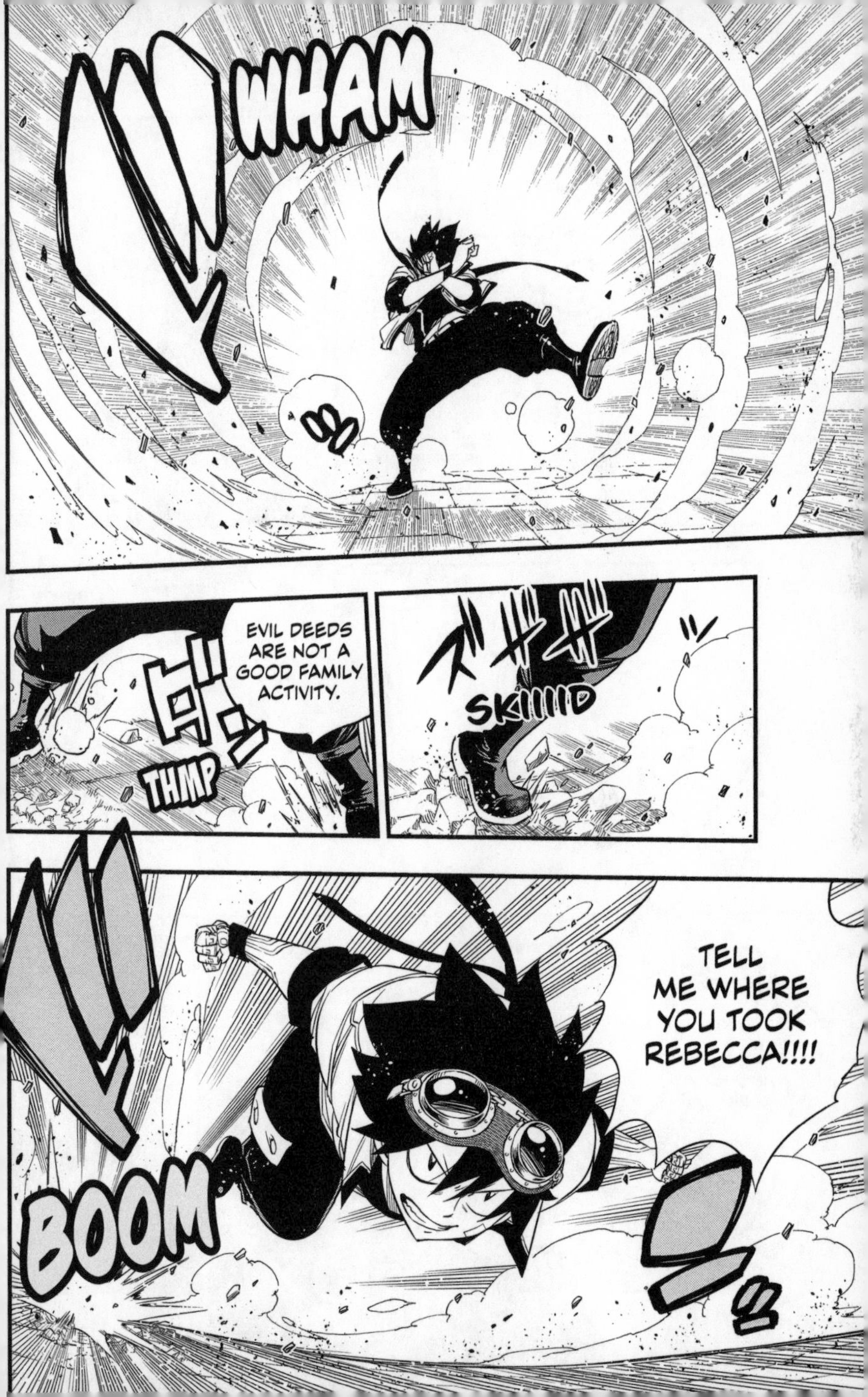
WHAM
SKIIIID
EVIL DEEDS ARE NOT A GOOD FAMILY ACTIVITY.
THMP
TELL ME WHERE YOU TOOK REBECCA!!!!
BOOM

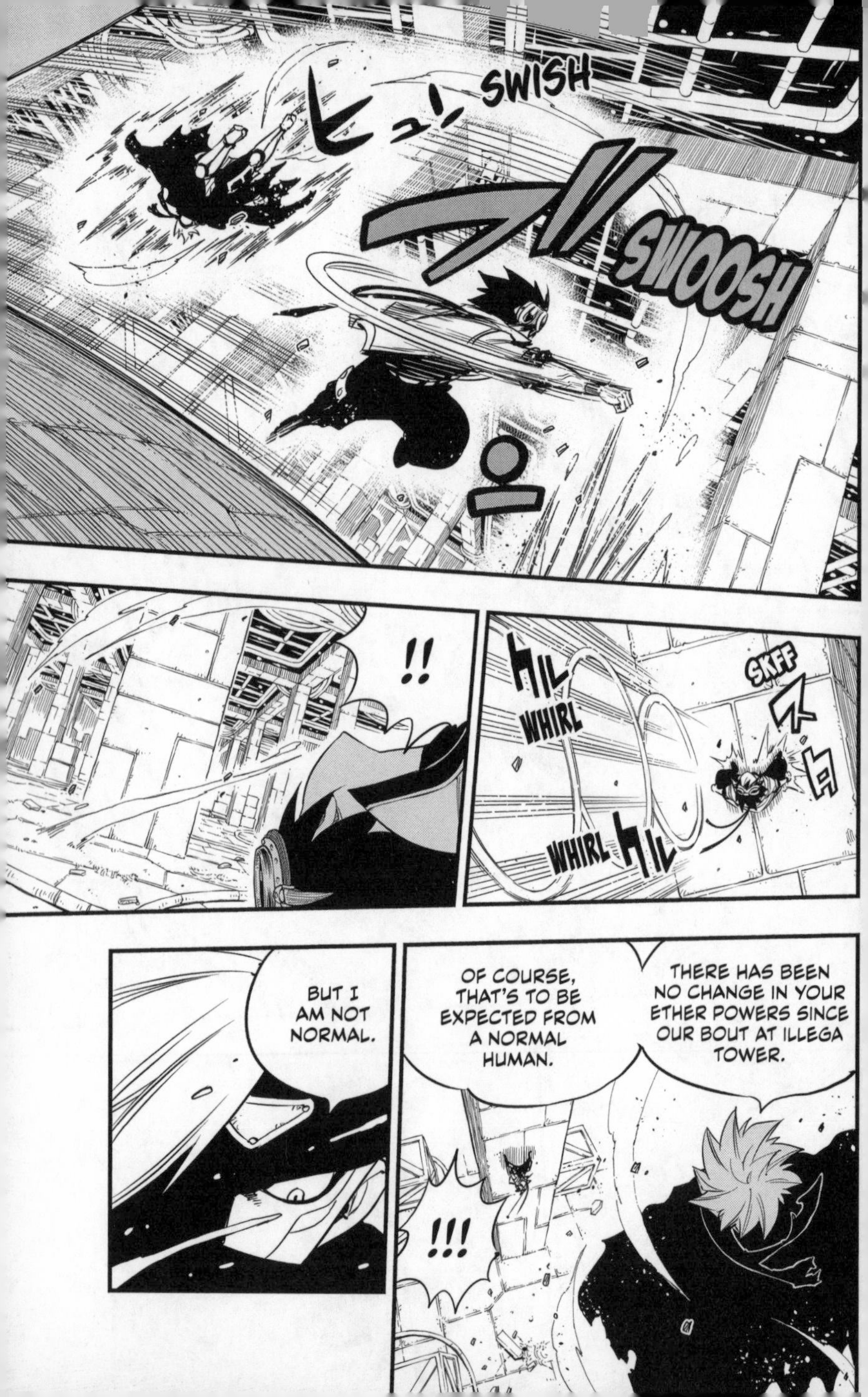
ヒュッ
SWISH
ブン
SWOOSH
ヒュ
ヒュ
ヒル
WHIRL
SKFF
スッ
WHIRL
ヒル
!!
THERE HAS BEEN NO CHANGE IN YOUR ETHER POWERS SINCE OUR BOUT AT ILLEGA TOWER.
OF COURSE, THAT'S TO BE EXPECTED FROM A NORMAL HUMAN.
!!!
BUT I AM NOT NORMAL.

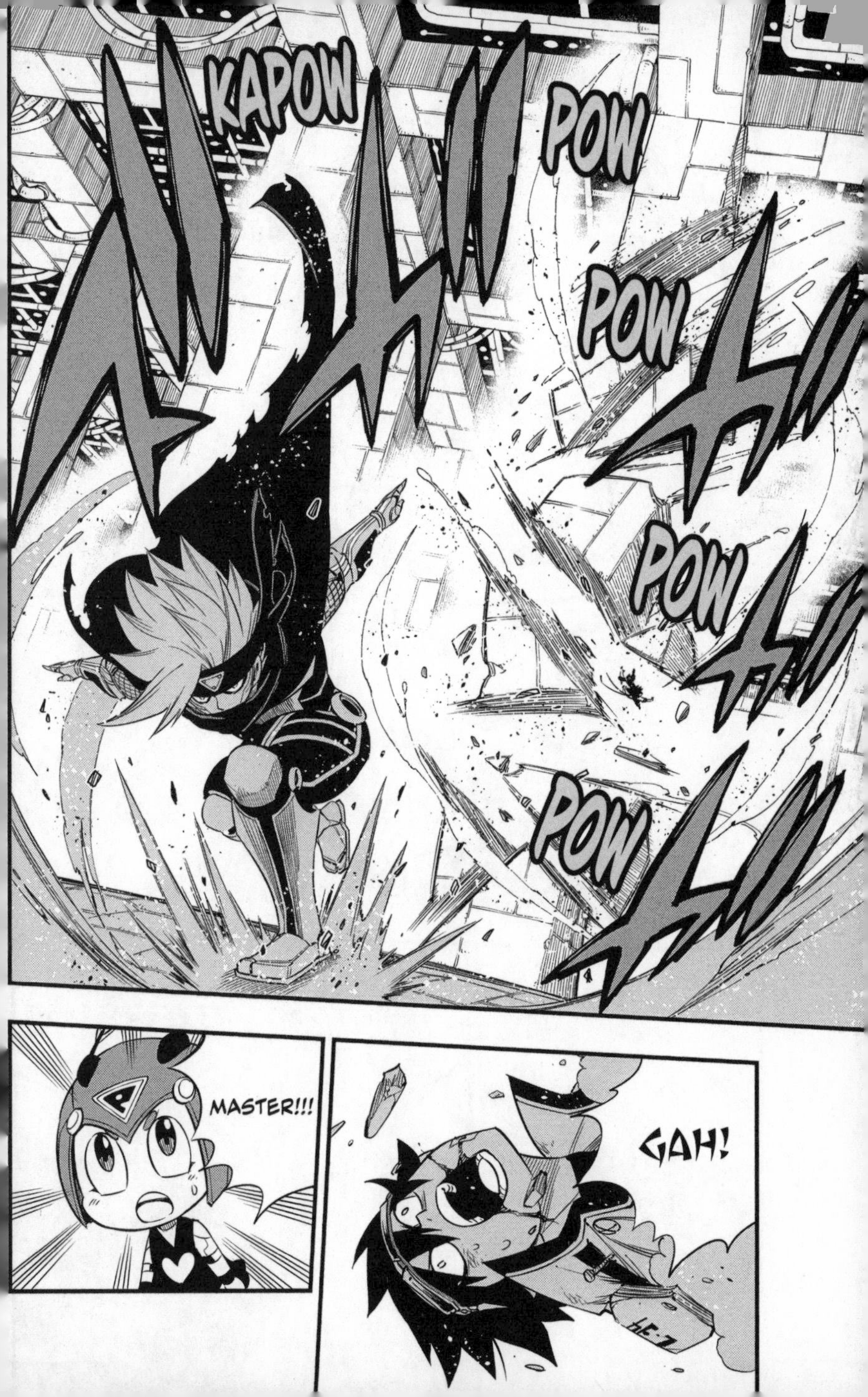
KAPOW
POW
POW
POW
POW
GAH!
MASTER!!!

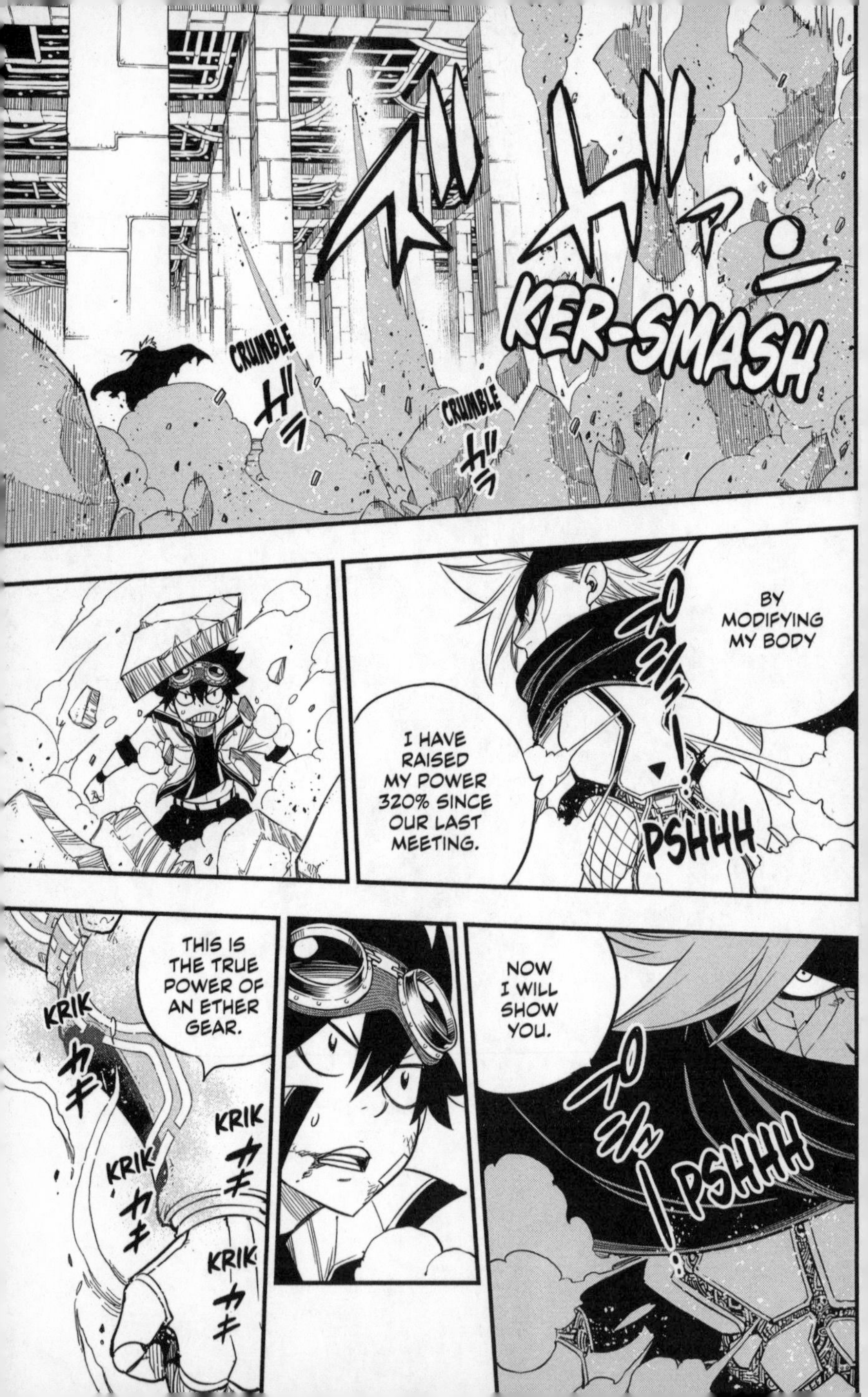
KER-SMASH
CRUMBLE
ガラ
CRUMBLE
ガラ
BY MODIFYING MY BODY
I HAVE RAISED MY POWER 320% SINCE OUR LAST MEETING.
PSHHH
NOW I WILL SHOW YOU.
PSHHH
THIS IS THE TRUE POWER OF AN ETHER GEAR.
KRIK
カキ
KRIK
カキ
KRIK
カキ
KRIK
カキ

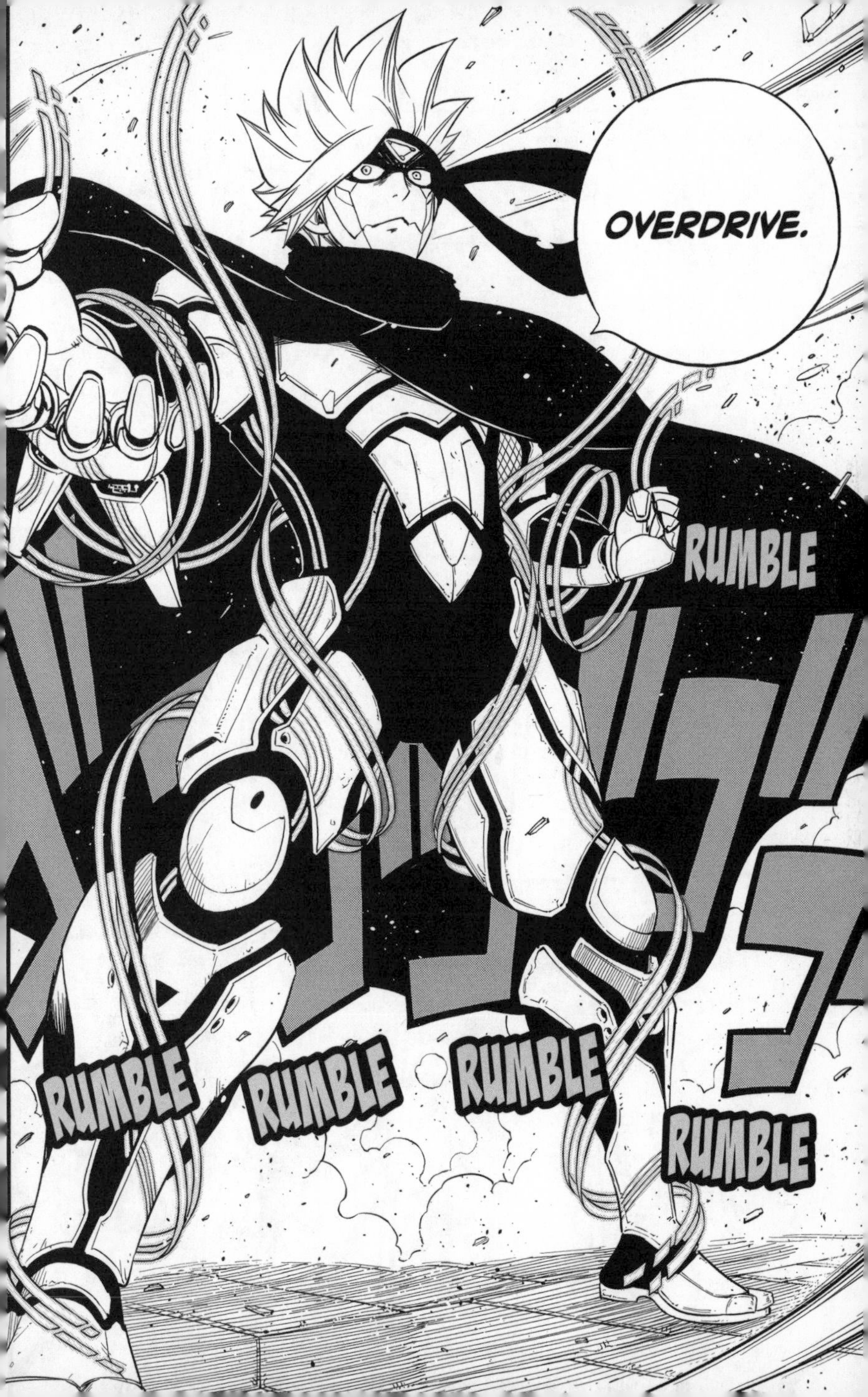
OVERDRIVE.
RUMBLE
RUMBLE
RUMBLE
RUMBLE
RUMBLE

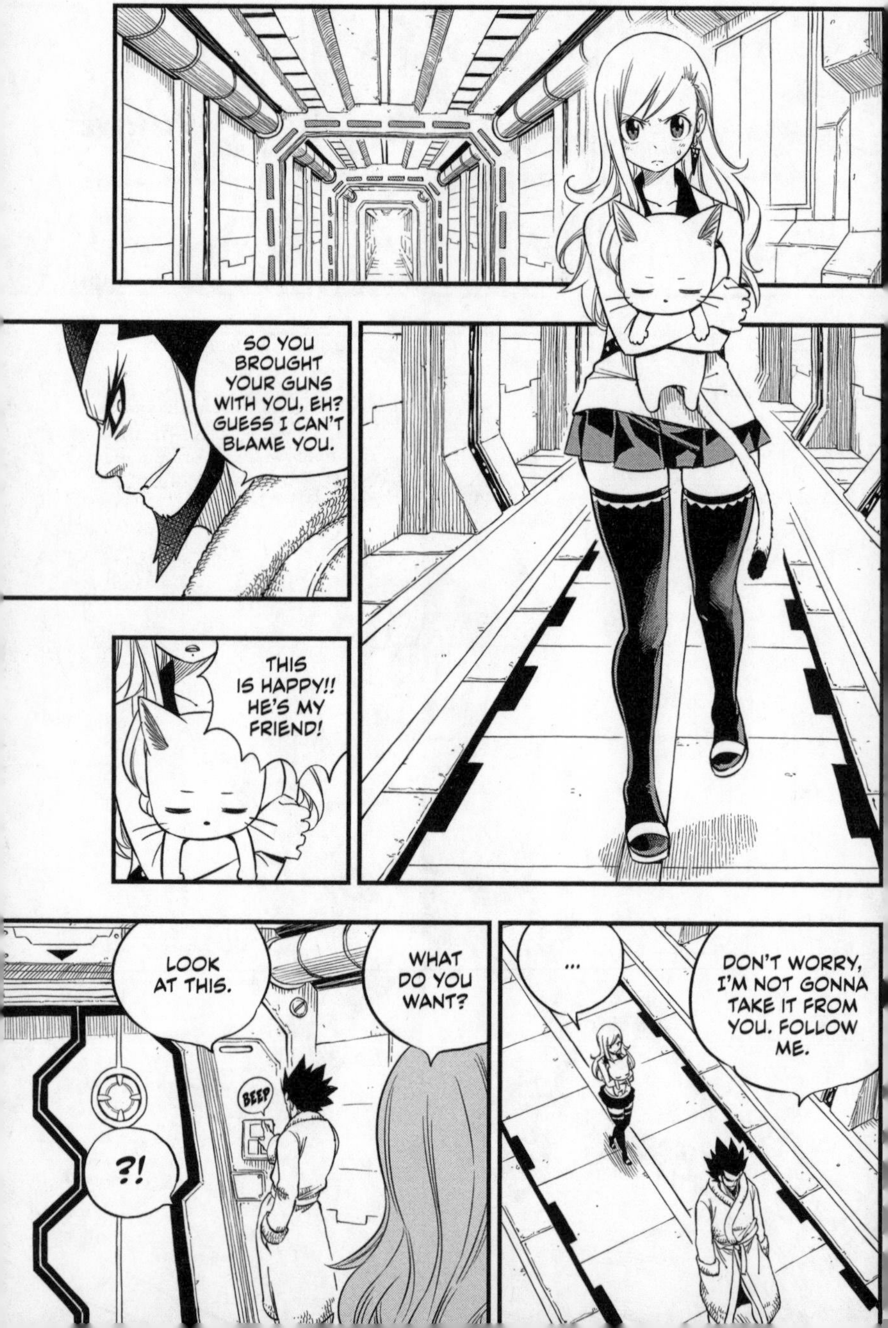
SO YOU BROUGHT YOUR GUNS WITH YOU, EH? GUESS I CAN'T BLAME YOU.
THIS IS HAPPY!! HE'S MY FRIEND!
DON'T WORRY, I'M NOT GONNA TAKE IT FROM YOU. FOLLOW ME.
...
WHAT DO YOU WANT?
LOOK AT THIS.
BEEP
?!

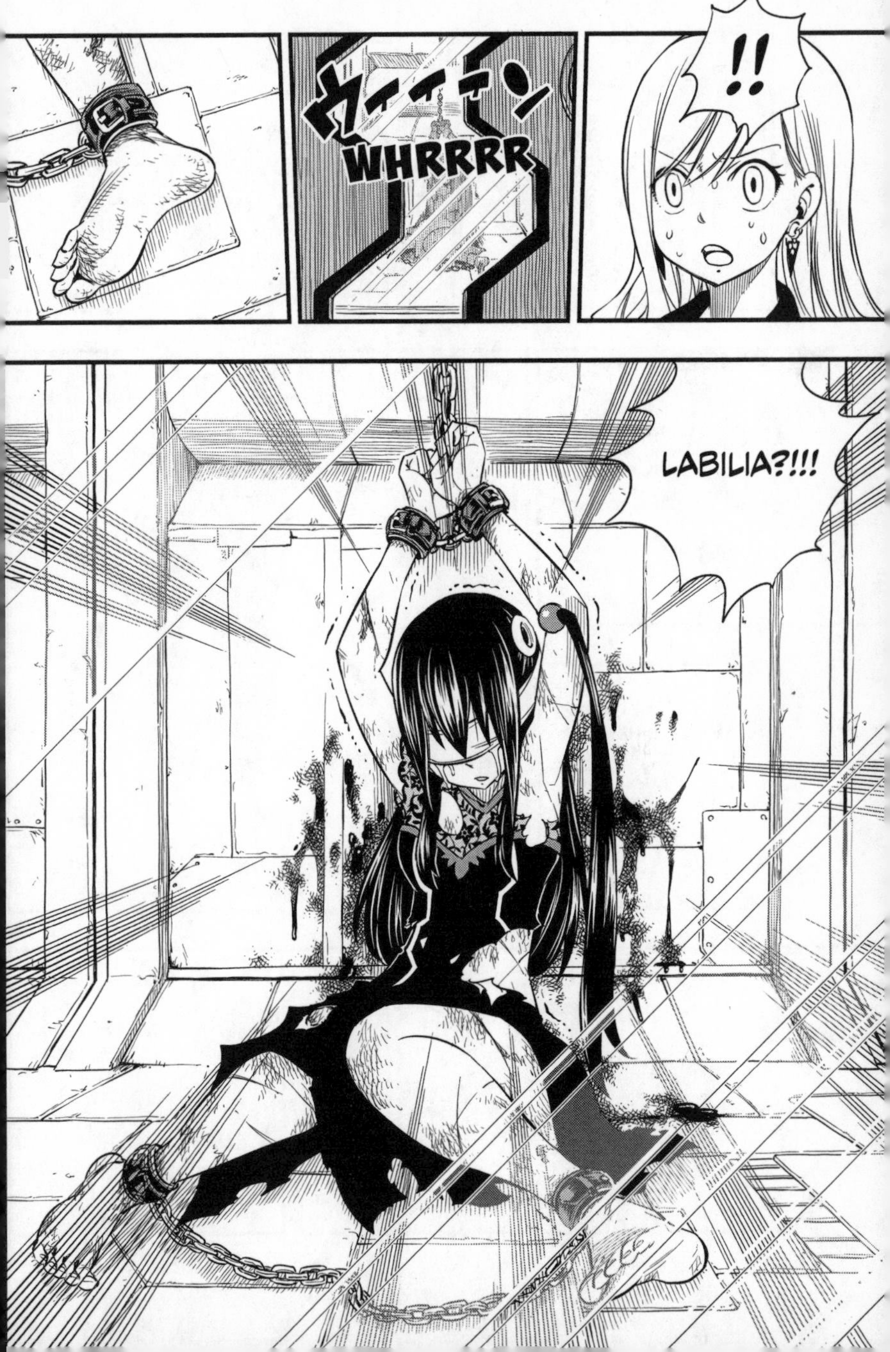
!!
ウィィィン
WHRRRR
LABILIA?!!!

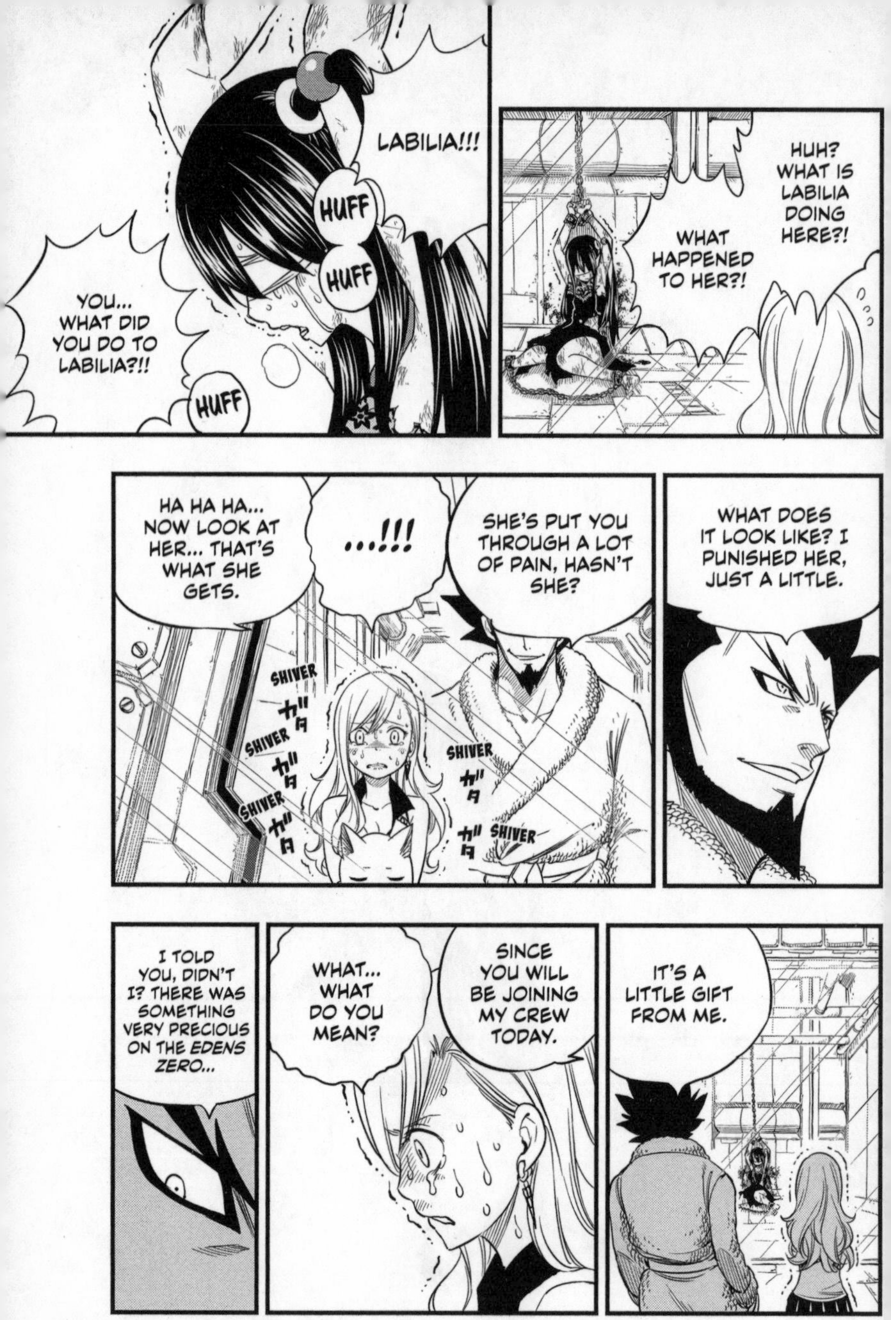
HUH? WHAT IS LABILIA DOING HERE?!
WHAT HAPPENED TO HER?!
LABILIA!!!
HUFF
HUFF
YOU... WHAT DID YOU DO TO LABILIA?!!
HUFF
WHAT DOES IT LOOK LIKE? I PUNISHED HER, JUST A LITTLE.
SHE'S PUT YOU THROUGH A LOT OF PAIN, HASN'T SHE?
...!!!
HA HA HA... NOW LOOK AT HER... THAT'S WHAT SHE GETS.
SHIVER
ガタ
SHIVER
ガタ
SHIVER
ガタ
SHIVER
ガタ
SHIVER
ガタ
IT'S A LITTLE GIFT FROM ME.
SINCE YOU WILL BE JOINING MY CREW TODAY.
WHAT... WHAT DO YOU MEAN?
I TOLD YOU, DIDN'T I? THERE WAS SOMETHING VERY PRECIOUS ON THE *EDENS ZERO*...

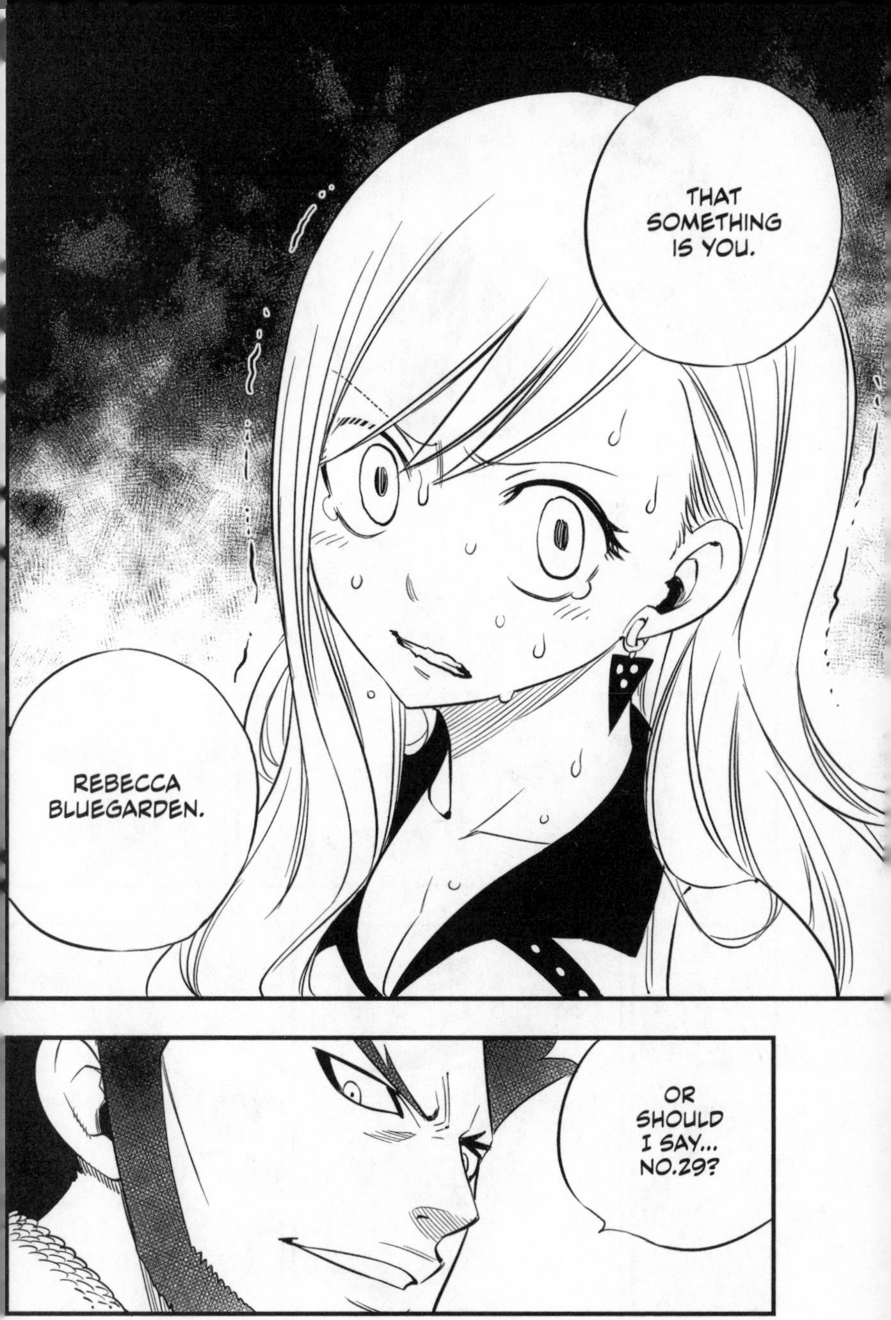
THAT SOMETHING IS YOU.
REBECCA BLUEGARDEN.
OR SHOULD I SAY... NO.29?

EDENSZERO

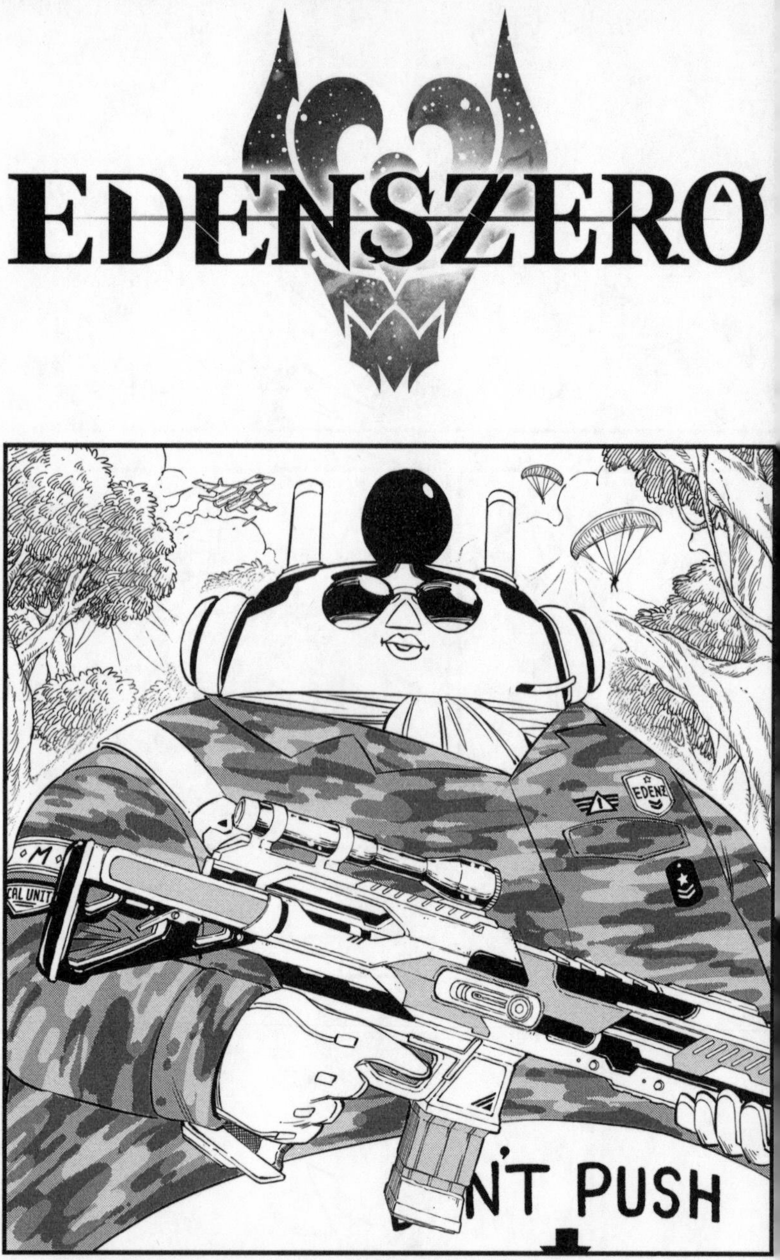
EDENZ
N'T PUSH

CHAPTER 79: THAT WHICH OBSTRUCTS AND THAT WHICH STEALS

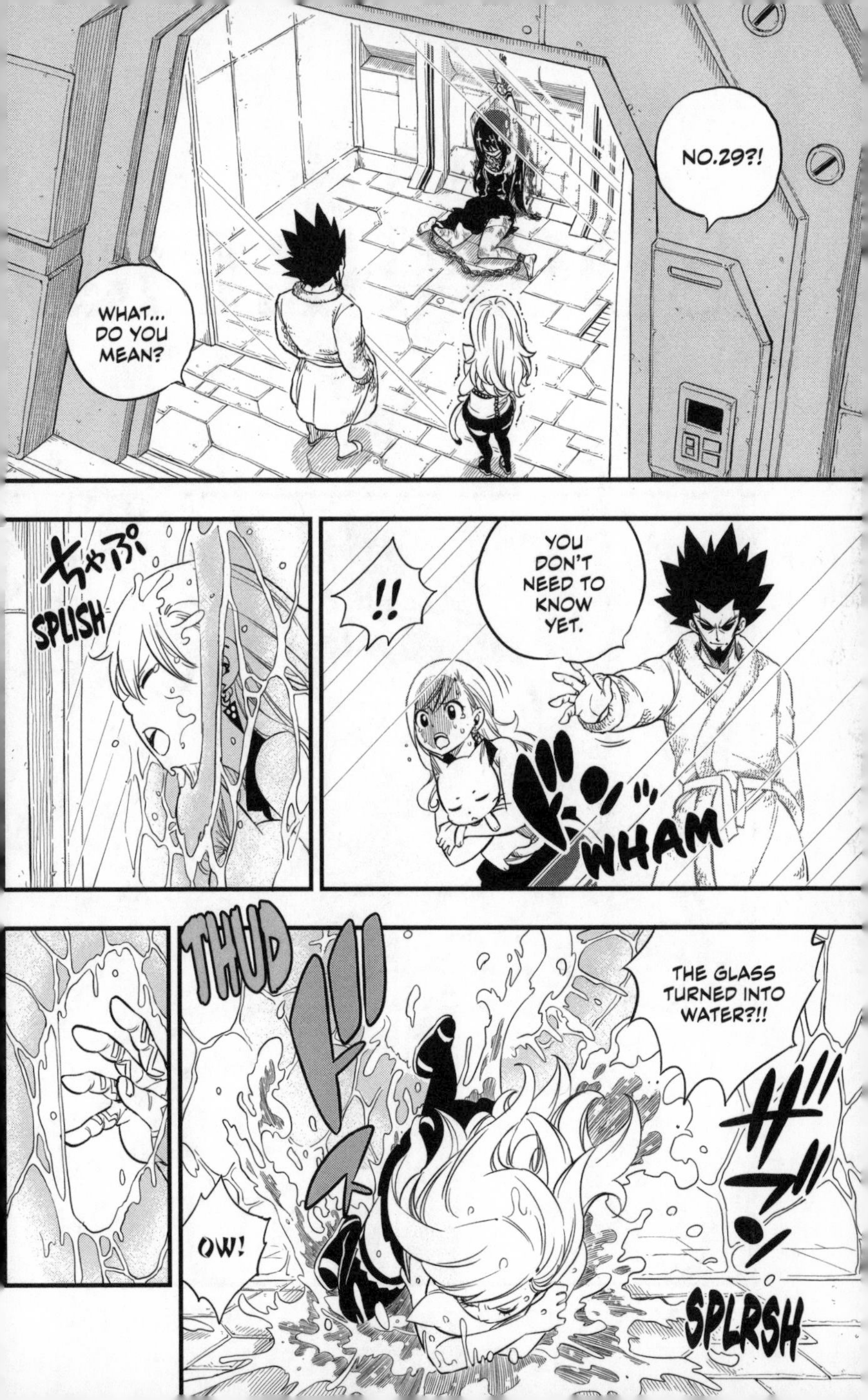
NO.29?!
WHAT... DO YOU MEAN?
YOU DON'T NEED TO KNOW YET.
!!
WHAM
ちゃぷ
SPLISH
THE GLASS TURNED INTO WATER?!!
THUD
SPLRSH
OW!

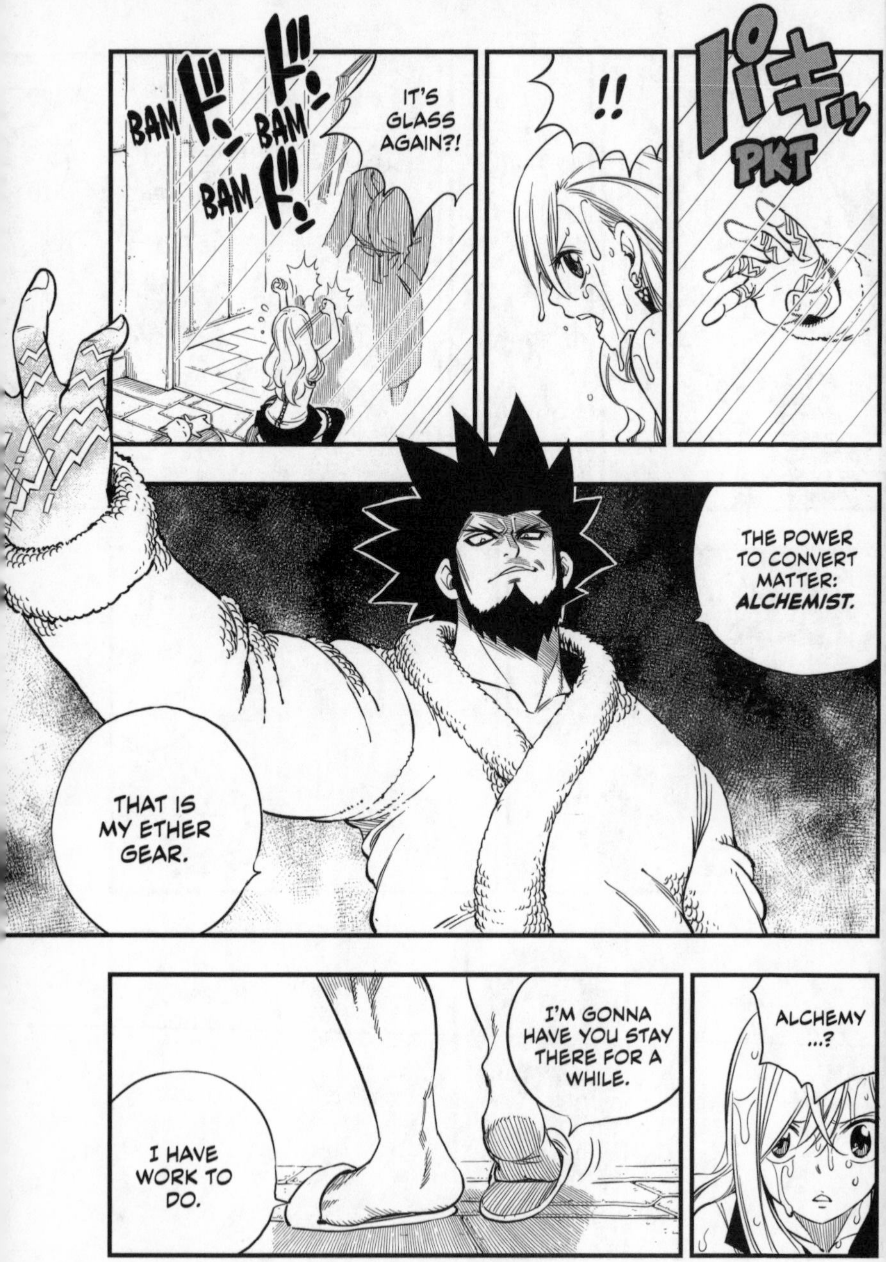
パキッ
PKT
!!
BAM ドン
BAM ドン
BAM ドン
IT'S GLASS AGAIN?!
THE POWER TO CONVERT MATTER: ***ALCHEMIST.***
THAT IS MY ETHER GEAR.
ALCHEMY ...?
I'M GONNA HAVE YOU STAY THERE FOR A WHILE.
I HAVE WORK TO DO.

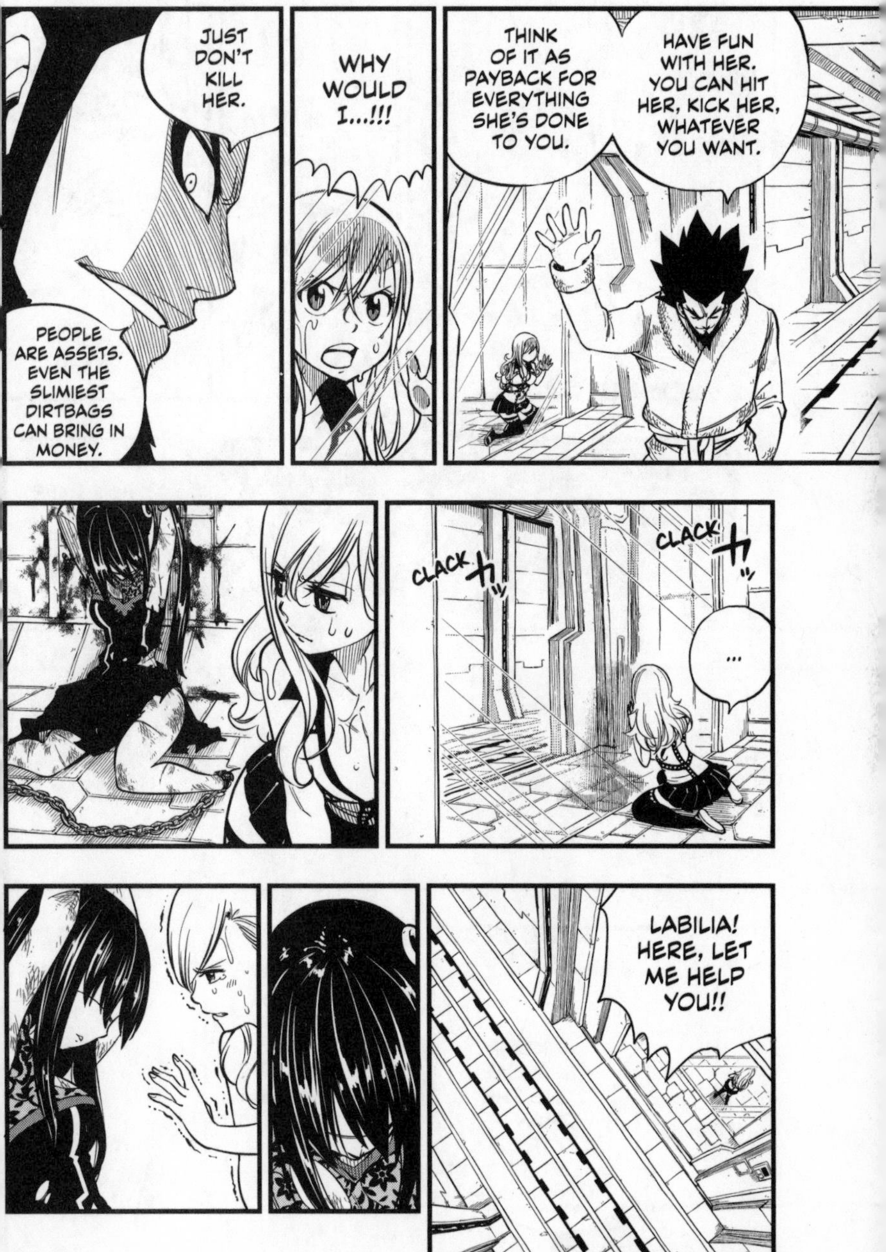
HAVE FUN WITH HER. YOU CAN HIT HER, KICK HER, WHATEVER YOU WANT.
THINK OF IT AS PAYBACK FOR EVERYTHING SHE'S DONE TO YOU.
WHY WOULD I...!!!
JUST DON'T KILL HER.
PEOPLE ARE ASSETS. EVEN THE SLIMIEST DIRTBAGS CAN BRING IN MONEY.
CLACK カッ
CLACK カッ
...
LABILIA! HERE, LET ME HELP YOU!!

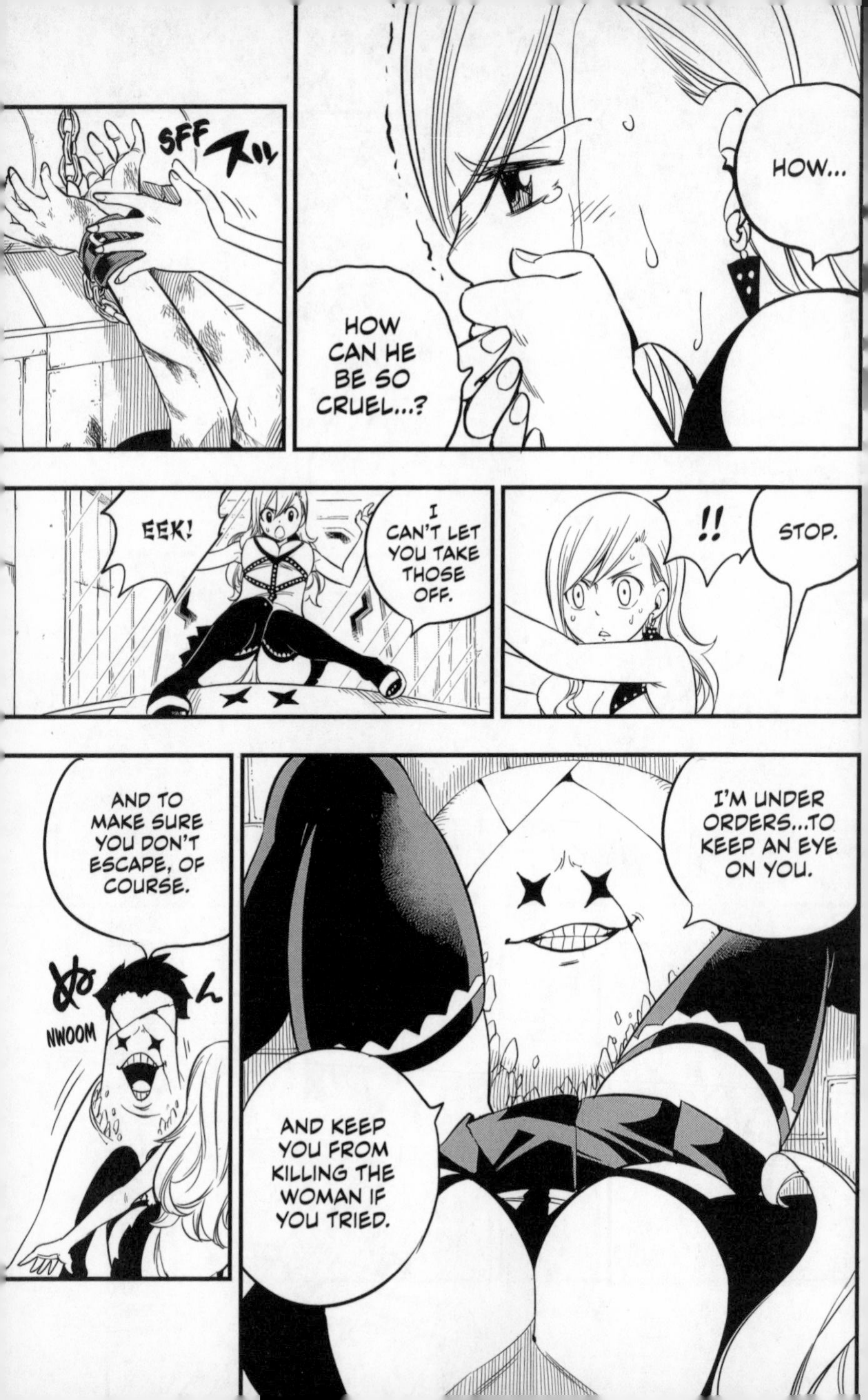
HOW...
HOW CAN HE BE SO CRUEL...?
SFF スル
!!
STOP.
I CAN'T LET YOU TAKE THOSE OFF.
EEK!
I'M UNDER ORDERS...TO KEEP AN EYE ON YOU.
AND KEEP YOU FROM KILLING THE WOMAN IF YOU TRIED.
AND TO MAKE SURE YOU DON'T ESCAPE, OF COURSE.
ぬん NWOOM

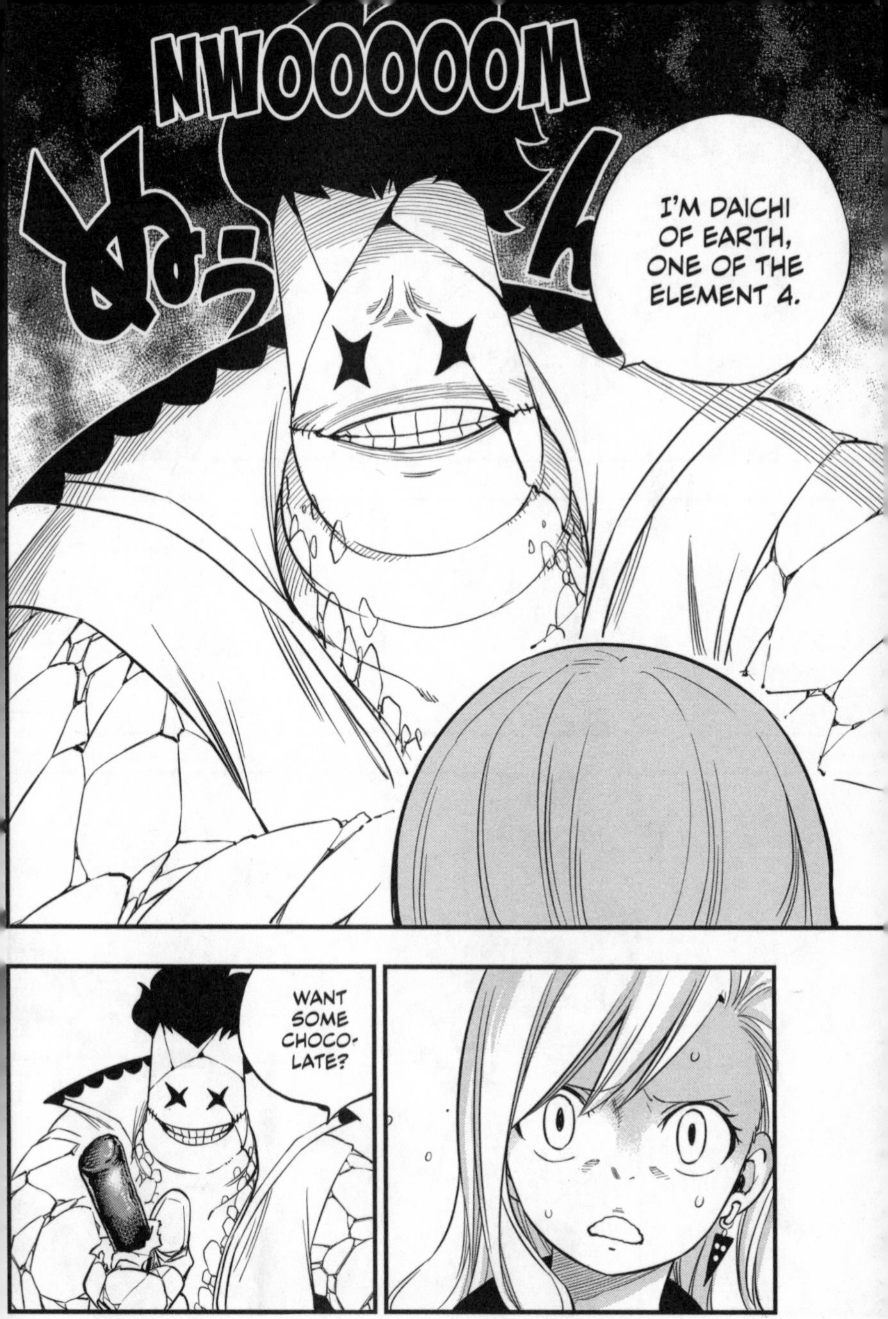
NWOOOOOM
ぬぅん
I'M DAICHI OF EARTH, ONE OF THE ELEMENT 4.
WANT SOME CHOCO-LATE?

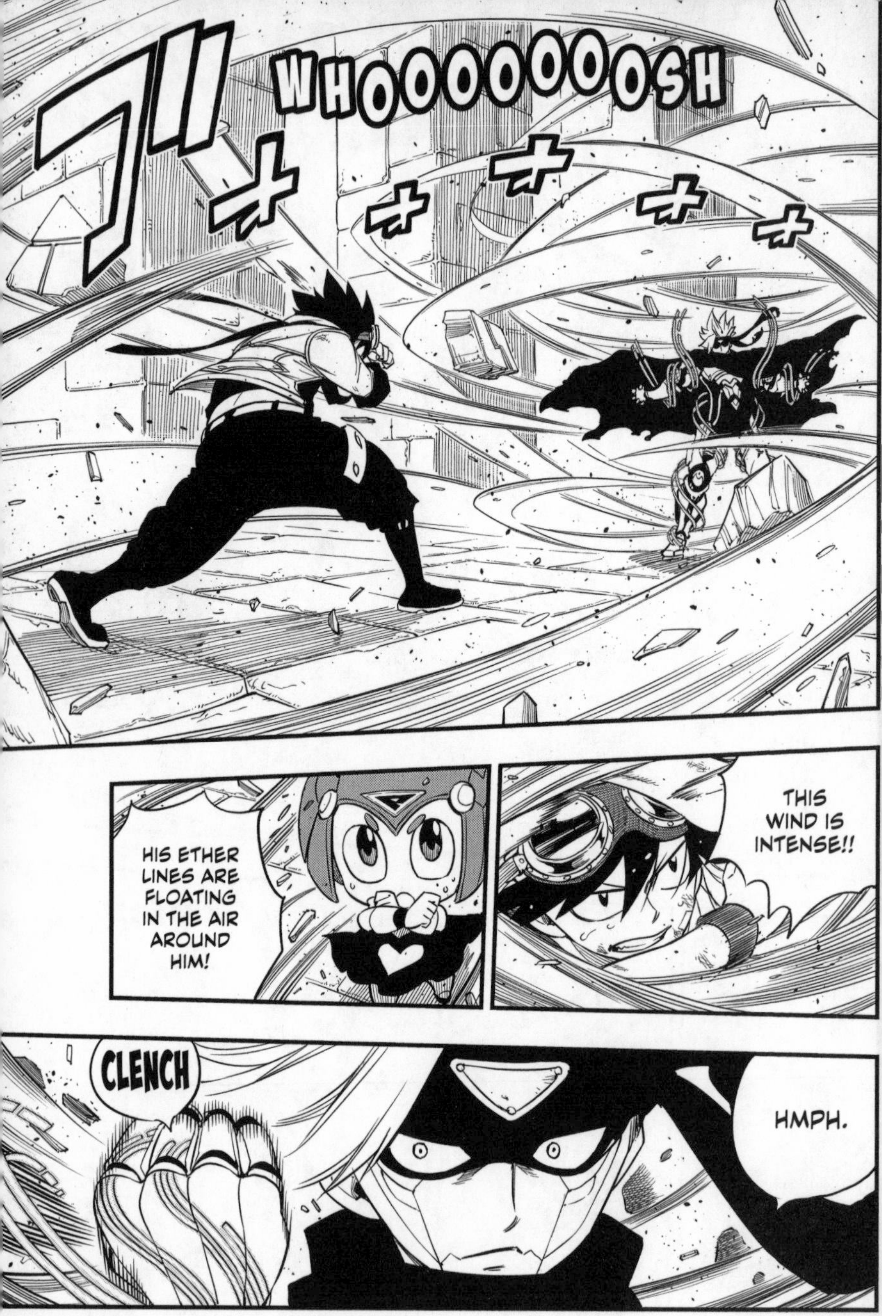
WHOOOOOOOSH
THIS WIND IS INTENSE!!
HIS ETHER LINES ARE FLOATING IN THE AIR AROUND HIM!
HMPH.
CLENCH

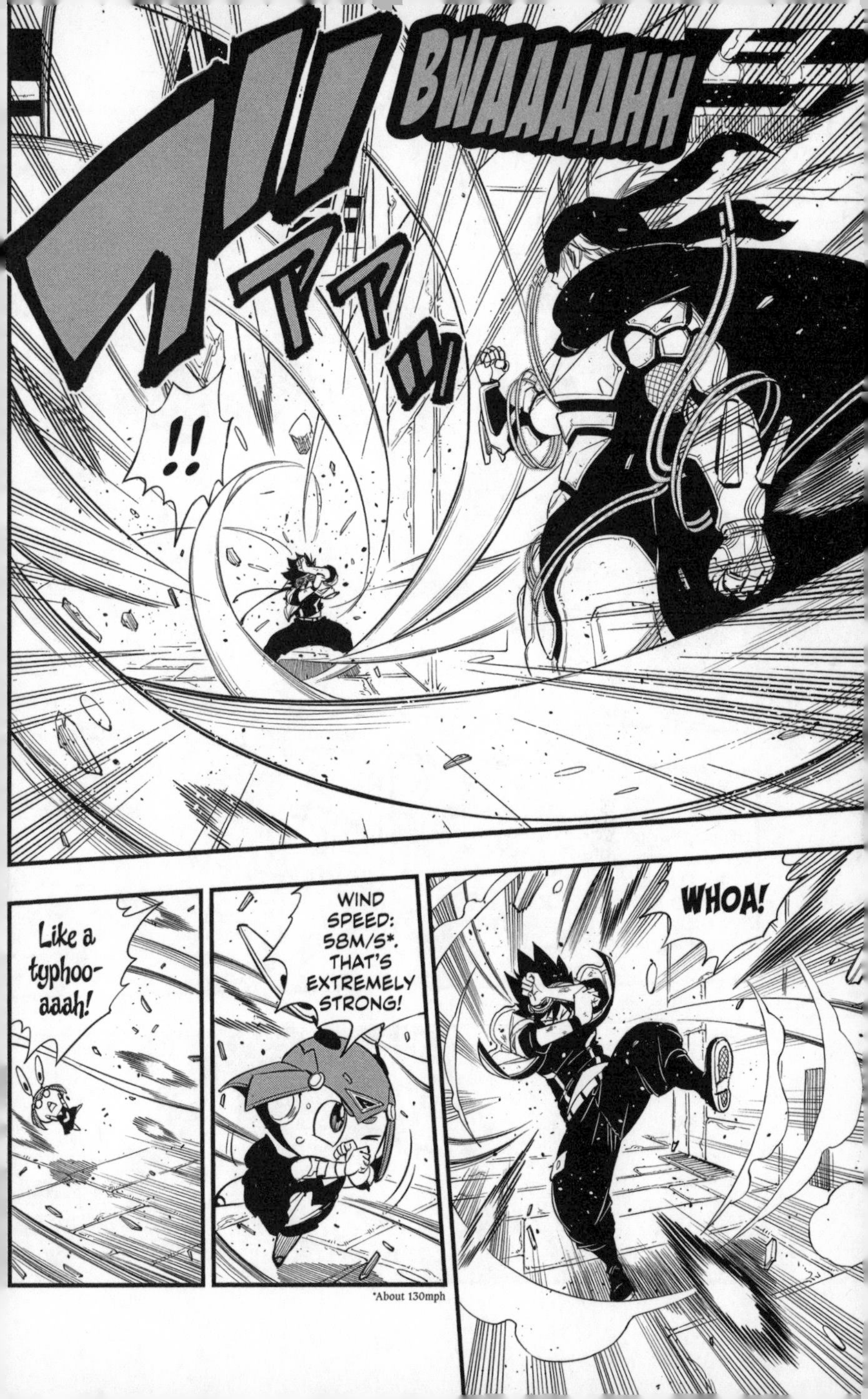
BWAAAAHH
!!
WHOA!
WIND SPEED: 58M/S*. THAT'S EXTREMELY STRONG!
Like a typhoo-aaah!

*About 130mph

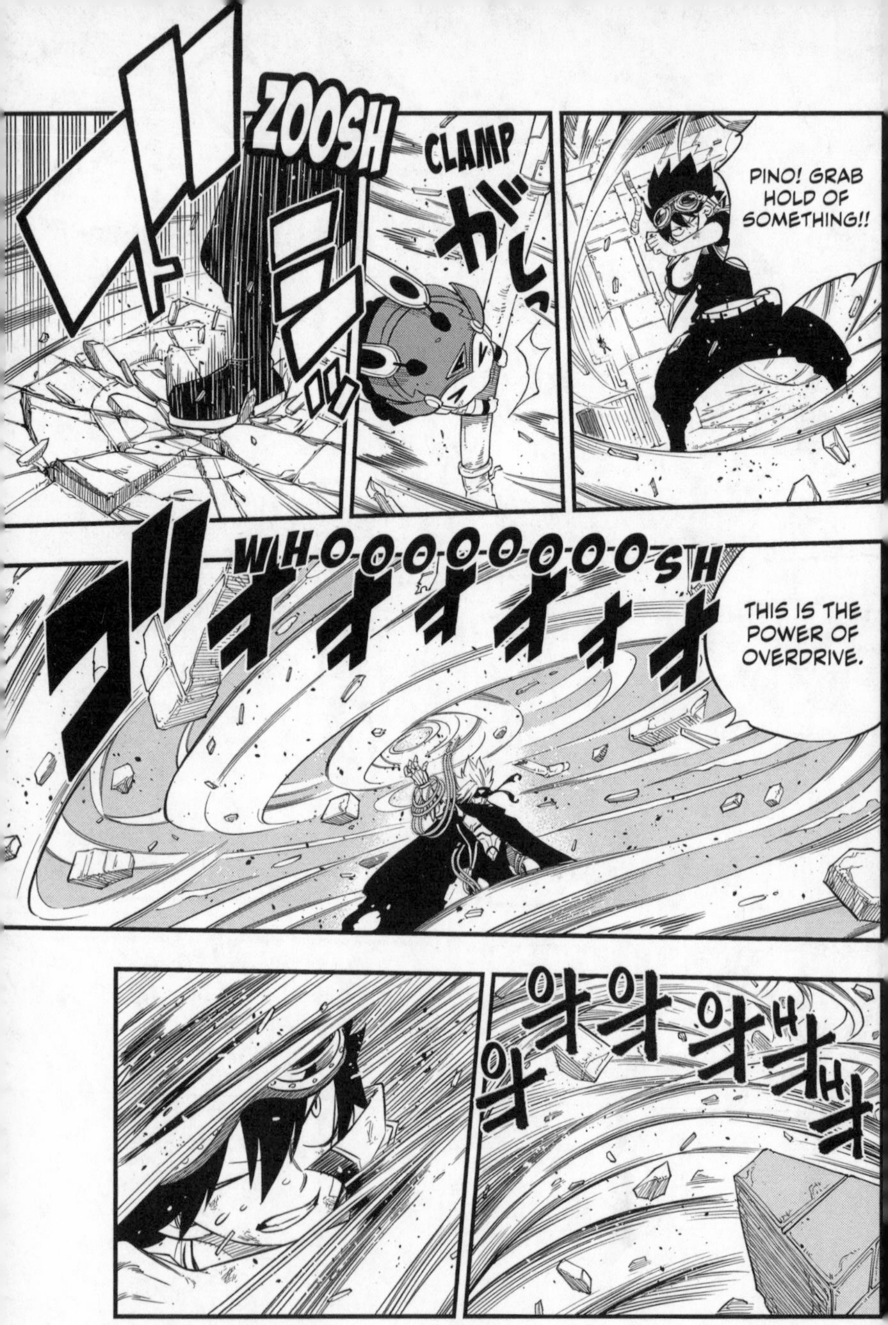
PINO! GRAB HOLD OF SOMETHING!!
CLAMP
ZOOSH
THIS IS THE POWER OF OVERDRIVE.
WHOOOOOOOOOSH

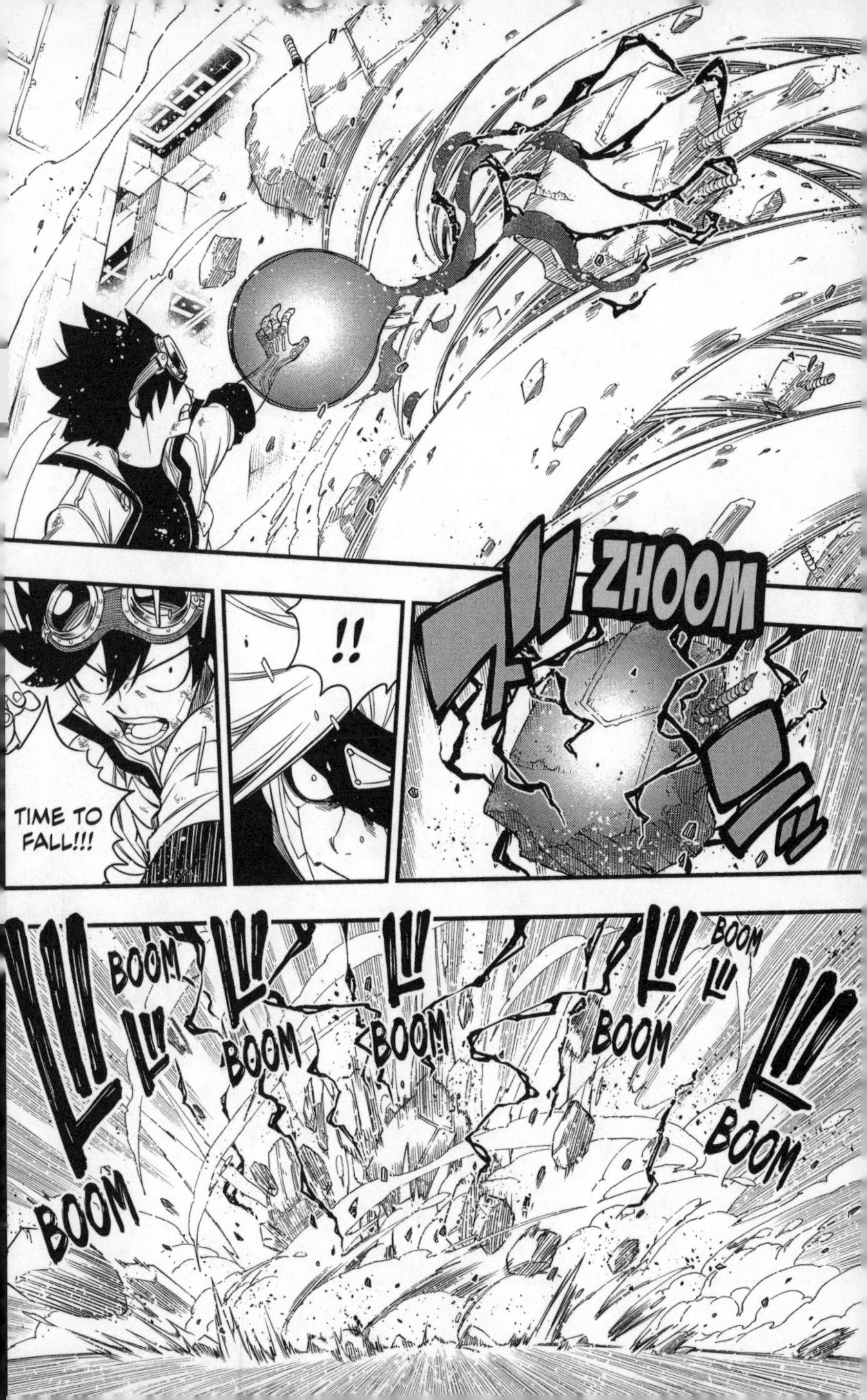

ZHOOM
!!
TIME TO FALL!!!
BOOM
BOOM
BOOM
BOOM
BOOM
BOOM
BOOM

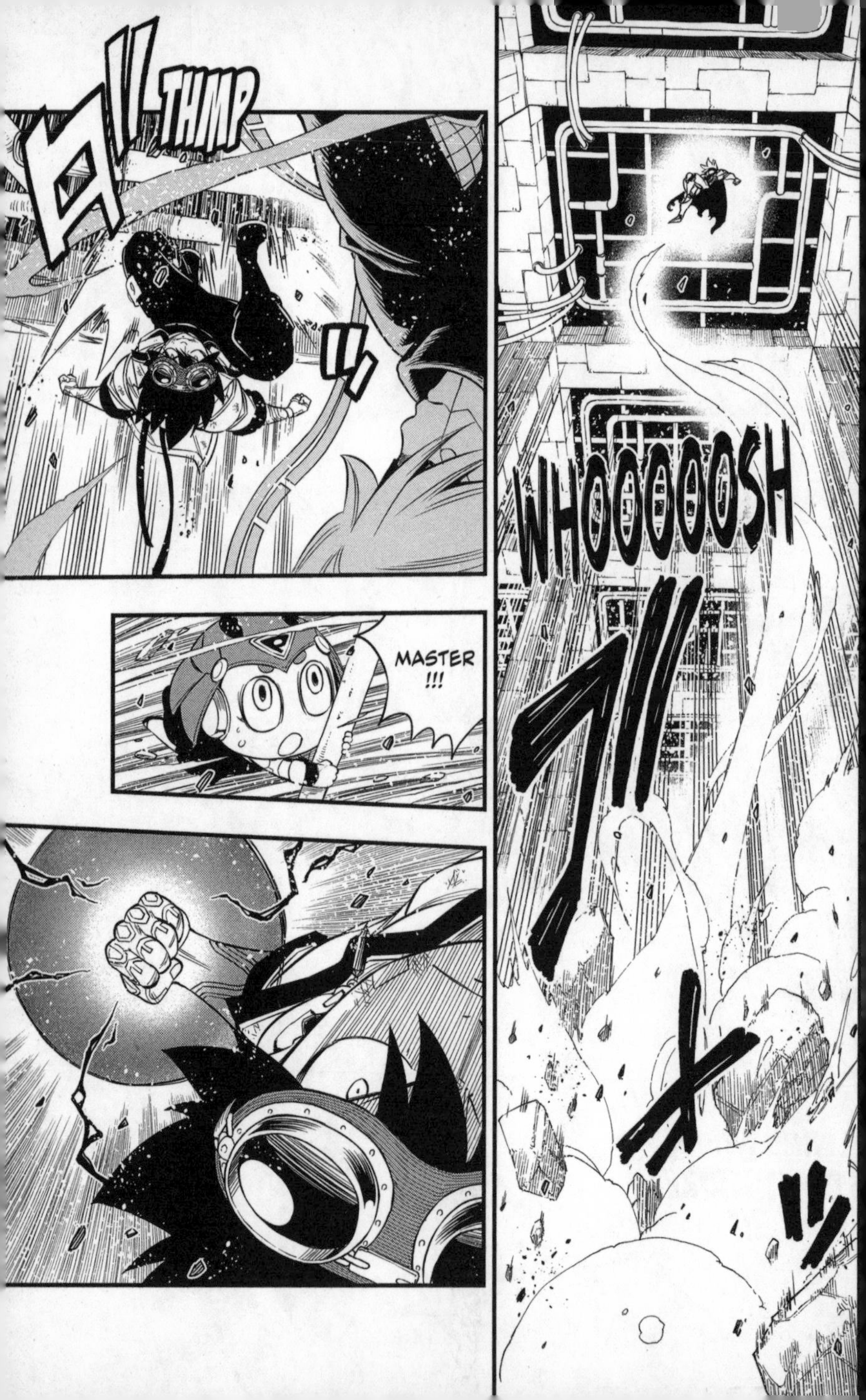
WHOOOOSH
THMP
MASTER !!!

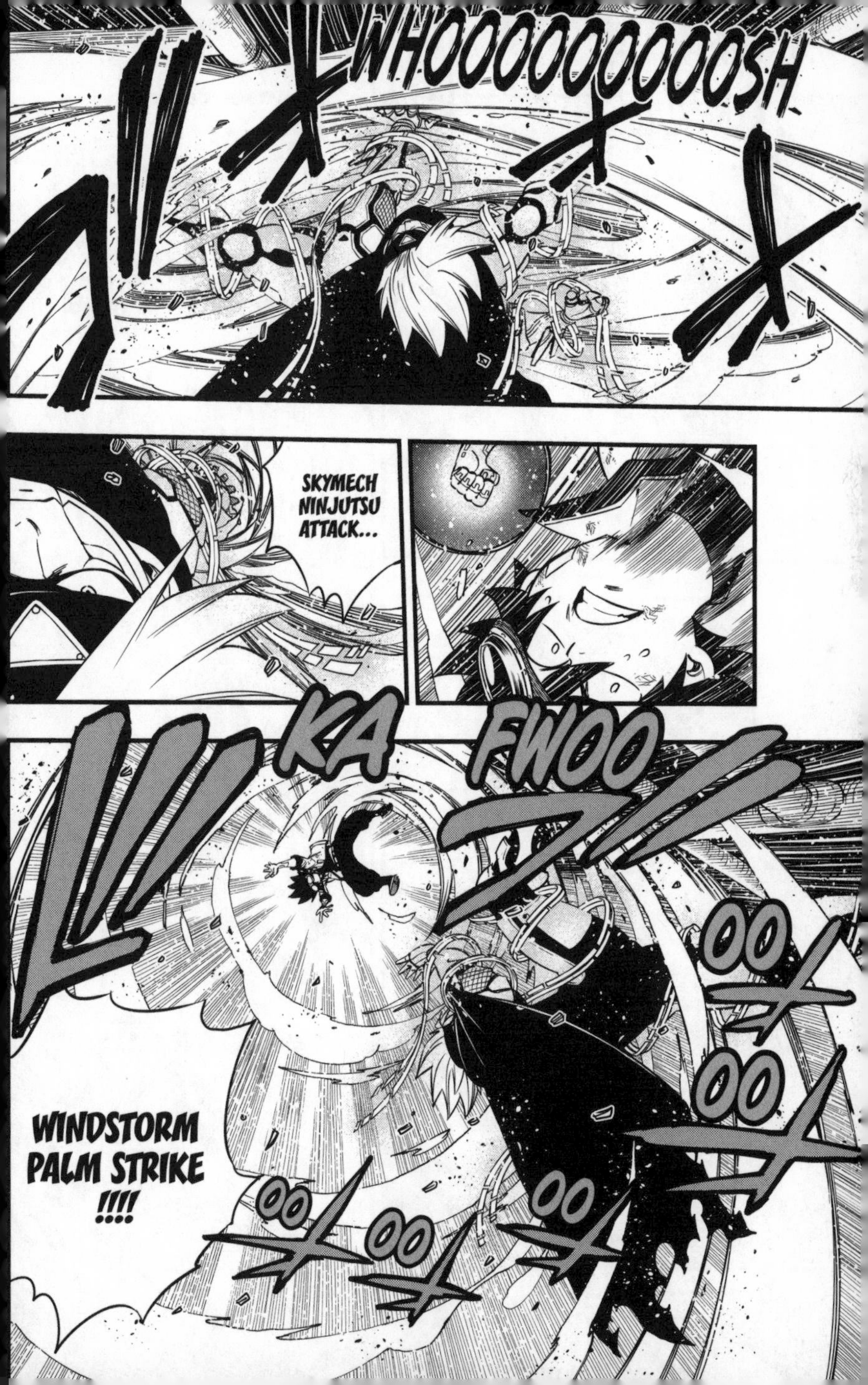
WHOOOOOOOOOSH
SKYMECH NINJUTSU ATTACK...
KA
FWOO
WINDSTORM PALM STRIKE !!!!

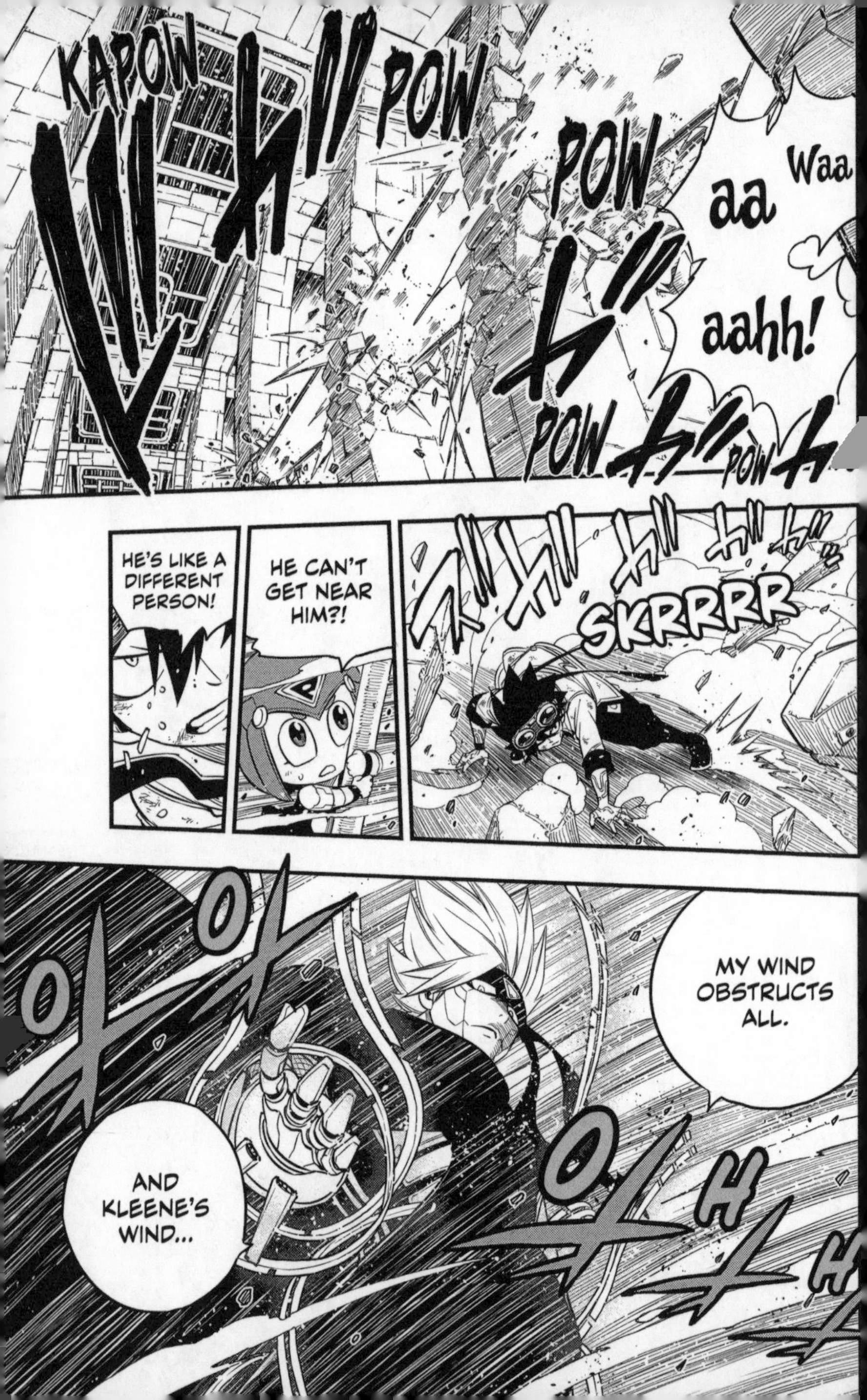
Waa
aa
aahh!
POW
POW
POW
POW
KAPOW
SKRRRR
HE CAN'T GET NEAR HIM?!
HE'S LIKE A DIFFERENT PERSON!
MY WIND OBSTRUCTS ALL.
AND KLEENE'S WIND...

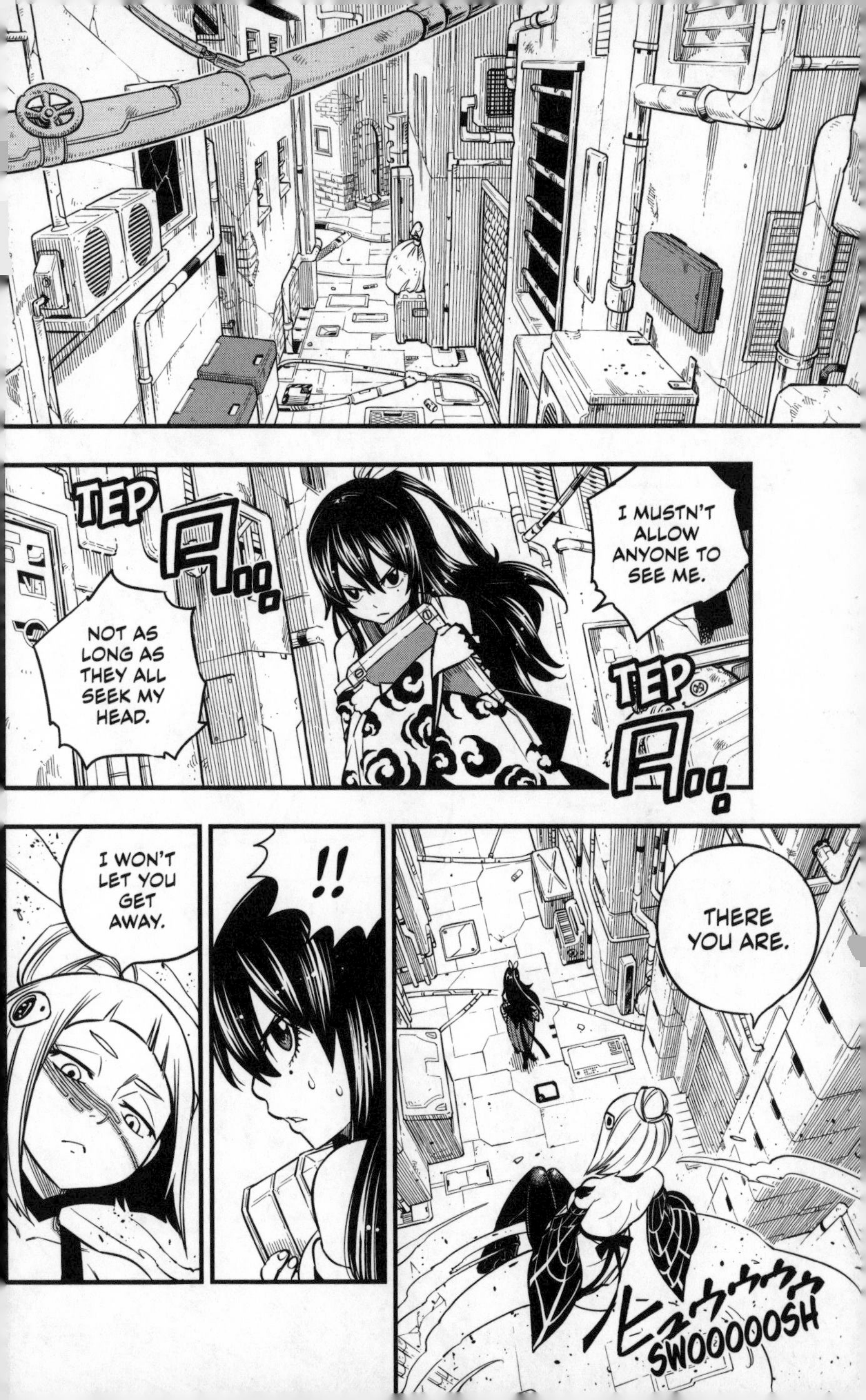
I MUSTN'T ALLOW ANYONE TO SEE ME.
TEP
NOT AS LONG AS THEY ALL SEEK MY HEAD.
TEP
THERE YOU ARE.
SWOOOOOSH
!!
I WON'T LET YOU GET AWAY.

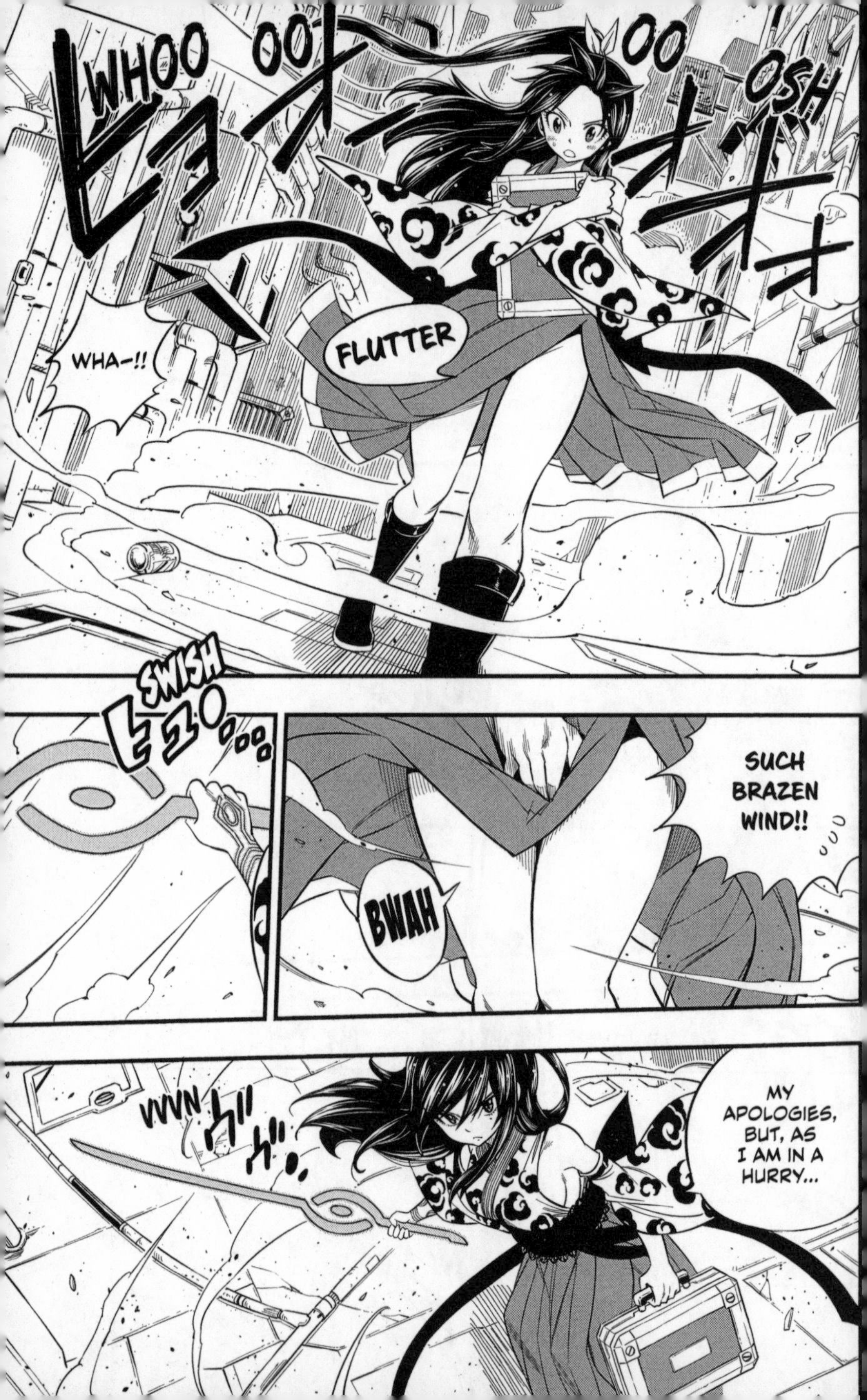
WHOO OO OO OSH
FLUTTER
WHA-!!
SUCH BRAZEN WIND!!
BWAH
SWISH
MY APOLOGIES, BUT, AS I AM IN A HURRY...
VVVN

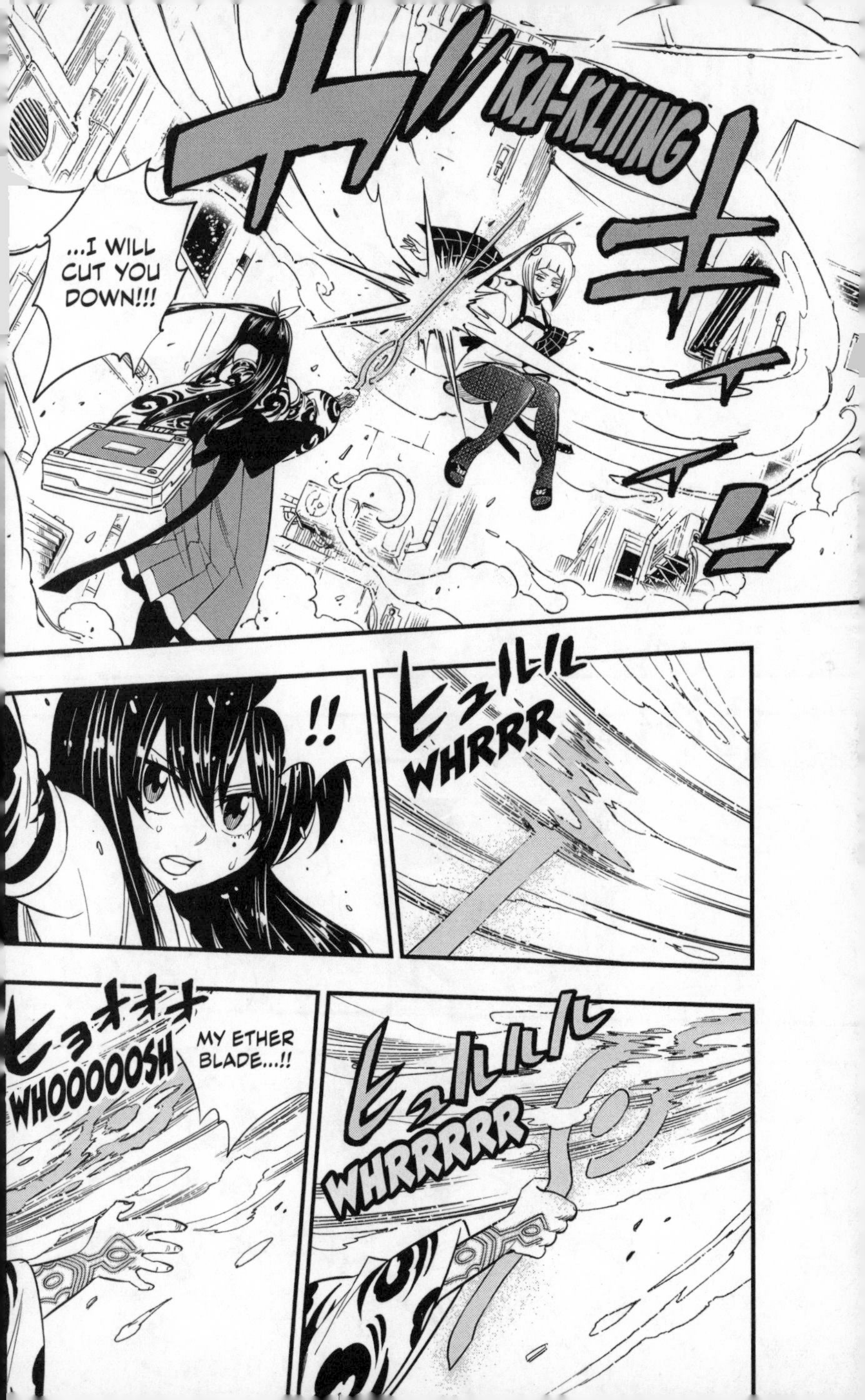
KA-KLIIING
...I WILL CUT YOU DOWN!!!
ヒュルル
WHRRR
!!
ヒュルルル
WHRRRRR
ヒョオオオ
WHOOOOOSH
MY ETHER BLADE...!!

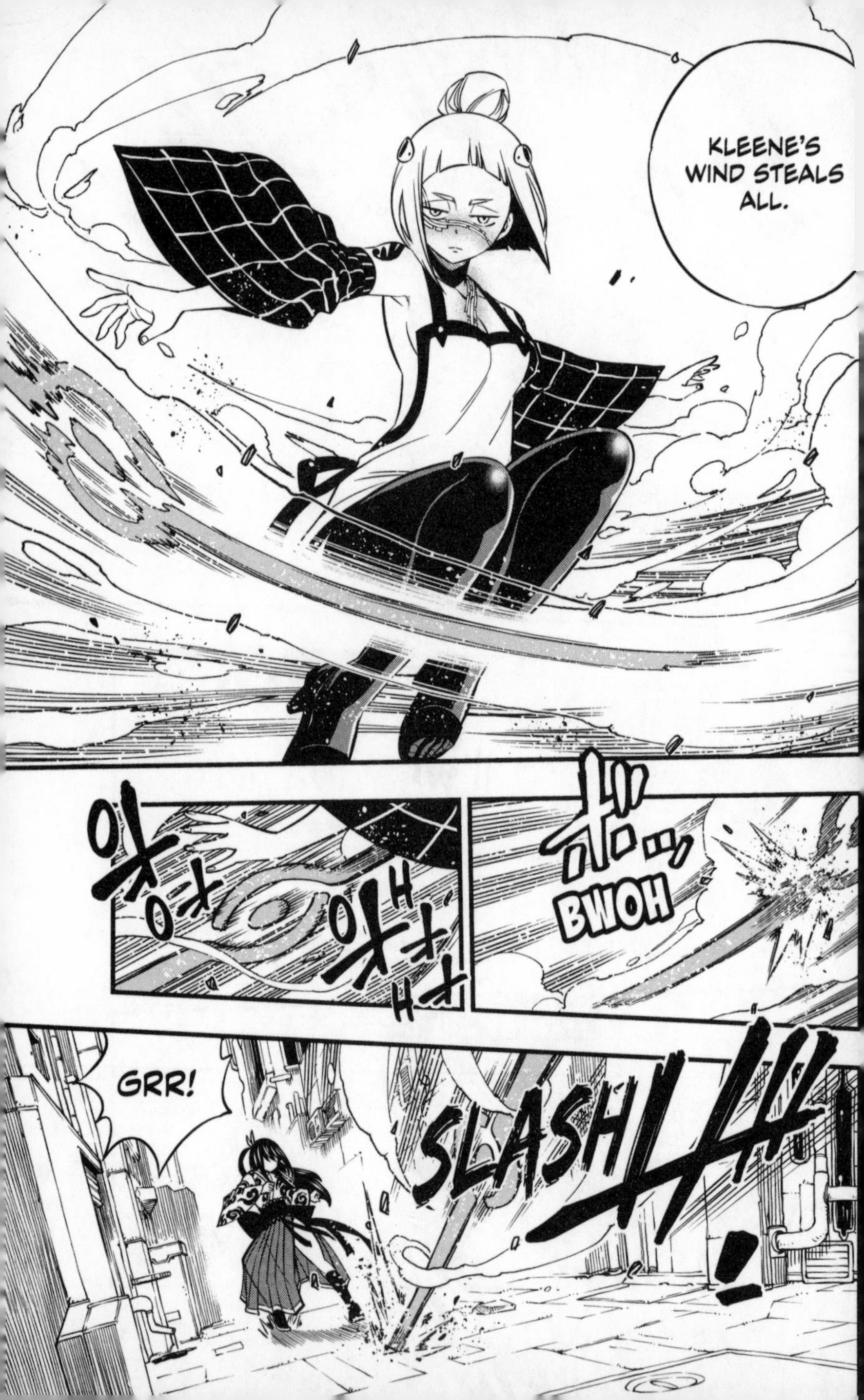
KLEENE'S WIND STEALS ALL.
BWOH
GRR!
SLASH!!

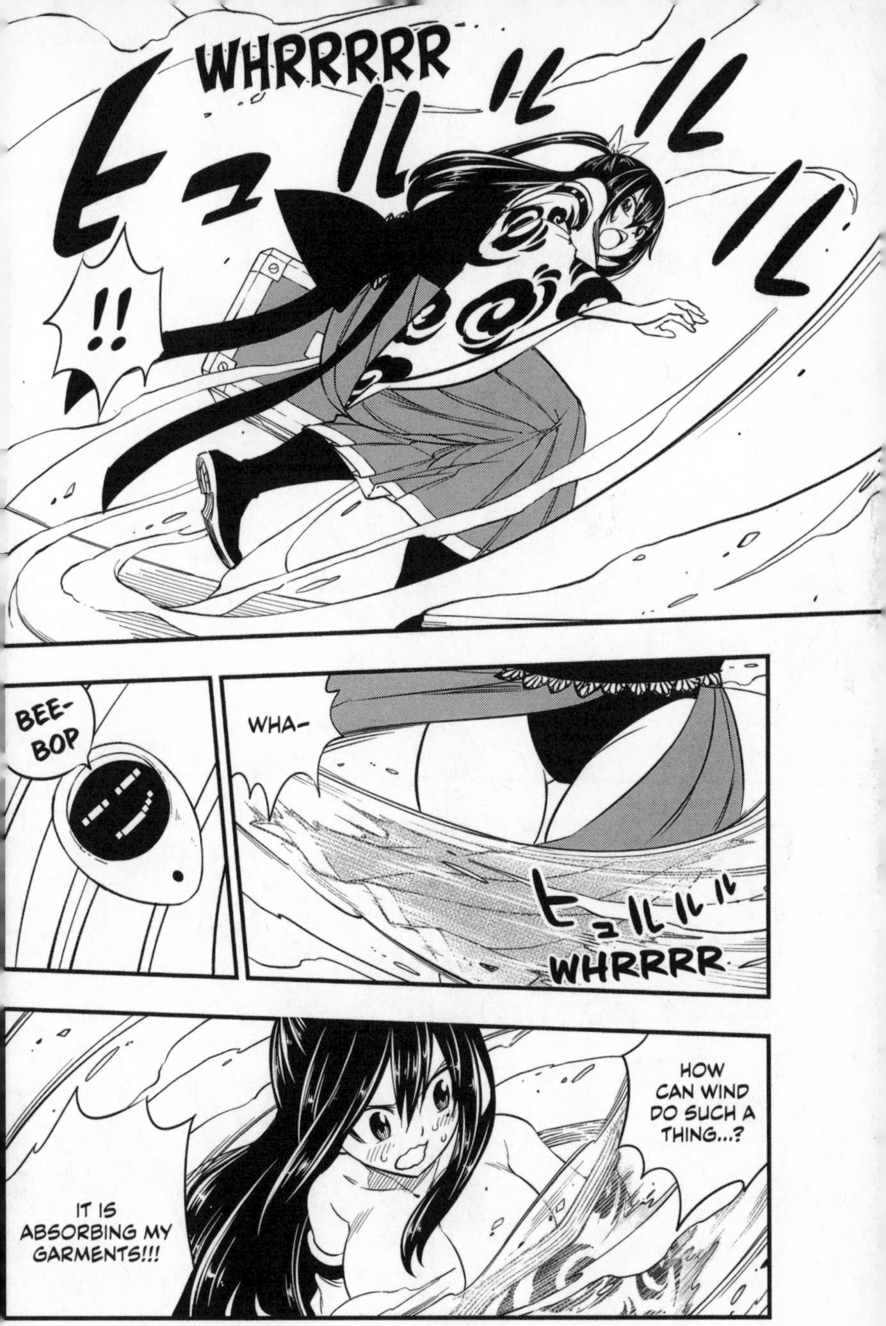
WHRRRRR
ヒュルルルル
!!
WHA-
ヒュルルル
WHRRRR
BEE-BOP
HOW CAN WIND DO SUCH A THING...?
IT IS ABSORBING MY GARMENTS!!!

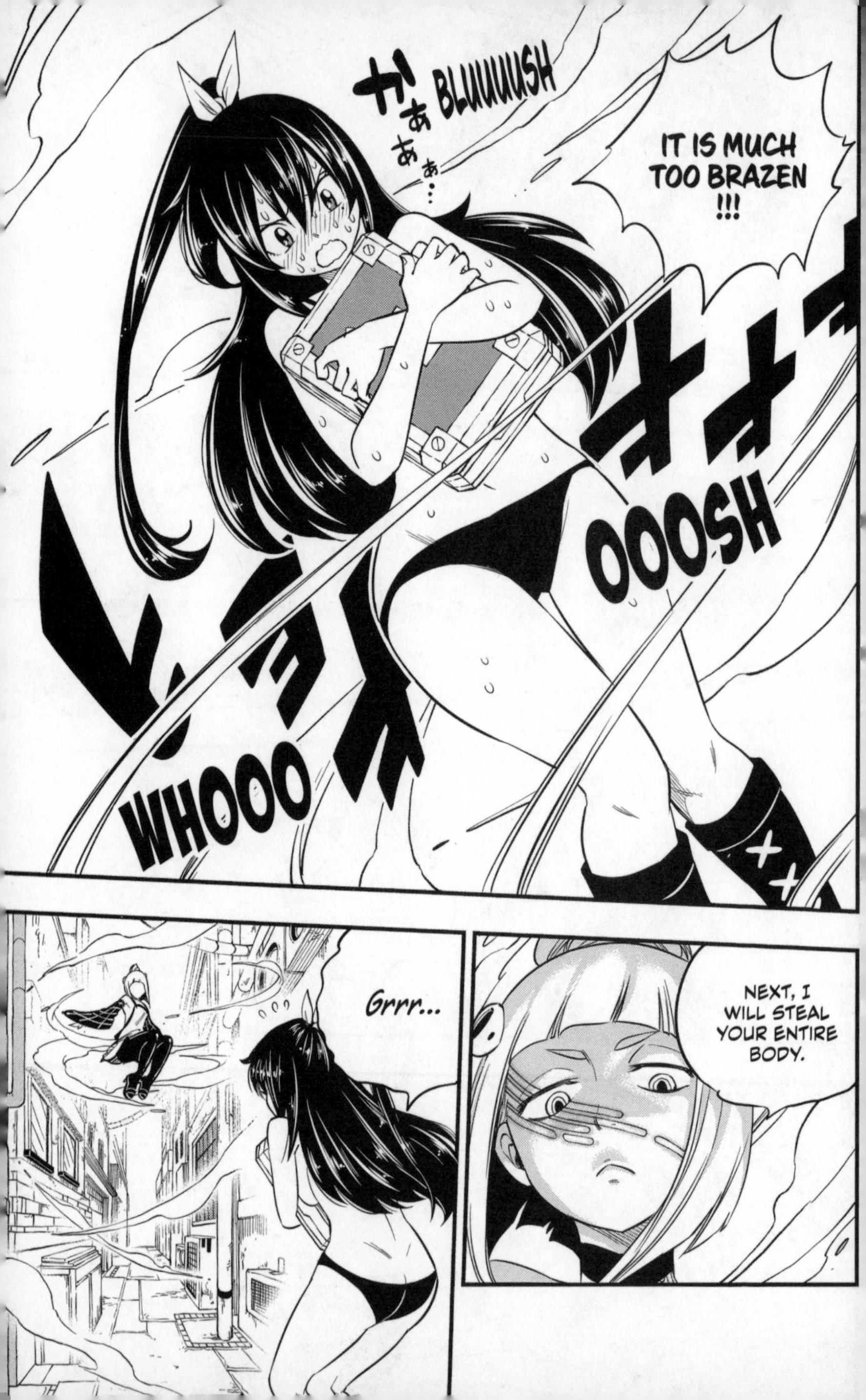
BLUUUUSH
IT IS MUCH TOO BRAZEN !!!
WHOOO OOOSH
NEXT, I WILL STEAL YOUR ENTIRE BODY.
Grrr...

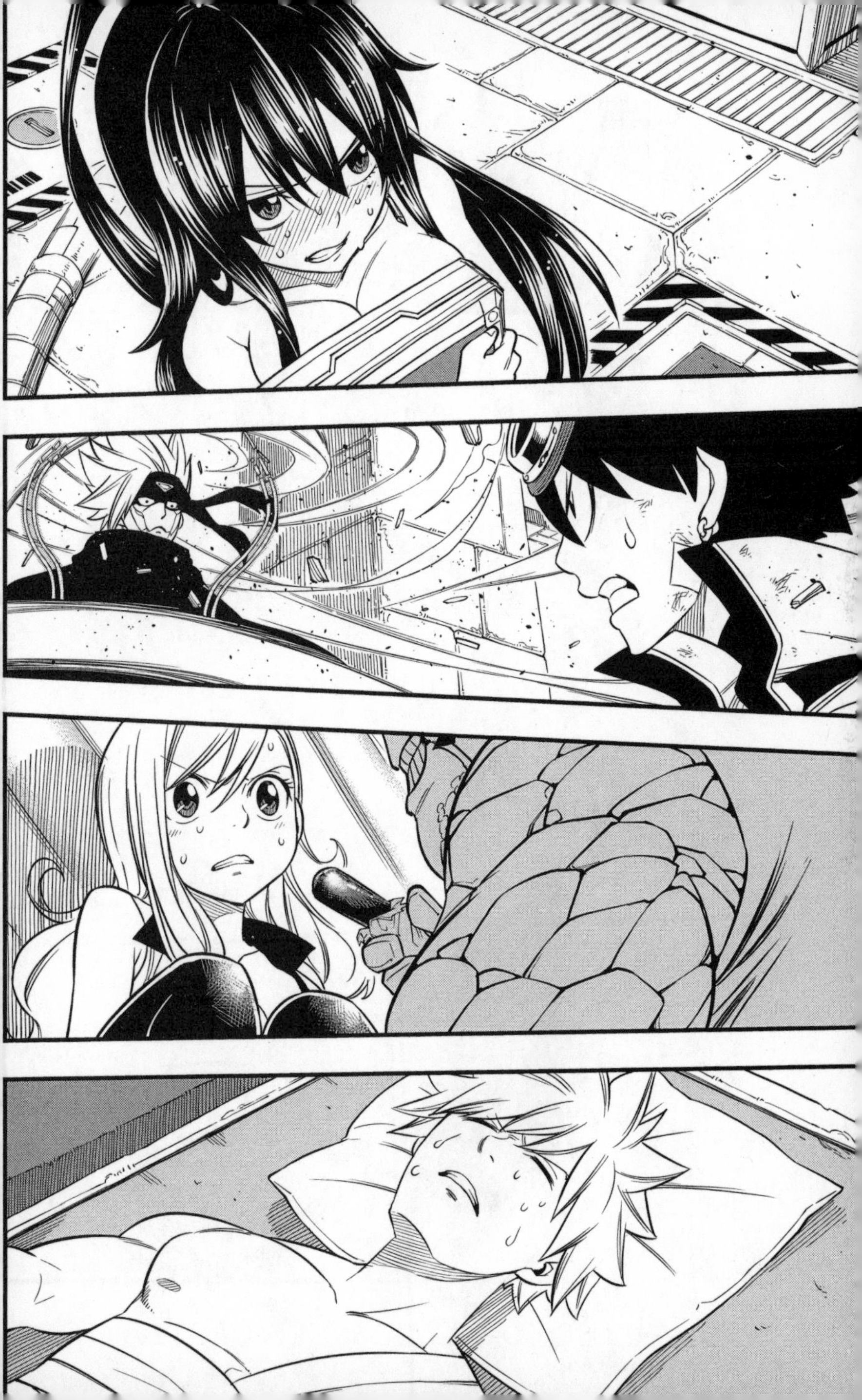

EDENS ZERO

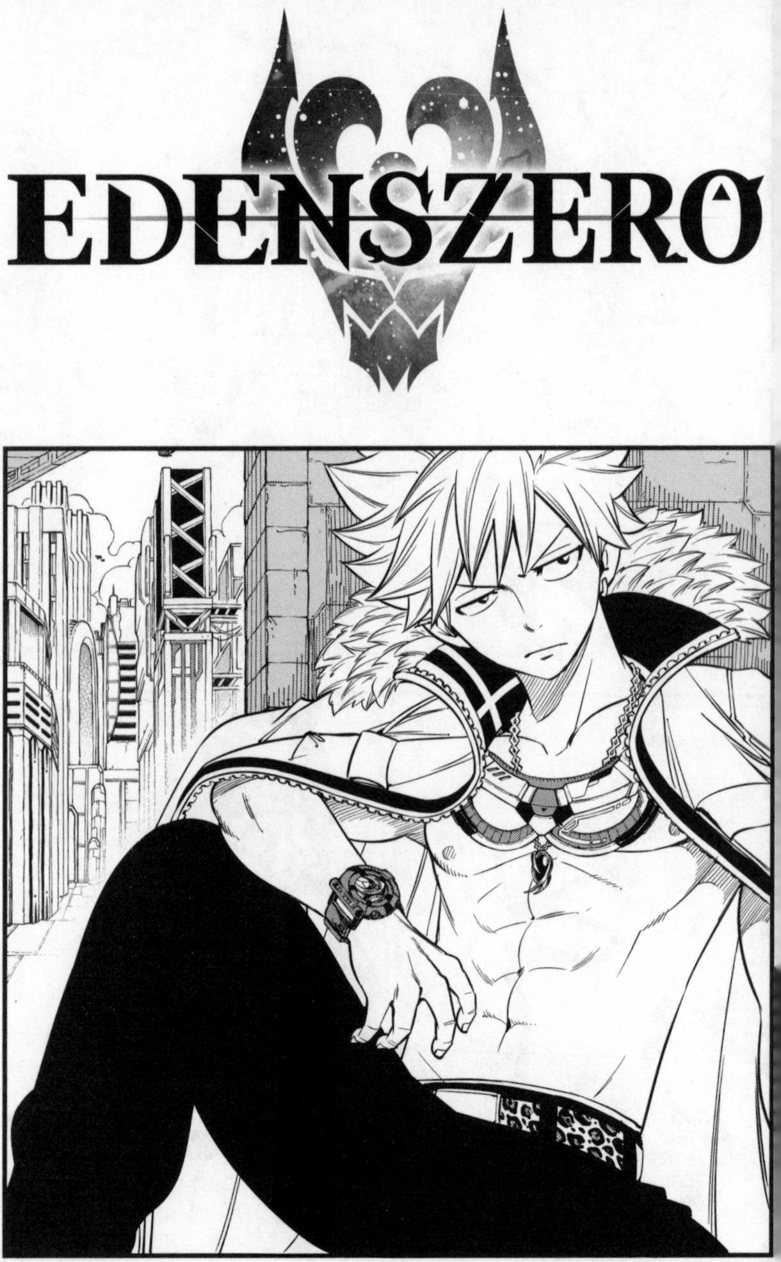

CHAPTER 80: 60-DAY COMMEMORATIVE COIN

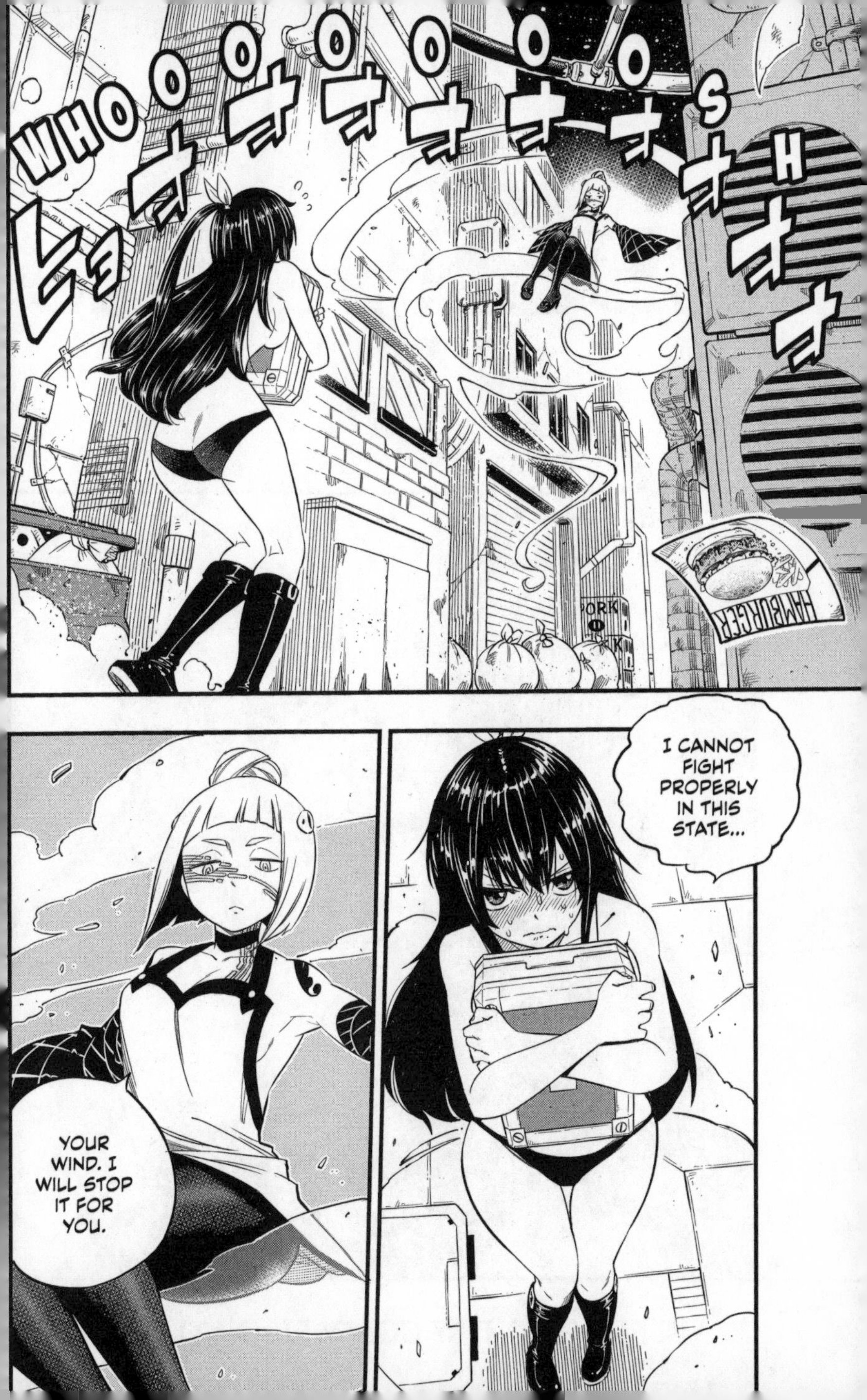
WHOOOOOOOSH
ヒョオオオオオオオオ
PORK
HAMBURGER
I CANNOT FIGHT PROPERLY IN THIS STATE...
YOUR WIND. I WILL STOP IT FOR YOU.

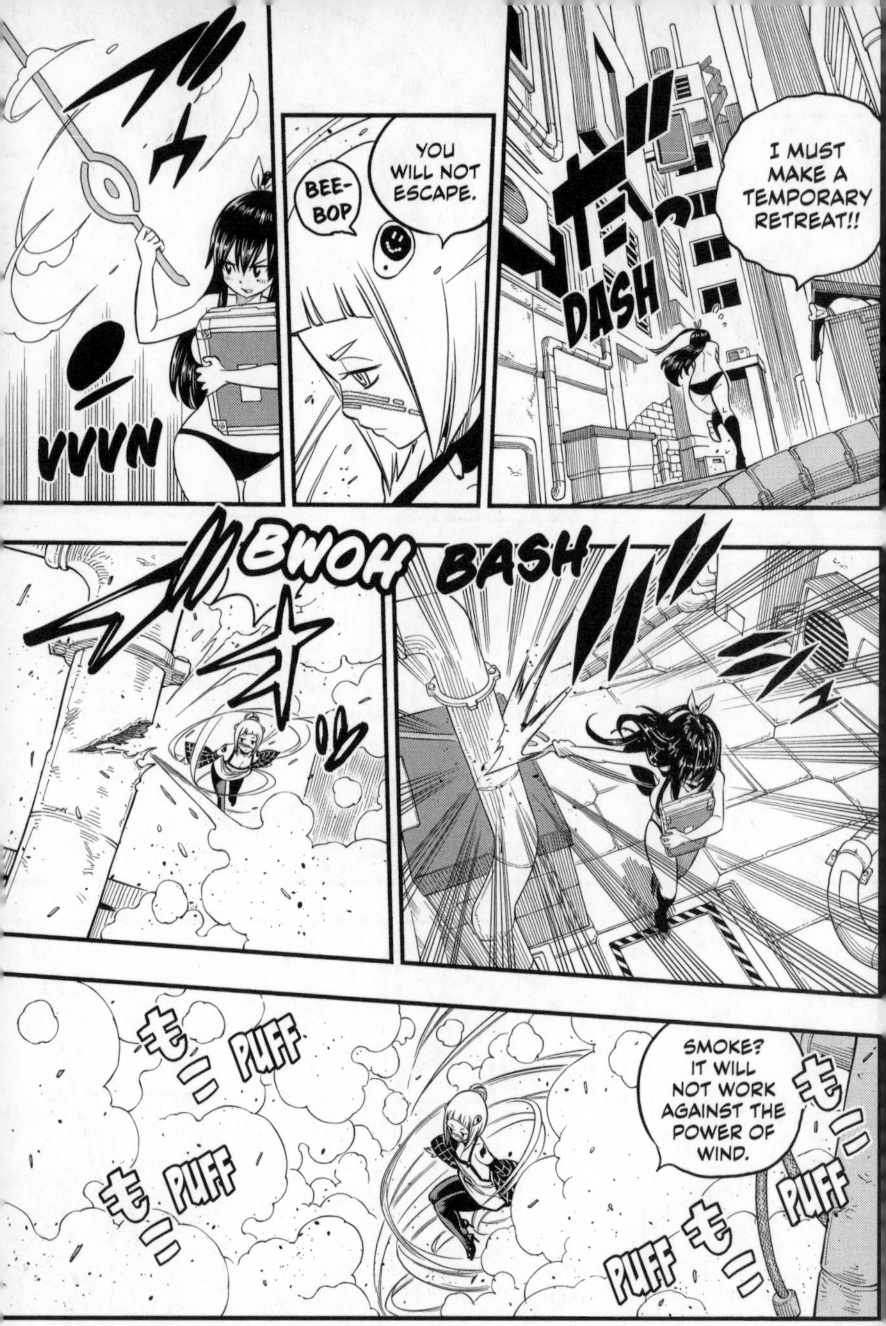
I MUST MAKE A TEMPORARY RETREAT!!
DASH
YOU WILL NOT ESCAPE.
BEE-BOP
VVVN
BASH
BWOH
SMOKE? IT WILL NOT WORK AGAINST THE POWER OF WIND.
PUFF
PUFF
PUFF
PUFF

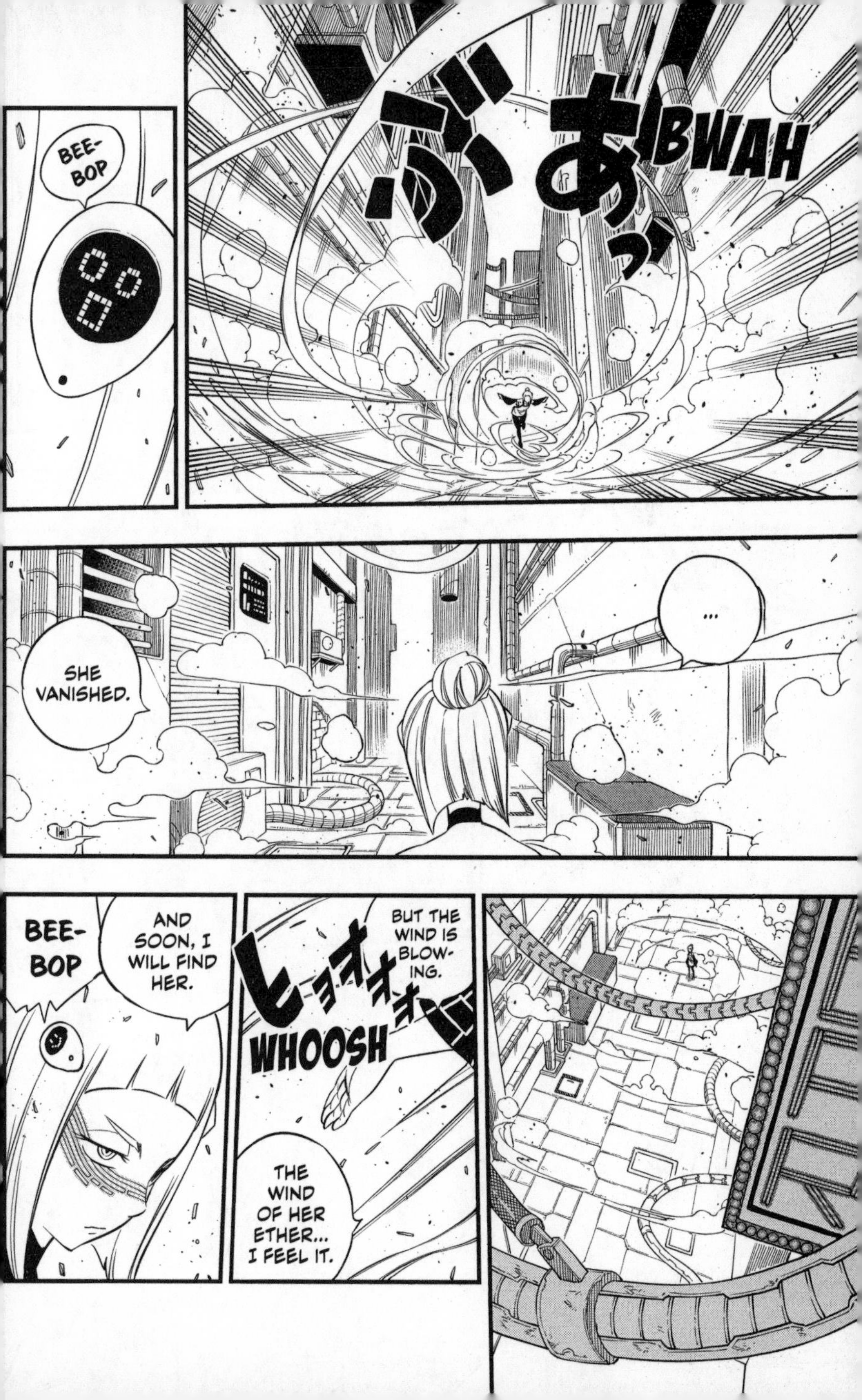
ぶあっ
BWAH
BEE-BOP
...
SHE VANISHED.
BUT THE WIND IS BLOWING.
ヒョオオオ
WHOOSH
THE WIND OF HER ETHER... I FEEL IT.
AND SOON, I WILL FIND HER.
BEE-BOP

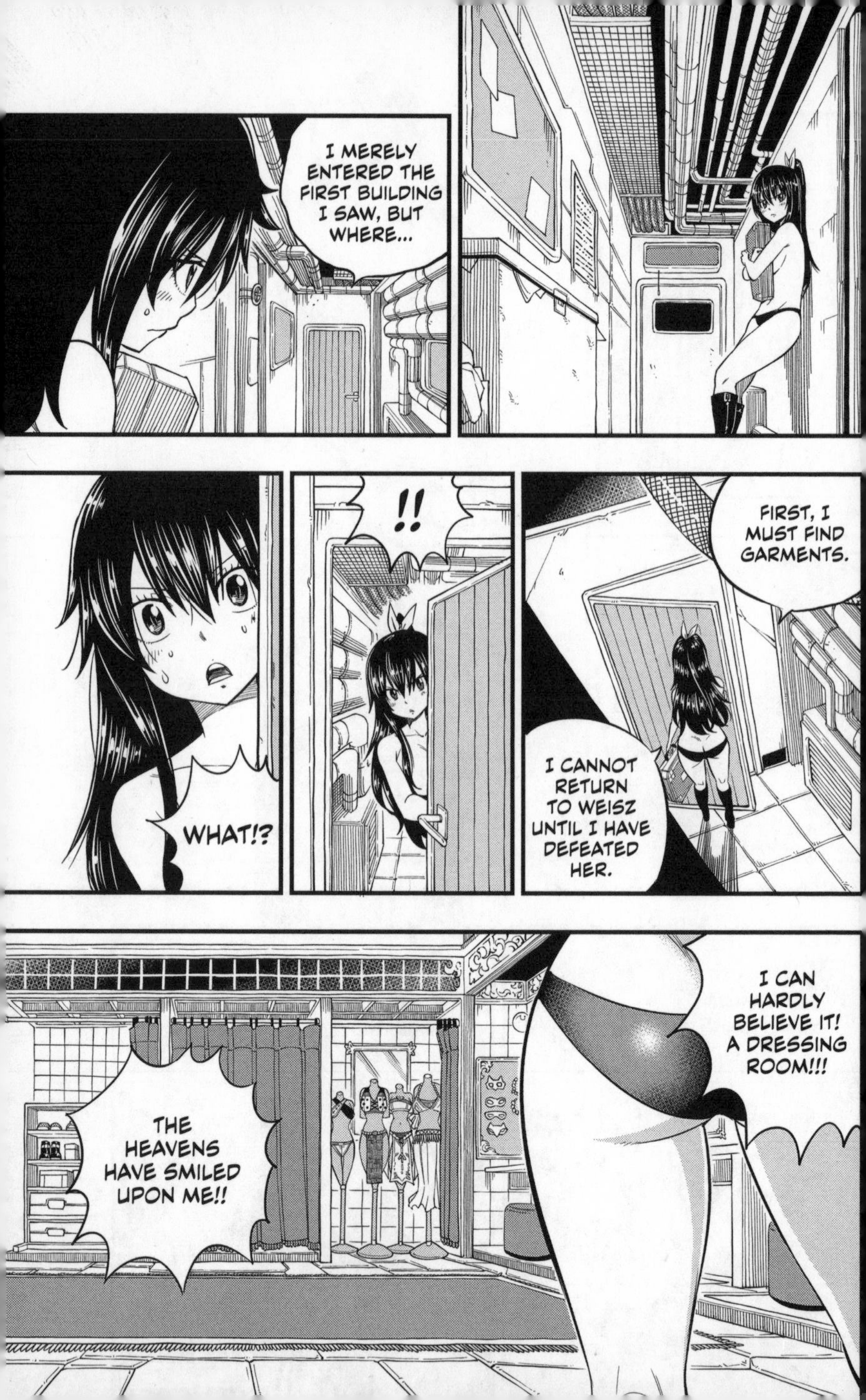
I MERELY ENTERED THE FIRST BUILDING I SAW, BUT WHERE...
FIRST, I MUST FIND GARMENTS.
I CANNOT RETURN TO WEISZ UNTIL I HAVE DEFEATED HER.
!!
WHAT!?
I CAN HARDLY BELIEVE IT! A DRESSING ROOM!!!
THE HEAVENS HAVE SMILED UPON ME!!

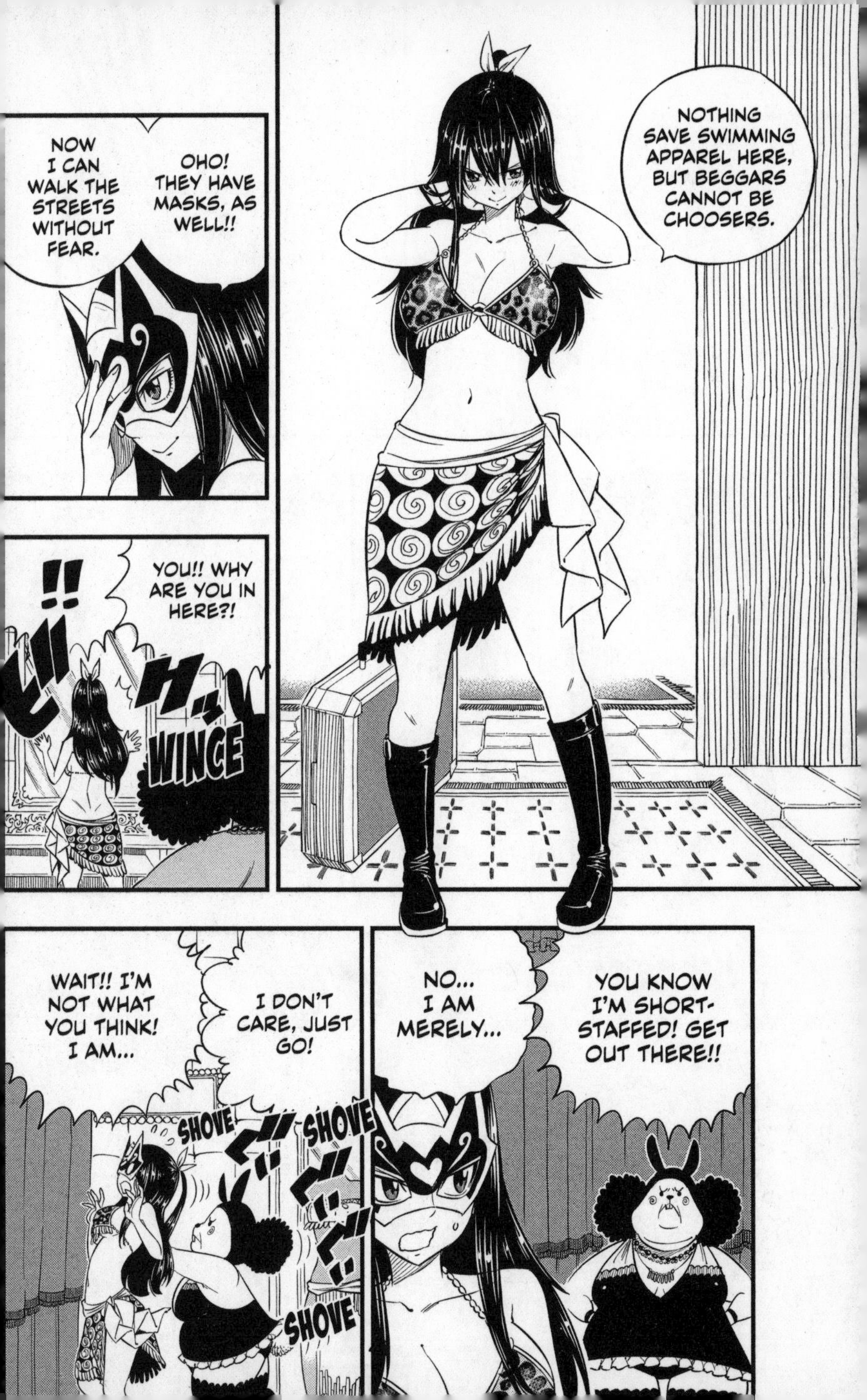
NOTHING SAVE SWIMMING APPAREL HERE, BUT BEGGARS CANNOT BE CHOOSERS.
OHO! THEY HAVE MASKS, AS WELL!!
NOW I CAN WALK THE STREETS WITHOUT FEAR.
YOU!! WHY ARE YOU IN HERE?!
WINCE
YOU KNOW I'M SHORT-STAFFED! GET OUT THERE!!
NO... I AM MERELY...
I DON'T CARE, JUST GO!
WAIT!! I'M NOT WHAT YOU THINK! I AM...
SHOVE
SHOVE
SHOVE

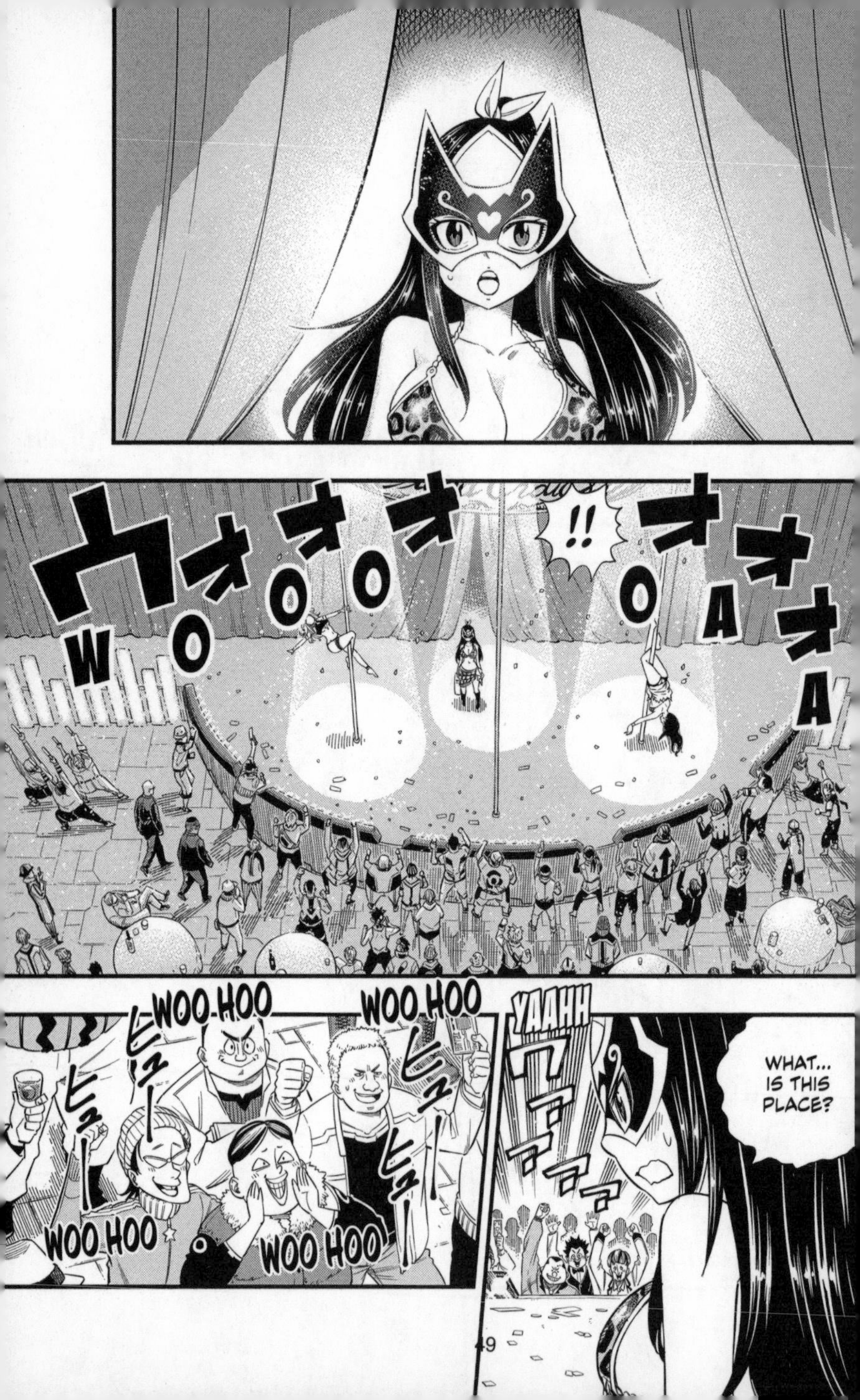
ウオオオオオオオ
WOOOOOAAA
!!
WHAT... IS THIS PLACE?
ワァァァァァ
YAAHH
WOO HOO
WOO HOO
WOO HOO
WOO HOO

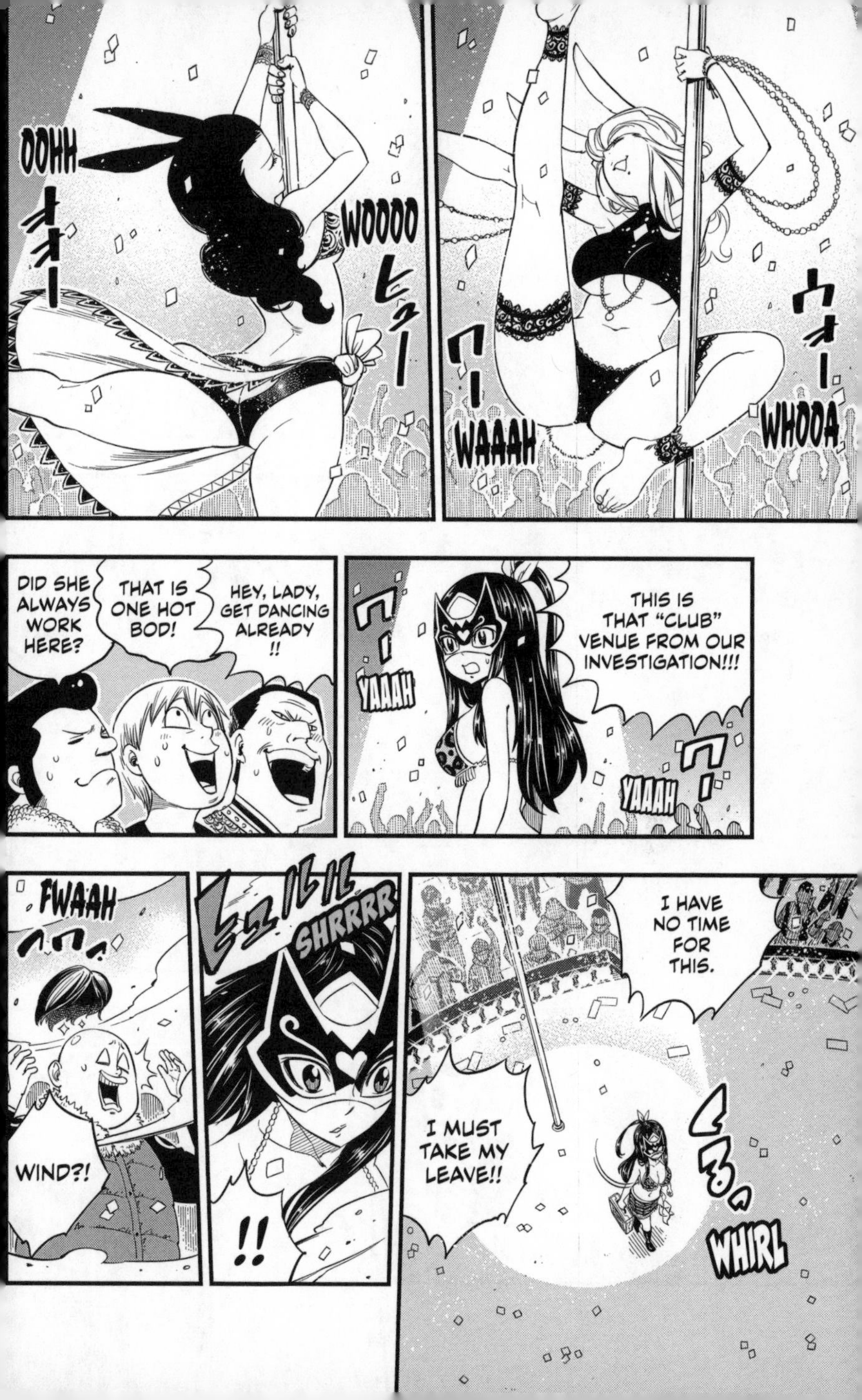
ウォー
WHOOA
ワー
WAAAH
WOOOO
ヒュー
OOHH
オォー
THIS IS THAT "CLUB" VENUE FROM OUR INVESTIGATION!!!
ワー
YAAAH
ワー
YAAAH
HEY, LADY, GET DANCING ALREADY !!
THAT IS ONE HOT BOD!
DID SHE ALWAYS WORK HERE?
I HAVE NO TIME FOR THIS.
I MUST TAKE MY LEAVE!!
くるっ
WHIRL
ヒュルル
SHRRRR
!!
FWAAH
WIND?!

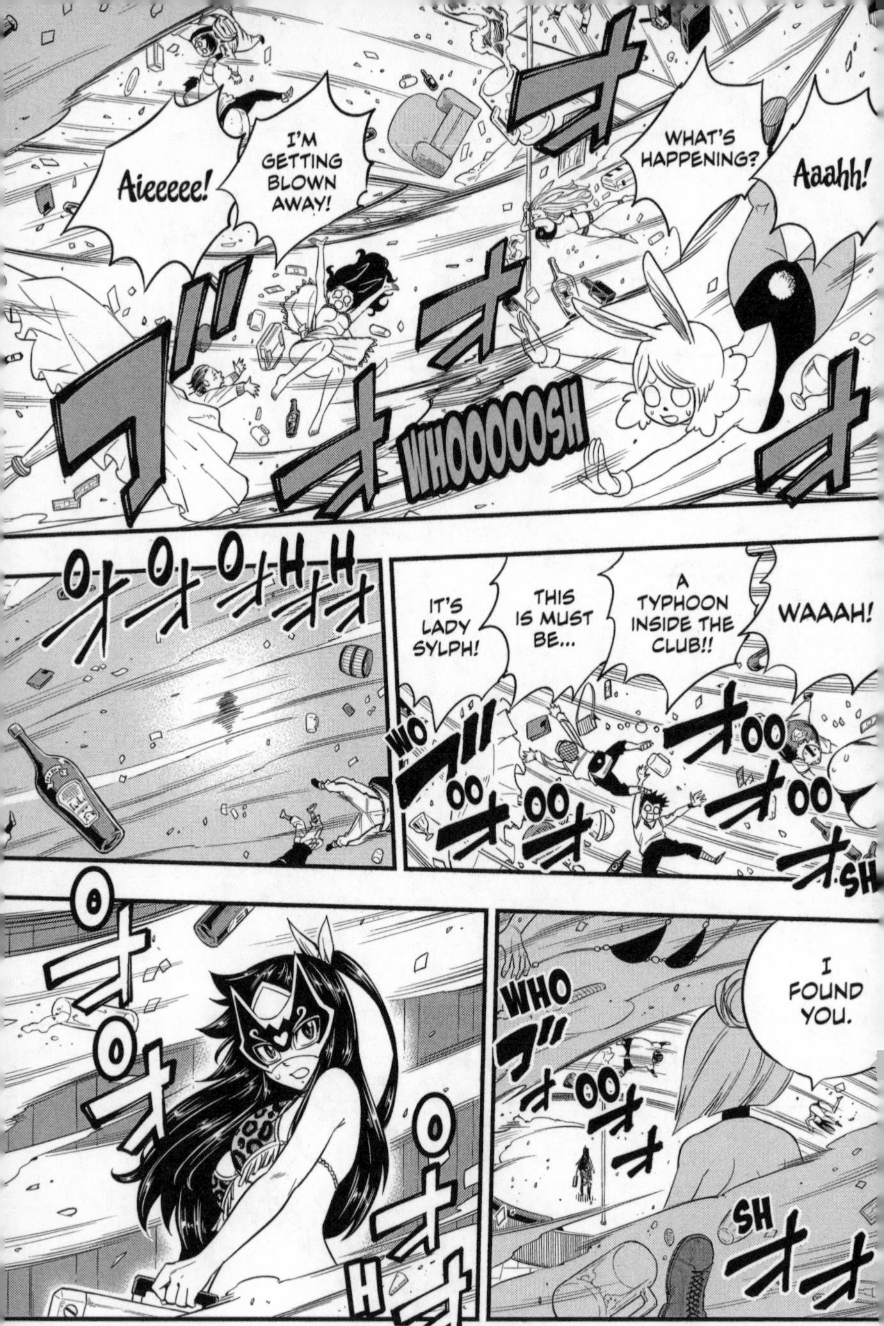
Aaahh!
WHAT'S HAPPENING?
I'M GETTING BLOWN AWAY!
Aieeeee!
WHOOOOOSH
WAAAH!
A TYPHOON INSIDE THE CLUB!!
THIS IS MUST BE...
IT'S LADY SYLPH!
WO
OO
OO
OO
OO
SH
OOOHH
I FOUND YOU.
WHO
OO
SH
O
O
O
H

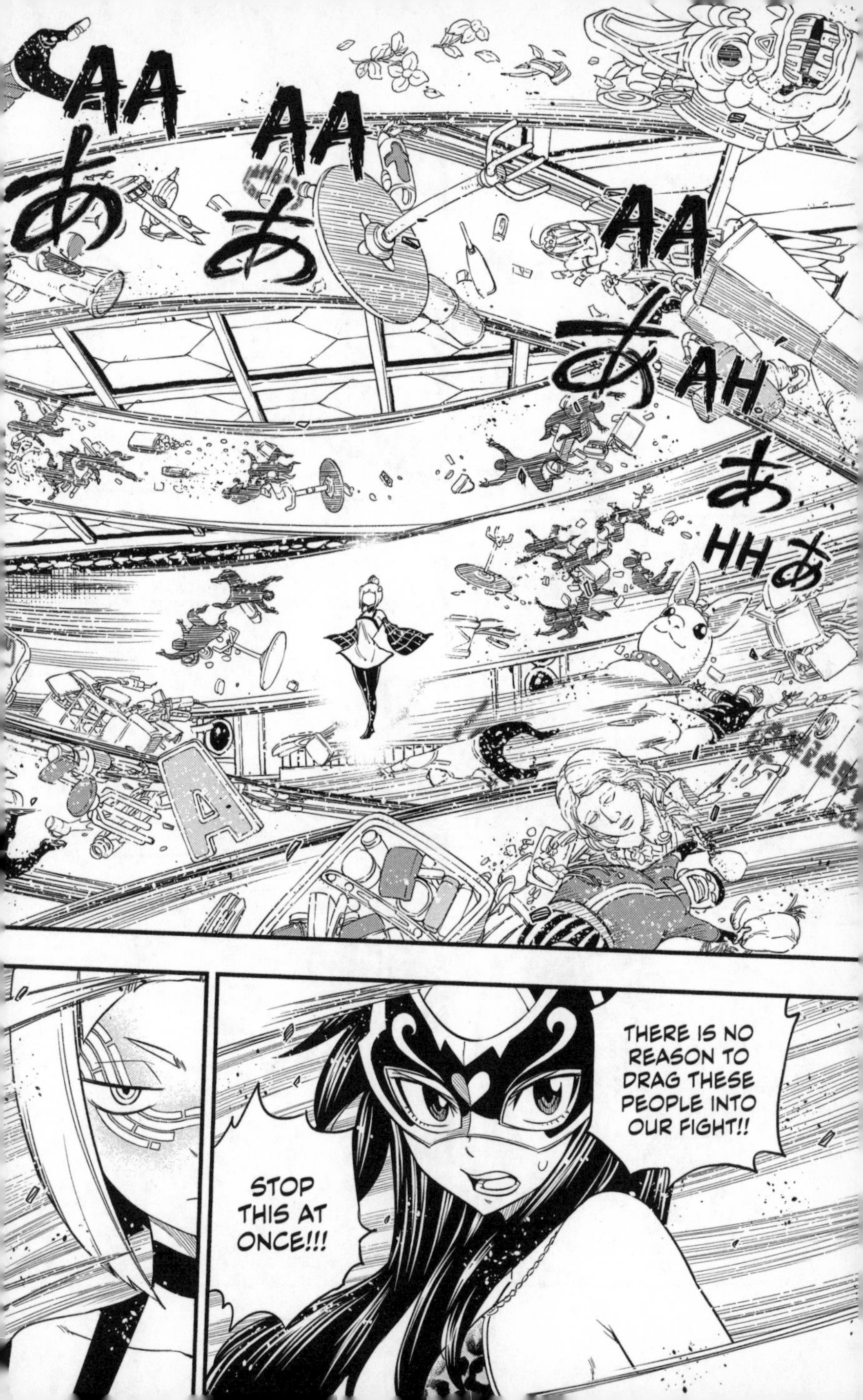

AA あ
AA あ
AA あ
AH あ
HH あ
THERE IS NO REASON TO DRAG THESE PEOPLE INTO OUR FIGHT!!
STOP THIS AT ONCE!!!

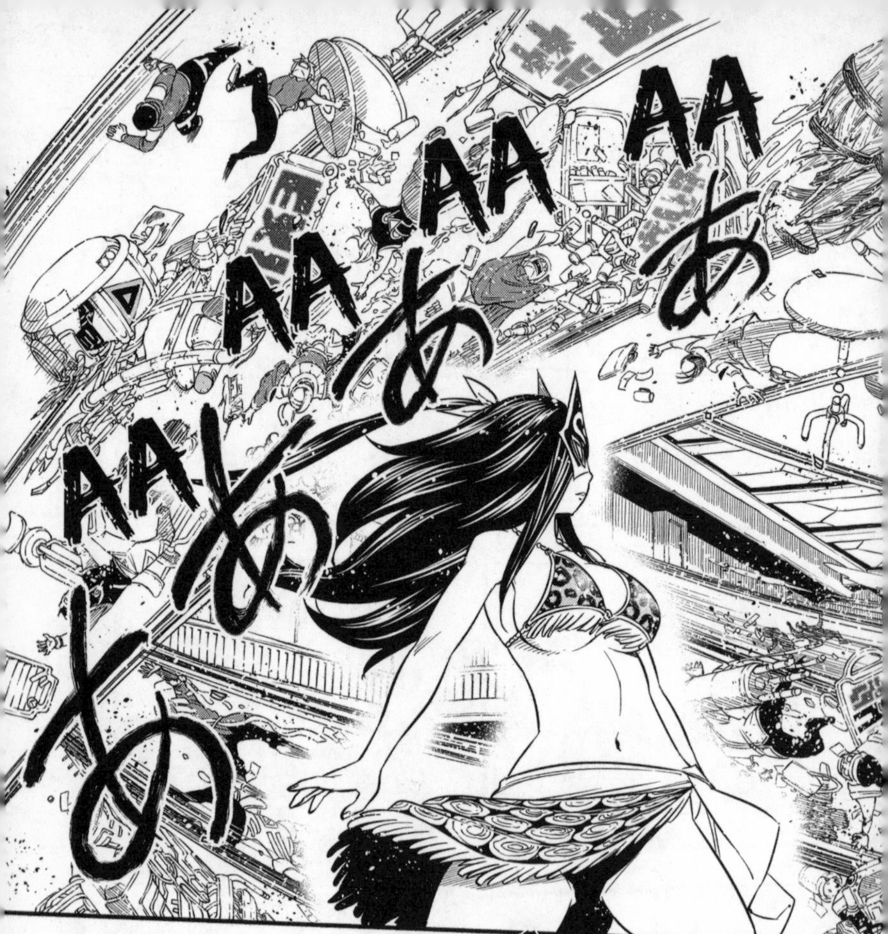
AAAAAAAAAA
ああああ
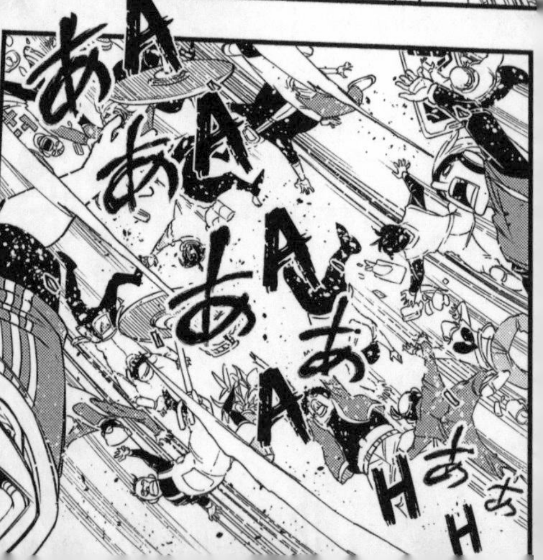
あAあAAあAあAあHあH
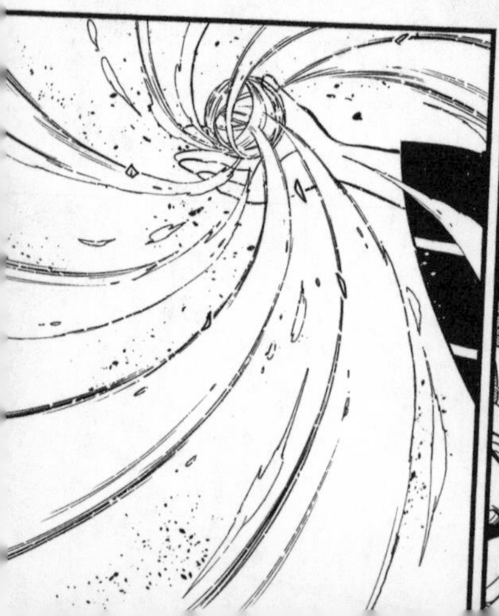

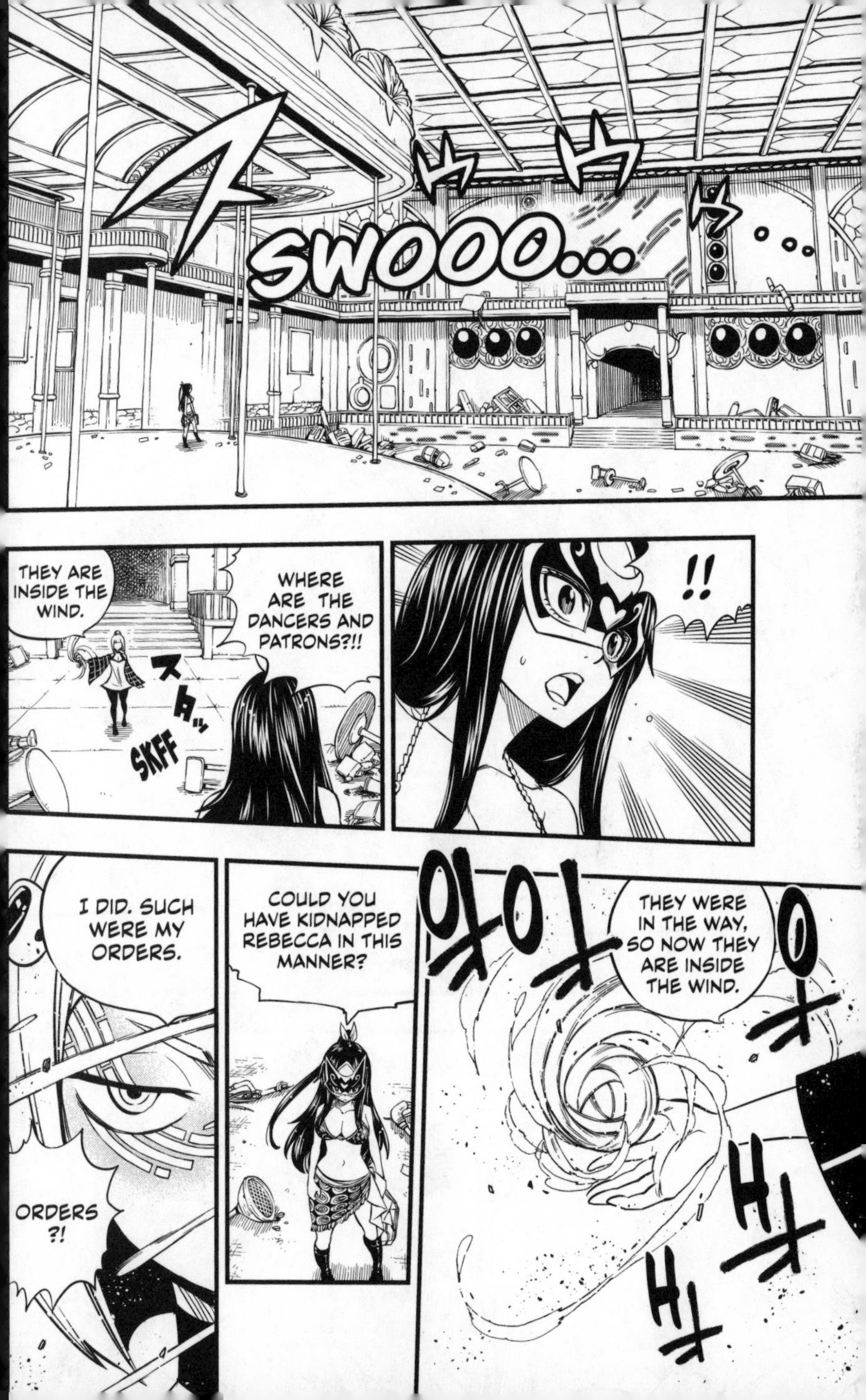
SWOOO...
!!
WHERE ARE THE DANCERS AND PATRONS?!!
THEY ARE INSIDE THE WIND.
SKFF
THEY WERE IN THE WAY, SO NOW THEY ARE INSIDE THE WIND.
COULD YOU HAVE KIDNAPPED REBECCA IN THIS MANNER?
I DID. SUCH WERE MY ORDERS.
ORDERS ?!

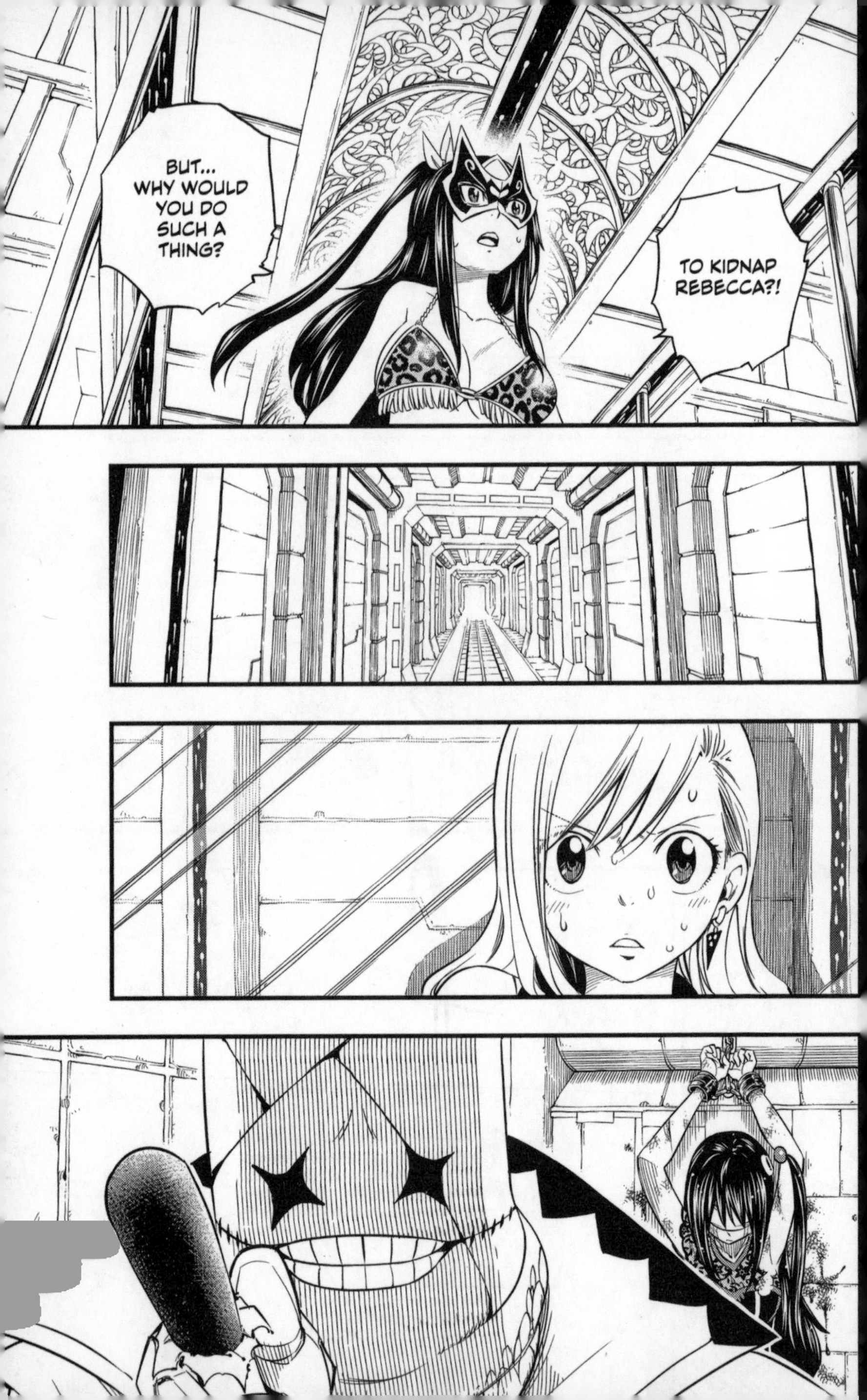
BUT... WHY WOULD YOU DO SUCH A THING?
TO KIDNAP REBECCA?!

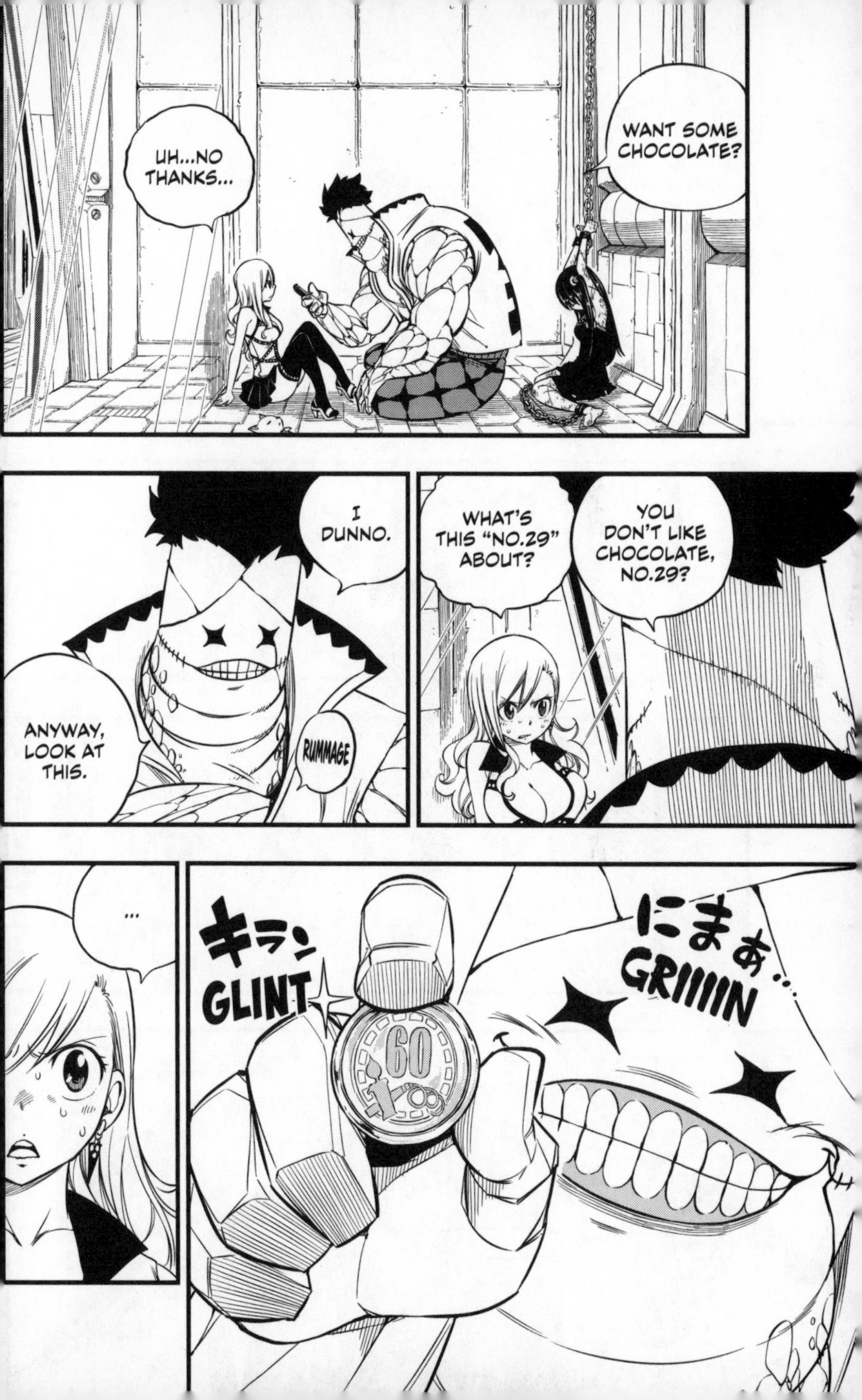
WANT SOME CHOCOLATE?
UH...NO THANKS...
YOU DON'T LIKE CHOCOLATE, NO.29?
WHAT'S THIS "NO.29" ABOUT?
I DUNNO.
RUMMAGE
ANYWAY, LOOK AT THIS.
にまぁ…
GRIIIIIN
キラン
GLINT
60
...

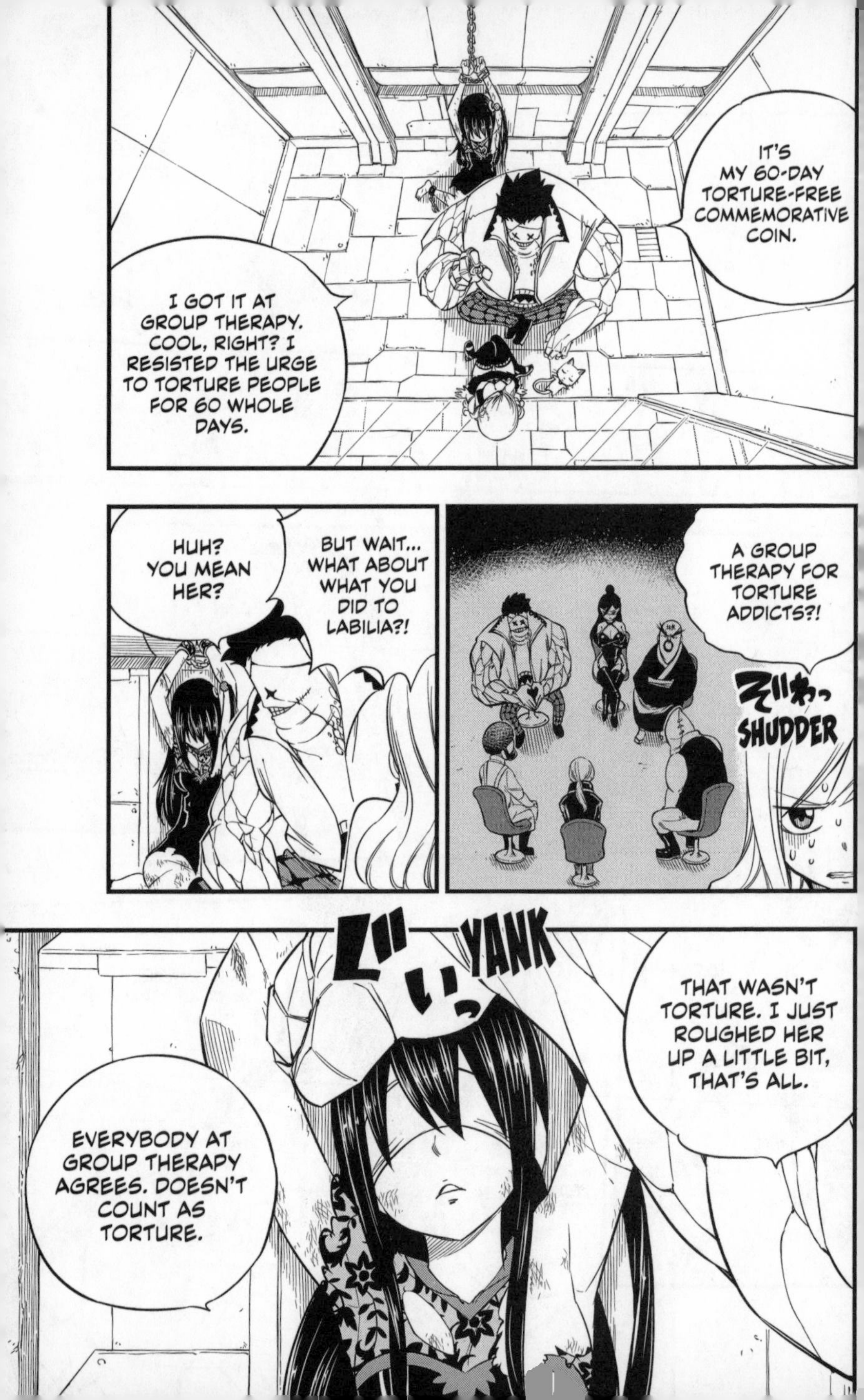
IT'S MY 60-DAY TORTURE-FREE COMMEMORATIVE COIN.
I GOT IT AT GROUP THERAPY. COOL, RIGHT? I RESISTED THE URGE TO TORTURE PEOPLE FOR 60 WHOLE DAYS.
A GROUP THERAPY FOR TORTURE ADDICTS?!
ぞわっ SHUDDER
BUT WAIT... WHAT ABOUT WHAT YOU DID TO LABILIA?!
HUH? YOU MEAN HER?
YANK
THAT WASN'T TORTURE. I JUST ROUGHED HER UP A LITTLE BIT, THAT'S ALL.
EVERYBODY AT GROUP THERAPY AGREES. DOESN'T COUNT AS TORTURE.

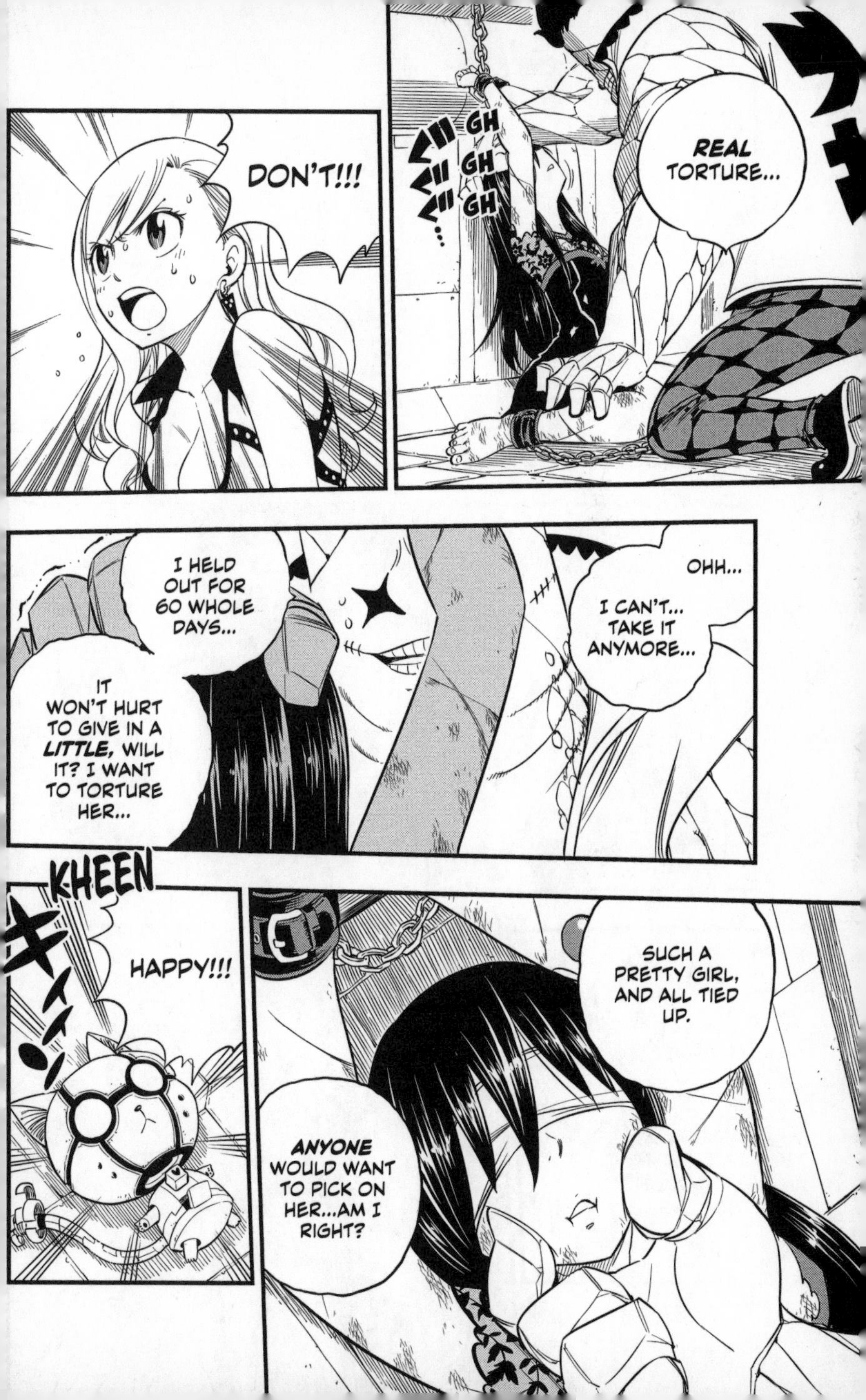
REAL TORTURE...
GH GH GH...
DON'T!!!
OHH...
I CAN'T... TAKE IT ANYMORE...
I HELD OUT FOR 60 WHOLE DAYS...
IT WON'T HURT TO GIVE IN A LITTLE, WILL IT? I WANT TO TORTURE HER...
SUCH A PRETTY GIRL, AND ALL TIED UP.
ANYONE WOULD WANT TO PICK ON HER...AM I RIGHT?
KHEEN
HAPPY!!!

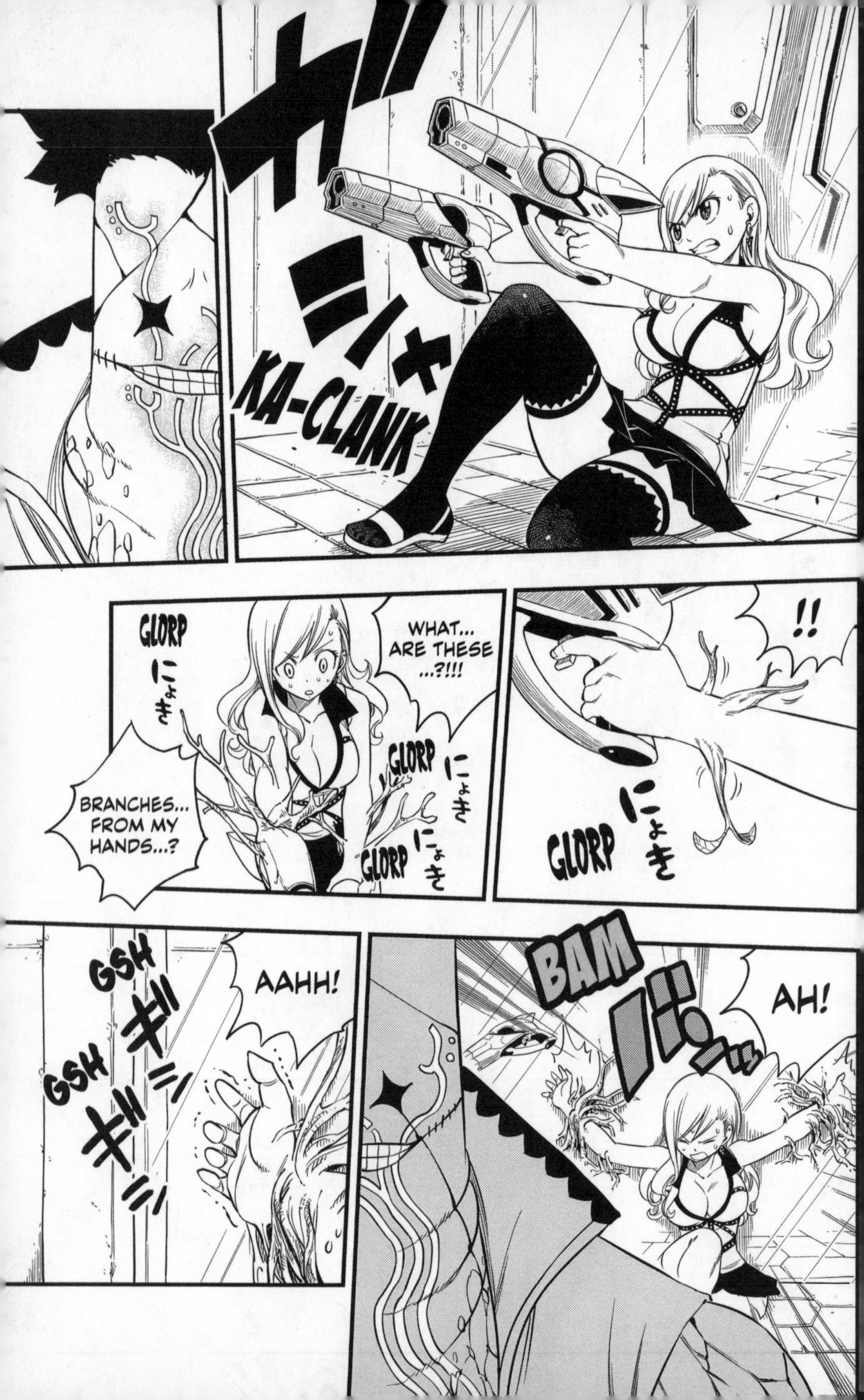

KA-CLANK
!!
GLORP
にょき
WHAT... ARE THESE ...?!!!
GLORP
にょき
GLORP
にょき
GLORP
にょき
BRANCHES... FROM MY HANDS...?
BAM
AH!
AAHH!
GSH
GSH

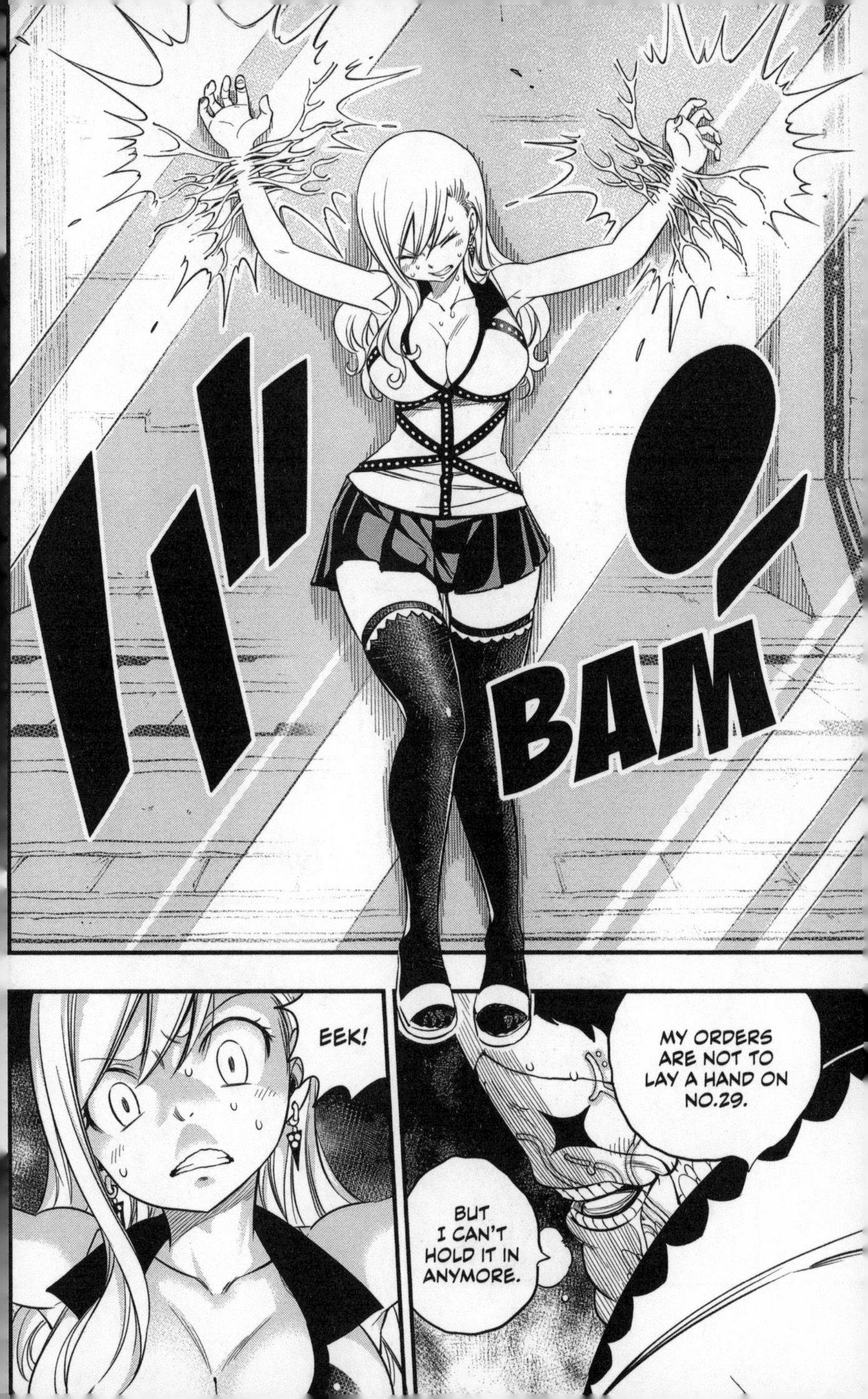
BAM
MY ORDERS ARE NOT TO LAY A HAND ON NO.29.
BUT I CAN'T HOLD IT IN ANYMORE.
EEK!

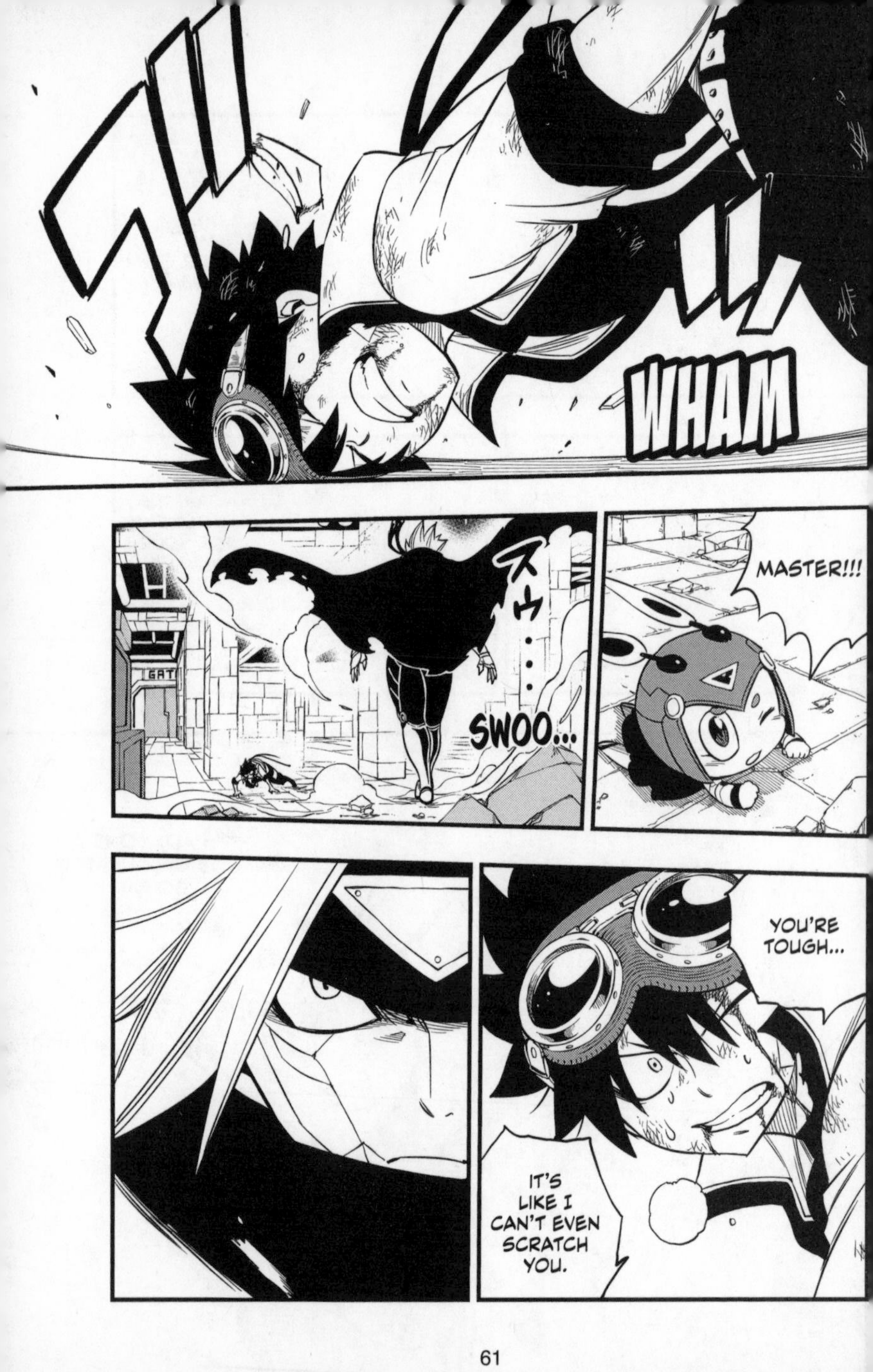
WHAM
MASTER!!!
スゥ…
SWOO...
YOU'RE TOUGH...
IT'S LIKE I CAN'T EVEN SCRATCH YOU.

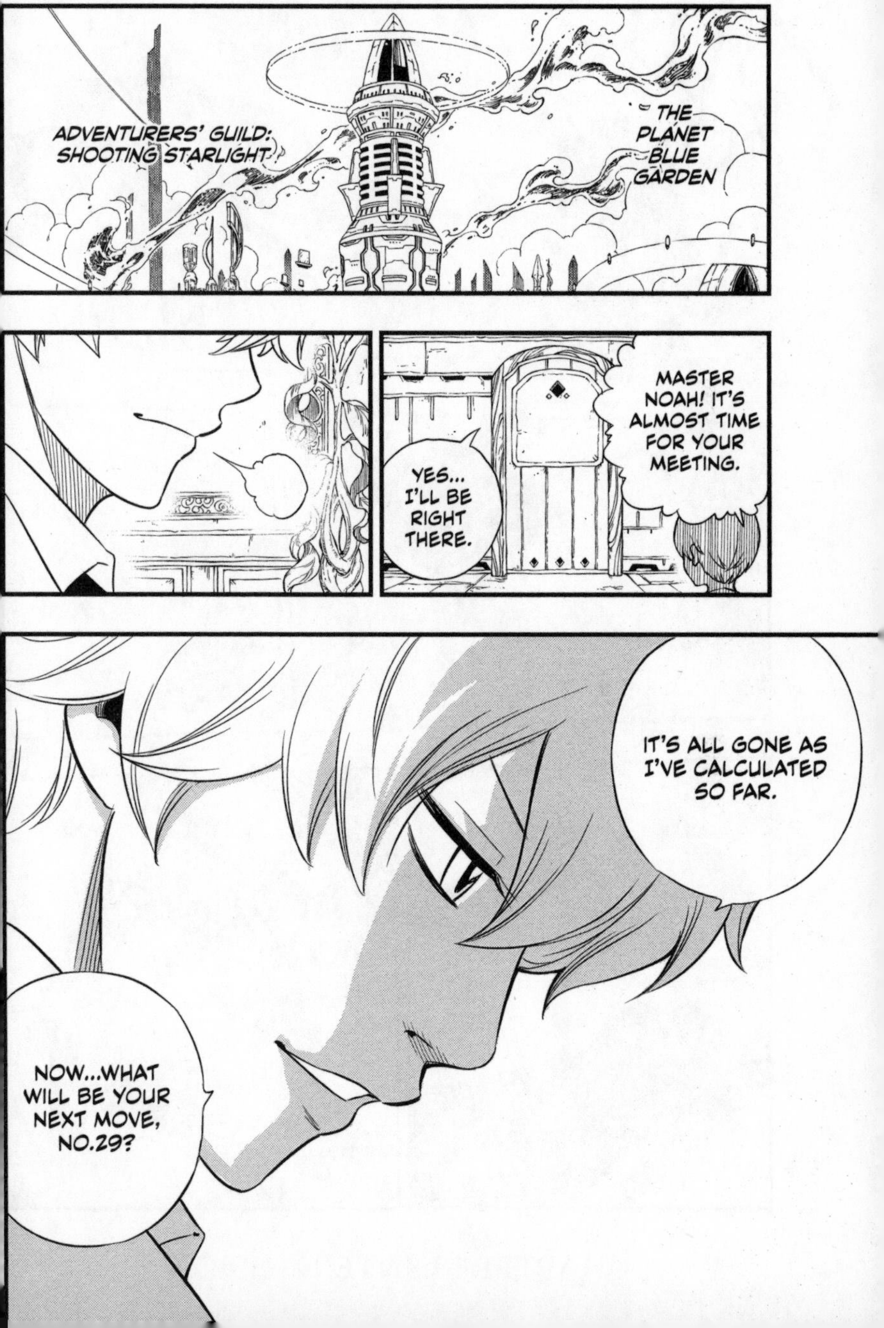
THE PLANET BLUE GARDEN
ADVENTURERS' GUILD: SHOOTING STARLIGHT
MASTER NOAH! IT'S ALMOST TIME FOR YOUR MEETING.
YES... I'LL BE RIGHT THERE.
IT'S ALL GONE AS I'VE CALCULATED SO FAR.
NOW...WHAT WILL BE YOUR NEXT MOVE, NO.29?

EDENSZERO

MORE INFO
CHANNEL

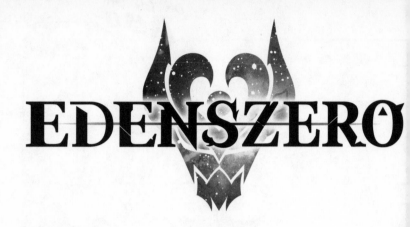

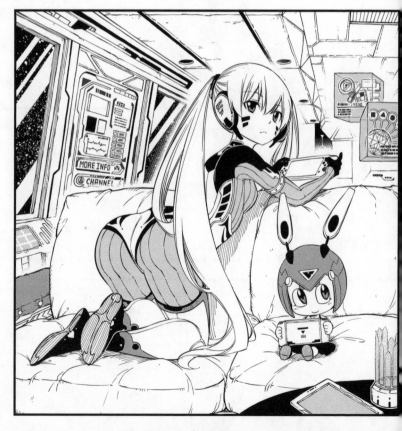

CHAPTER 81: INTERCESSION

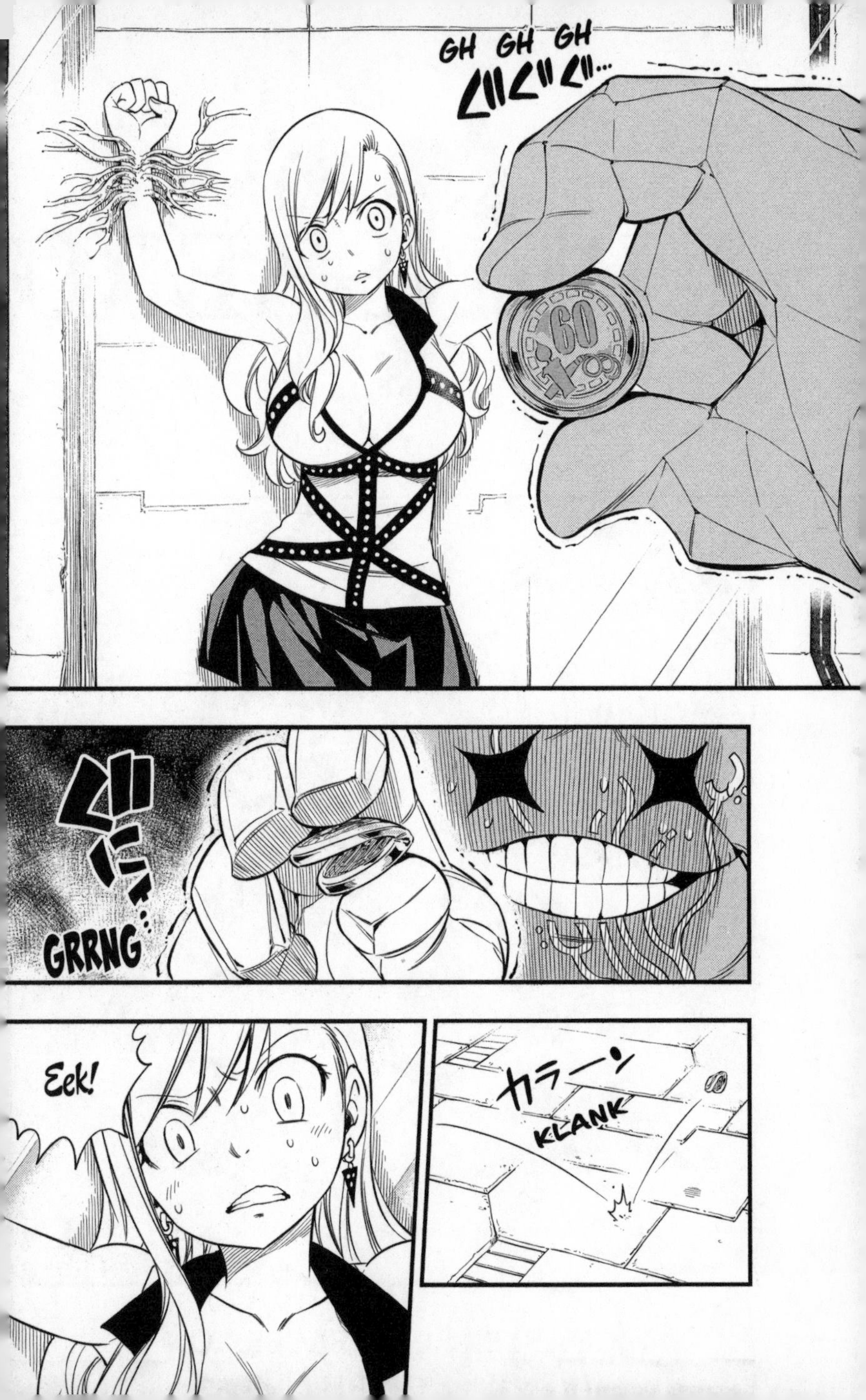
GH GH GH
くいくいくい…
ぐにゃ…
GRRNG
カラーン
KLANK
Eek!

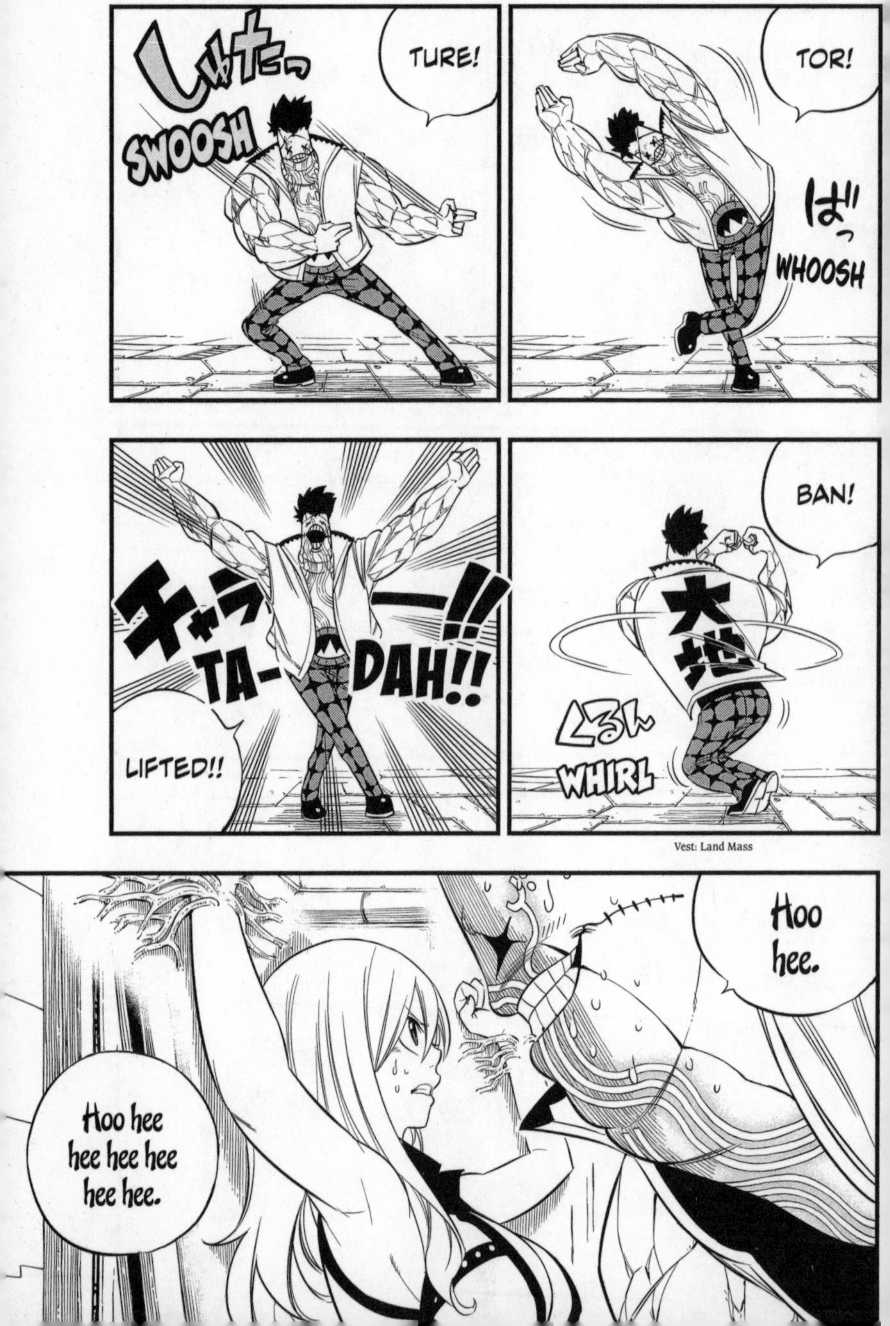
TOR!
ばっ
WHOOSH
TURE!
しゅたっ
SWOOSH
BAN!
大地
くるん
WHIRL
Vest: Land Mass
チャラー!!
TA-DAH!!
LIFTED!!
Hoo hee.
Hoo hee hee hee hee hee hee.

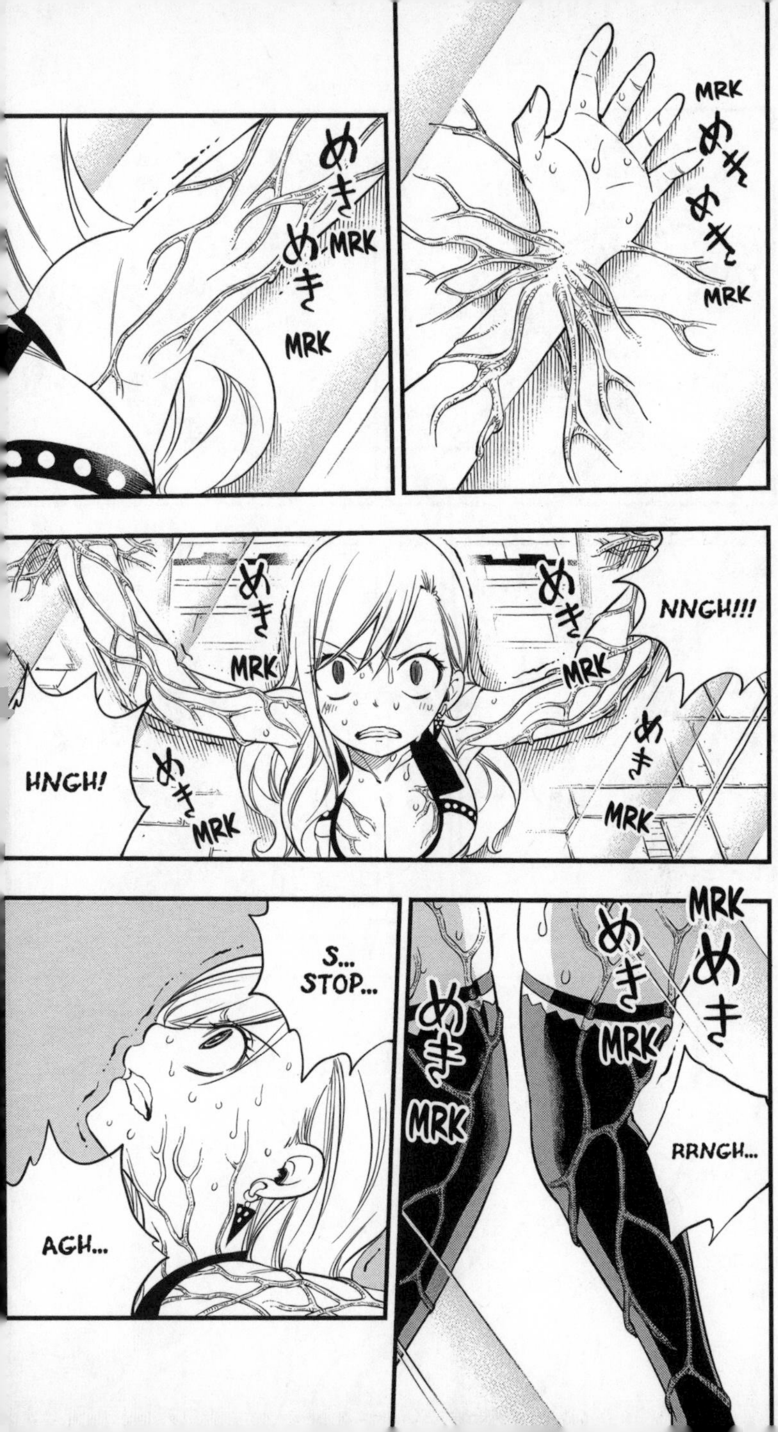
MRK
めき
めき
MRK
めき
めき
MRK
MRK
NNGH!!!
めき
MRK
めき
MRK
めき
MRK
めき
MRK
HNGH!
MRK
めき
MRK
めき
MRK
RRNGH...
S... STOP...
AGH...

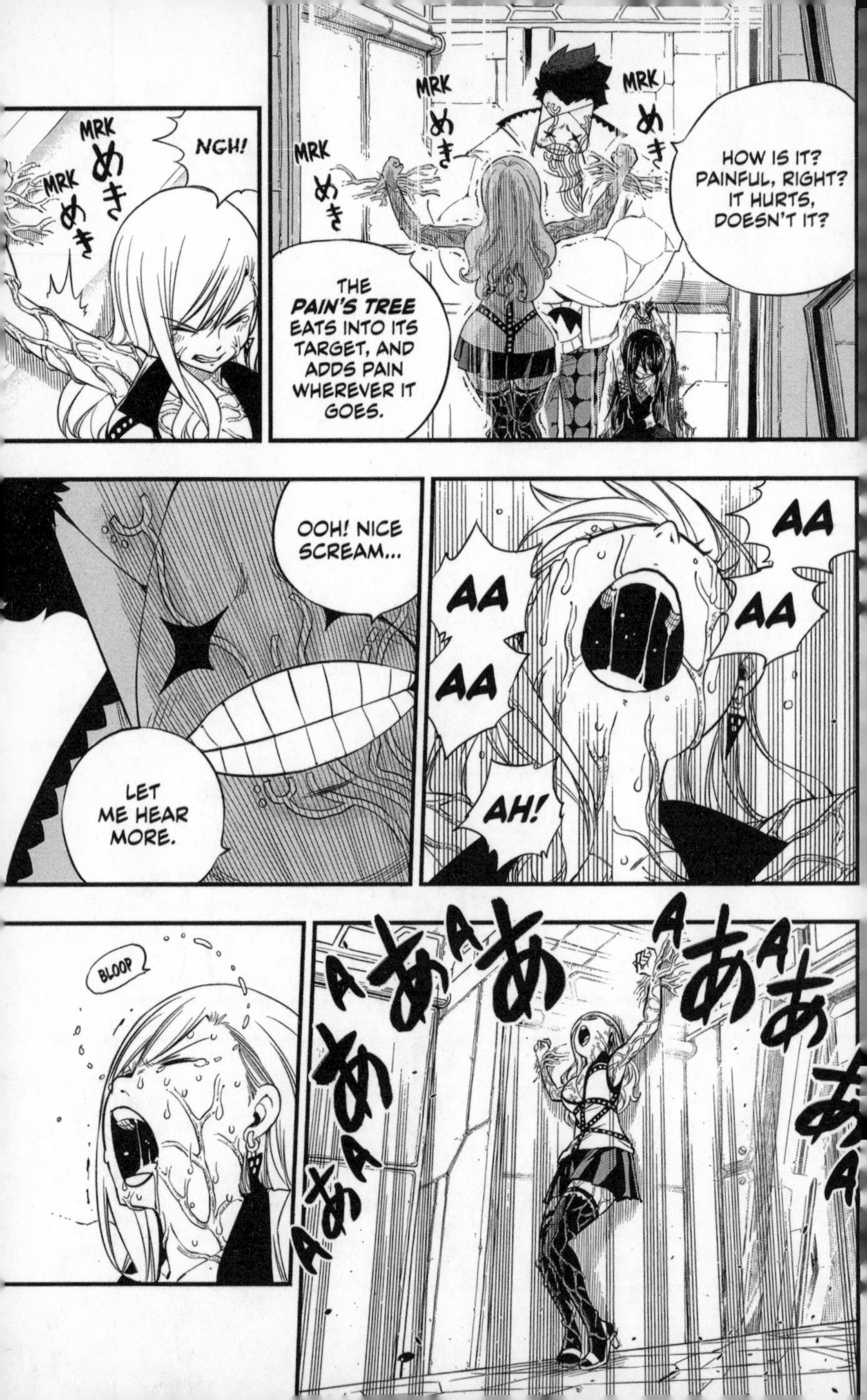
MRK
めき
MRK
めき
MRK
めき
HOW IS IT? PAINFUL, RIGHT? IT HURTS, DOESN'T IT?
THE *PAIN'S TREE* EATS INTO ITS TARGET, AND ADDS PAIN WHEREVER IT GOES.
MRK
めき
NGH!
MRK
めき
AA
AA
AA
AA
AH!
OOH! NICE SCREAM...
LET ME HEAR MORE.
A あ A あ A あ A あ A あ A
A あ A あ A あ A
BLOOP

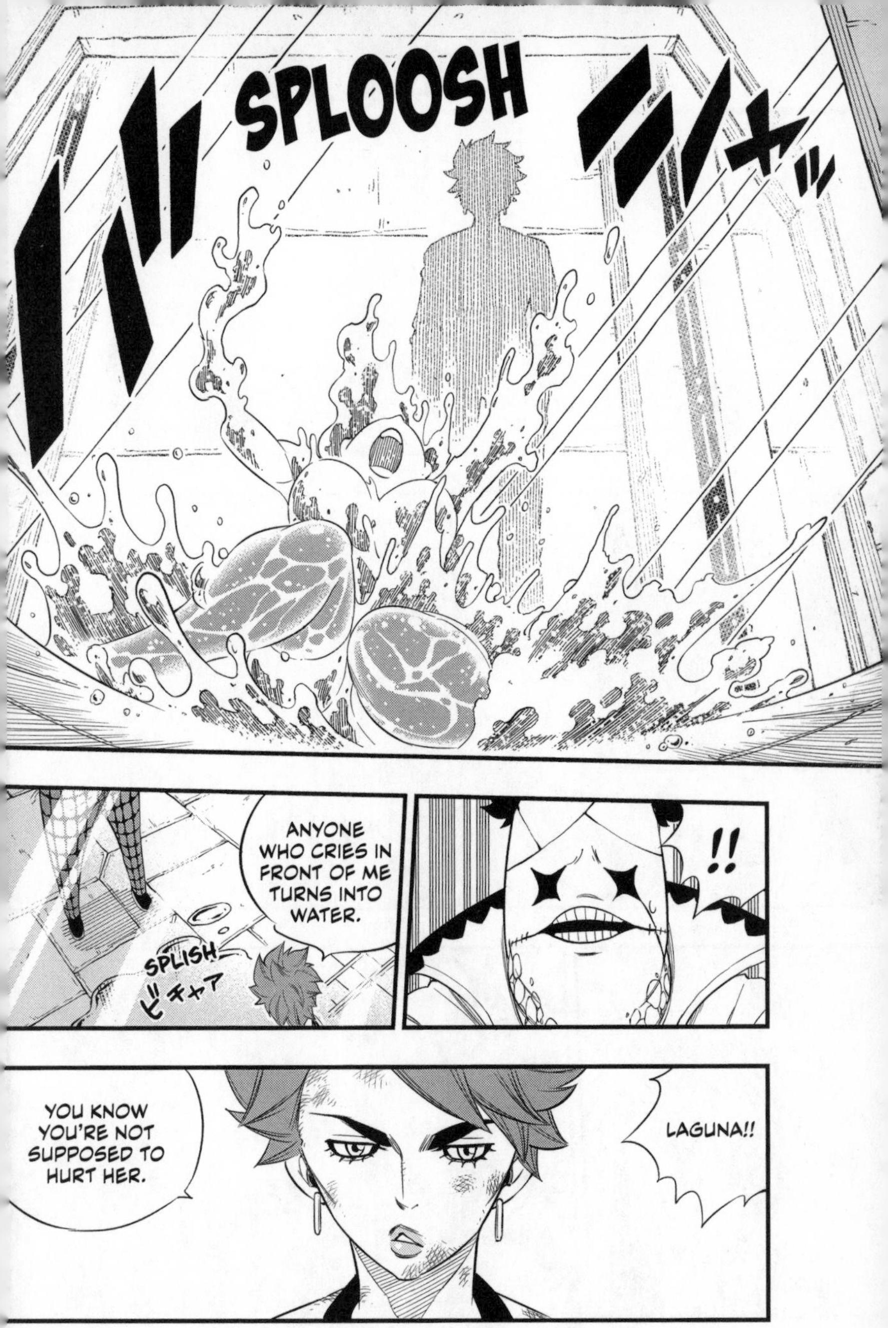
SPLOOSH
!!
ANYONE WHO CRIES IN FRONT OF ME TURNS INTO WATER.
SPLISH
ビチャア
LAGUNA!!
YOU KNOW YOU'RE NOT SUPPOSED TO HURT HER.

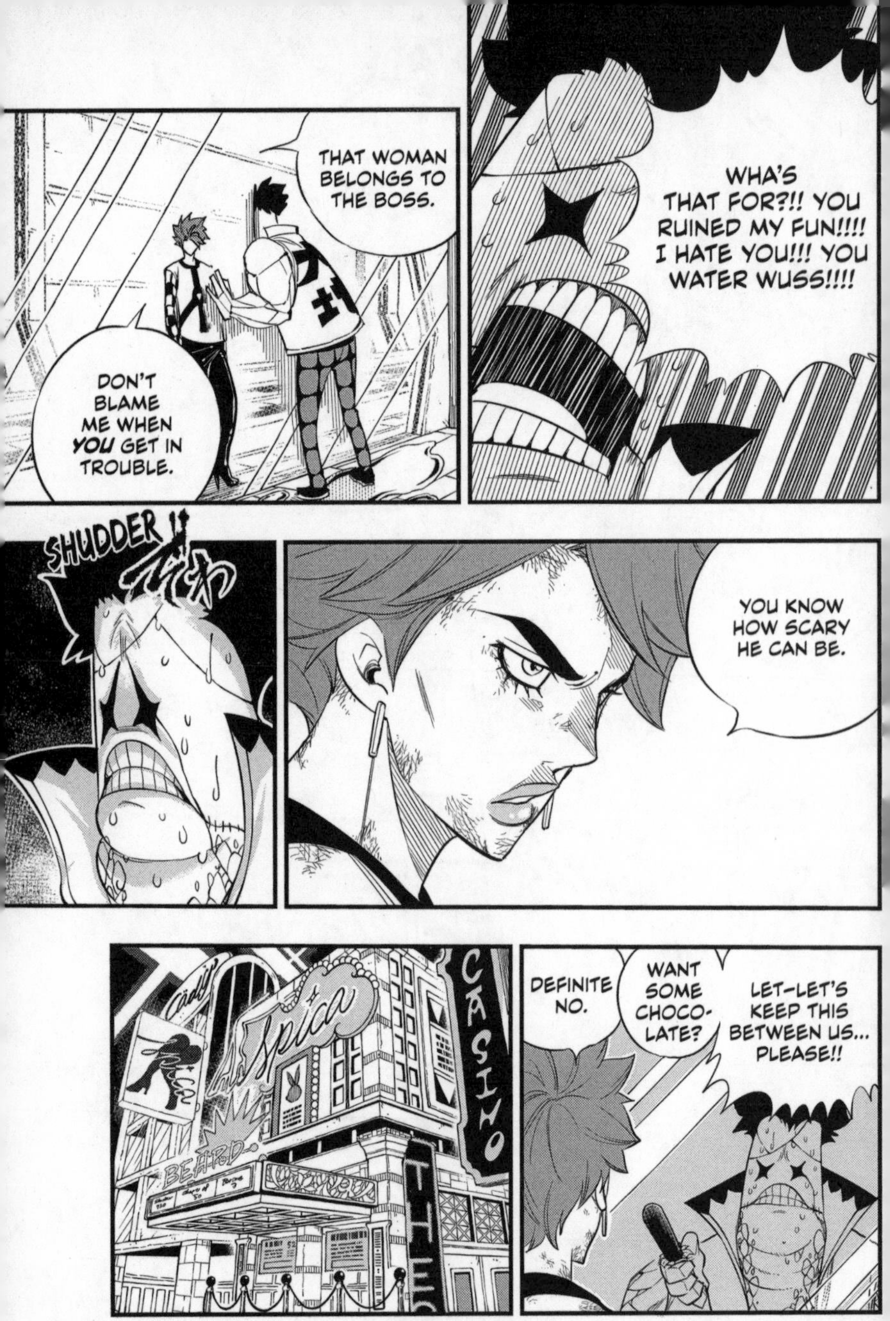
WHA'S THAT FOR?!! YOU RUINED MY FUN!!!! I HATE YOU!!! YOU WATER WUSS!!!!
THAT WOMAN BELONGS TO THE BOSS.
DON'T BLAME ME WHEN *YOU* GET IN TROUBLE.
YOU KNOW HOW SCARY HE CAN BE.
SHUDDER!!
LET-LET'S KEEP THIS BETWEEN US... PLEASE!!
WANT SOME CHOCO-LATE?
DEFINITE NO.
CASINO

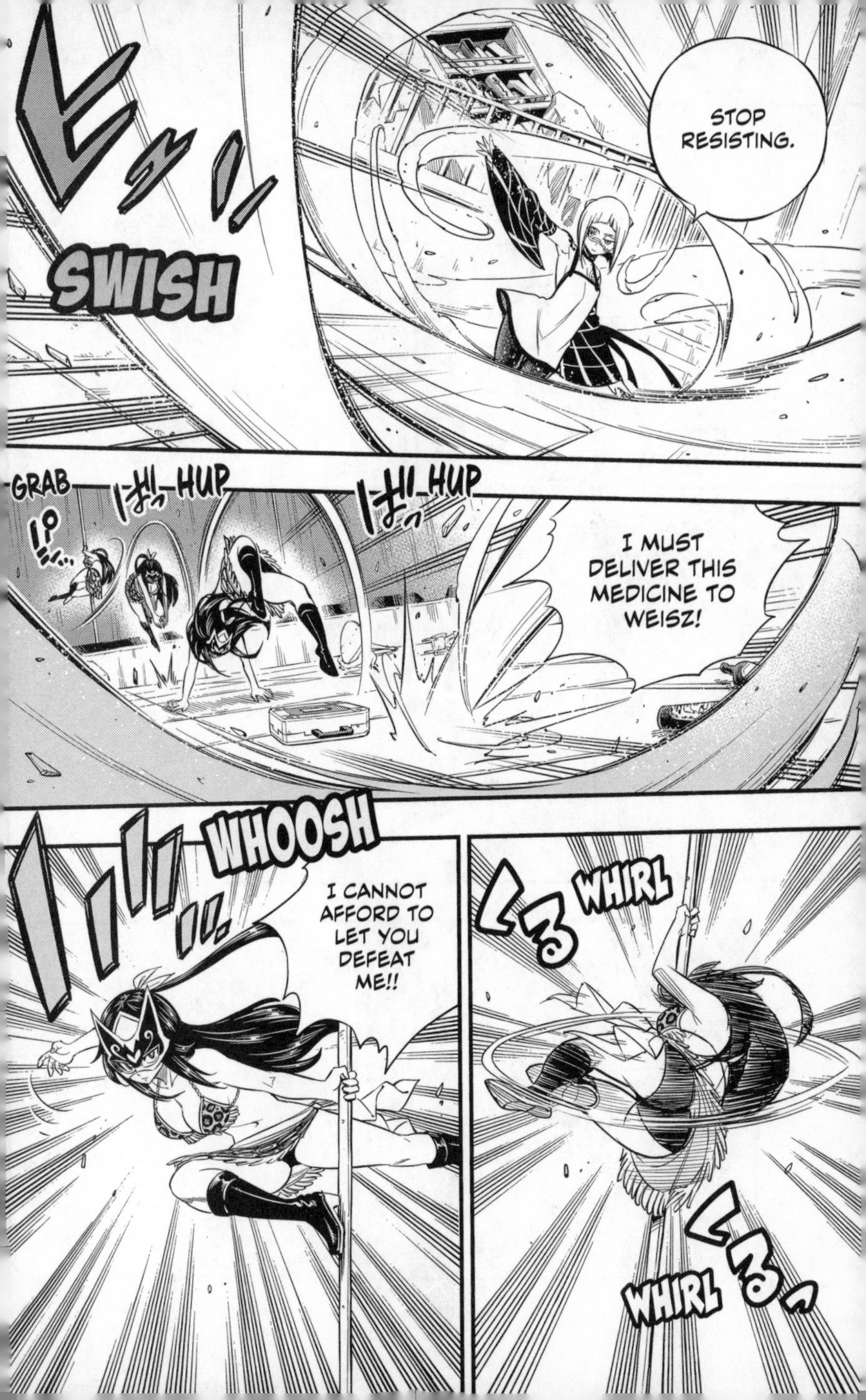
STOP RESISTING.
SWISH
I MUST DELIVER THIS MEDICINE TO WEISZ!
HUP
HUP
GRAB
WHIRL
WHIRL
WHOOSH
I CANNOT AFFORD TO LET YOU DEFEAT ME!!

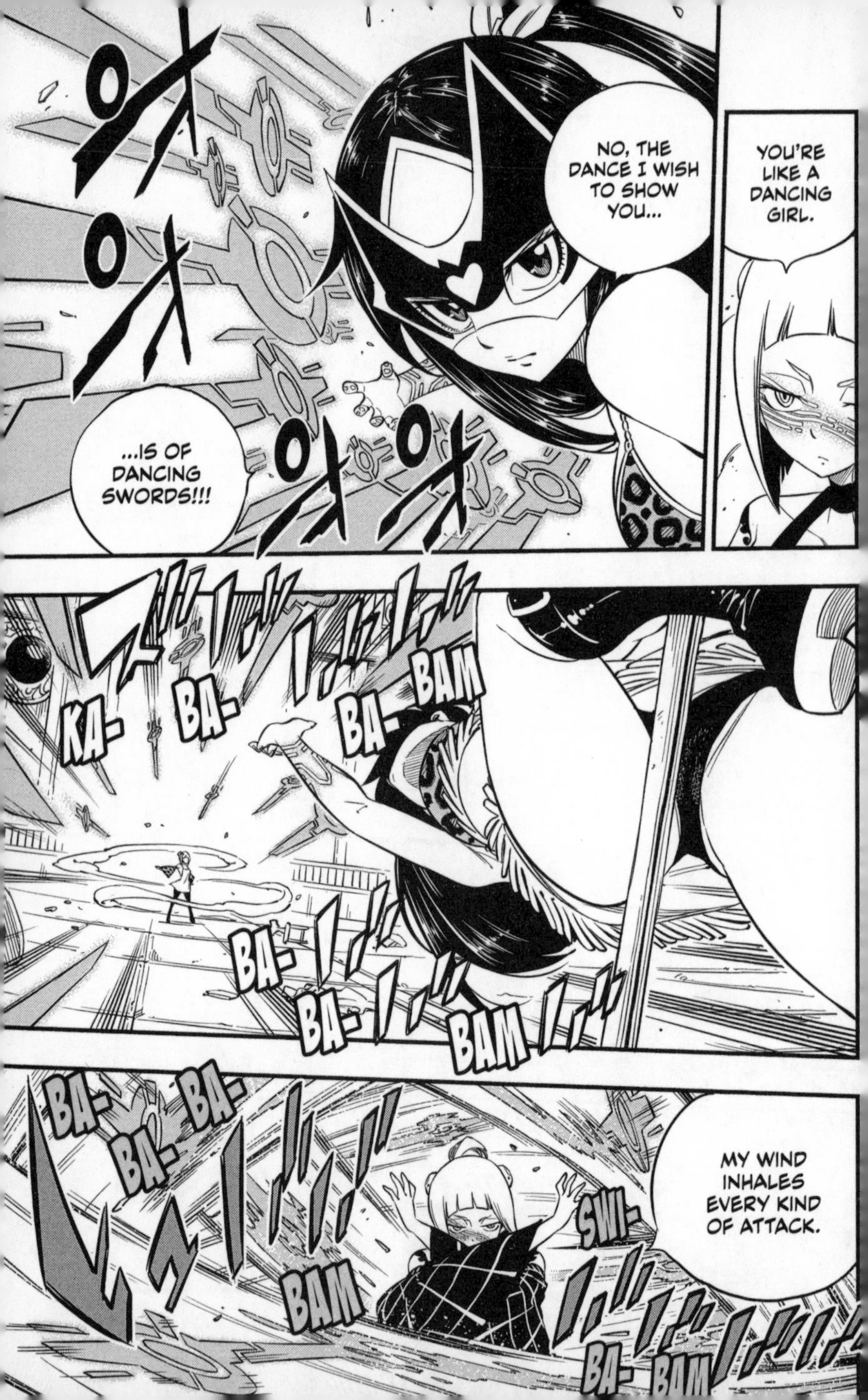

YOU'RE LIKE A DANCING GIRL.
NO, THE DANCE I WISH TO SHOW YOU...
...IS OF DANCING SWORDS!!!
KA- BA- BA- BAM
BA- BA- BAM
MY WIND INHALES EVERY KIND OF ATTACK.
SWI-
BA- BA- BA-
BAM
BA- BAM

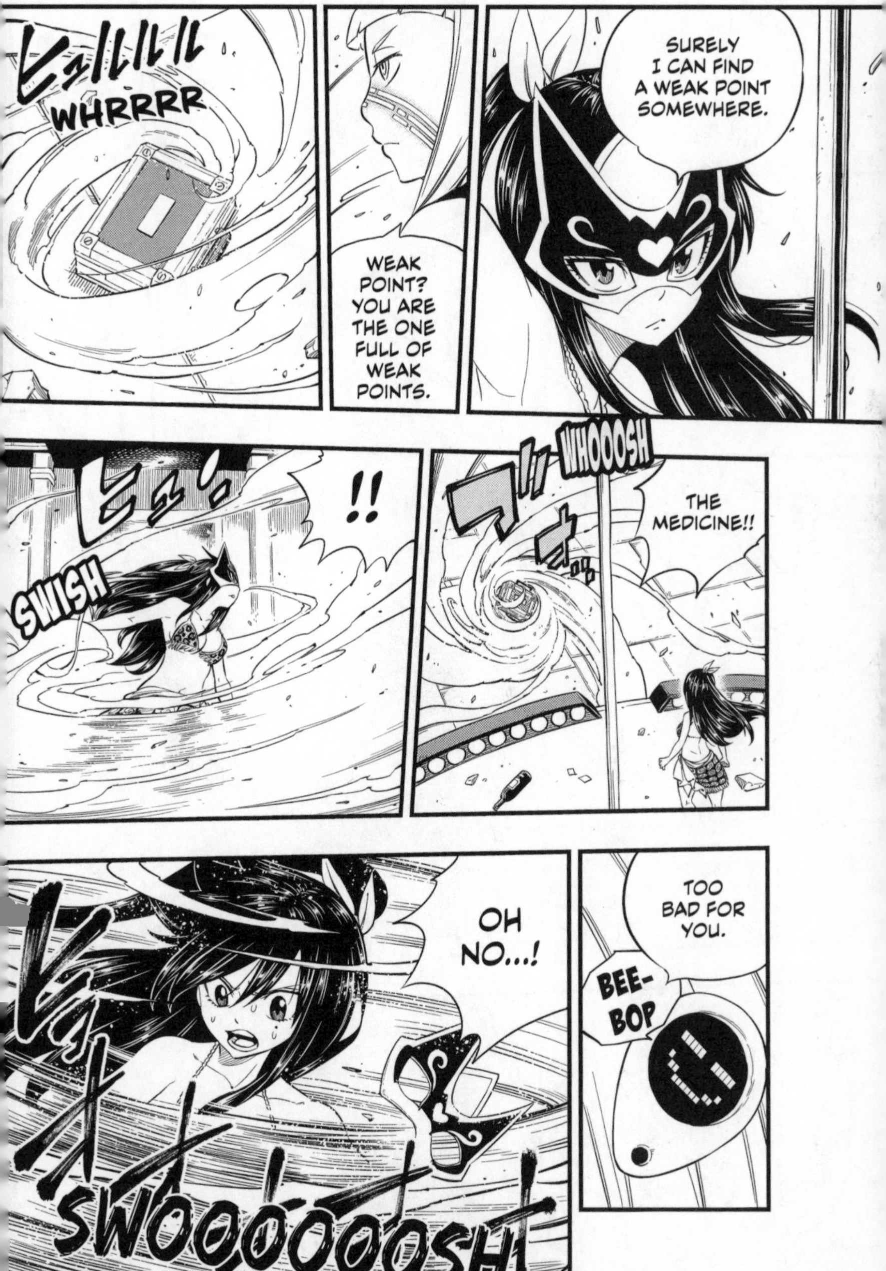
SURELY I CAN FIND A WEAK POINT SOMEWHERE.
WEAK POINT? YOU ARE THE ONE FULL OF WEAK POINTS.
WHRRRR
WHOOOSH
THE MEDICINE!!
!!
SWISH
TOO BAD FOR YOU.
BEE-BOP
OH NO...!
SWOOOOOOOSH

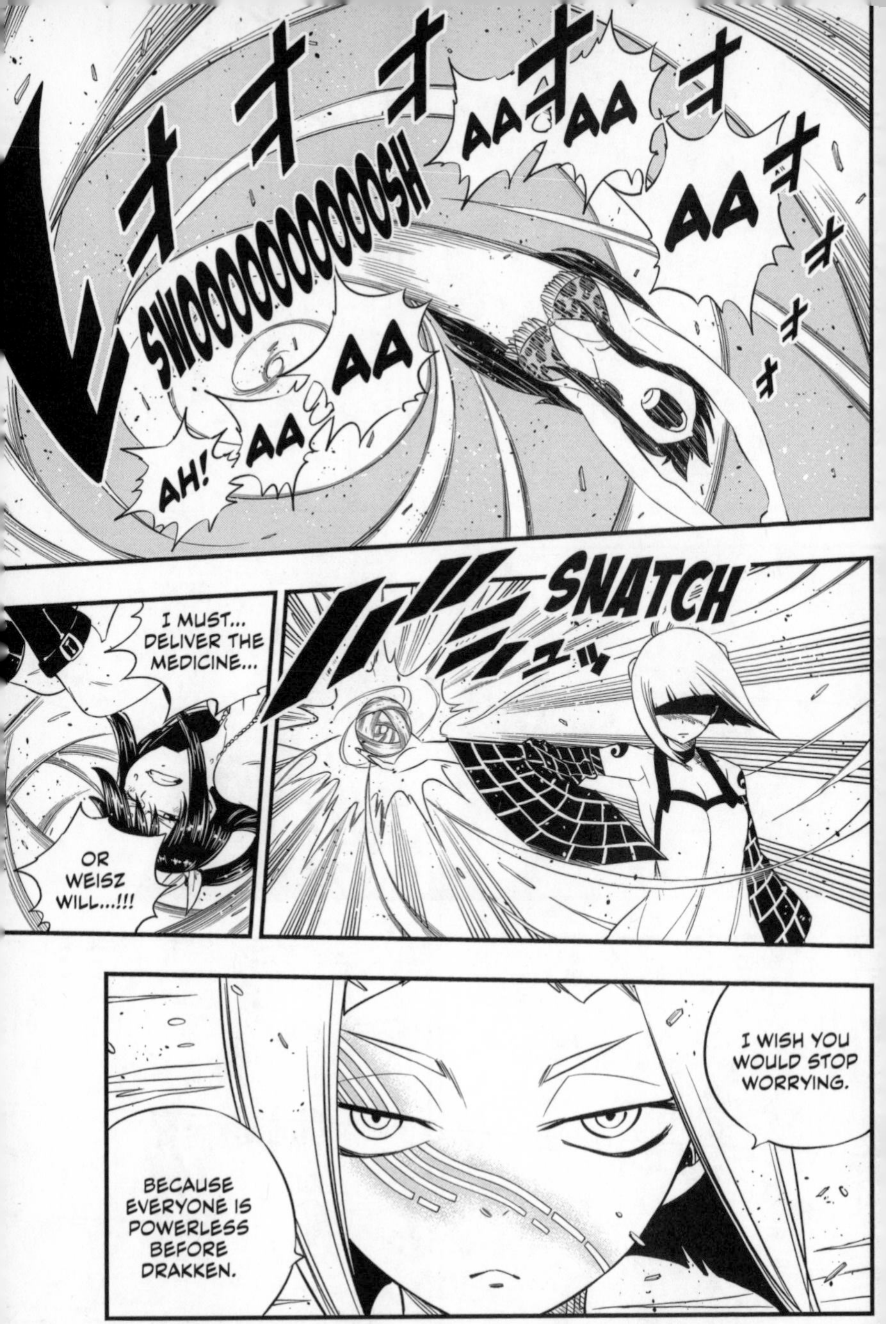
SWOOOOOOOOOOSH
AA AA
AA
AA AA AH!
SNATCH
I MUST... DELIVER THE MEDICINE...
OR WEISZ WILL...!!!
I WISH YOU WOULD STOP WORRYING.
BECAUSE EVERYONE IS POWERLESS BEFORE DRAKKEN.

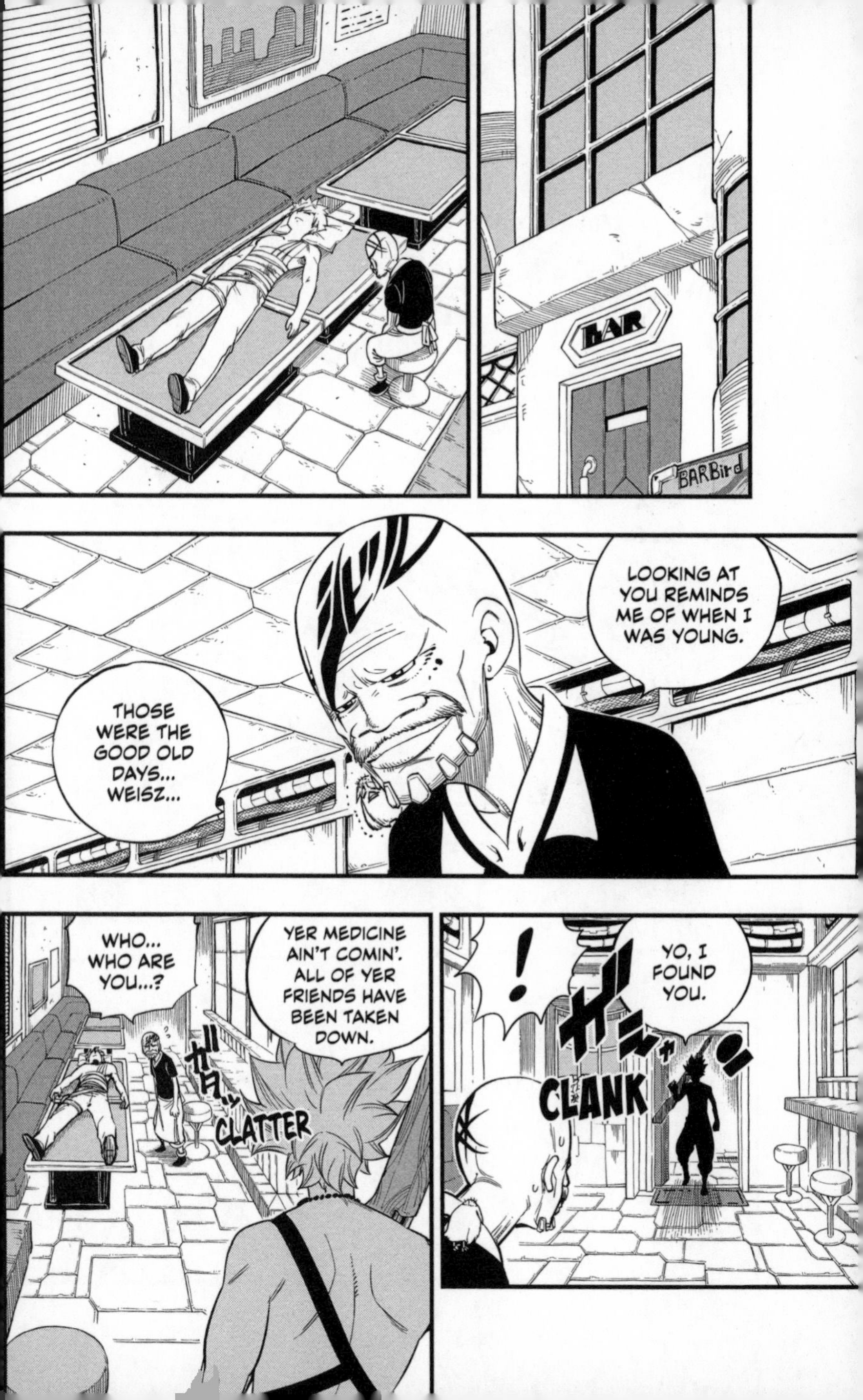
BAR
BARBird
LOOKING AT YOU REMINDS ME OF WHEN I WAS YOUNG.
THOSE WERE THE GOOD OLD DAYS... WEISZ...
YO, I FOUND YOU.
!
CLANK
YER MEDICINE AIN'T COMIN'. ALL OF YER FRIENDS HAVE BEEN TAKEN DOWN.
WHO... WHO ARE YOU...?
CLATTER

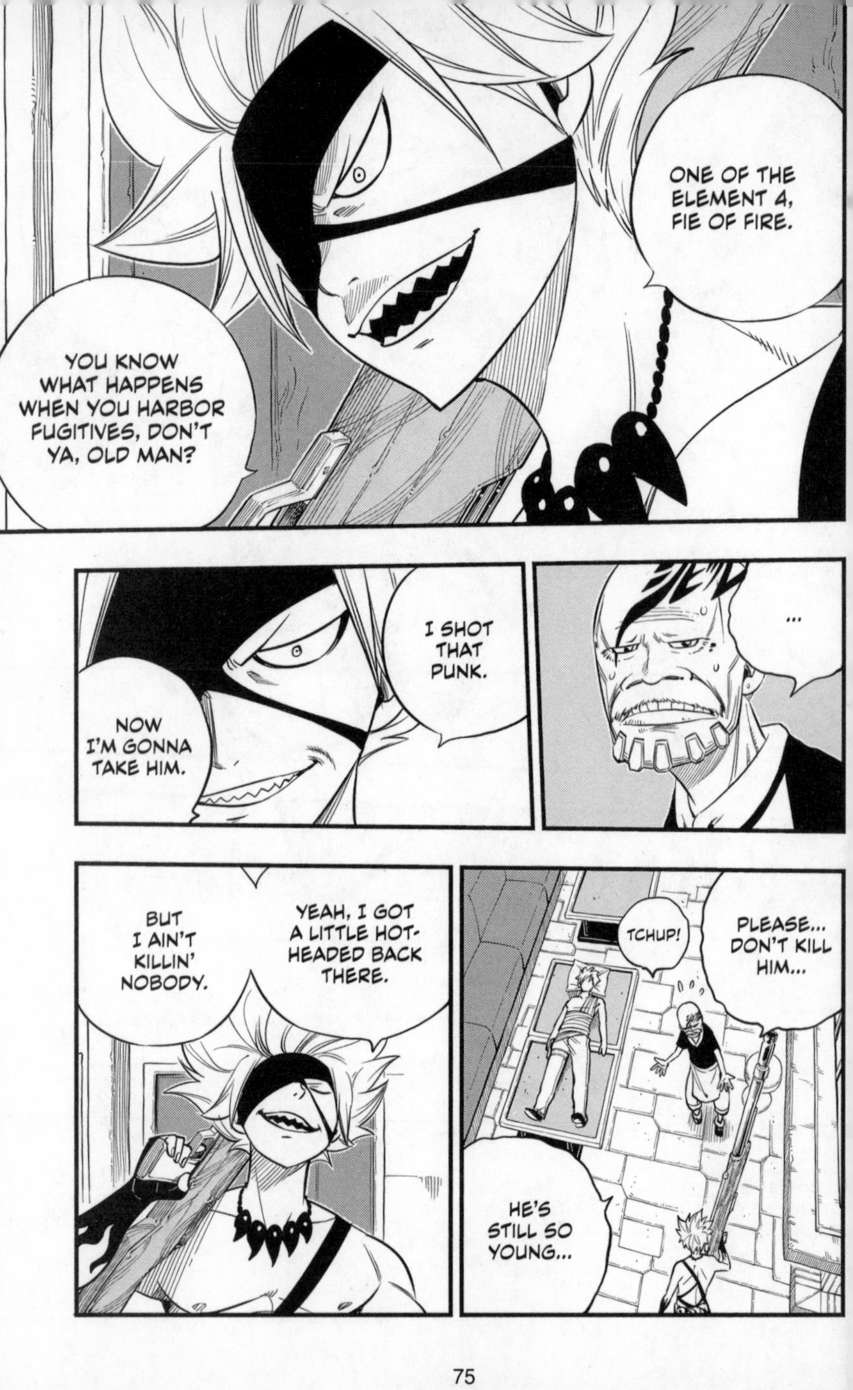
ONE OF THE ELEMENT 4, FIE OF FIRE.
YOU KNOW WHAT HAPPENS WHEN YOU HARBOR FUGITIVES, DON'T YA, OLD MAN?
...
I SHOT THAT PUNK.
NOW I'M GONNA TAKE HIM.
PLEASE... DON'T KILL HIM...
TCHUP!
HE'S STILL SO YOUNG...
YEAH, I GOT A LITTLE HOT-HEADED BACK THERE.
BUT I AIN'T KILLIN' NOBODY.

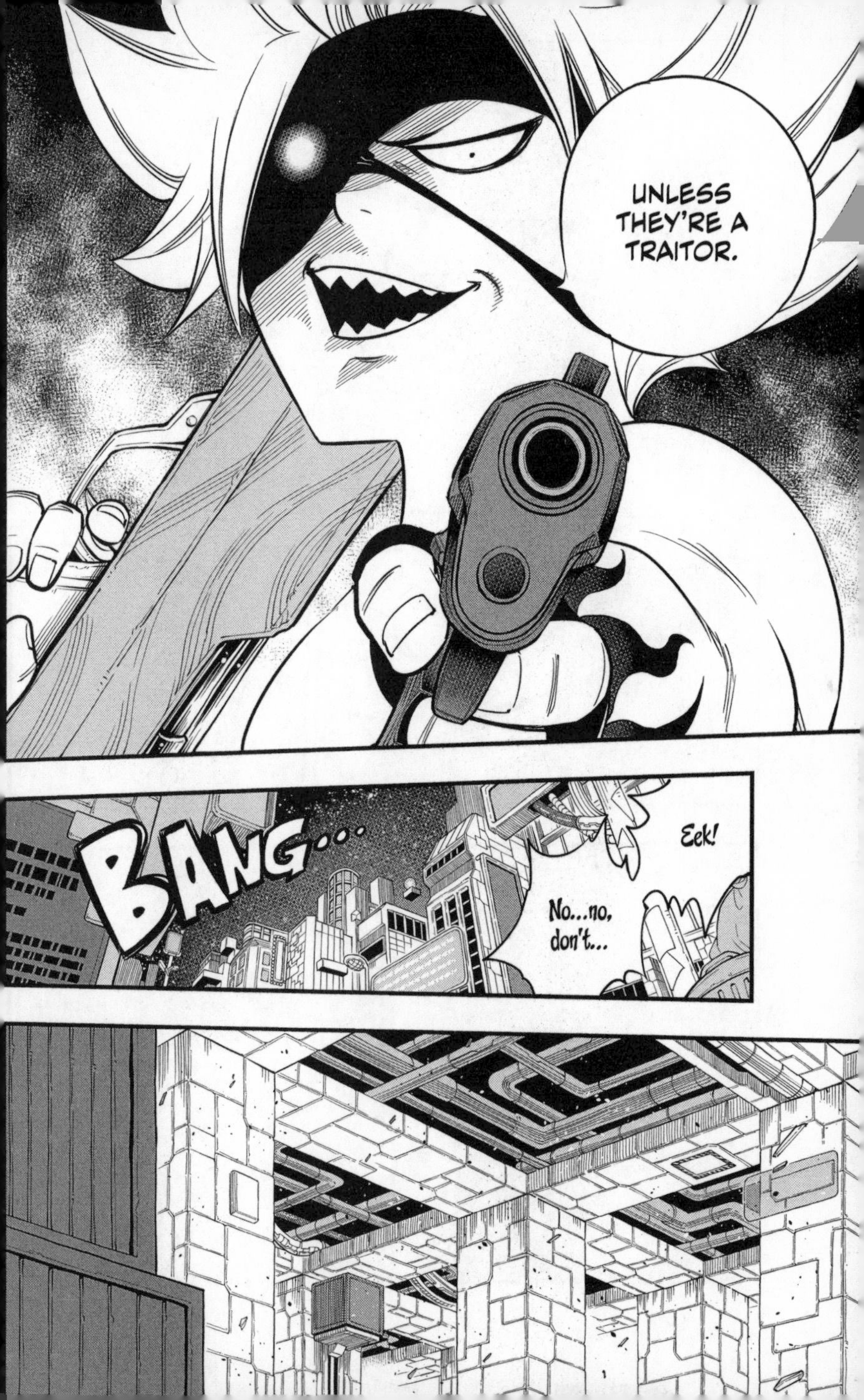
UNLESS THEY'RE A TRAITOR.
BANG...
Eek!
No...no, don't...

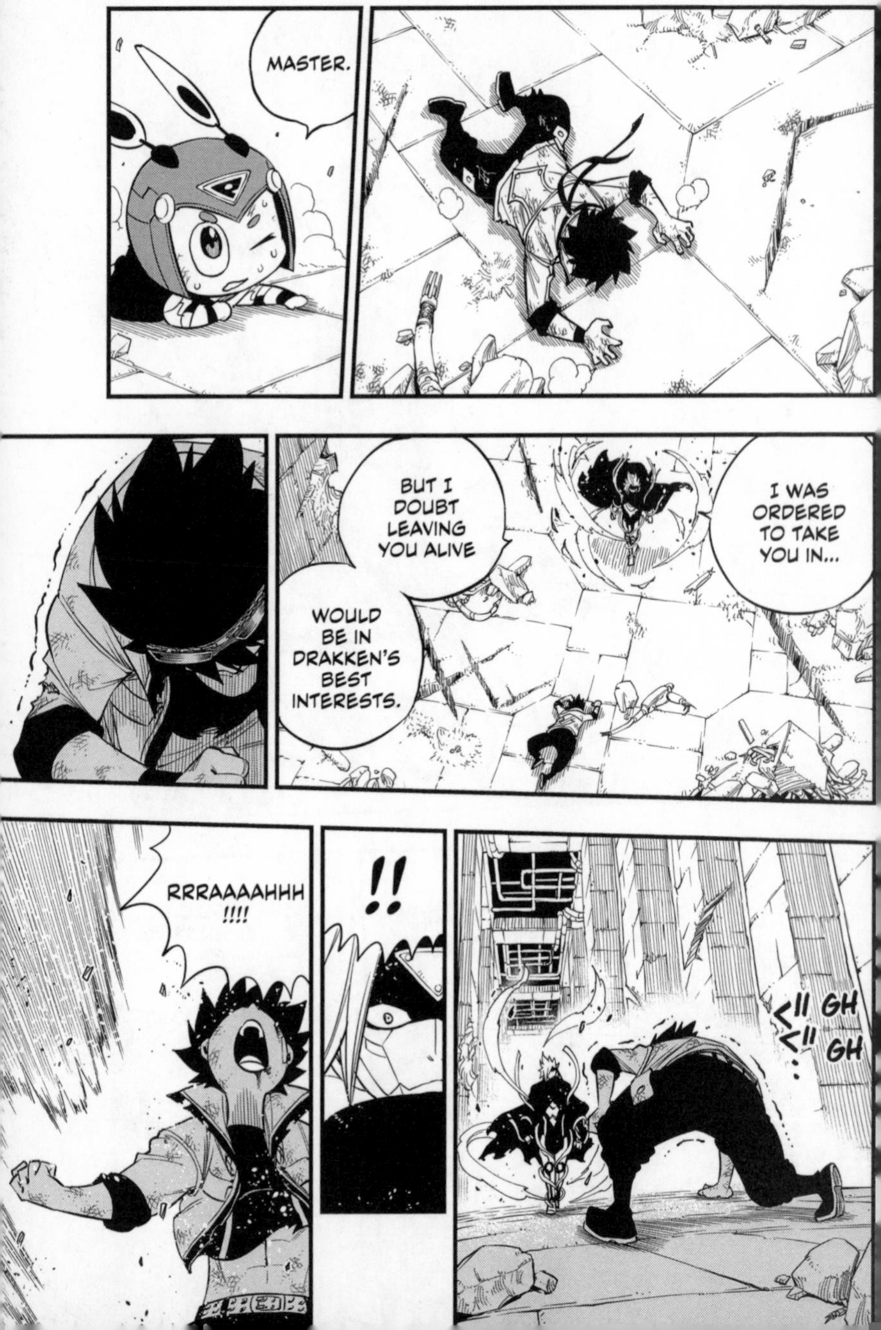
MASTER.
I WAS ORDERED TO TAKE YOU IN...
BUT I DOUBT LEAVING YOU ALIVE
WOULD BE IN DRAKKEN'S BEST INTERESTS.
GH GH
!!
RRRAAAAHHH!!!!

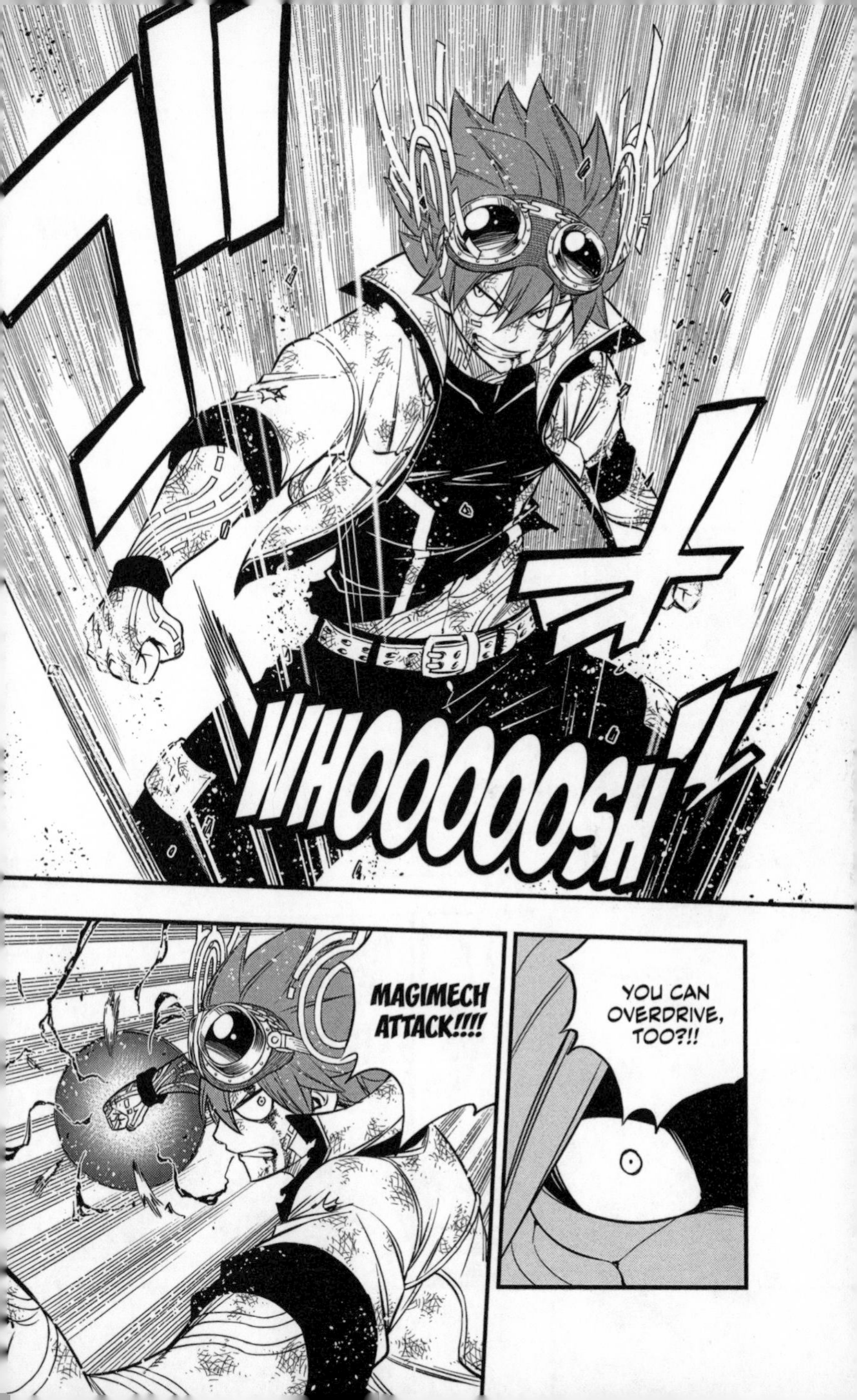
WHOOOOOSH!
YOU CAN OVERDRIVE, TOO?!!
MAGIMECH ATTACK!!!!

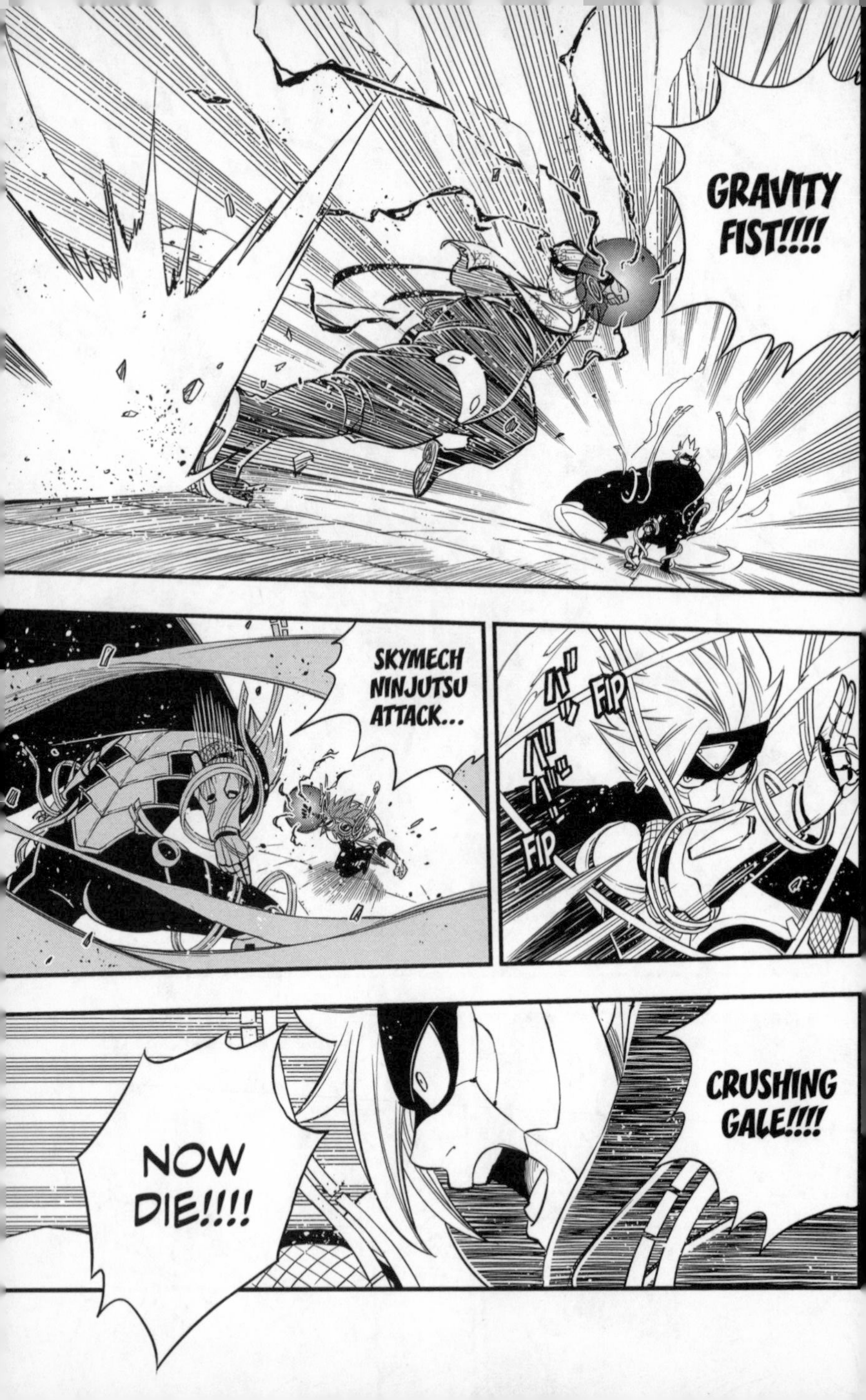
GRAVITY FIST!!!!
FIP
FIP
SKYMECH NINJUTSU ATTACK...
CRUSHING GALE!!!!
NOW DIE!!!!

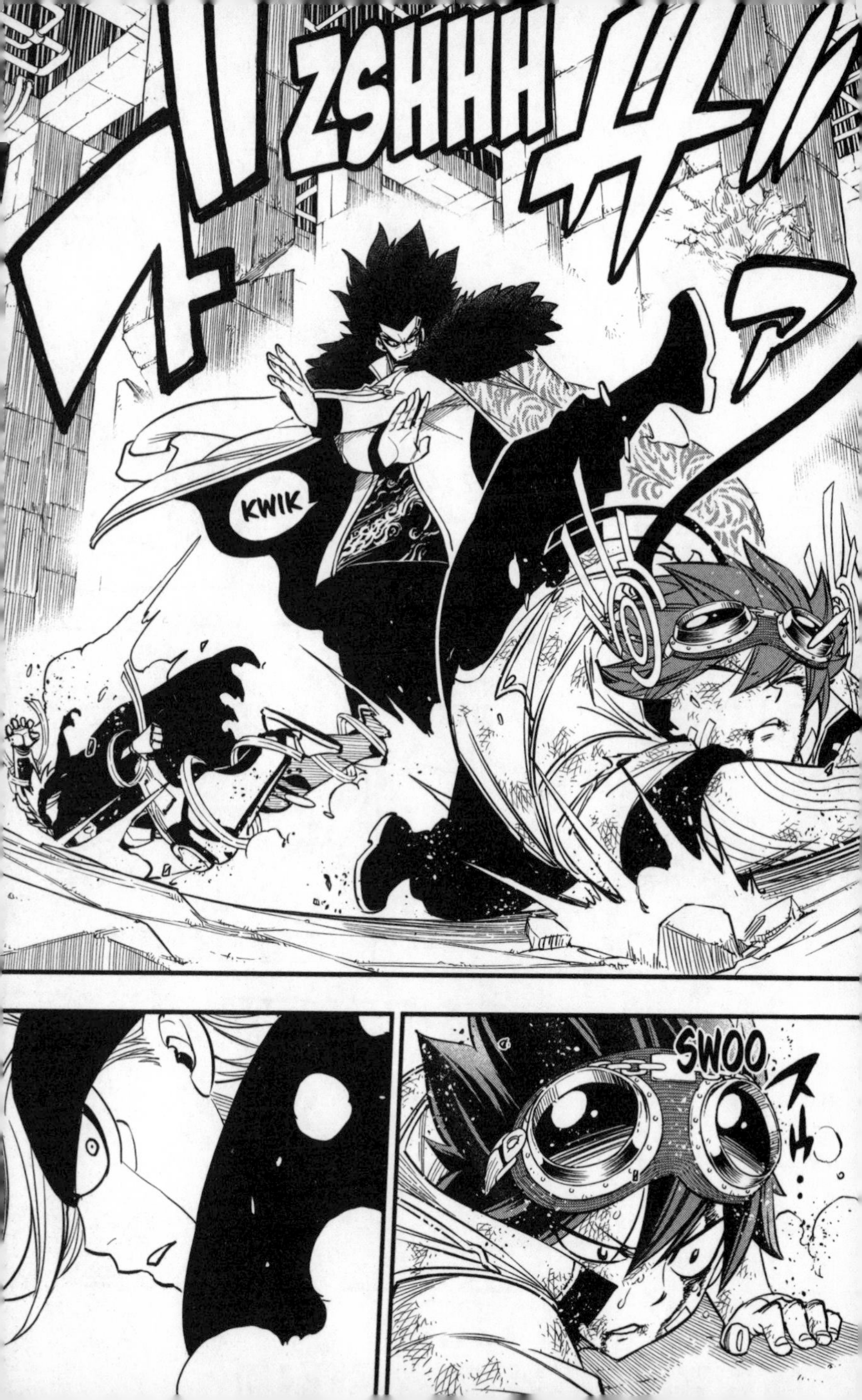
ZSHHH
KWIK
SWOO

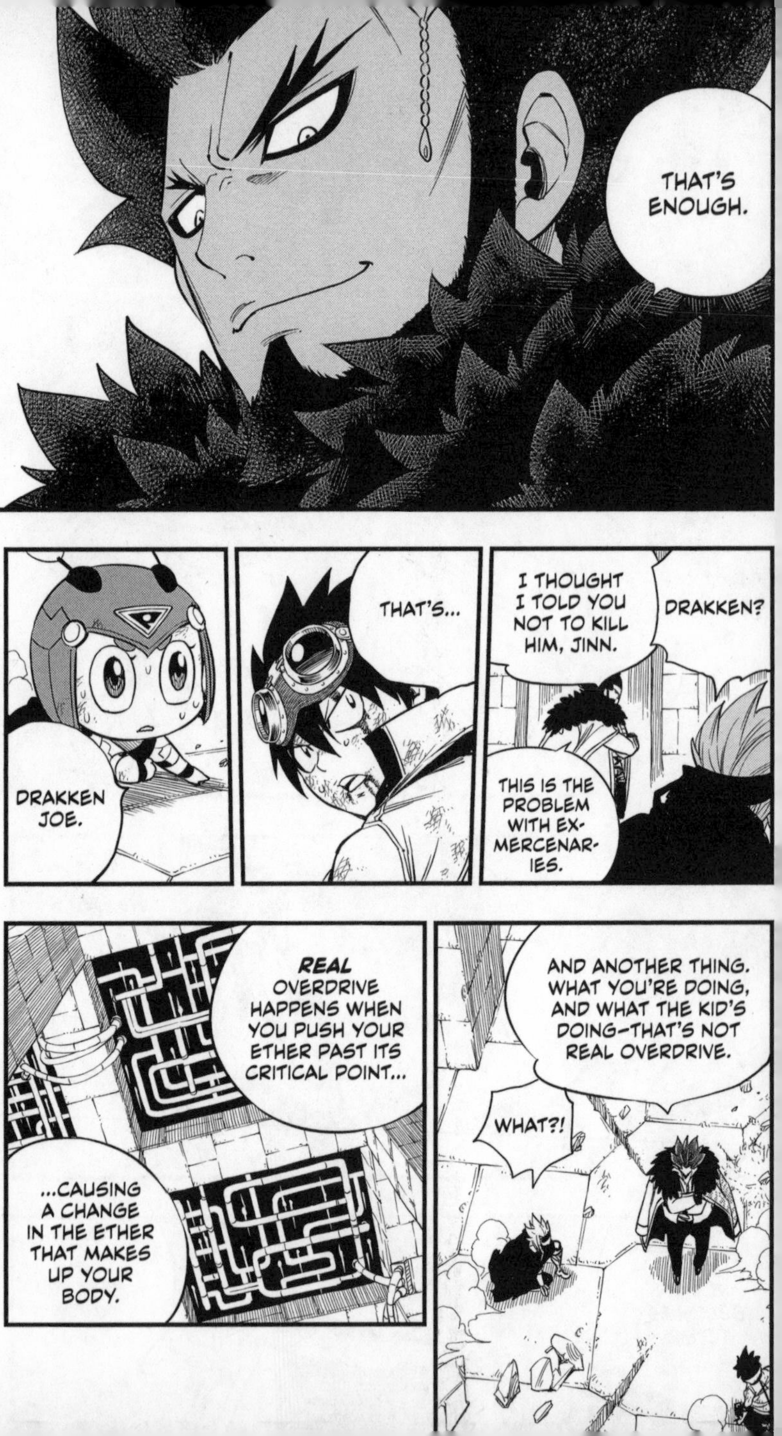
THAT'S ENOUGH.
DRAKKEN?
I THOUGHT I TOLD YOU NOT TO KILL HIM, JINN.
THIS IS THE PROBLEM WITH EX-MERCENARIES.
THAT'S...
DRAKKEN JOE.
AND ANOTHER THING. WHAT YOU'RE DOING, AND WHAT THE KID'S DOING—THAT'S NOT REAL OVERDRIVE.
WHAT?!
REAL OVERDRIVE HAPPENS WHEN YOU PUSH YOUR ETHER PAST ITS CRITICAL POINT...
...CAUSING A CHANGE IN THE ETHER THAT MAKES UP YOUR BODY.

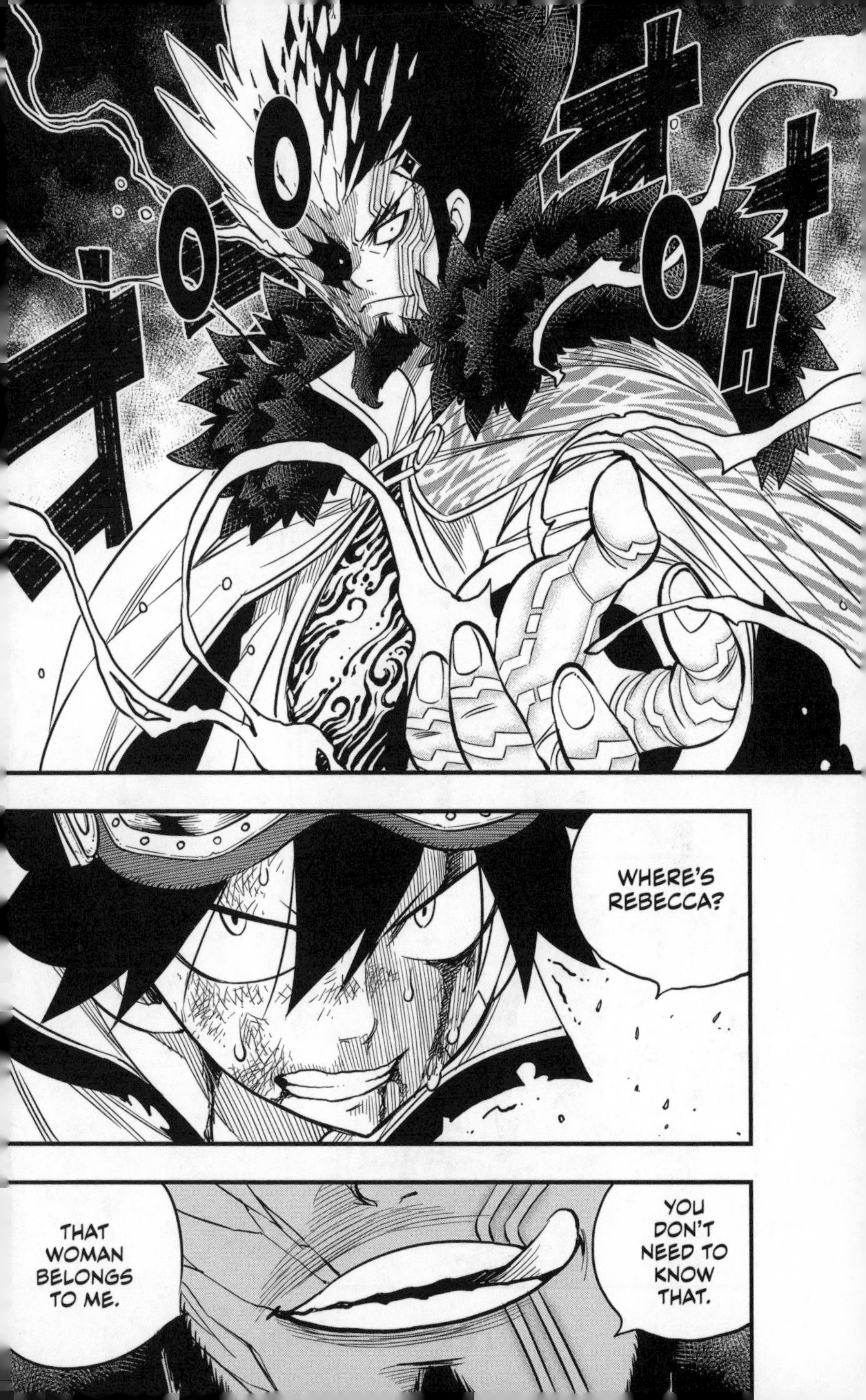
WHERE'S REBECCA?
YOU DON'T NEED TO KNOW THAT.
THAT WOMAN BELONGS TO ME.

EDENS ZERO

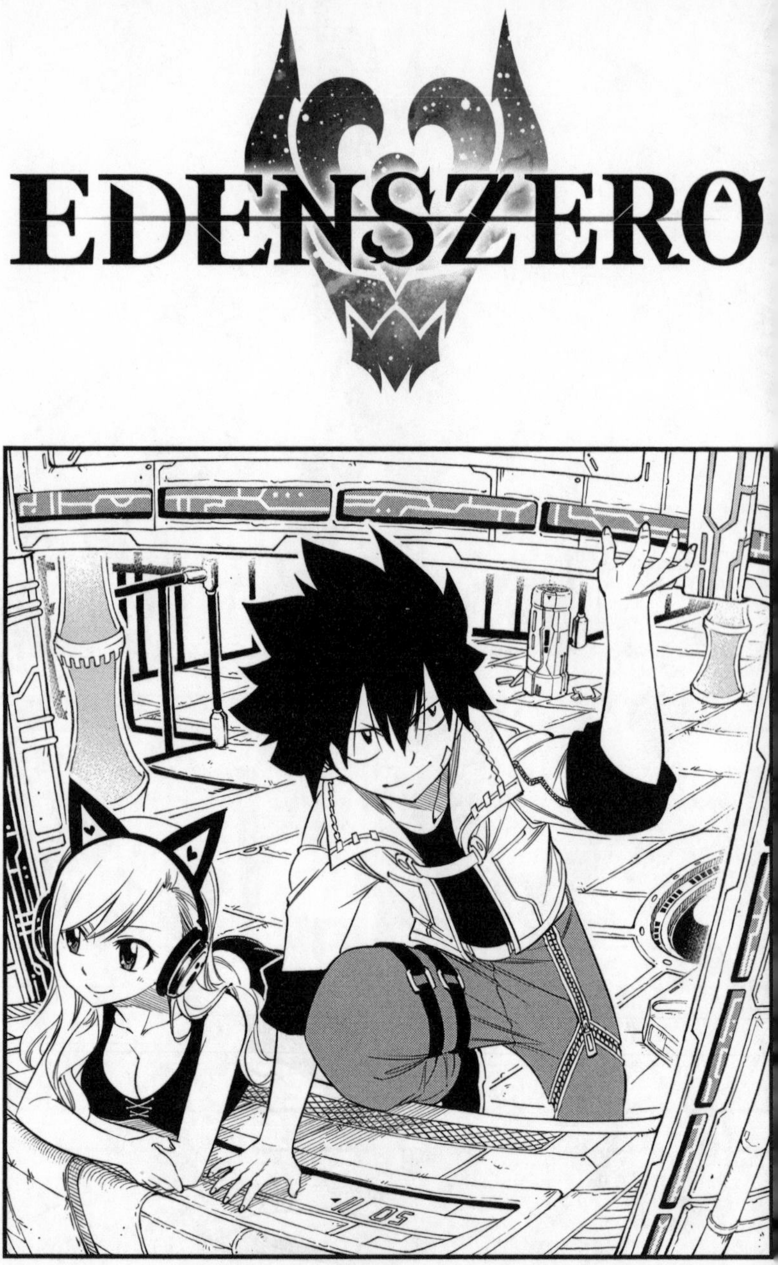

CHAPTER 82: SCOLDING

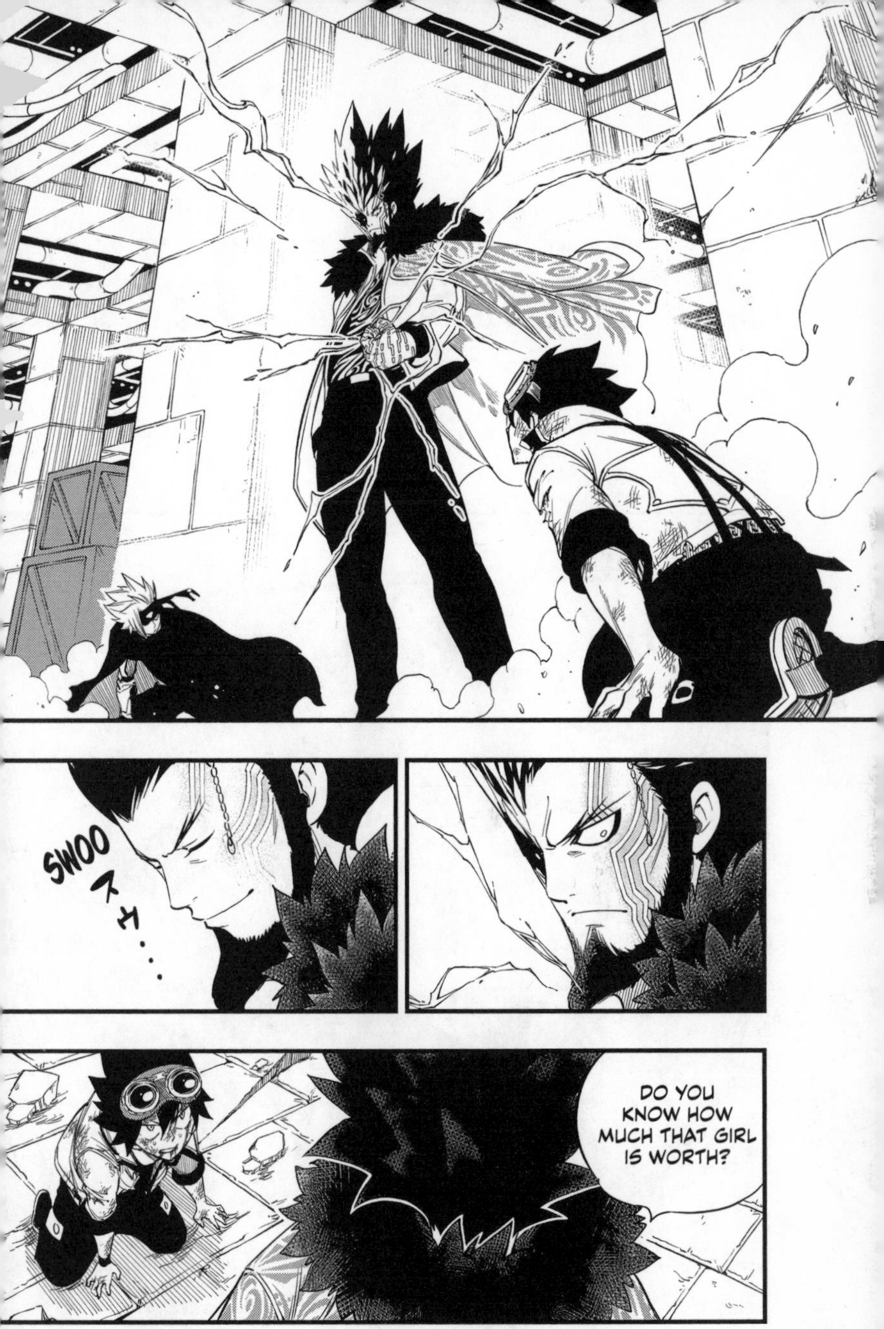
SWOO
DO YOU KNOW HOW MUCH THAT GIRL IS WORTH?

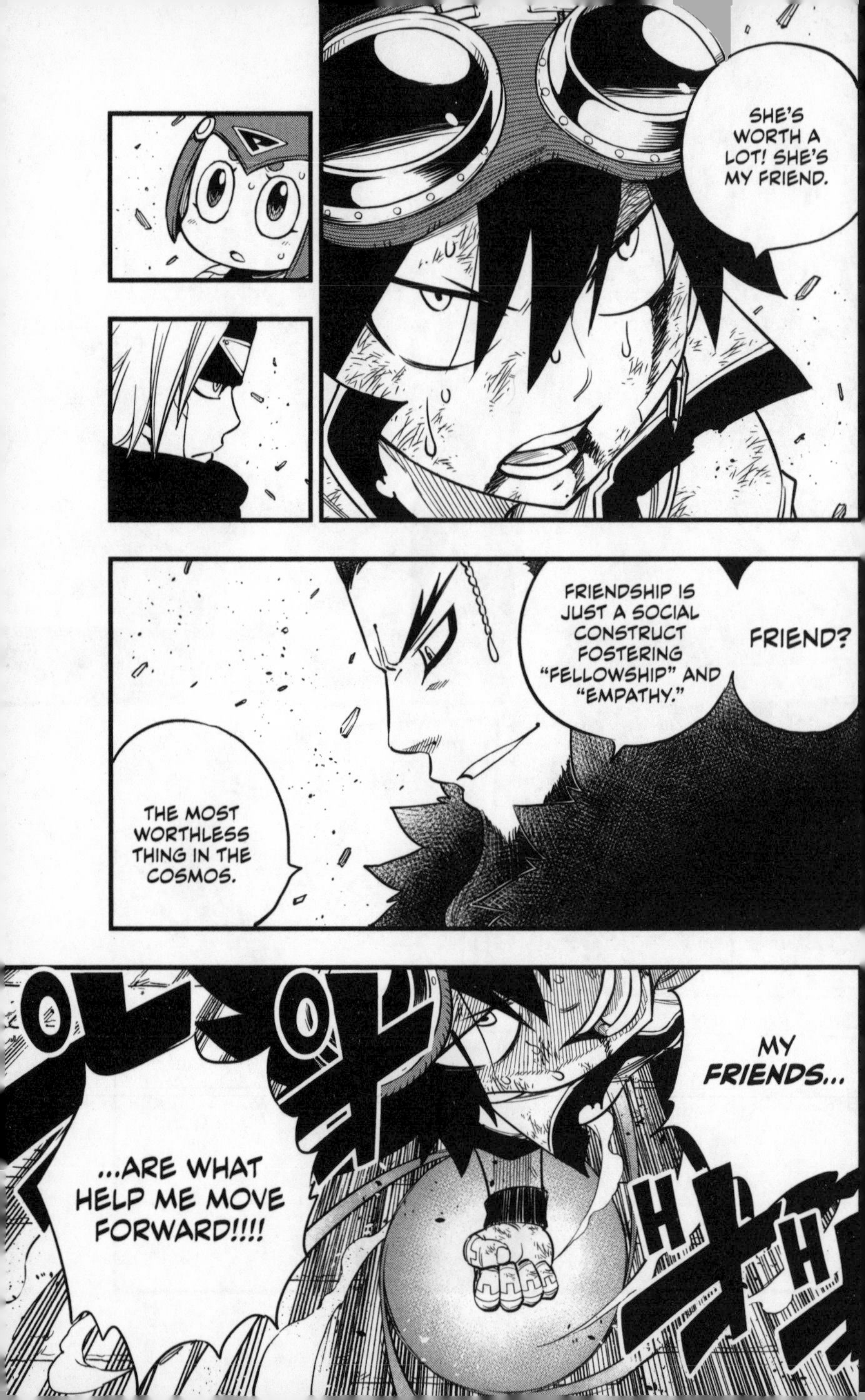
SHE'S WORTH A LOT! SHE'S MY FRIEND.
FRIEND?
FRIENDSHIP IS JUST A SOCIAL CONSTRUCT FOSTERING "FELLOWSHIP" AND "EMPATHY."
THE MOST WORTHLESS THING IN THE COSMOS.
MY FRIENDS...
...ARE WHAT HELP ME MOVE FORWARD!!!!

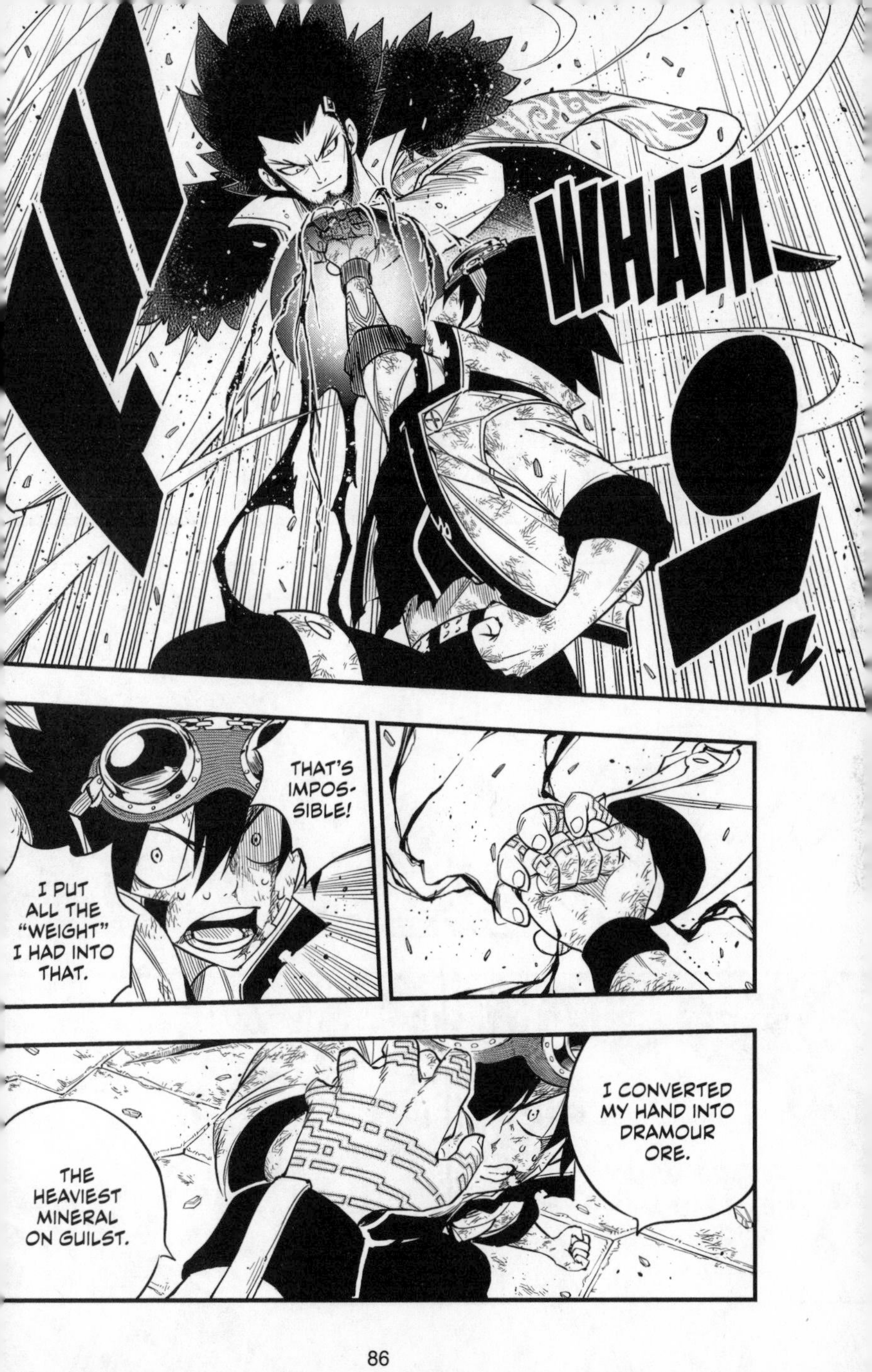
WHAM
THAT'S IMPOSSIBLE!
I PUT ALL THE "WEIGHT" I HAD INTO THAT.
I CONVERTED MY HAND INTO DRAMOUR ORE.
THE HEAVIEST MINERAL ON GUILST.

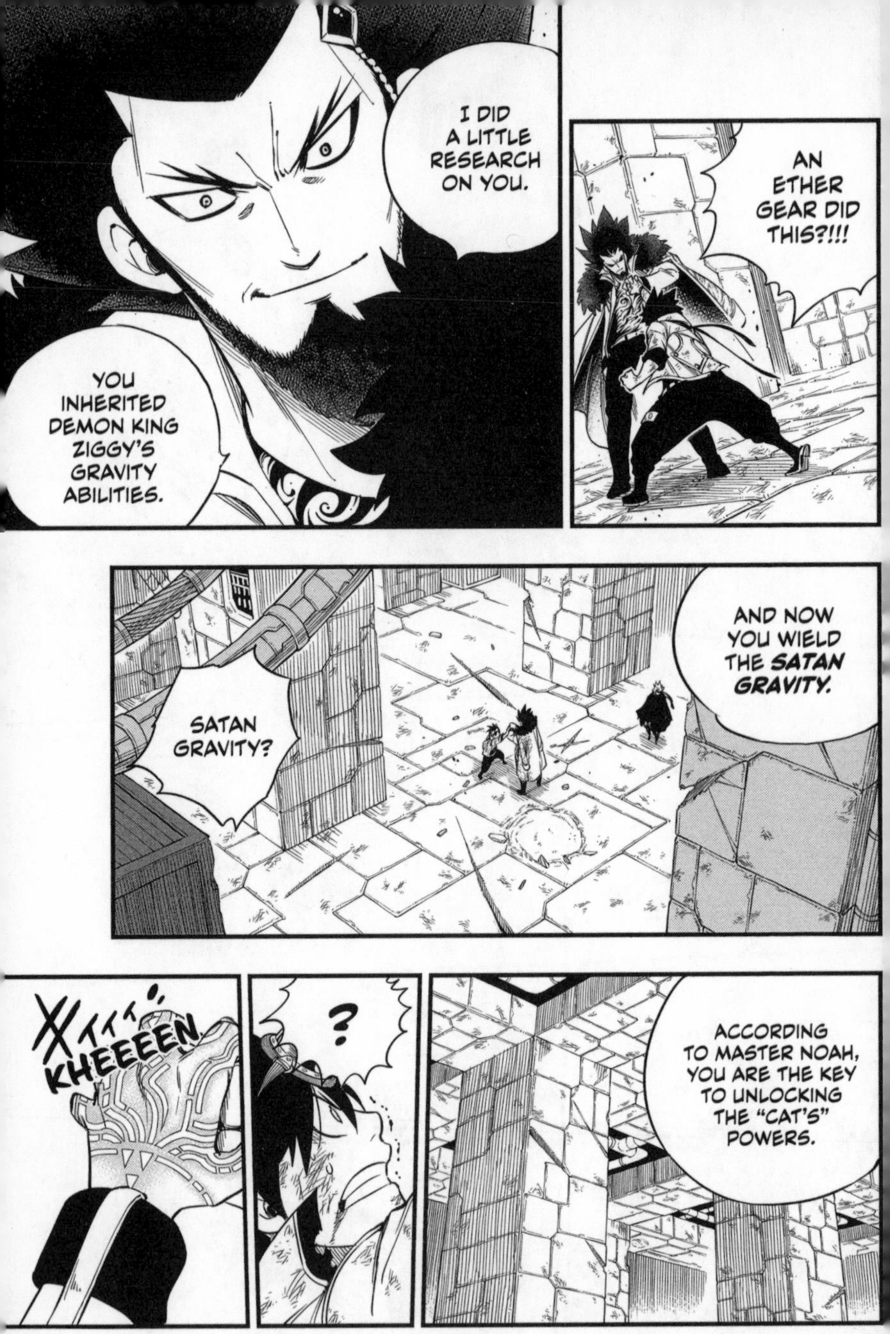
AN ETHER GEAR DID THIS?!!!
I DID A LITTLE RESEARCH ON YOU.
YOU INHERITED DEMON KING ZIGGY'S GRAVITY ABILITIES.
AND NOW YOU WIELD THE ***SATAN GRAVITY.***
SATAN GRAVITY?
ACCORDING TO MASTER NOAH, YOU ARE THE KEY TO UNLOCKING THE "CAT'S" POWERS.
?
KHEEEEN

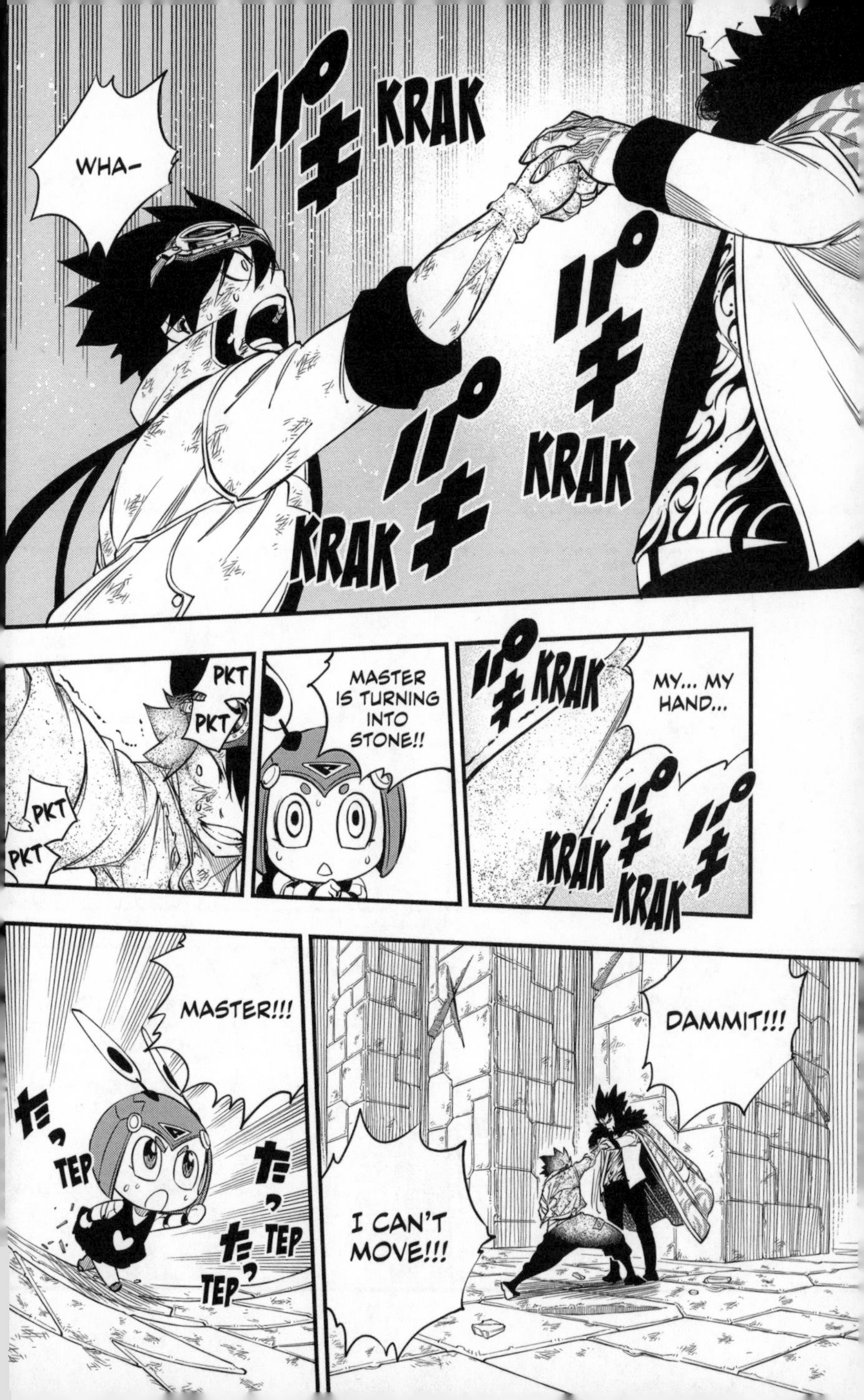

パキ KRAK
WHA-
パキ KRAK
パキ KRAK
MY... MY HAND...
パキ KRAK
パキ KRAK
パキ KRAK
MASTER IS TURNING INTO STONE!!
PKT
PKT
PKT
PKT
DAMMIT!!!
I CAN'T MOVE!!!
MASTER!!!
たっ TEP
たっ TEP
たっ TEP

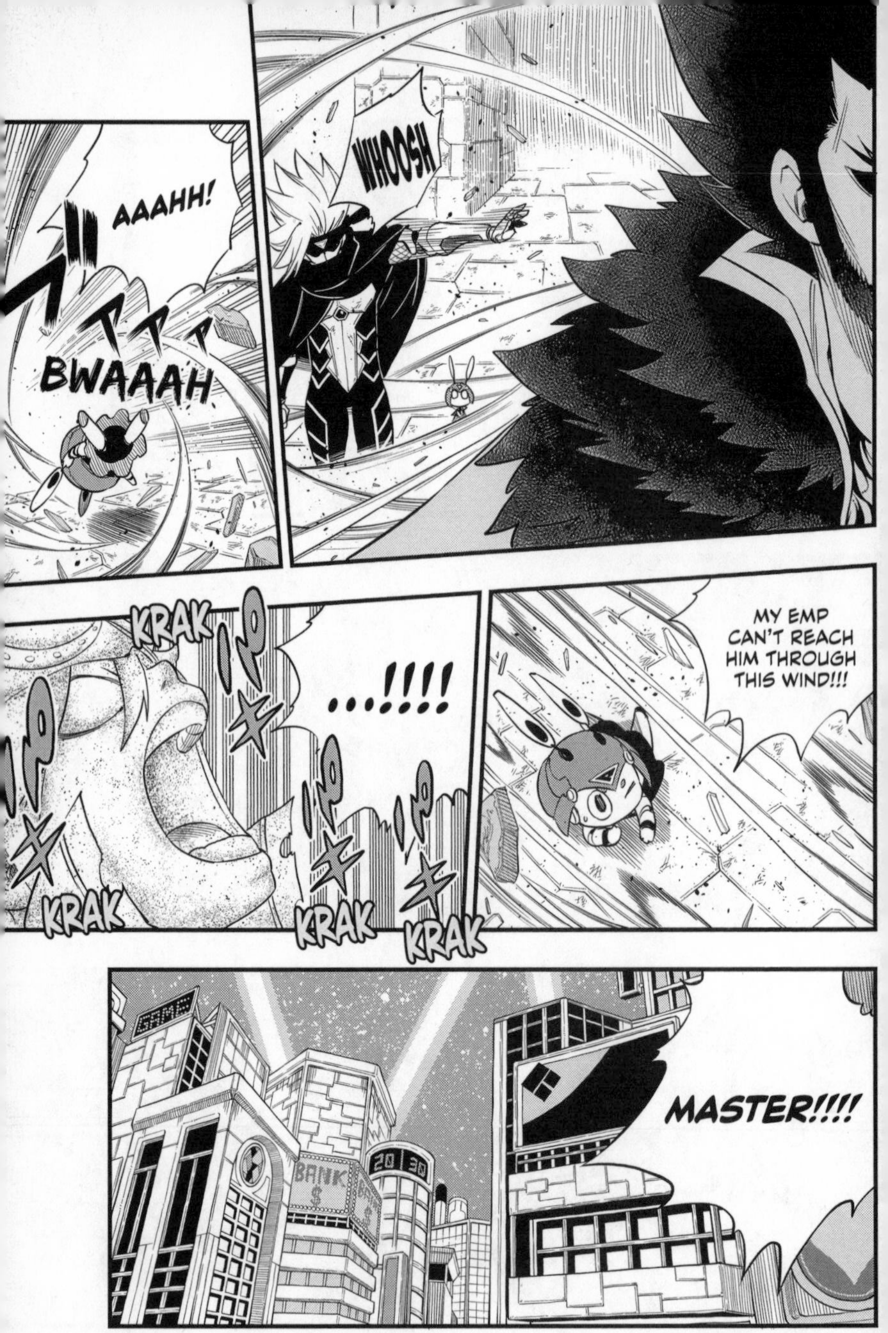
WHOOSH
AAAHH!
BWAAAH
MY EMP CAN'T REACH HIM THROUGH THIS WIND!!!
KRAK
...!!!!
KRAK
KRAK
KRAK
MASTER!!!!

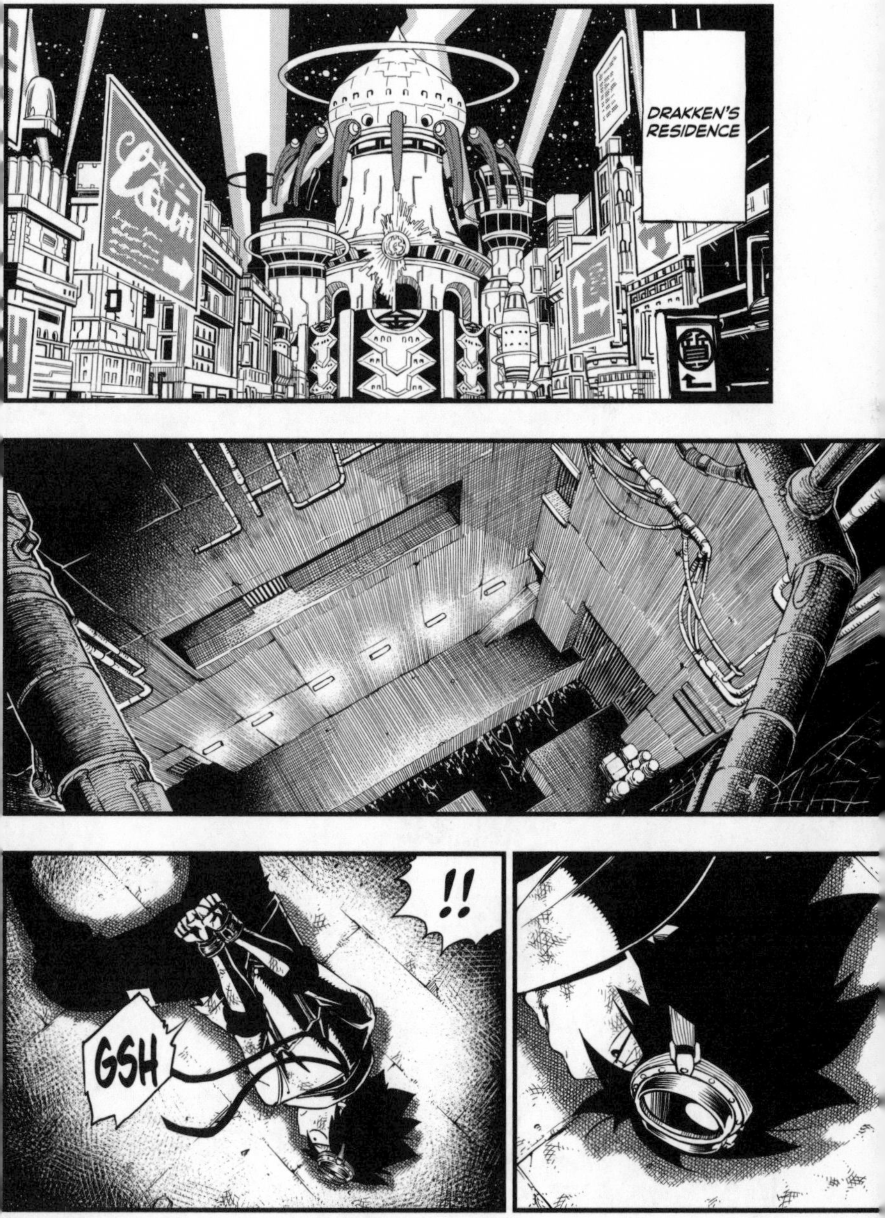
DRAKKEN'S RESIDENCE
!!
GSH

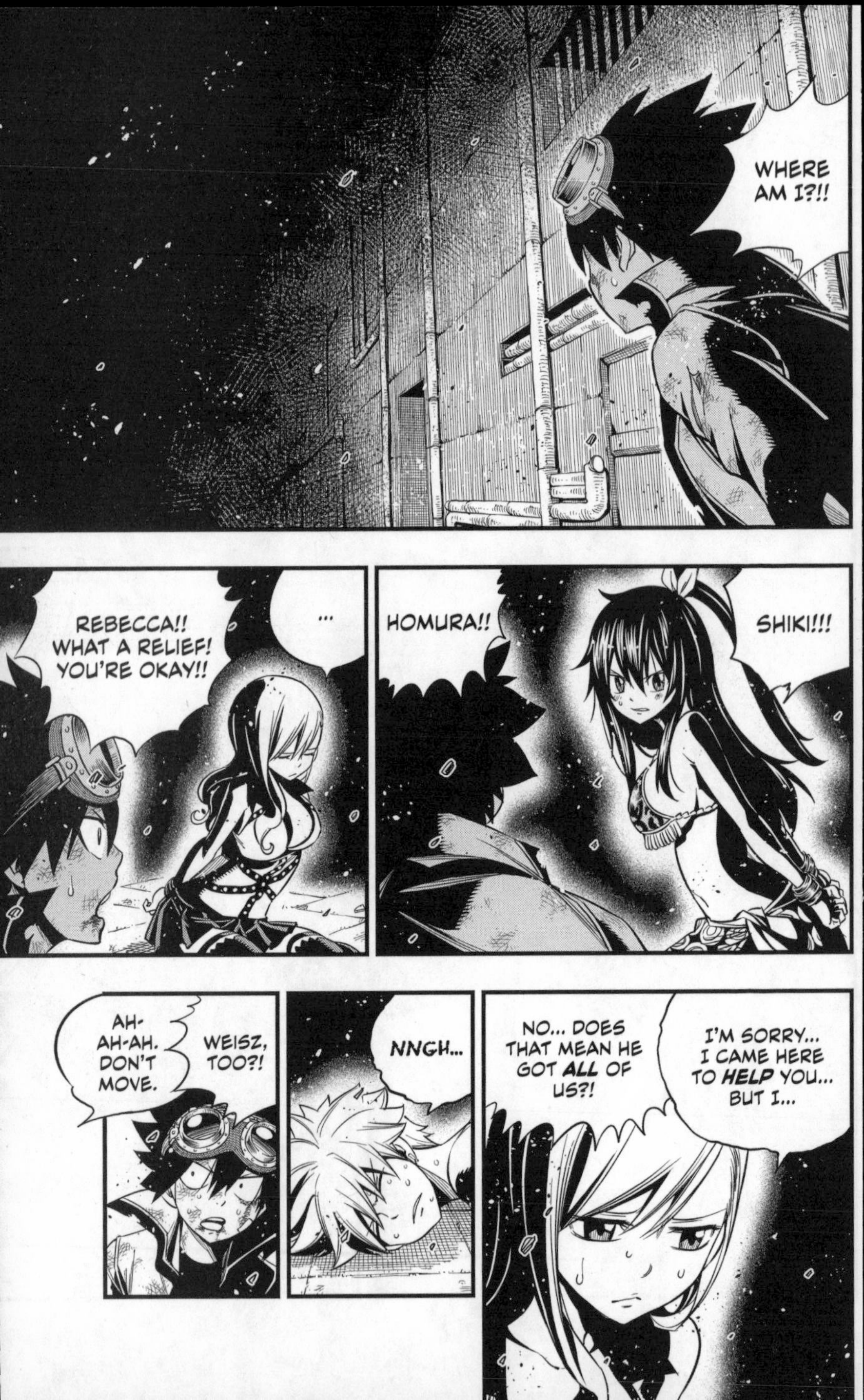
WHERE AM I?!!
SHIKI!!!
HOMURA!!
...
REBECCA!! WHAT A RELIEF! YOU'RE OKAY!!
I'M SORRY... I CAME HERE TO HELP YOU... BUT I...
NO... DOES THAT MEAN HE GOT ALL OF US?!
NNGH...
WEISZ, TOO?!
AH-AH-AH. DON'T MOVE.

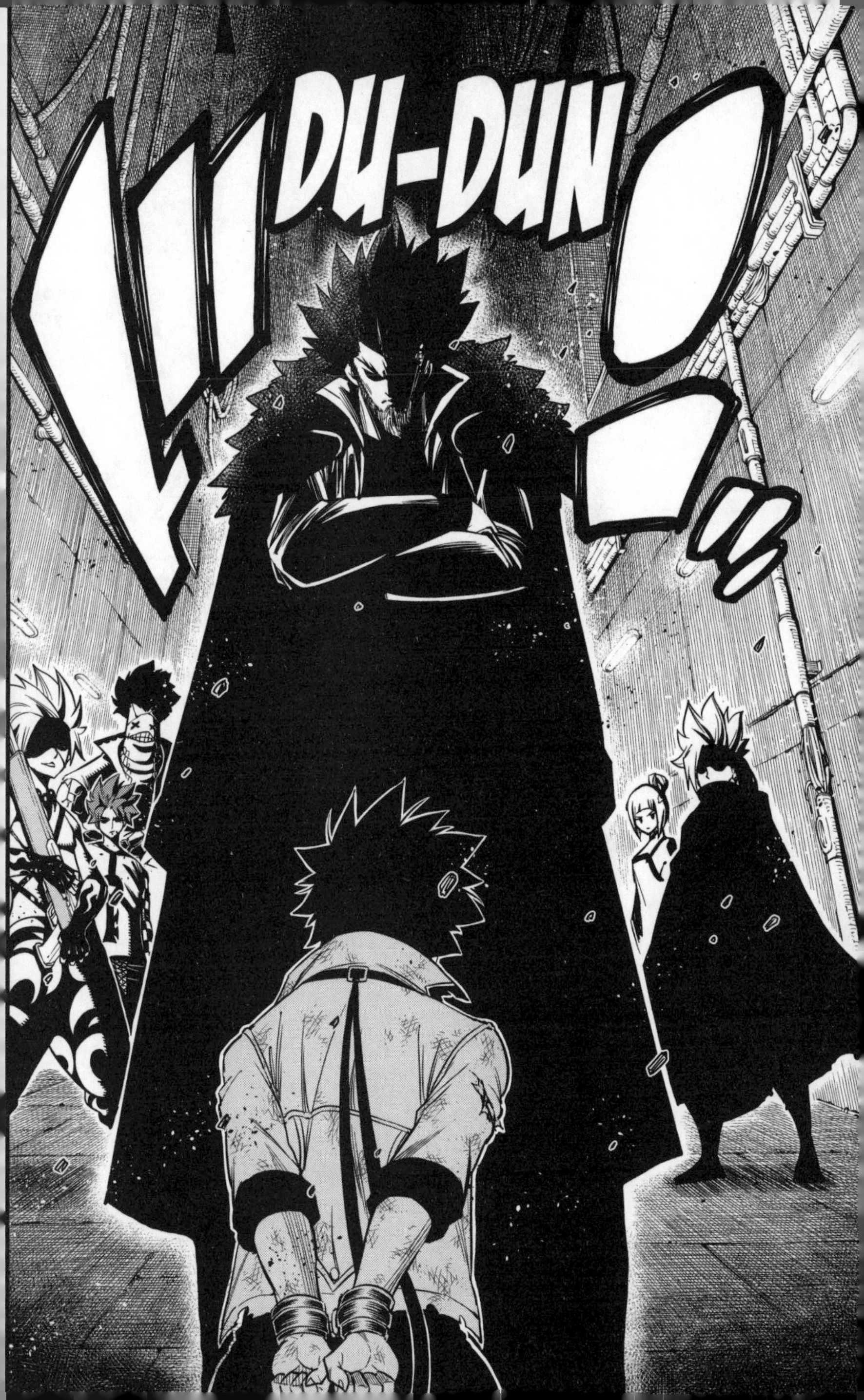
DU-DUN

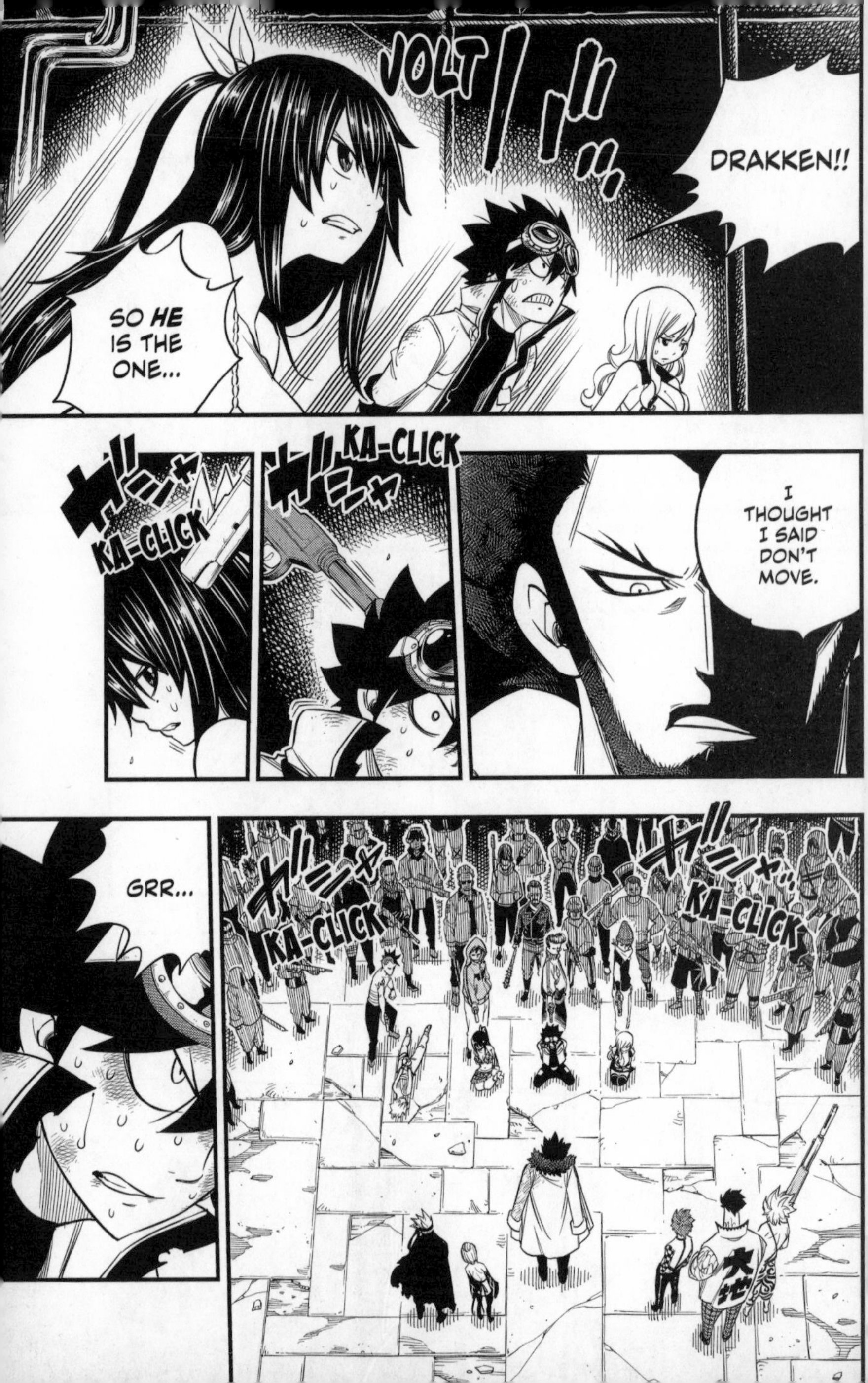
JOLT
DRAKKEN!!
SO HE IS THE ONE...
I THOUGHT I SAID DON'T MOVE.
KA-CLICK
KA-CLICK
KA-CLICK
KA-CLICK
GRR...

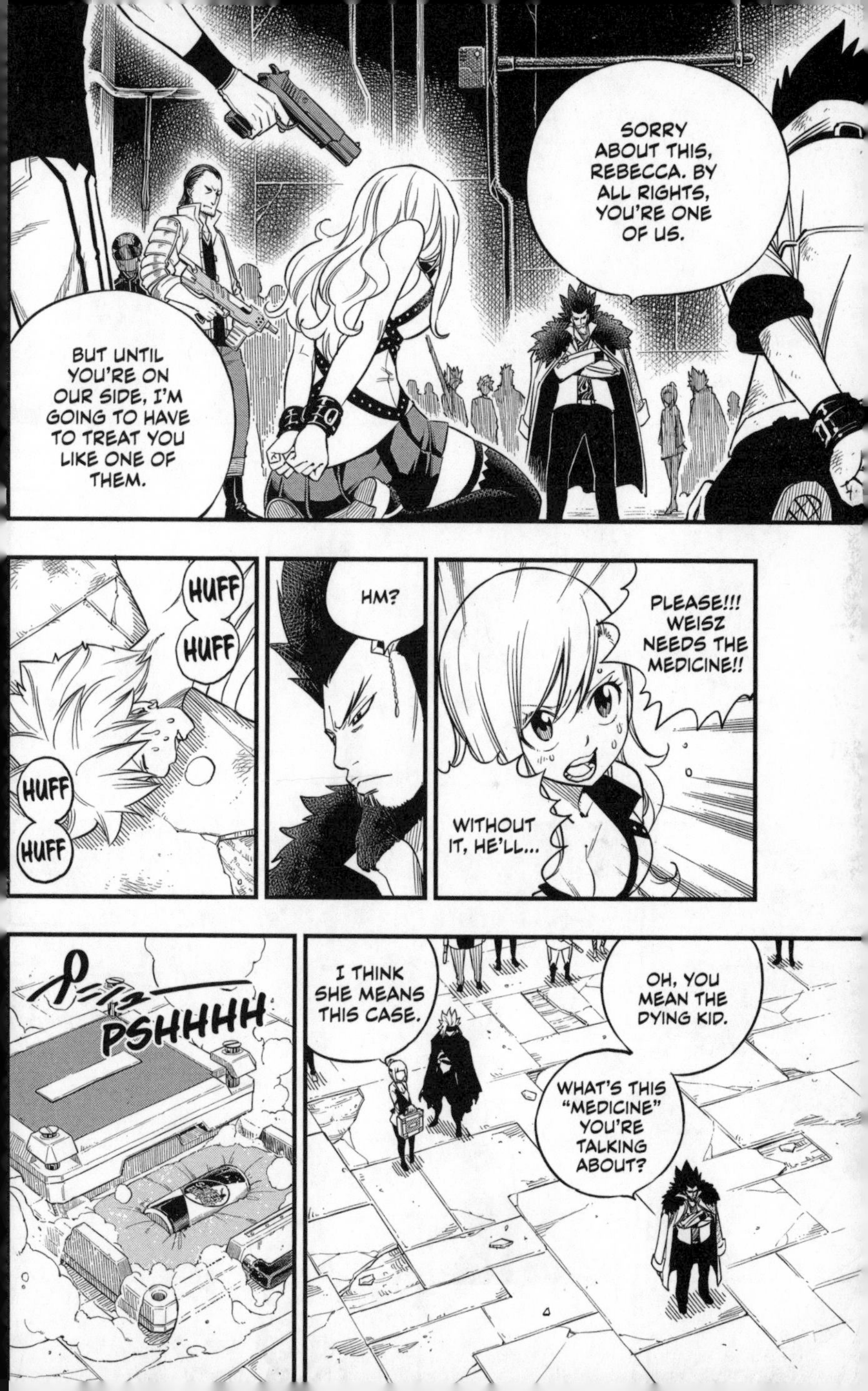
SORRY ABOUT THIS, REBECCA. BY ALL RIGHTS, YOU'RE ONE OF US.
BUT UNTIL YOU'RE ON OUR SIDE, I'M GOING TO HAVE TO TREAT YOU LIKE ONE OF THEM.
PLEASE!!! WEISZ NEEDS THE MEDICINE!!
WITHOUT IT, HE'LL...
HM?
HUFF
HUFF
HUFF
HUFF
OH, YOU MEAN THE DYING KID.
I THINK SHE MEANS THIS CASE.
WHAT'S THIS "MEDICINE" YOU'RE TALKING ABOUT?
PSHHHH

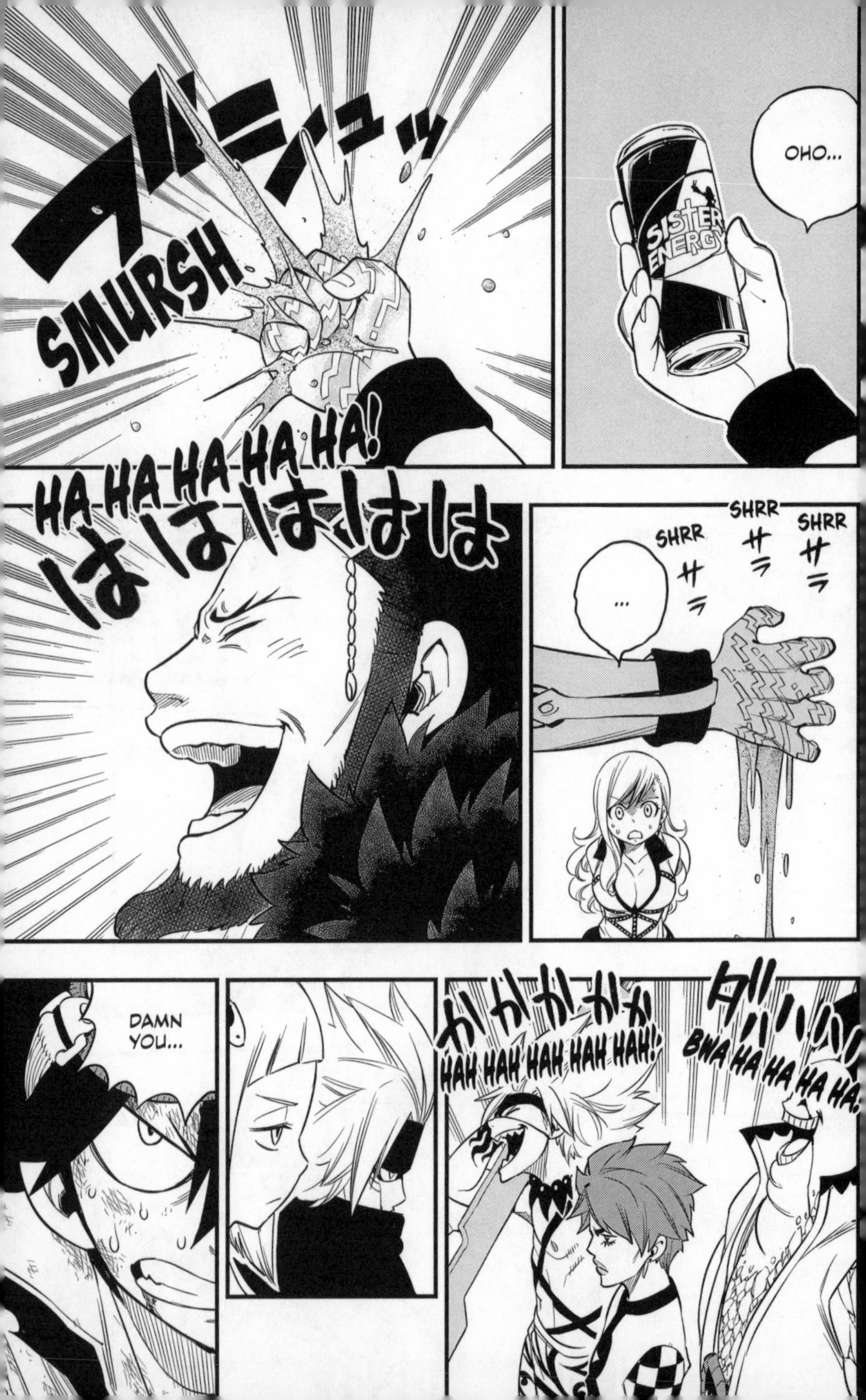
SISTER ENERGY
OHO...
SMURSH
SHRR
SHRR
SHRR
...
HA HA HA HA HA!
ははははは
BWA HA HA HA HA!
HAH HAH HAH HAH HAH!
DAMN YOU...

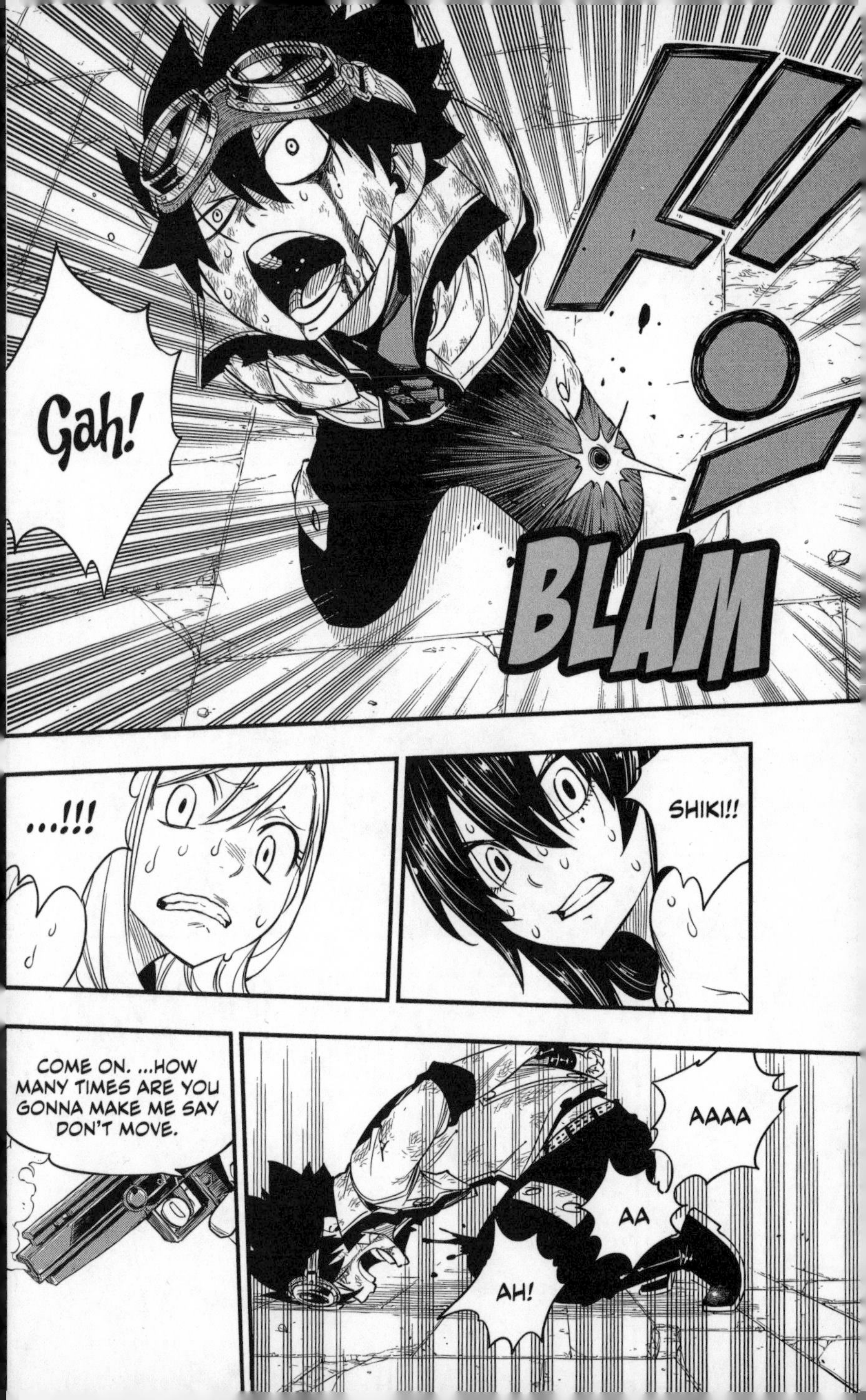

Gah!
BLAM
SHIKI!!
...!!!
AAAA
AA
AH!
COME ON. ...HOW MANY TIMES ARE YOU GONNA MAKE ME SAY DON'T MOVE.

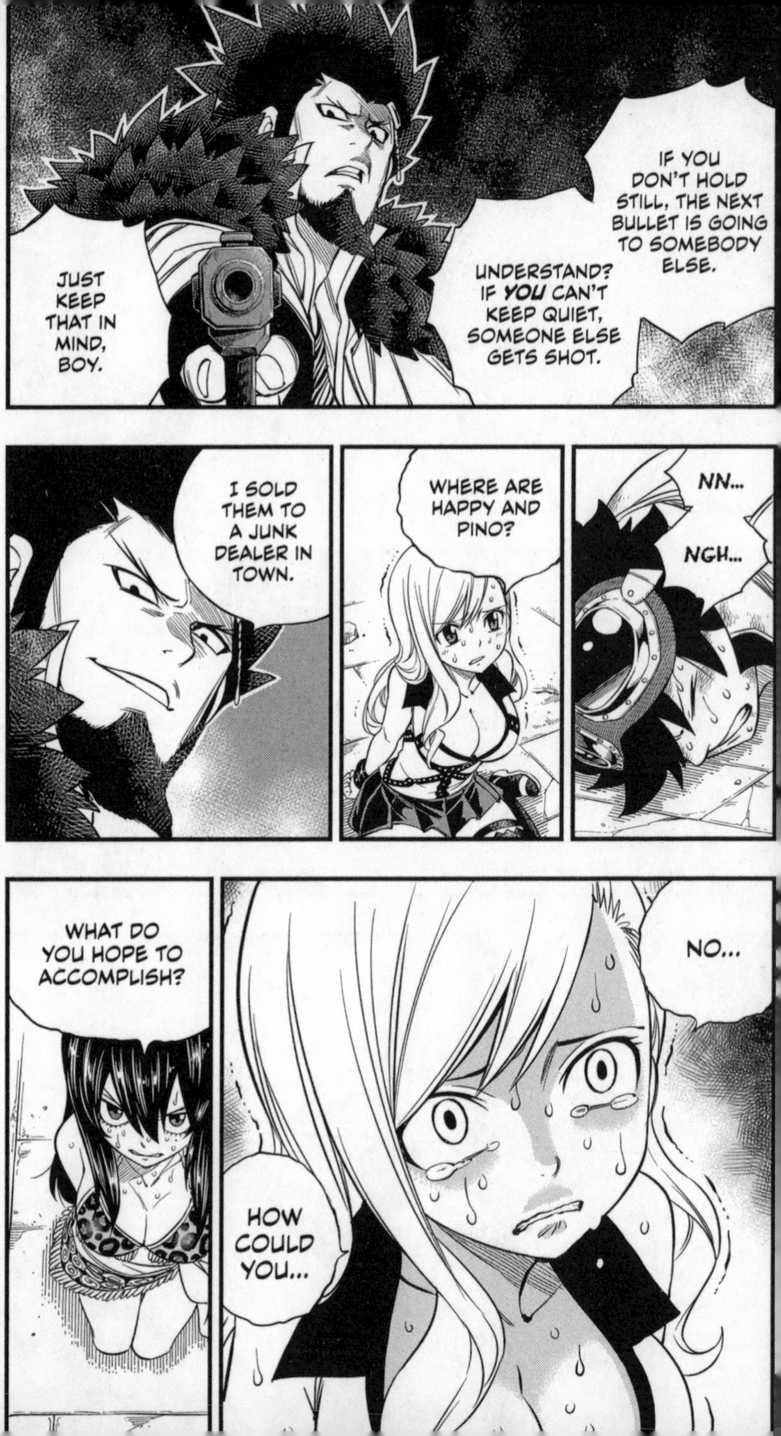
IF YOU DON'T HOLD STILL, THE NEXT BULLET IS GOING TO SOMEBODY ELSE.
UNDERSTAND? IF ***YOU*** CAN'T KEEP QUIET, SOMEONE ELSE GETS SHOT.
JUST KEEP THAT IN MIND, BOY.
NN...
NGH...
WHERE ARE HAPPY AND PINO?
I SOLD THEM TO A JUNK DEALER IN TOWN.
NO...
HOW COULD YOU...
WHAT DO YOU HOPE TO ACCOMPLISH?

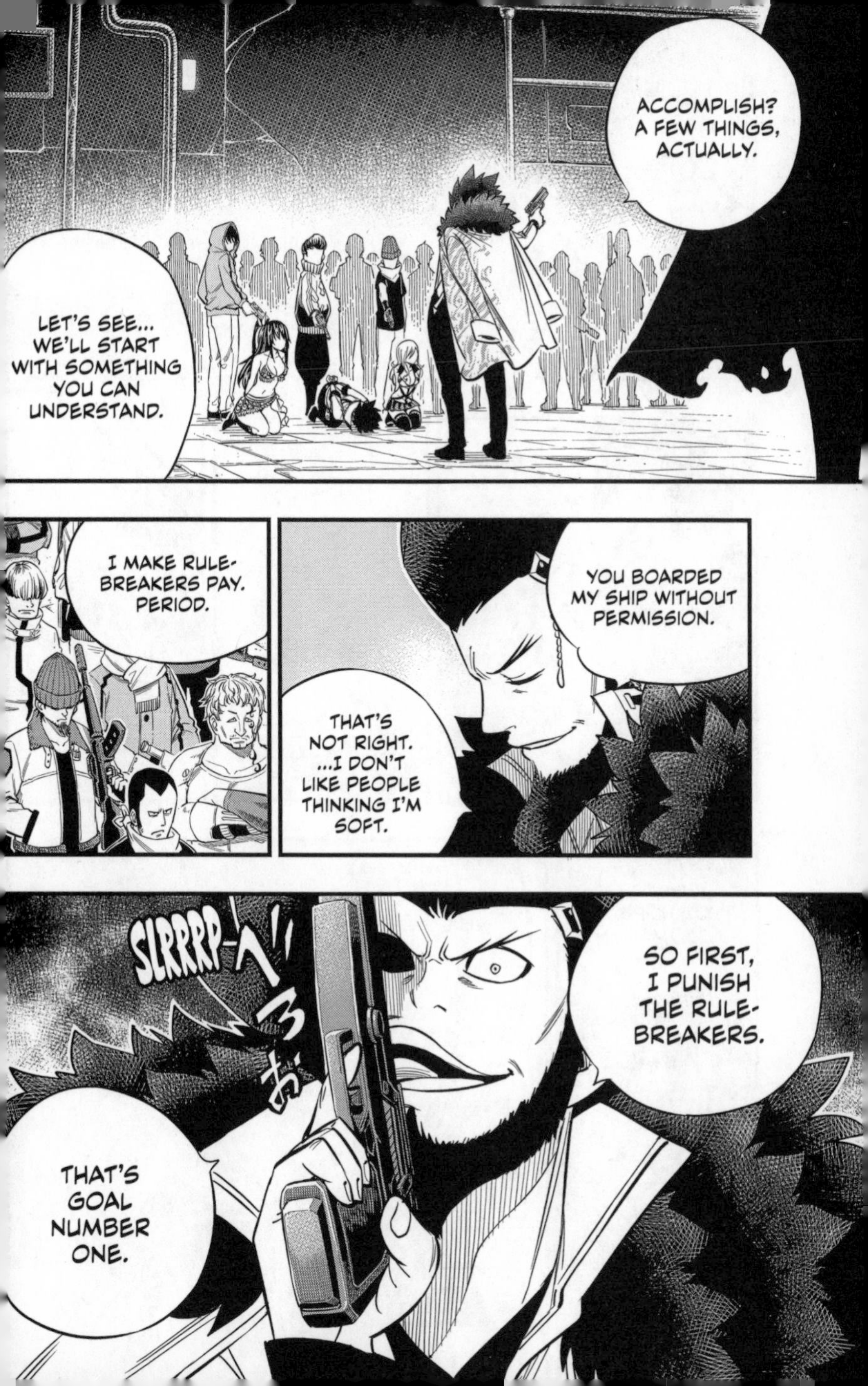
ACCOMPLISH? A FEW THINGS, ACTUALLY.
LET'S SEE... WE'LL START WITH SOMETHING YOU CAN UNDERSTAND.
YOU BOARDED MY SHIP WITHOUT PERMISSION.
THAT'S NOT RIGHT. ...I DON'T LIKE PEOPLE THINKING I'M SOFT.
I MAKE RULE-BREAKERS PAY. PERIOD.
SO FIRST, I PUNISH THE RULE-BREAKERS.
SLRRRP
THAT'S GOAL NUMBER ONE.

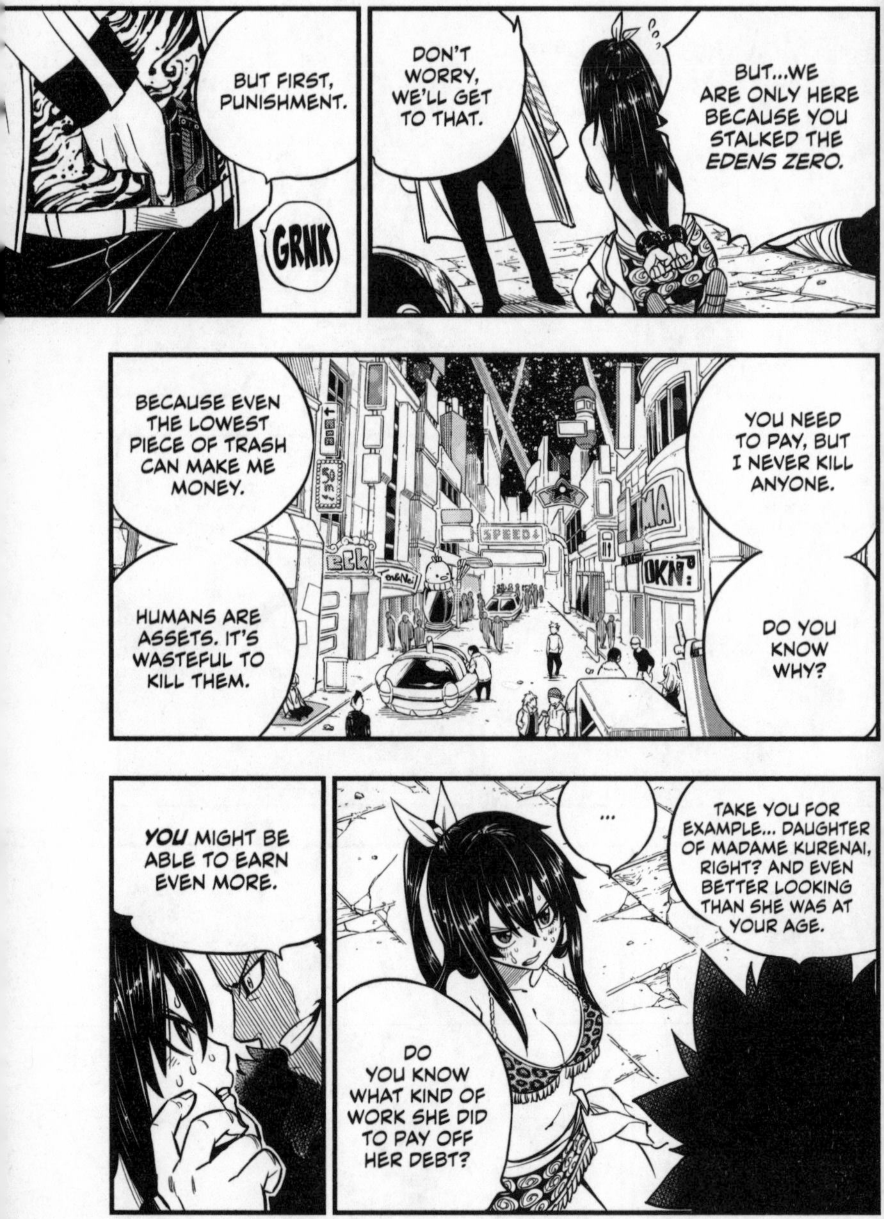
BUT...WE ARE ONLY HERE BECAUSE YOU STALKED THE *EDENS ZERO.*
DON'T WORRY, WE'LL GET TO THAT.
BUT FIRST, PUNISHMENT.
GRNK
YOU NEED TO PAY, BUT I NEVER KILL ANYONE.
DO YOU KNOW WHY?
BECAUSE EVEN THE LOWEST PIECE OF TRASH CAN MAKE ME MONEY.
HUMANS ARE ASSETS. IT'S WASTEFUL TO KILL THEM.
TAKE YOU FOR EXAMPLE... DAUGHTER OF MADAME KURENAI, RIGHT? AND EVEN BETTER LOOKING THAN SHE WAS AT YOUR AGE.
...
DO YOU KNOW WHAT KIND OF WORK SHE DID TO PAY OFF HER DEBT?
YOU MIGHT BE ABLE TO EARN EVEN MORE.

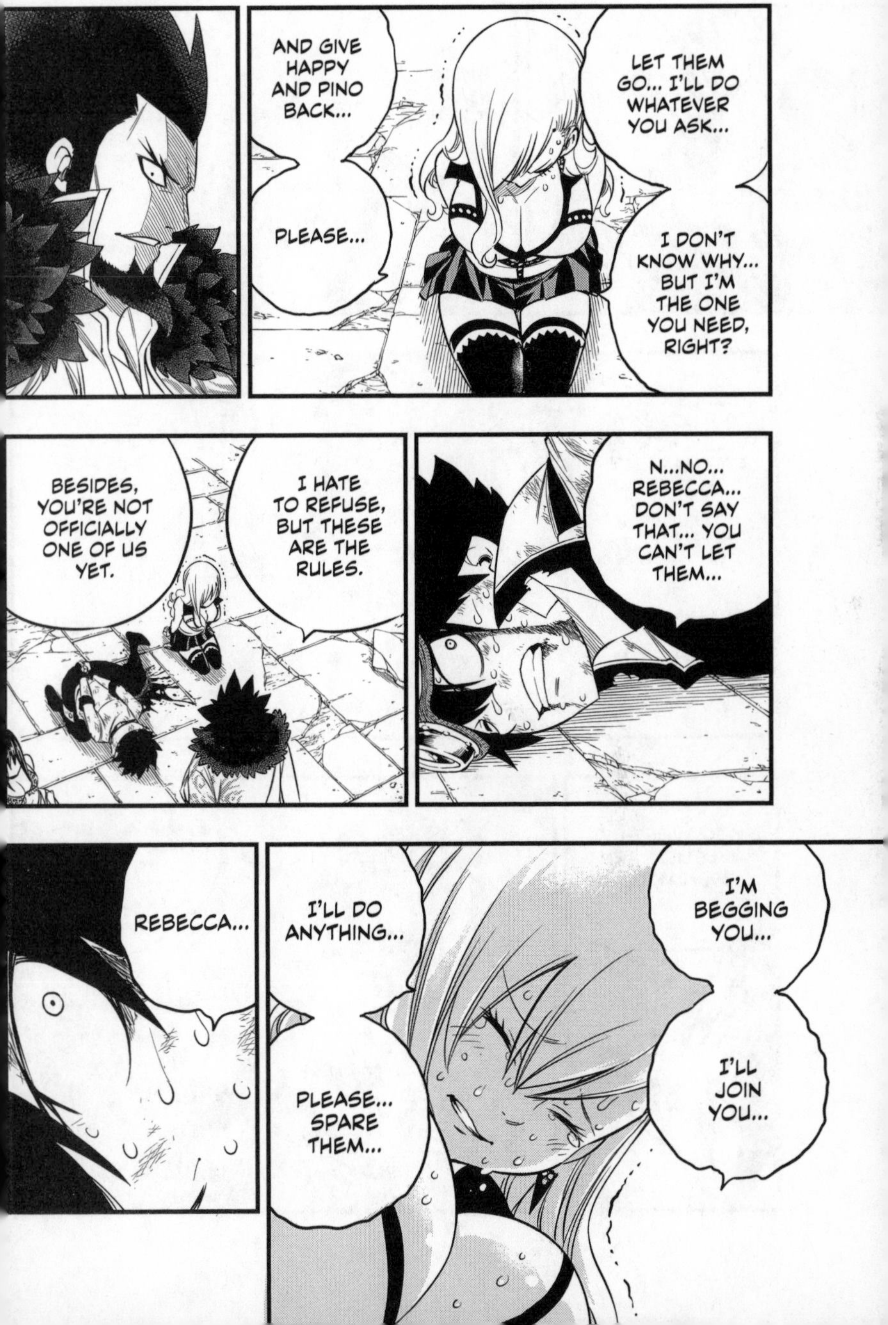
LET THEM GO... I'LL DO WHATEVER YOU ASK...
I DON'T KNOW WHY... BUT I'M THE ONE YOU NEED, RIGHT?
AND GIVE HAPPY AND PINO BACK...
PLEASE...
N...NO... REBECCA... DON'T SAY THAT... YOU CAN'T LET THEM...
I HATE TO REFUSE, BUT THESE ARE THE RULES.
BESIDES, YOU'RE NOT OFFICIALLY ONE OF US YET.
I'M BEGGING YOU...
I'LL JOIN YOU...
I'LL DO ANYTHING...
PLEASE... SPARE THEM...
REBECCA...

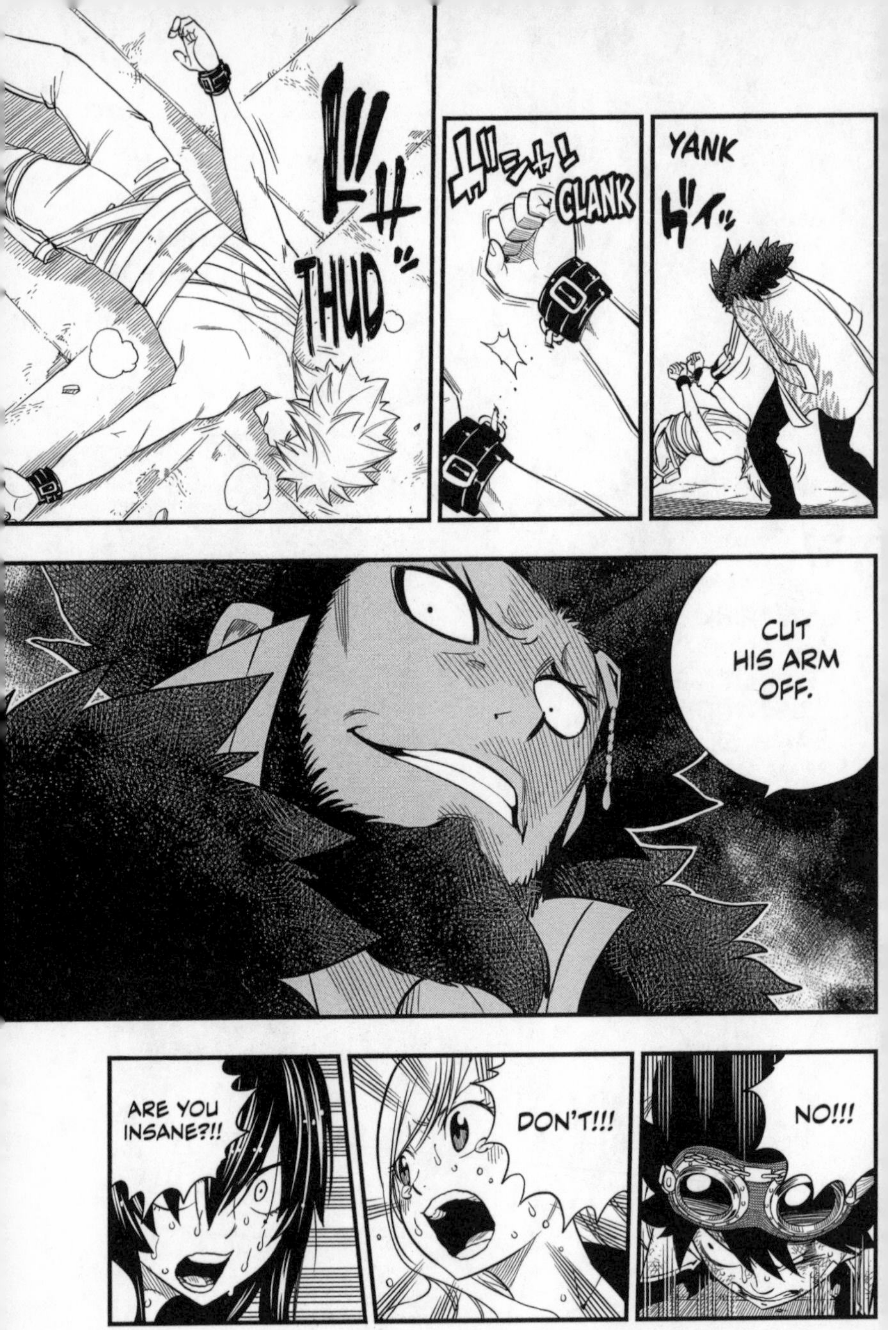
YANK
CLANK
THUD
CUT HIS ARM OFF.
NO!!!
DON'T!!!
ARE YOU INSANE?!!

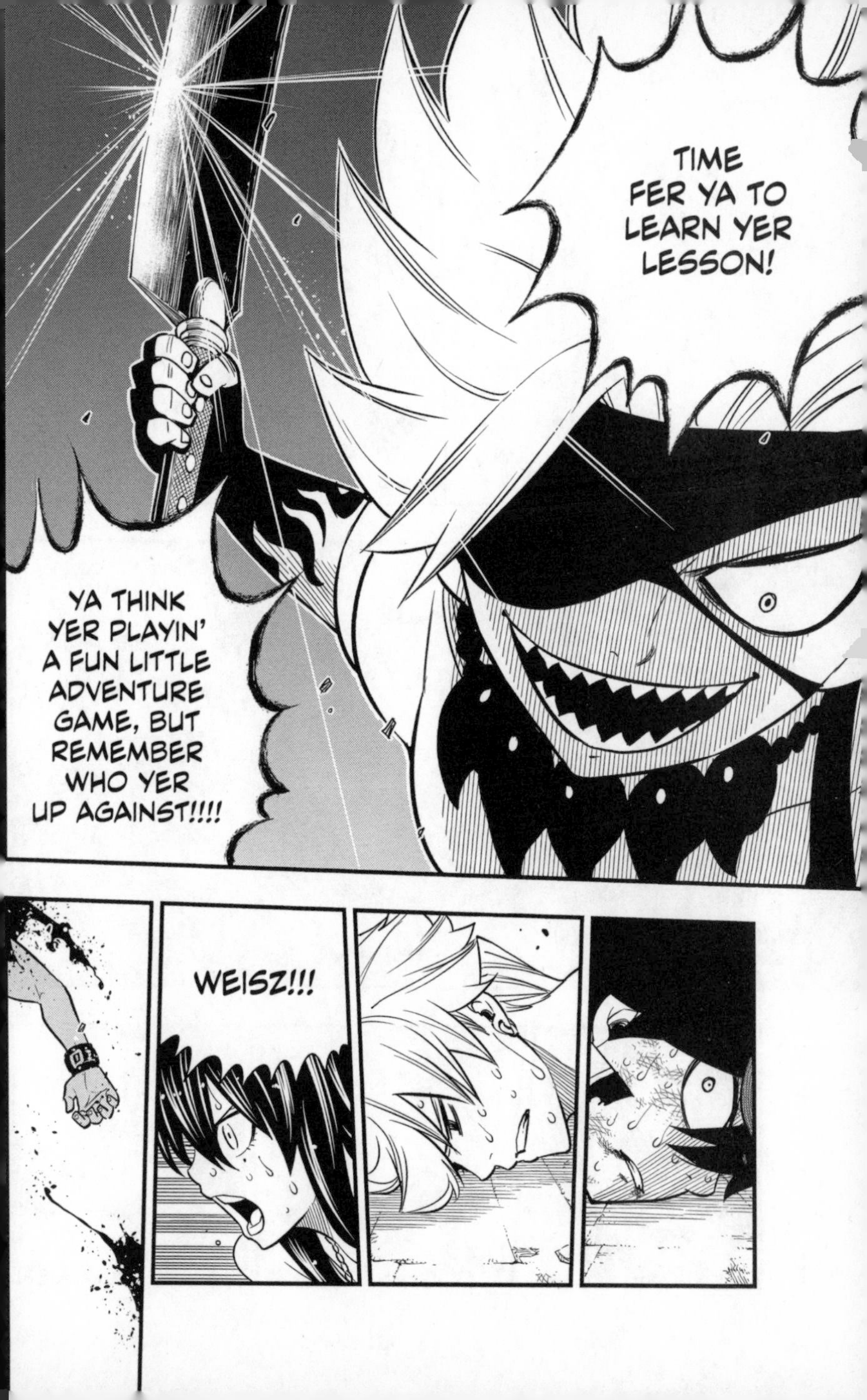
TIME FER YA TO LEARN YER LESSON!
YA THINK YER PLAYIN' A FUN LITTLE ADVENTURE GAME, BUT REMEMBER WHO YER UP AGAINST!!!!
WEISZ!!!

EDENSZERO
エデンズゼロ

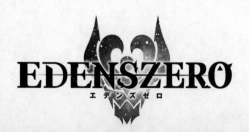

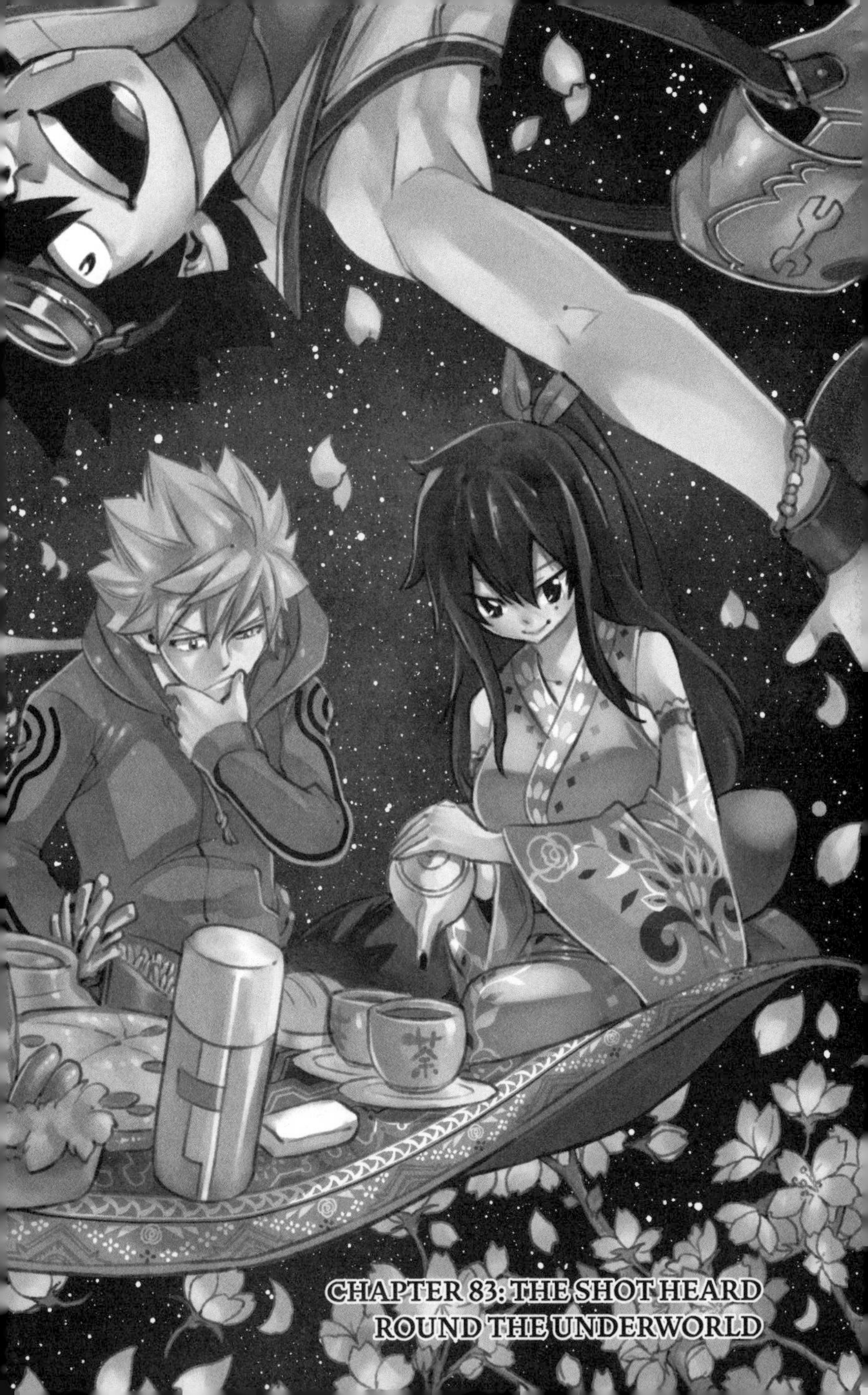

CHAPTER 83: THE SHOT HEARD ROUND THE UNDERWORLD

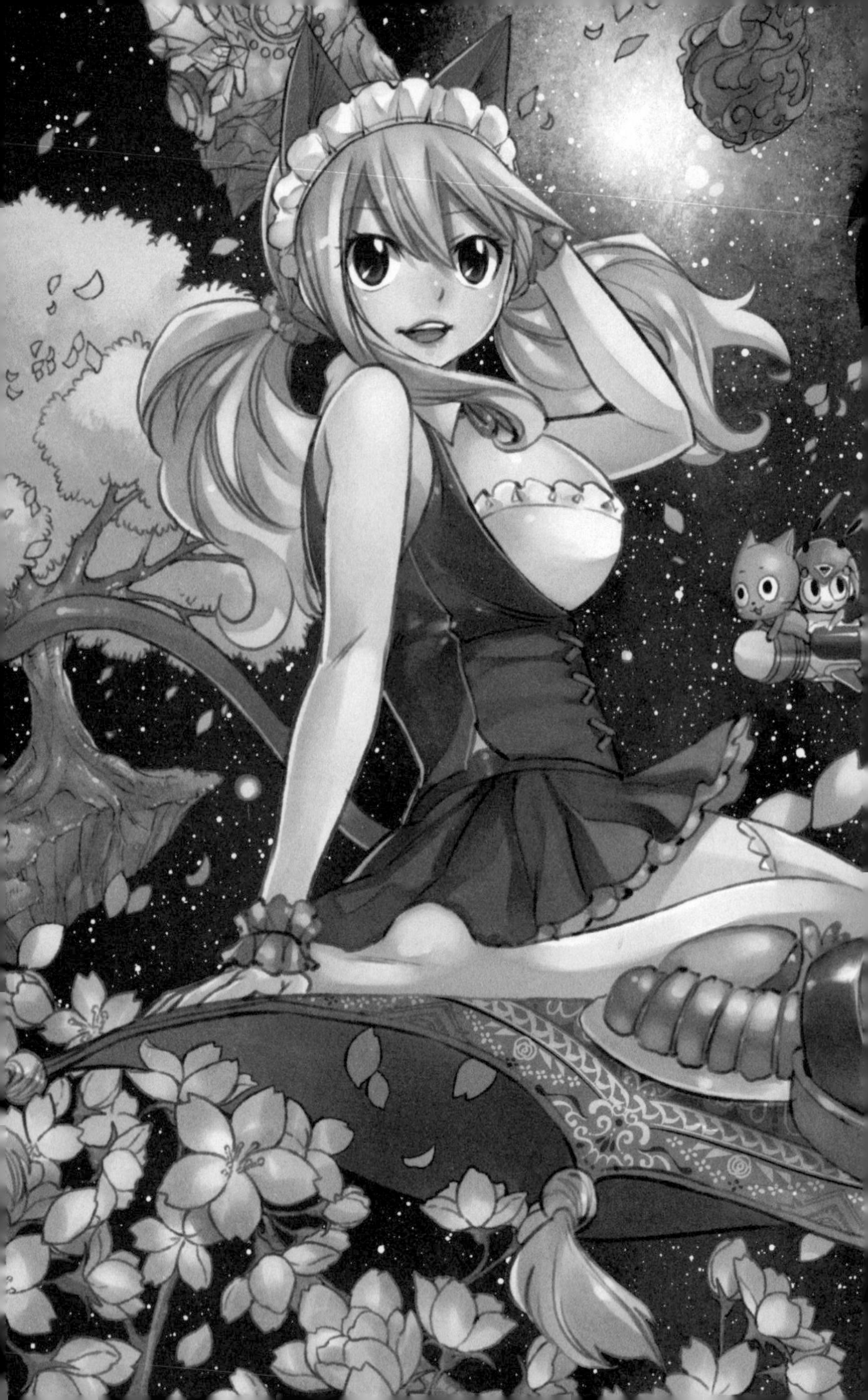

EDENSZERO

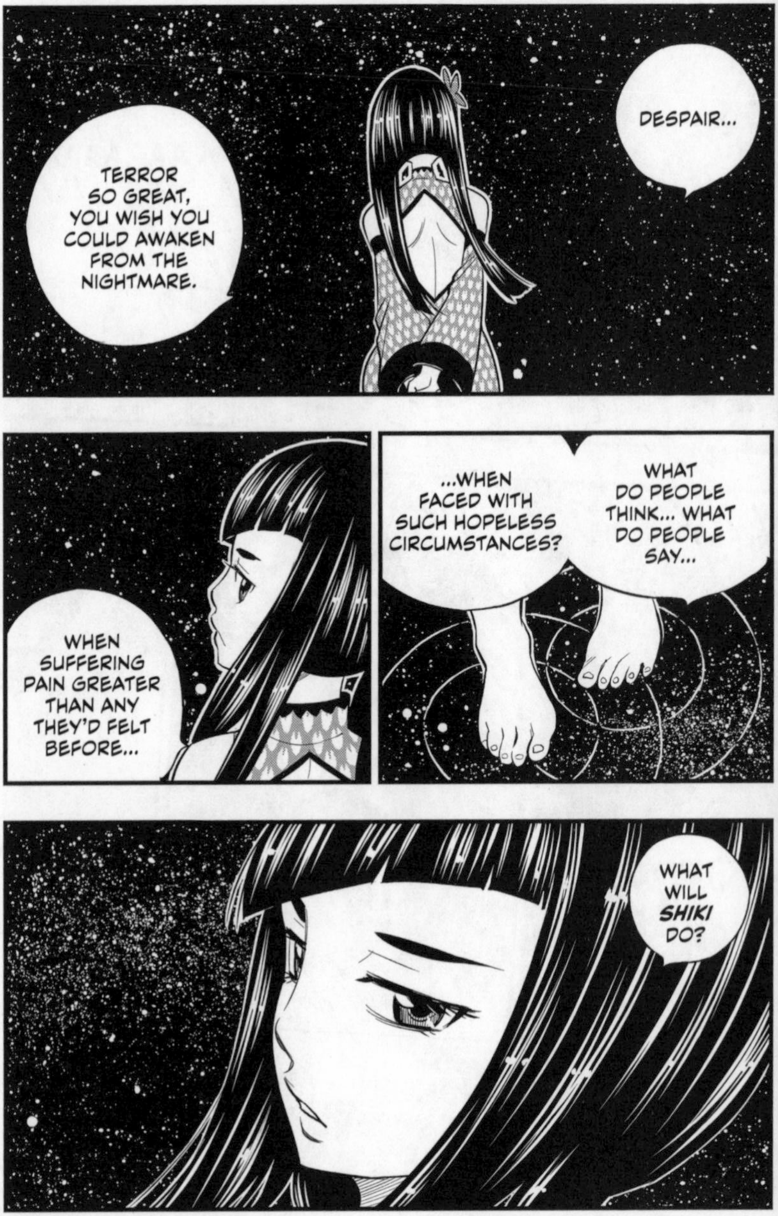
DESPAIR...
TERROR SO GREAT, YOU WISH YOU COULD AWAKEN FROM THE NIGHTMARE.
WHAT DO PEOPLE THINK... WHAT DO PEOPLE SAY...
...WHEN FACED WITH SUCH HOPELESS CIRCUMSTANCES?
WHEN SUFFERING PAIN GREATER THAN ANY THEY'D FELT BEFORE...
WHAT WILL *SHIKI* DO?

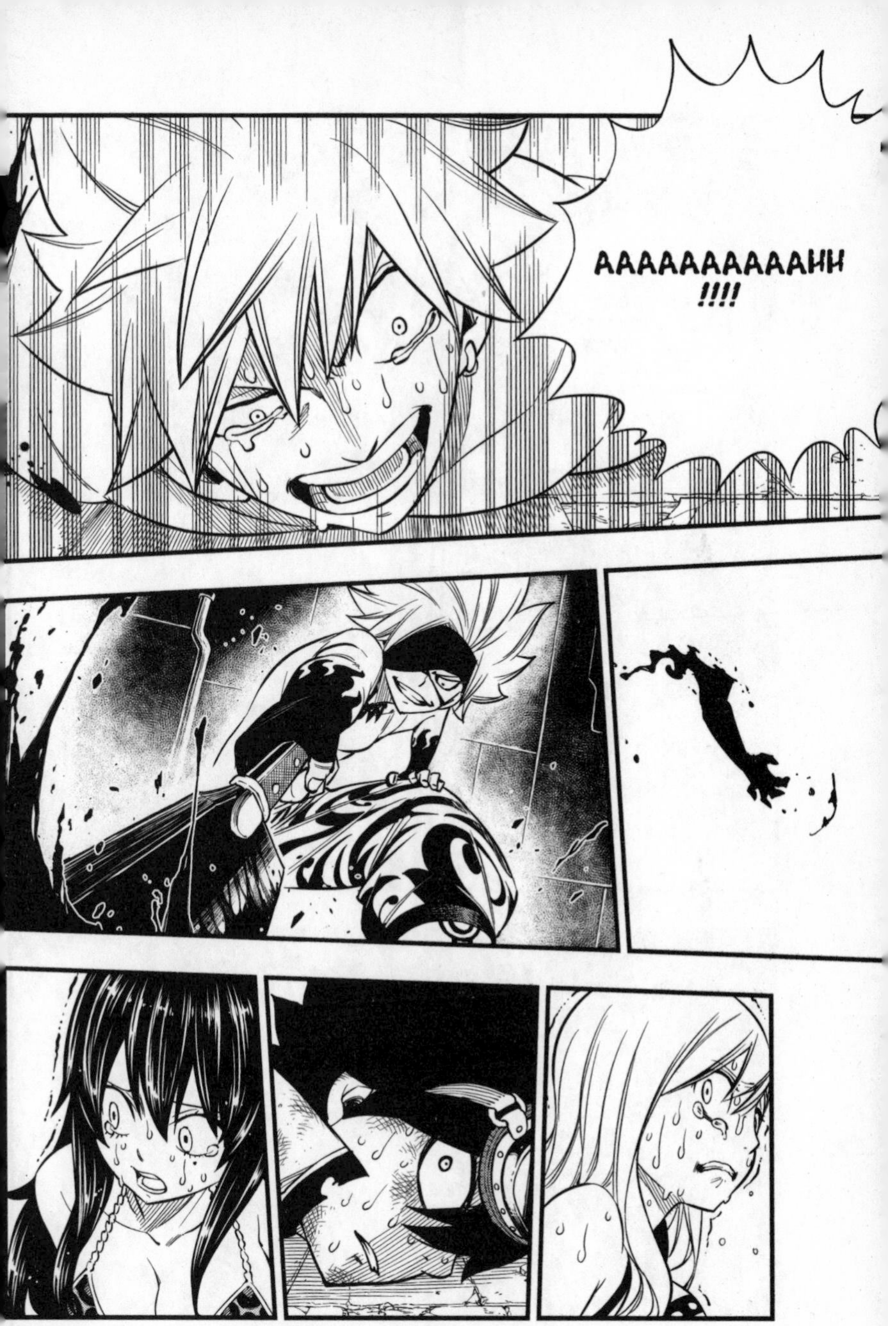
AAAAAAAAAAAHH
!!!!

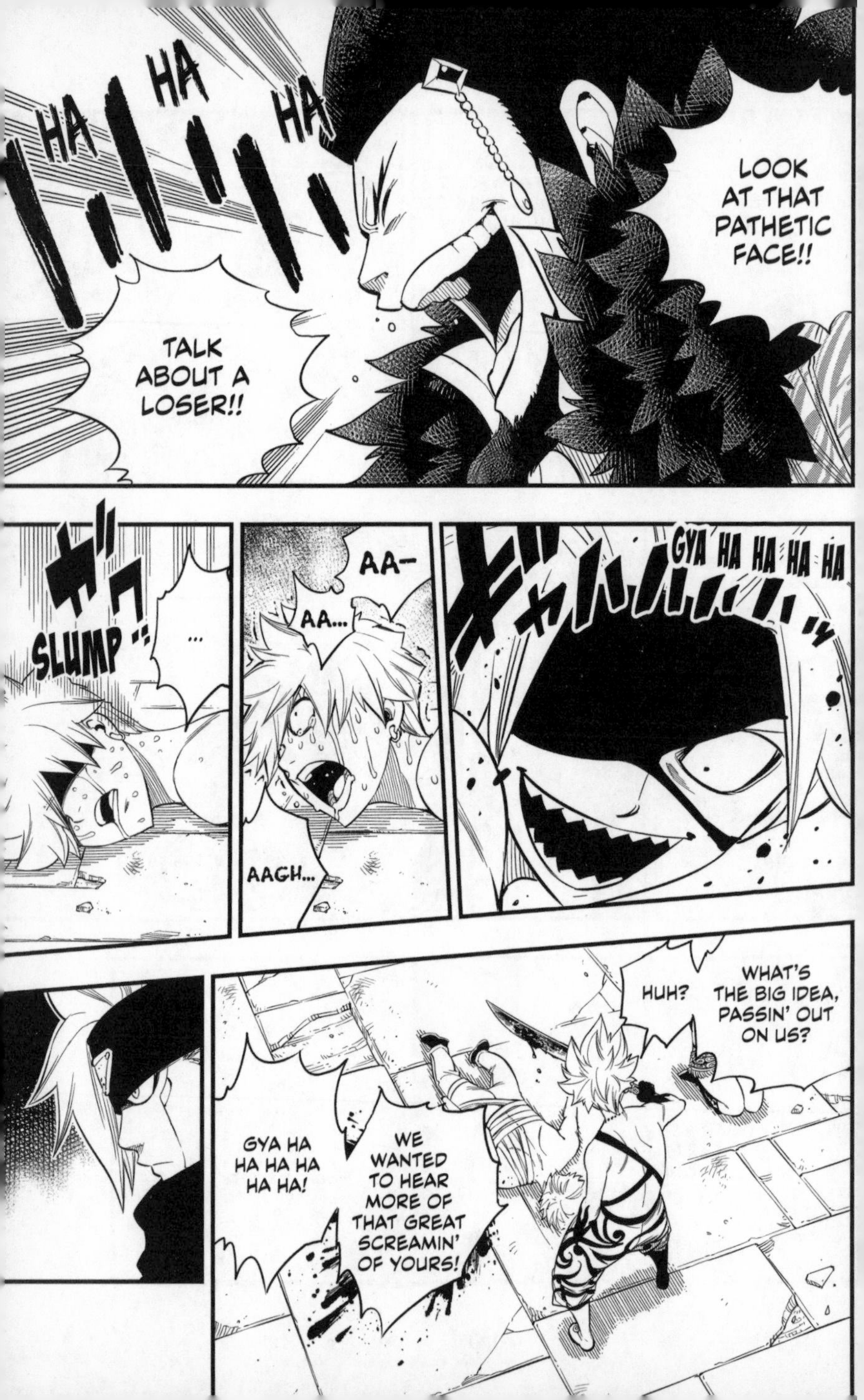

LOOK AT THAT PATHETIC FACE!!
HA HA HA
TALK ABOUT A LOSER!!
GYA HA HA HA HA
AA—
AA...
AAGH...
SLUMP!!
...
WHAT'S THE BIG IDEA, PASSIN' OUT ON US?
HUH?
WE WANTED TO HEAR MORE OF THAT GREAT SCREAMIN' OF YOURS!
GYA HA HA HA HA HA HA!

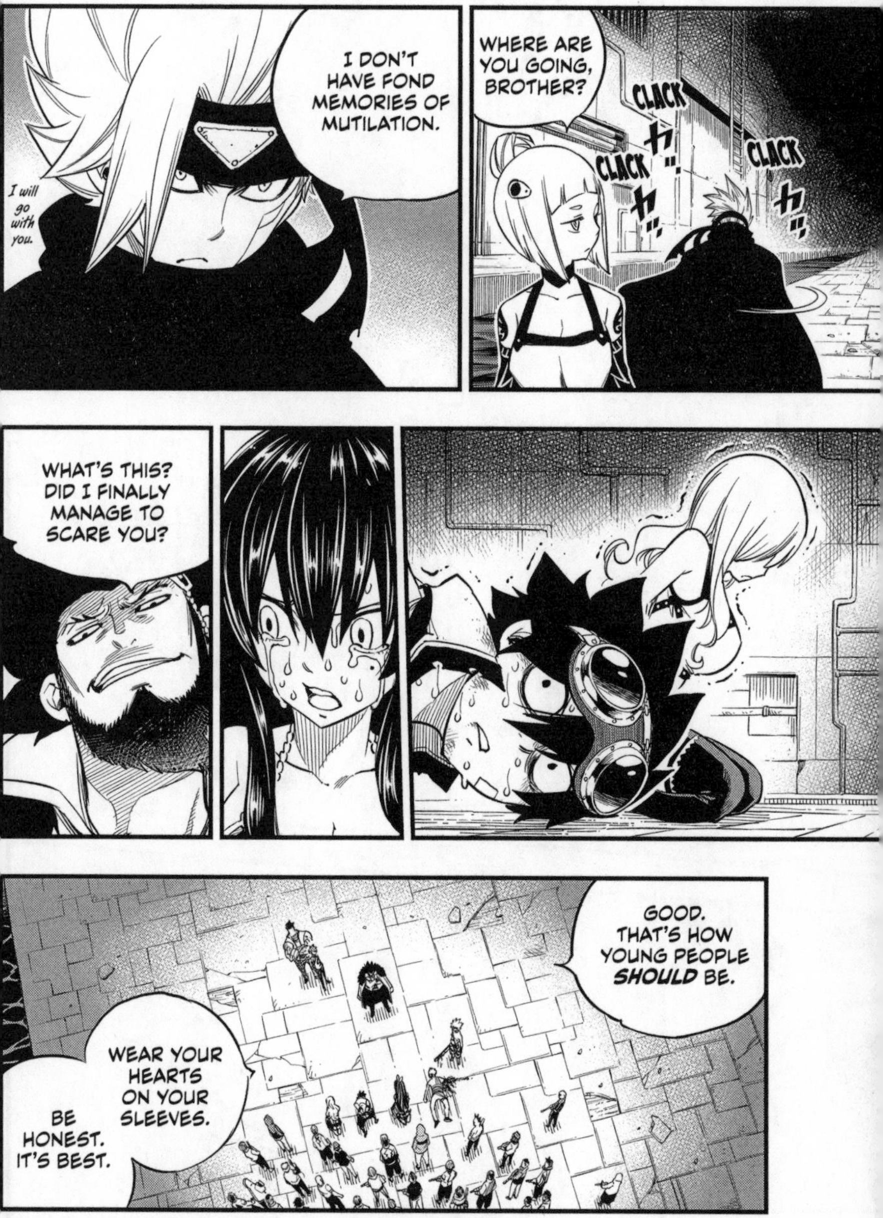
WHERE ARE YOU GOING, BROTHER?
CLACK
CLACK
CLACK
I DON'T HAVE FOND MEMORIES OF MUTILATION.
I will go with you.
WHAT'S THIS? DID I FINALLY MANAGE TO SCARE YOU?
GOOD. THAT'S HOW YOUNG PEOPLE **SHOULD** BE.
WEAR YOUR HEARTS ON YOUR SLEEVES.
BE HONEST. IT'S BEST.

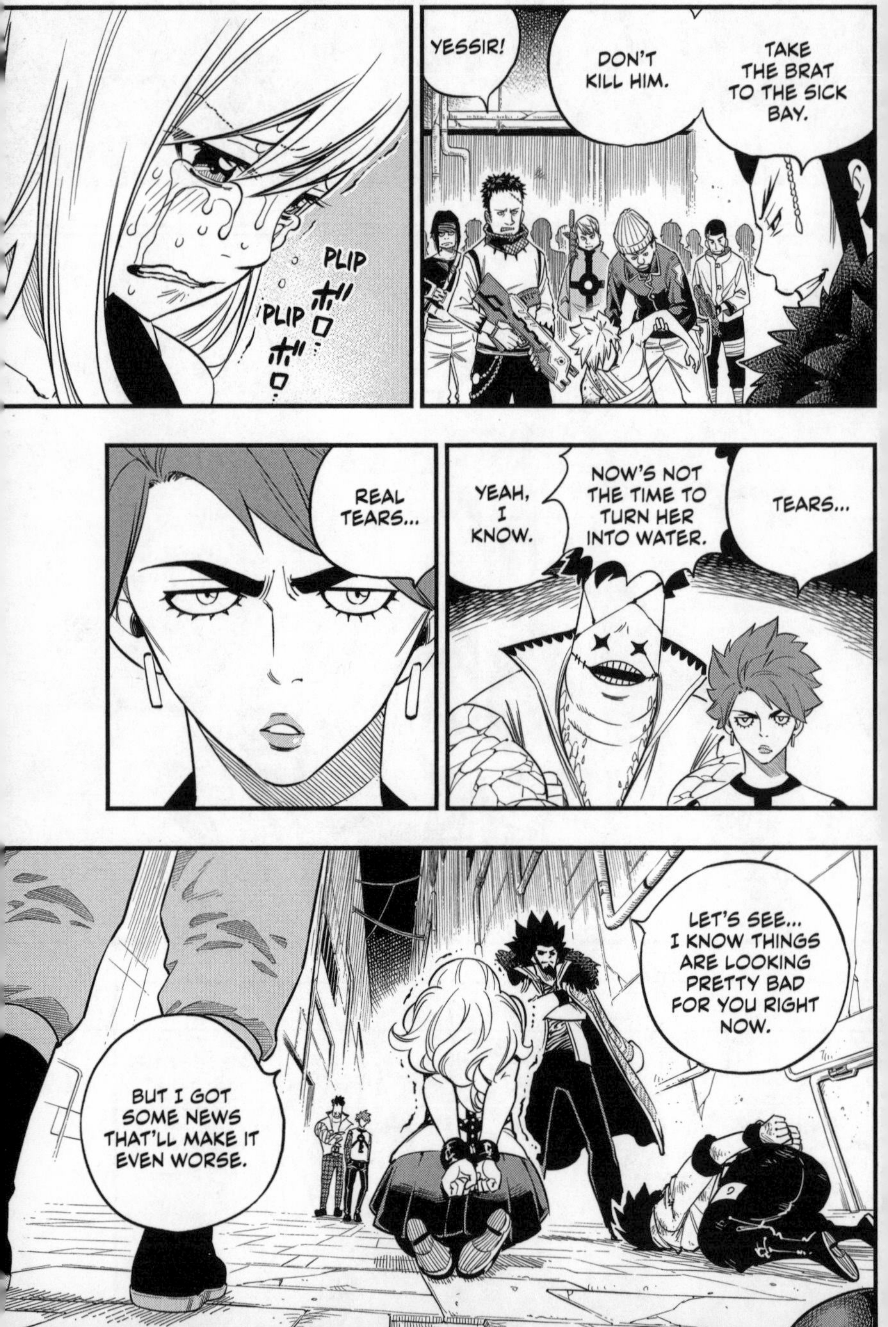
TAKE THE BRAT TO THE SICK BAY.
DON'T KILL HIM.
YESSIR!
PLIP
ボロ
PLIP
ボロ
TEARS...
NOW'S NOT THE TIME TO TURN HER INTO WATER.
YEAH, I KNOW.
REAL TEARS...
LET'S SEE... I KNOW THINGS ARE LOOKING PRETTY BAD FOR YOU RIGHT NOW.
BUT I GOT SOME NEWS THAT'LL MAKE IT EVEN WORSE.

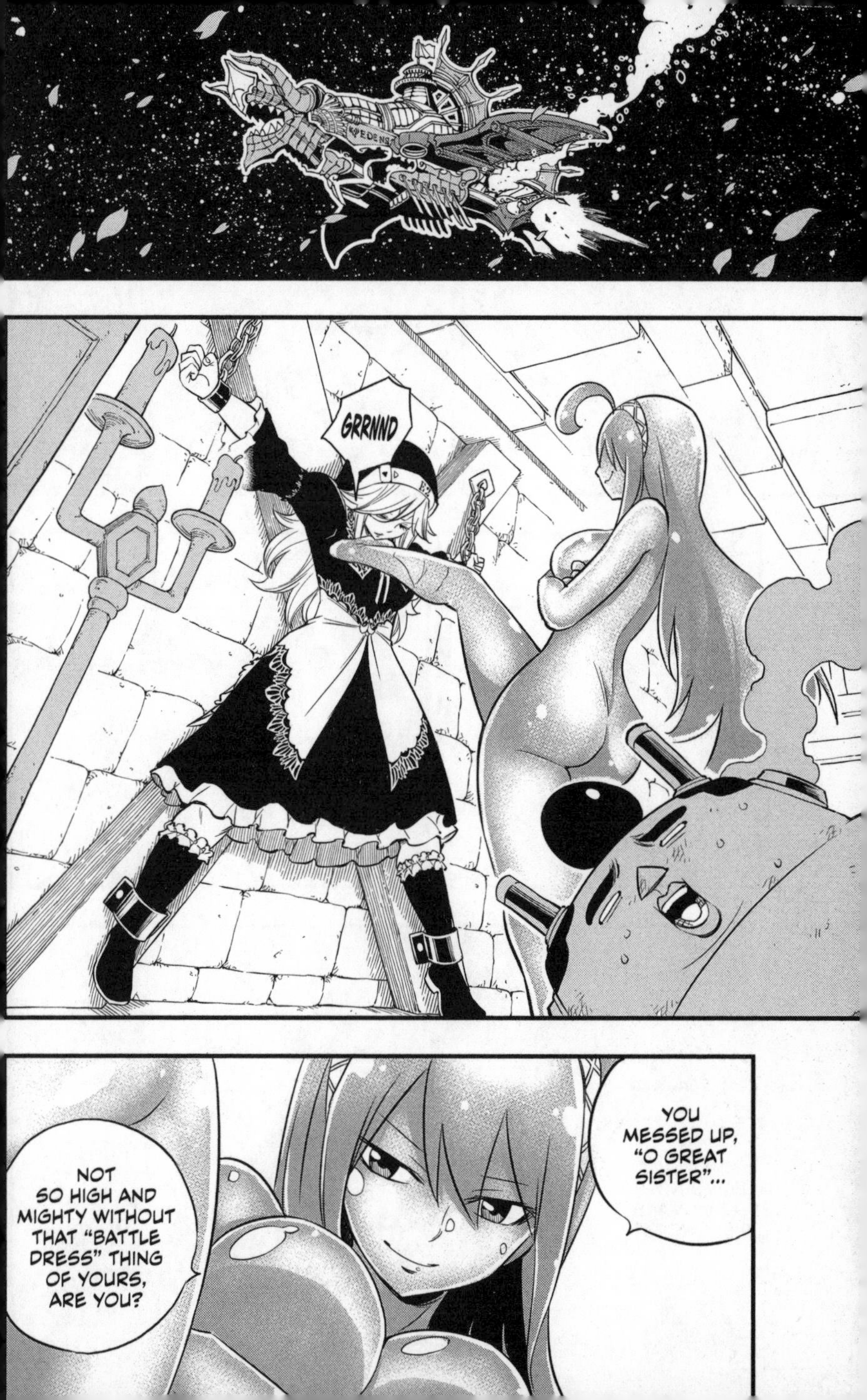
GRRNND
YOU MESSED UP, "O GREAT SISTER"...
NOT SO HIGH AND MIGHTY WITHOUT THAT "BATTLE DRESS" THING OF YOURS, ARE YOU?

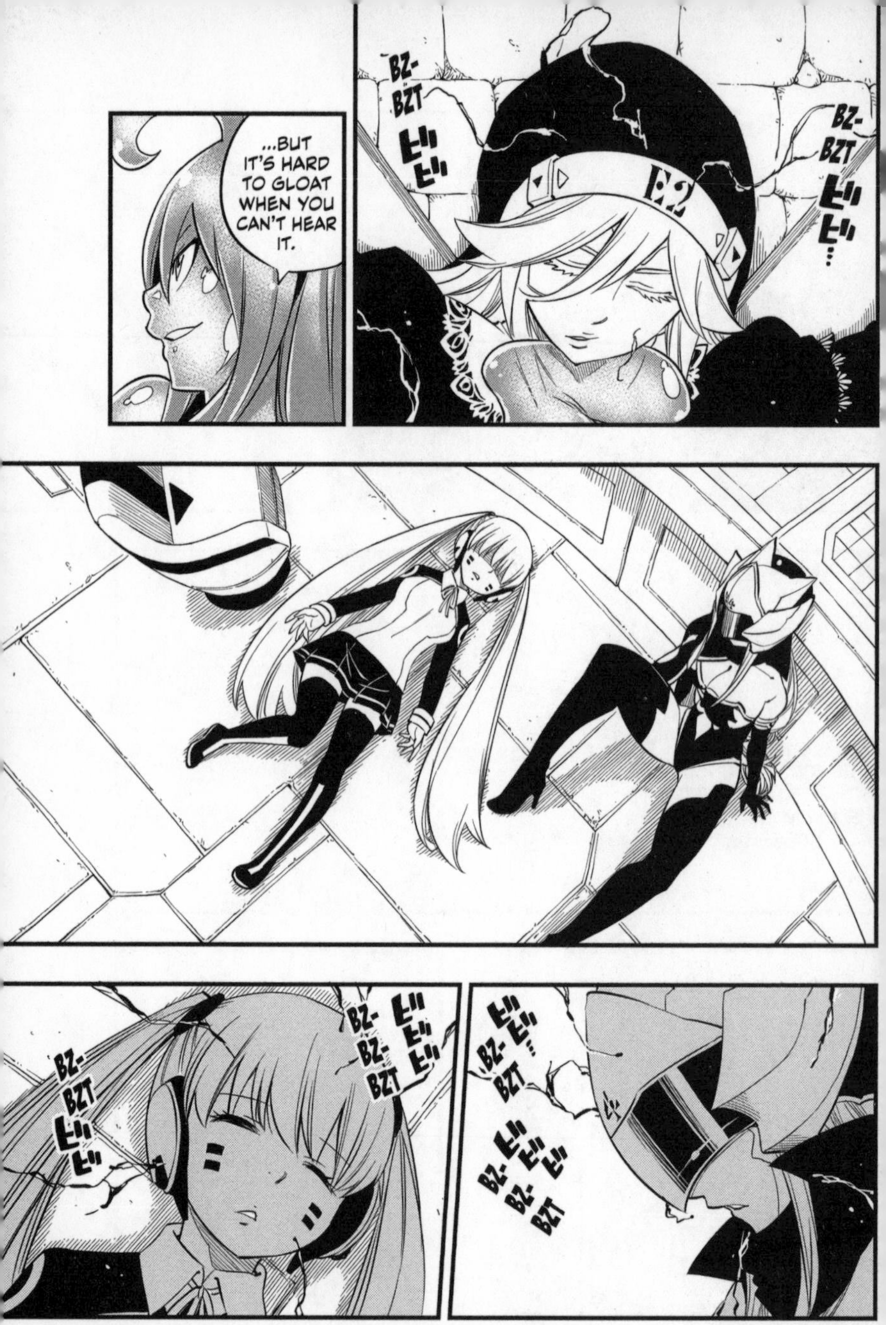
BZ-BZT
BZ-BZT...
...BUT IT'S HARD TO GLOAT WHEN YOU CAN'T HEAR IT.
BZ-BZT...
BZ-BZ-BZT
BZ-BZ-BZT
BZ-BZT

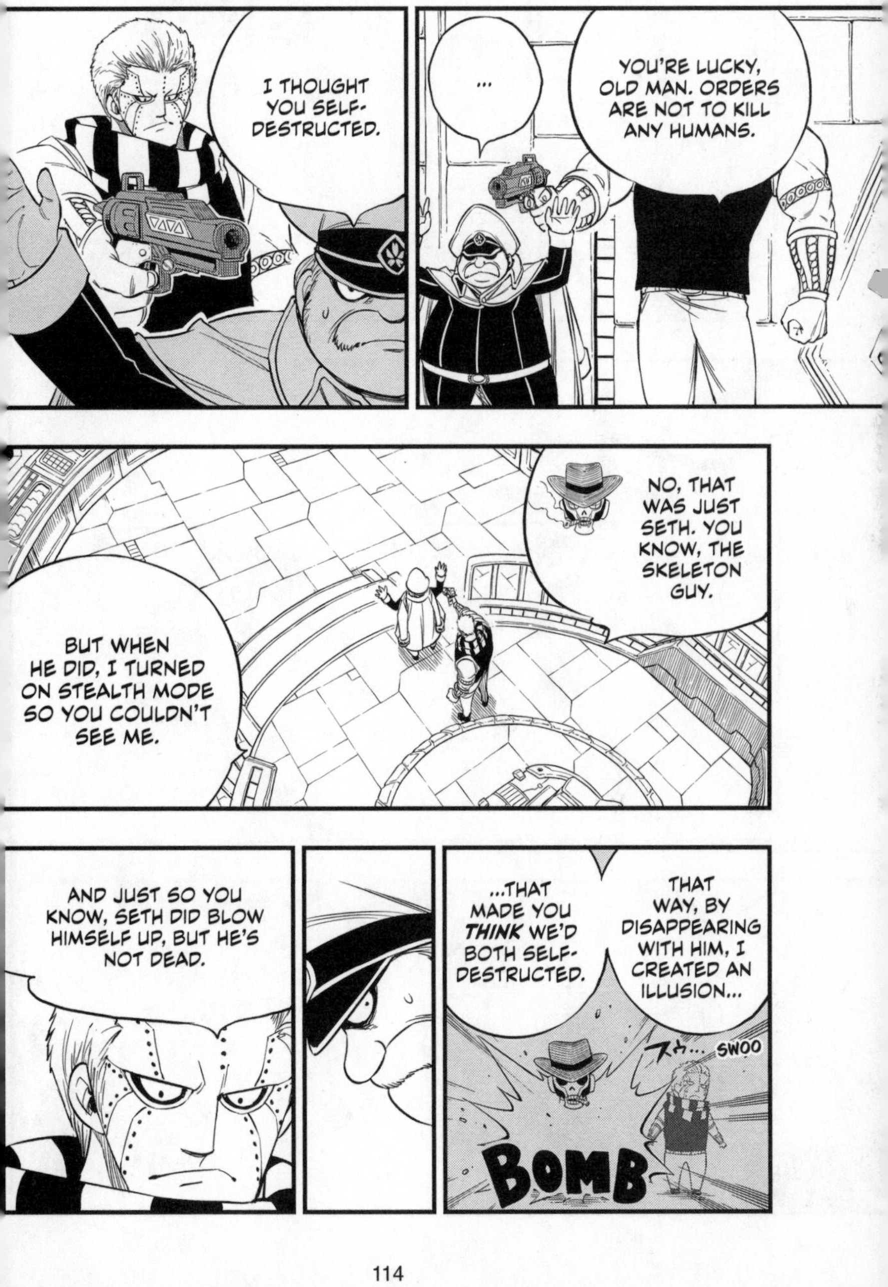
YOU'RE LUCKY, OLD MAN. ORDERS ARE NOT TO KILL ANY HUMANS.
...
I THOUGHT YOU SELF-DESTRUCTED.
NO, THAT WAS JUST SETH. YOU KNOW, THE SKELETON GUY.
BUT WHEN HE DID, I TURNED ON STEALTH MODE SO YOU COULDN'T SEE ME.
THAT WAY, BY DISAPPEARING WITH HIM, I CREATED AN ILLUSION...
...THAT MADE YOU *THINK* WE'D BOTH SELF-DESTRUCTED.
SWOO
BOMB
AND JUST SO YOU KNOW, SETH DID BLOW HIMSELF UP, BUT HE'S NOT DEAD.

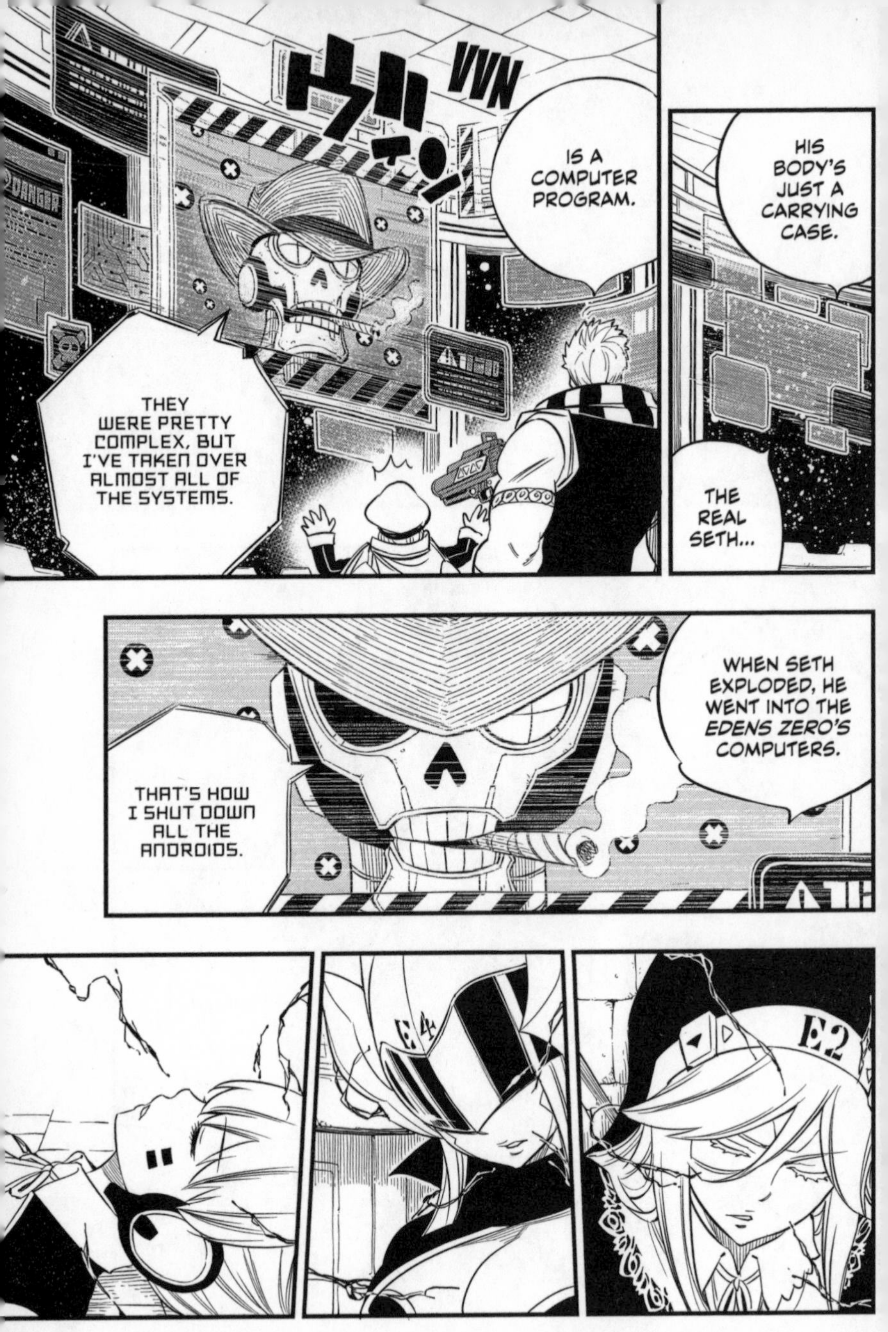
HIS BODY'S JUST A CARRYING CASE.
THE REAL SETH...
VVN
IS A COMPUTER PROGRAM.
THEY WERE PRETTY COMPLEX, BUT I'VE TAKEN OVER ALMOST ALL OF THE SYSTEMS.
WHEN SETH EXPLODED, HE WENT INTO THE *EDENS ZERO'S* COMPUTERS.
THAT'S HOW I SHUT DOWN ALL THE ANDROIDS.

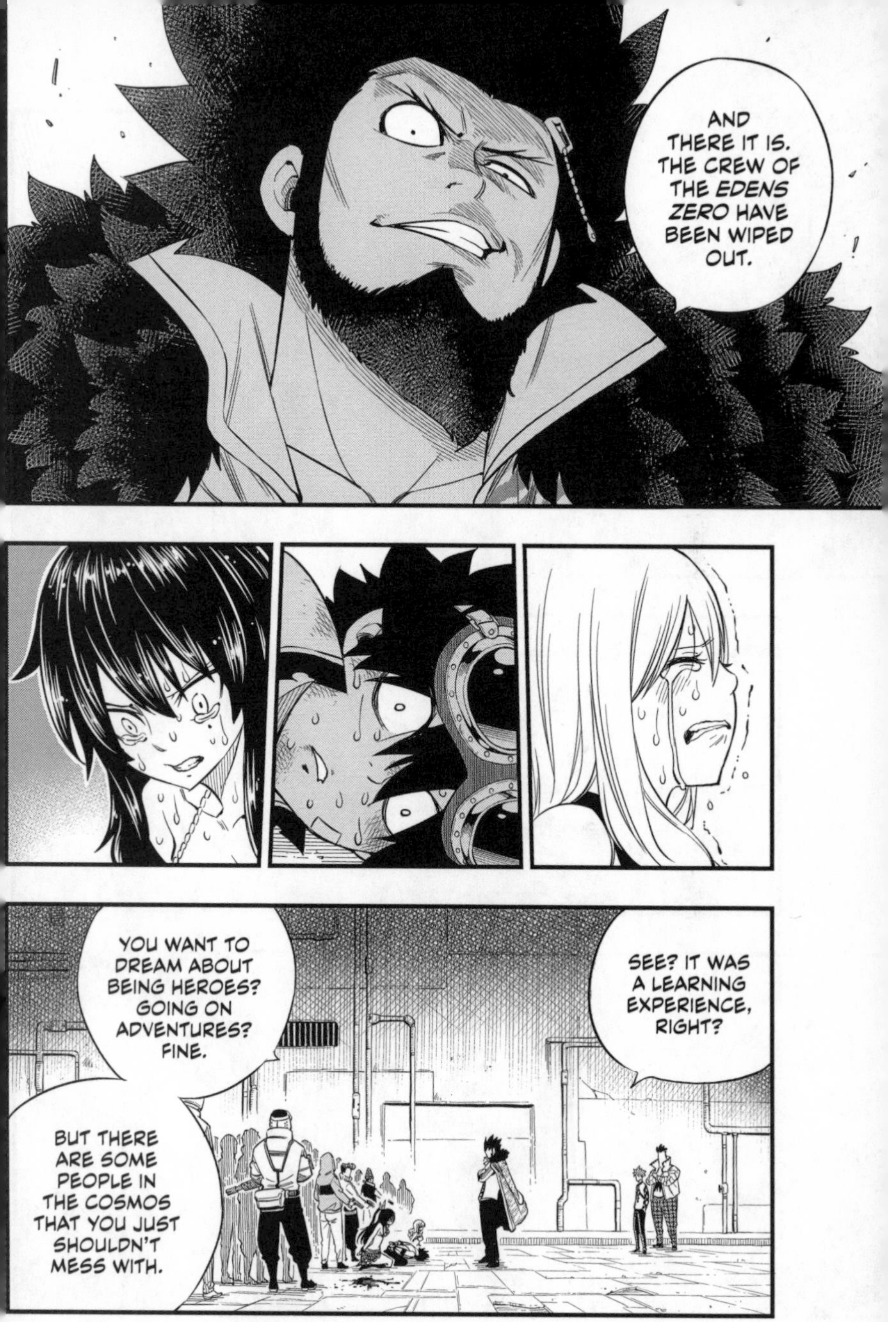
AND THERE IT IS. THE CREW OF THE *EDENS ZERO* HAVE BEEN WIPED OUT.
SEE? IT WAS A LEARNING EXPERIENCE, RIGHT?
YOU WANT TO DREAM ABOUT BEING HEROES? GOING ON ADVENTURES? FINE.
BUT THERE ARE SOME PEOPLE IN THE COSMOS THAT YOU JUST SHOULDN'T MESS WITH.

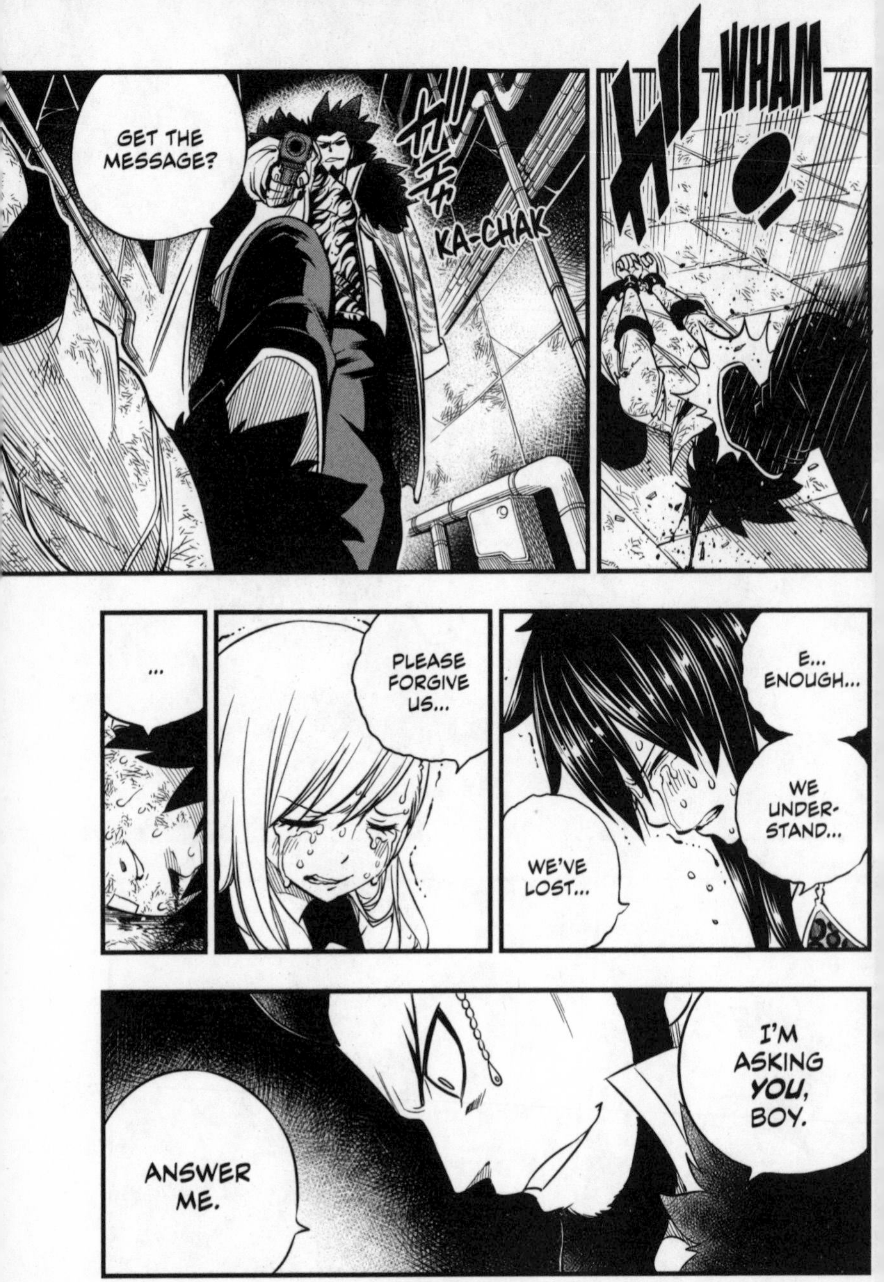
WHAM
GET THE MESSAGE?
KA-CHAK
E... ENOUGH...
WE UNDER-STAND...
WE'VE LOST...
PLEASE FORGIVE US...
...
I'M ASKING *YOU*, BOY.
ANSWER ME.

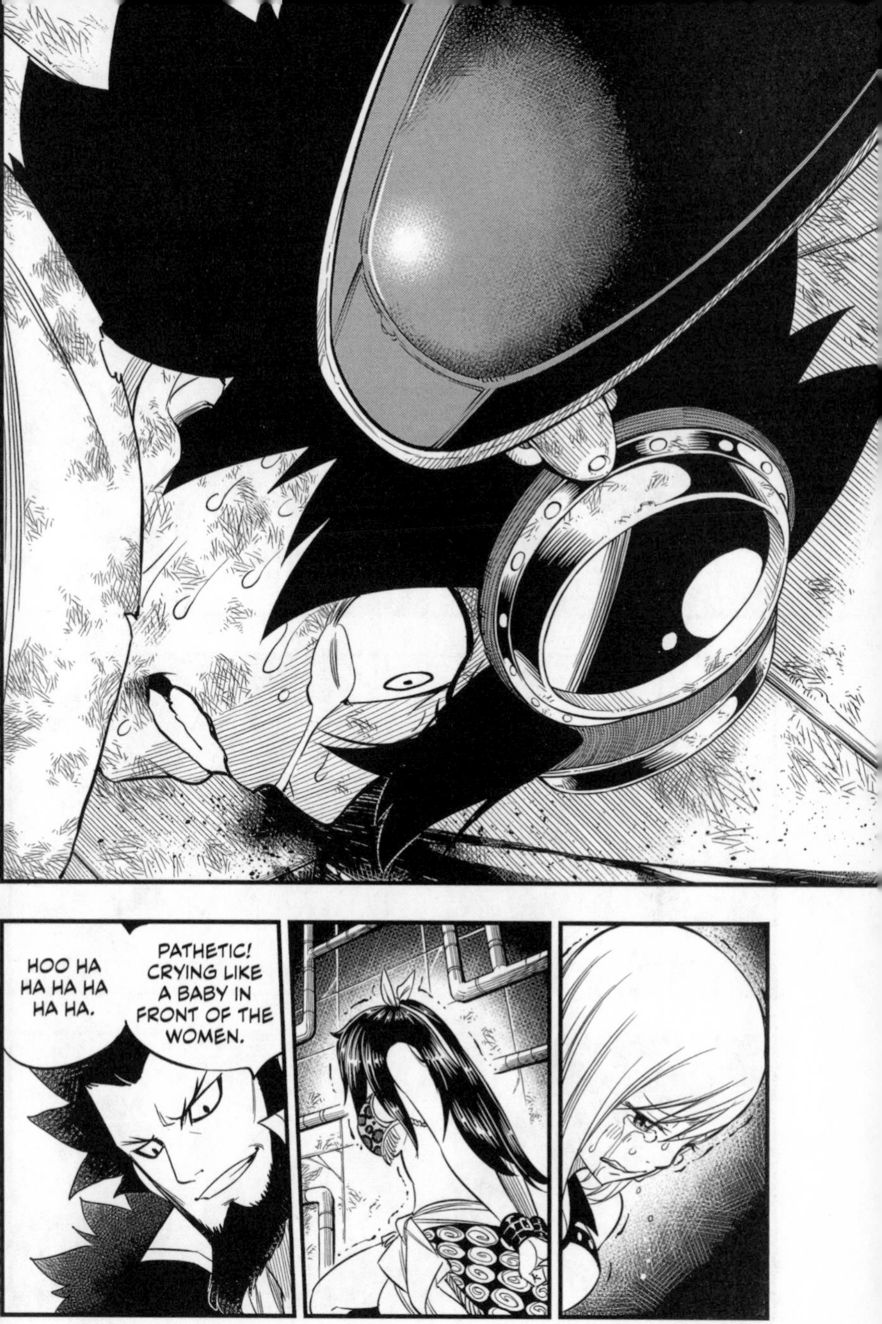
PATHETIC! CRYING LIKE A BABY IN FRONT OF THE WOMEN.
HOO HA HA HA HA HA HA.

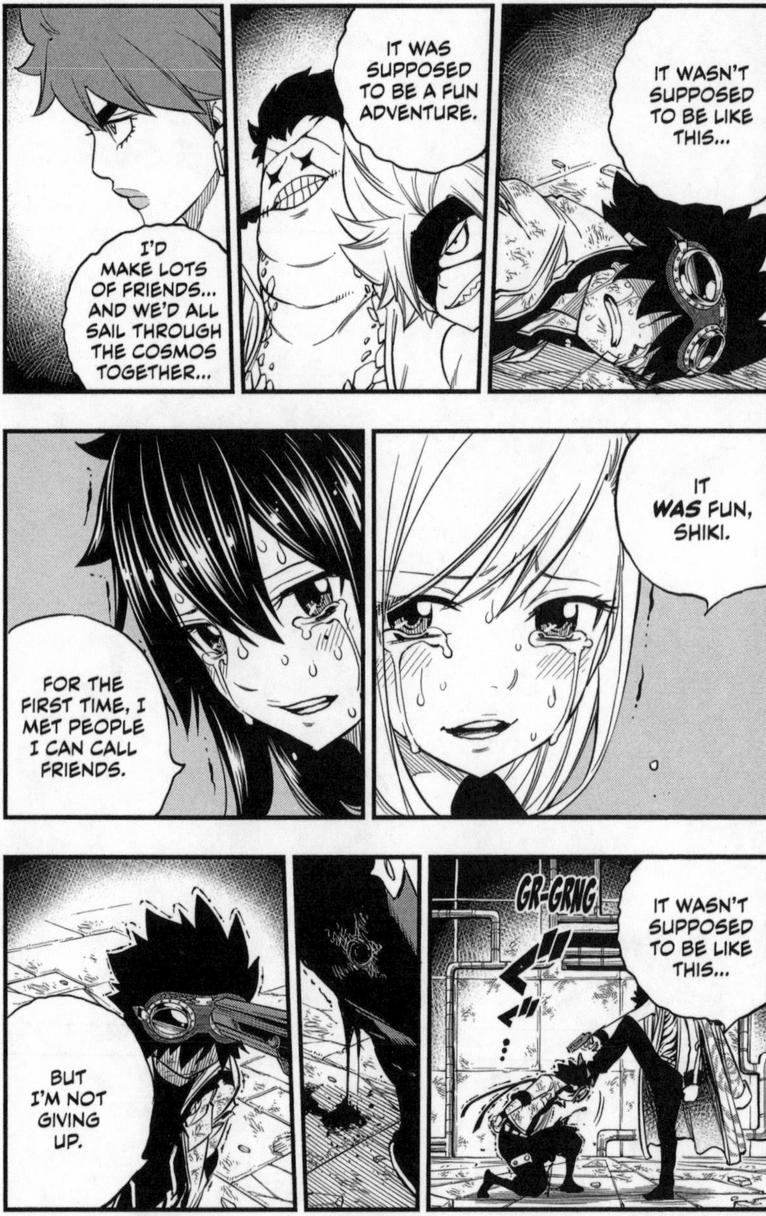
IT WASN'T SUPPOSED TO BE LIKE THIS...
IT WAS SUPPOSED TO BE A FUN ADVENTURE.
I'D MAKE LOTS OF FRIENDS... AND WE'D ALL SAIL THROUGH THE COSMOS TOGETHER...
IT *WAS* FUN, SHIKI.
FOR THE FIRST TIME, I MET PEOPLE I CAN CALL FRIENDS.
IT WASN'T SUPPOSED TO BE LIKE THIS...
GR-GRNG
BUT I'M NOT GIVING UP.

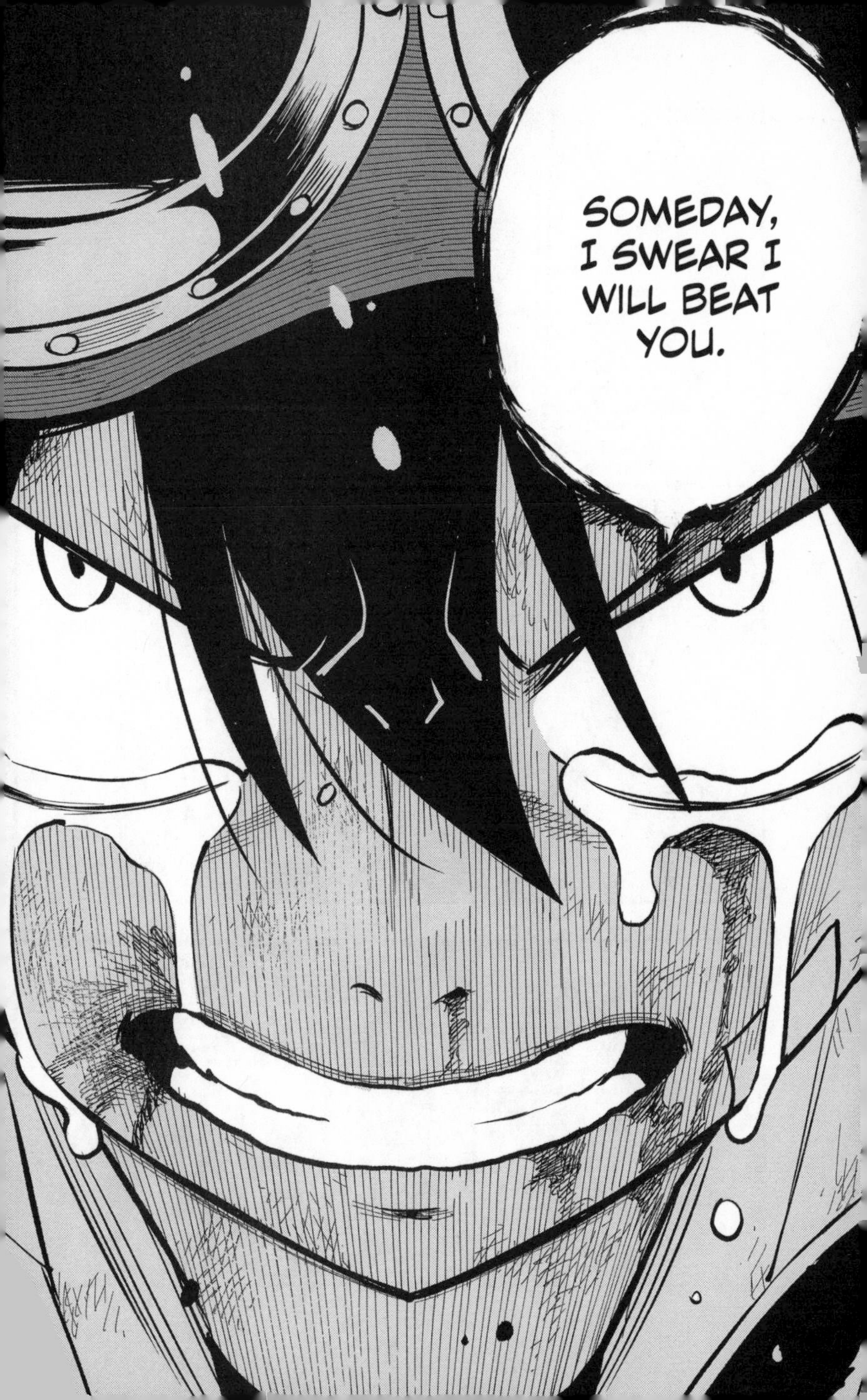
SOMEDAY, I SWEAR I WILL BEAT YOU.

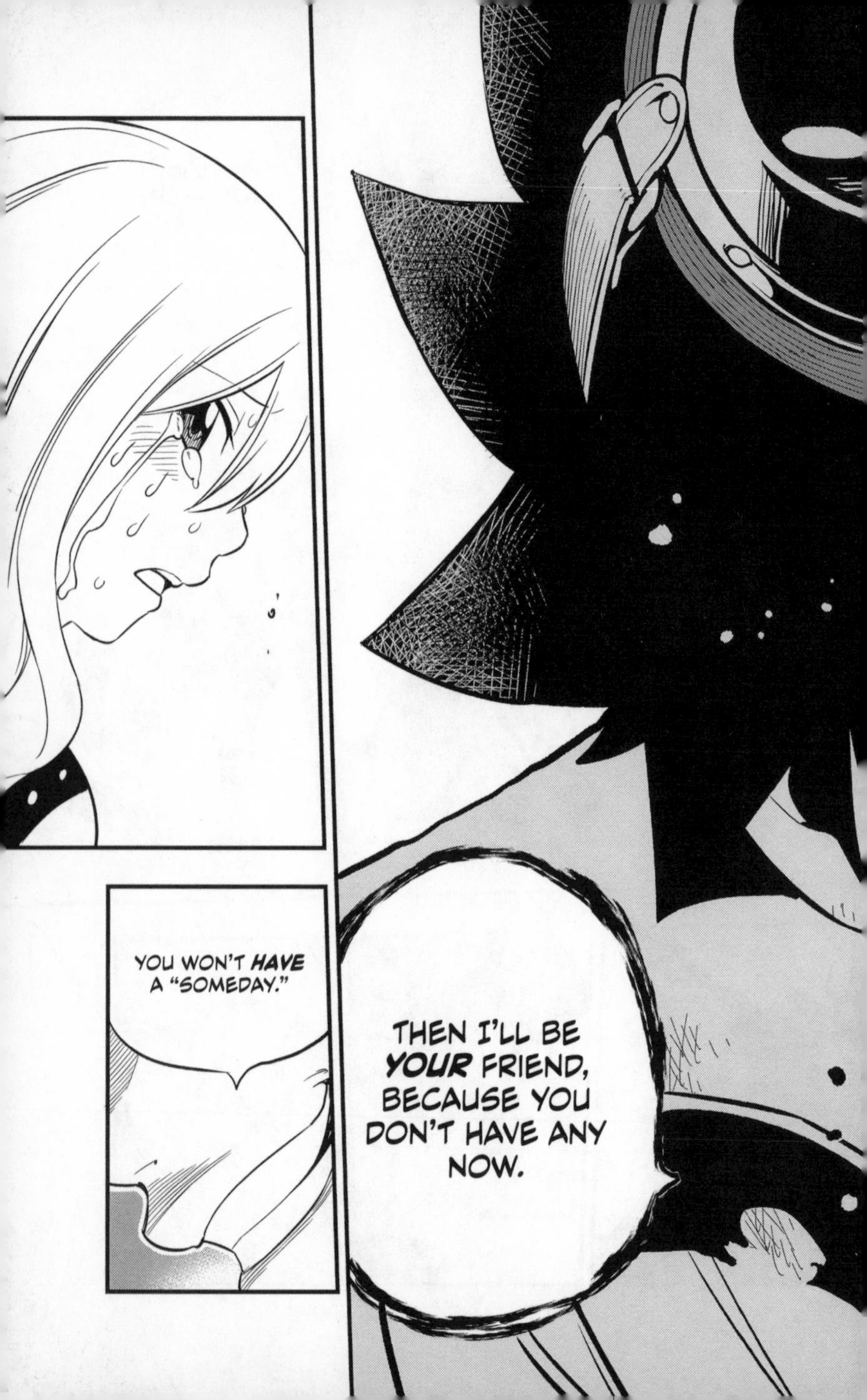
THEN I'LL BE *YOUR* FRIEND, BECAUSE YOU DON'T HAVE ANY NOW.
YOU WON'T *HAVE* A "SOMEDAY."

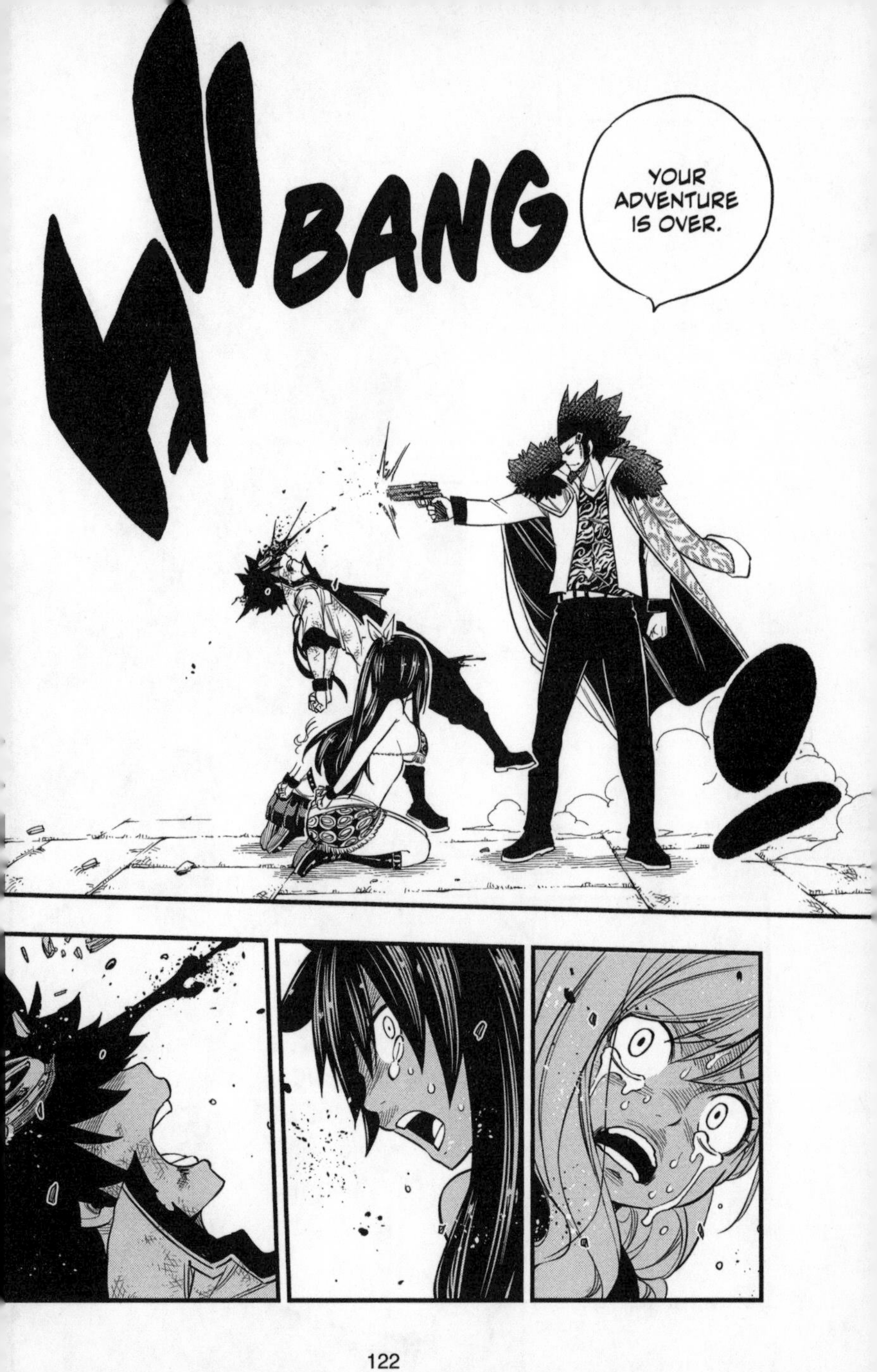
YOUR ADVENTURE IS OVER.
BANG

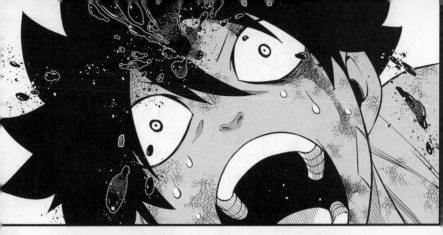

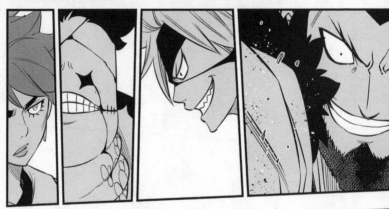

I DON'T KILL PEOPLE, AS A RULE.

BUT I DO MAKE EXCEPTIONS.

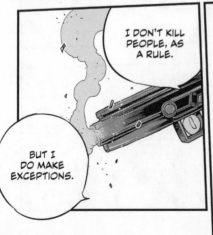

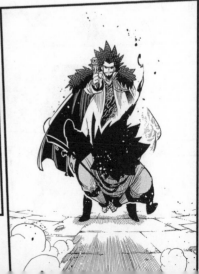

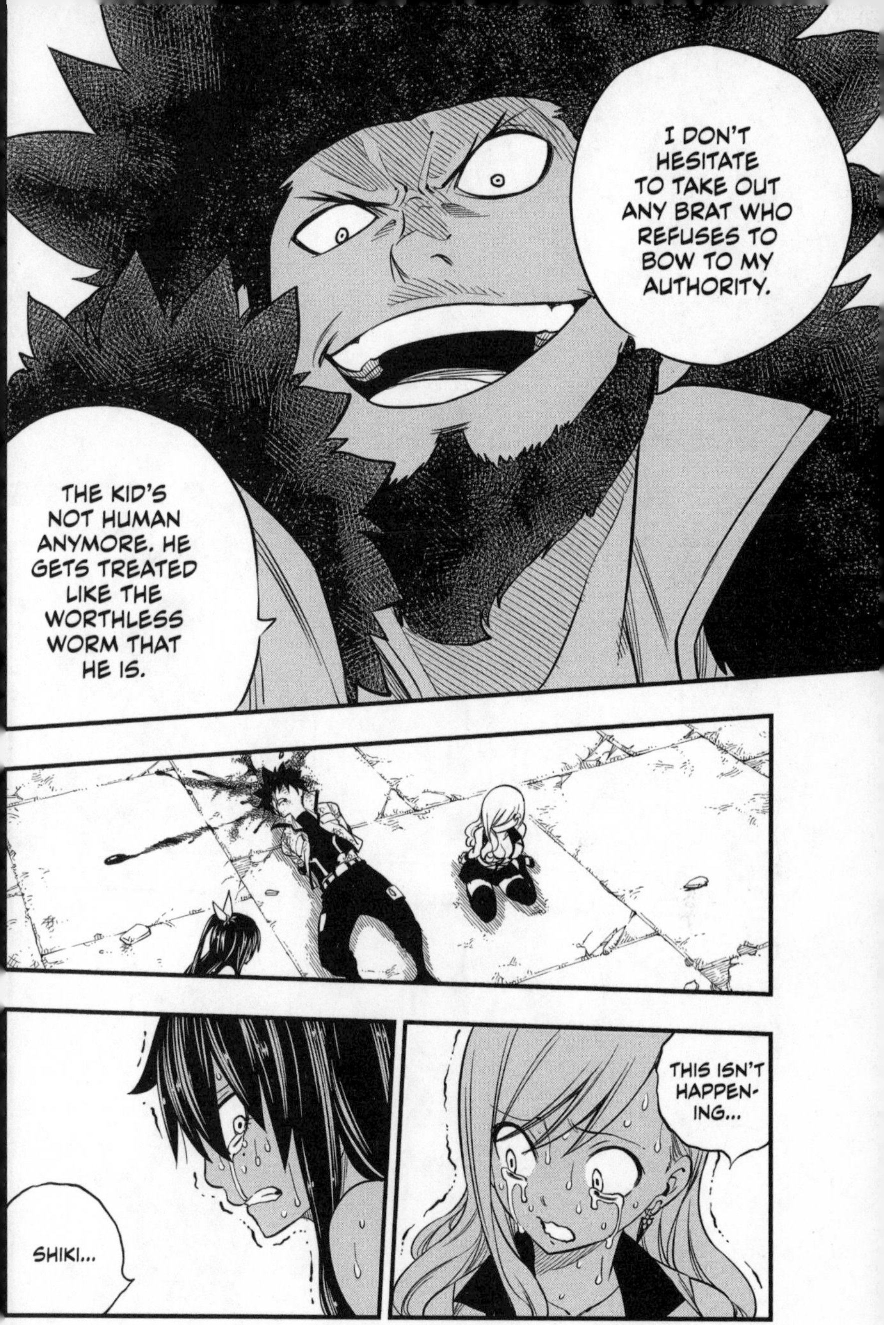
I DON'T HESITATE TO TAKE OUT ANY BRAT WHO REFUSES TO BOW TO MY AUTHORITY.
THE KID'S NOT HUMAN ANYMORE. HE GETS TREATED LIKE THE WORTHLESS WORM THAT HE IS.
THIS ISN'T HAPPEN-ING...
SHIKI...

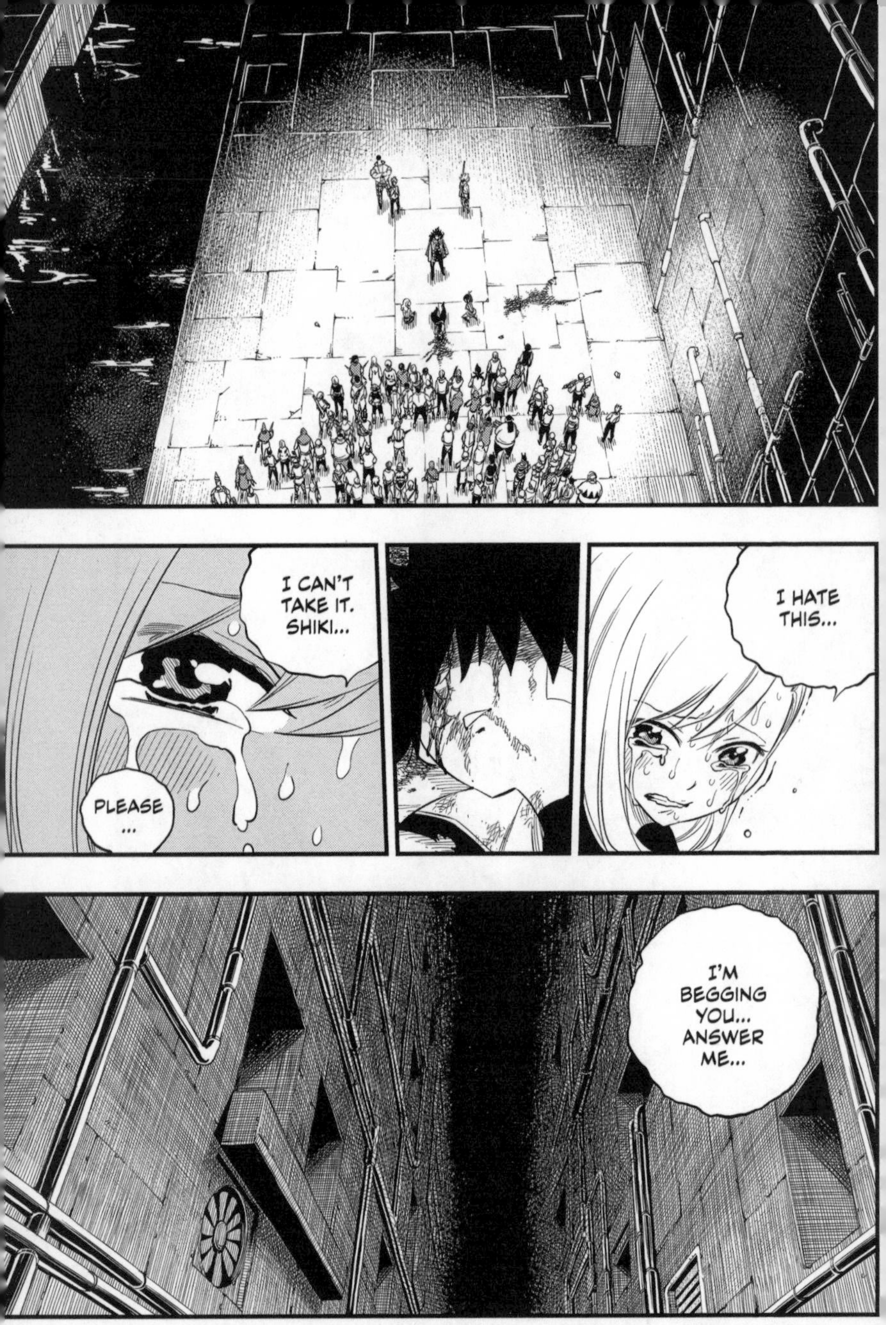
I HATE THIS...
I CAN'T TAKE IT. SHIKI...
PLEASE ...
I'M BEGGING YOU... ANSWER ME...

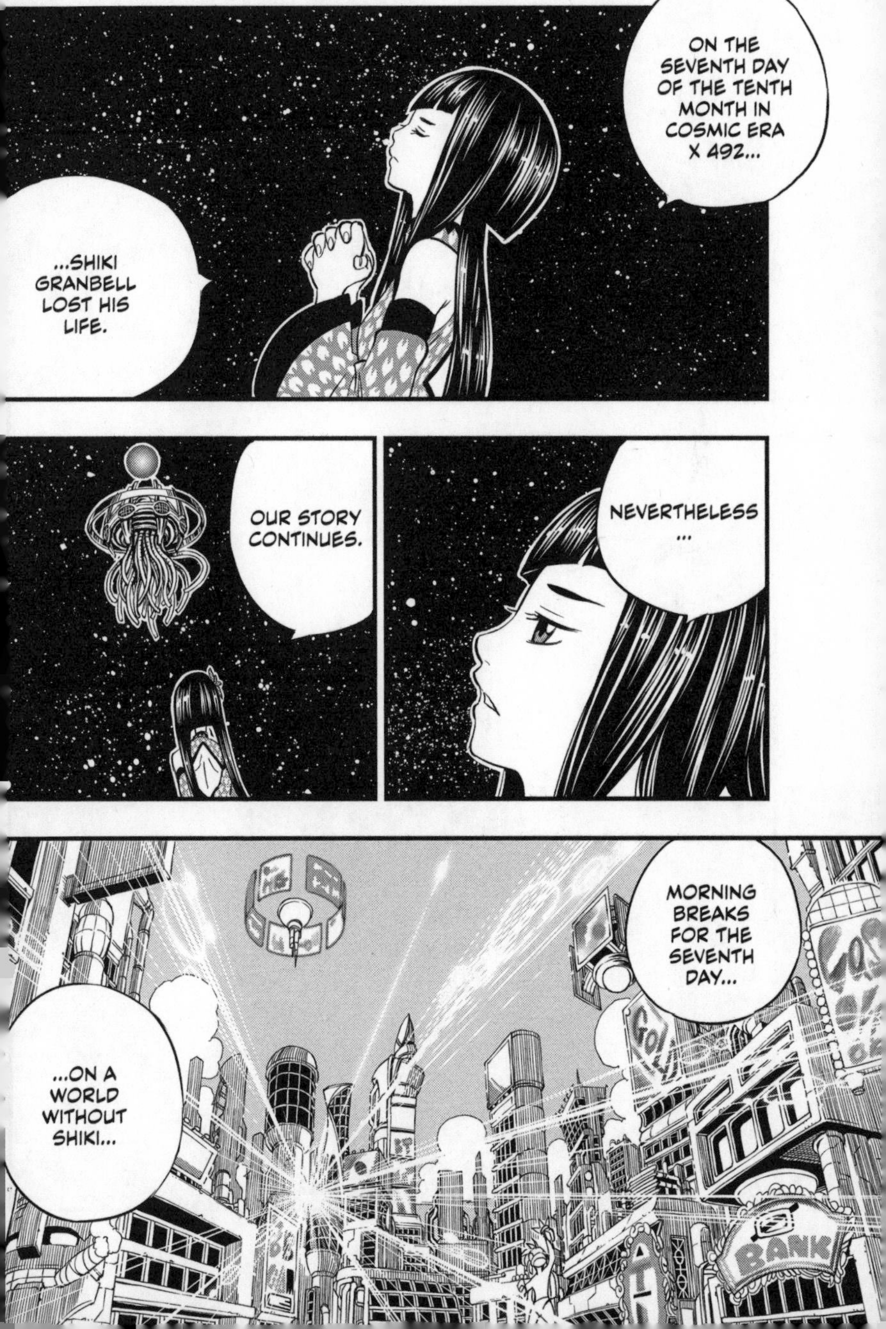
ON THE SEVENTH DAY OF THE TENTH MONTH IN COSMIC ERA X 492...
...SHIKI GRANBELL LOST HIS LIFE.
NEVERTHELESS ...
OUR STORY CONTINUES.
MORNING BREAKS FOR THE SEVENTH DAY...
...ON A WORLD WITHOUT SHIKI...
BANK

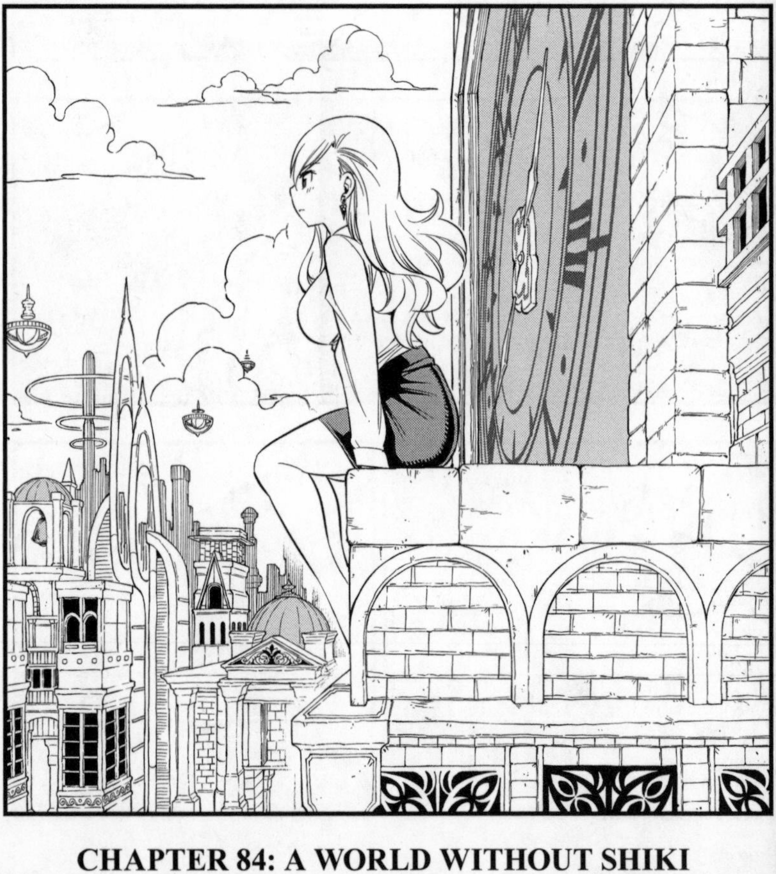

CHAPTER 84: A WORLD WITHOUT SHIKI

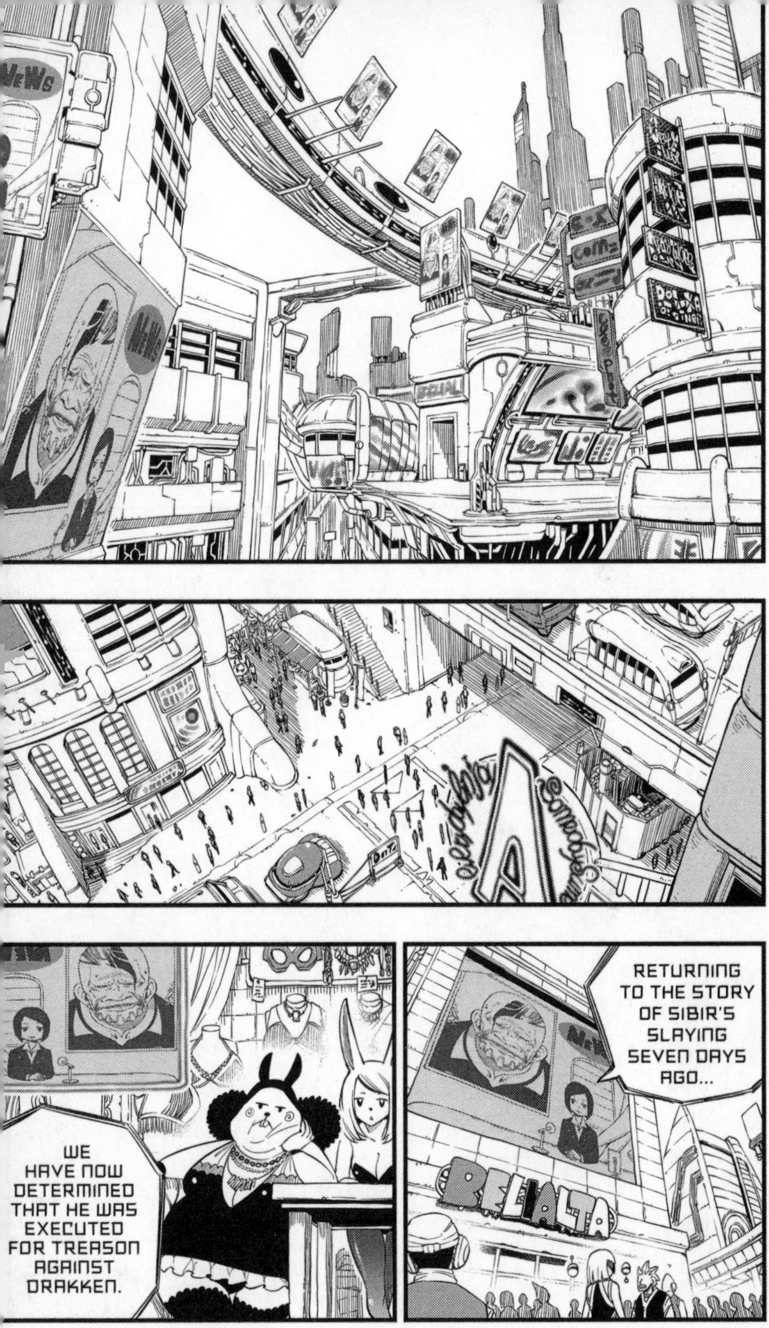
RETURNING TO THE STORY OF SIBIR'S SLAYING SEVEN DAYS AGO...
WE HAVE NOW DETERMINED THAT HE WAS EXECUTED FOR TREASON AGAINST DRAKKEN.

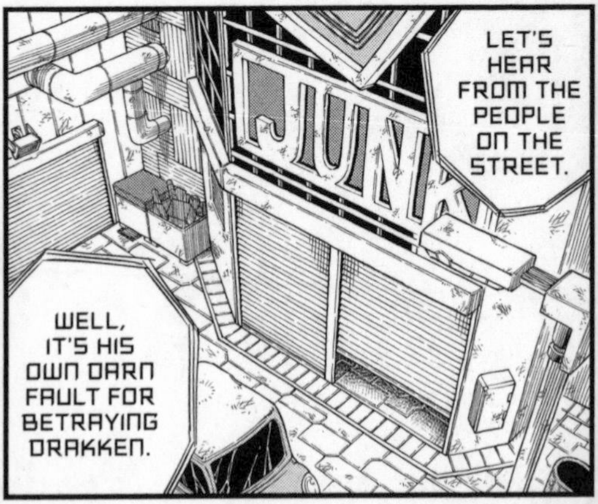
LET'S HEAR FROM THE PEOPLE ON THE STREET.
WELL, IT'S HIS OWN DARN FAULT FOR BETRAYING DRAKKEN.

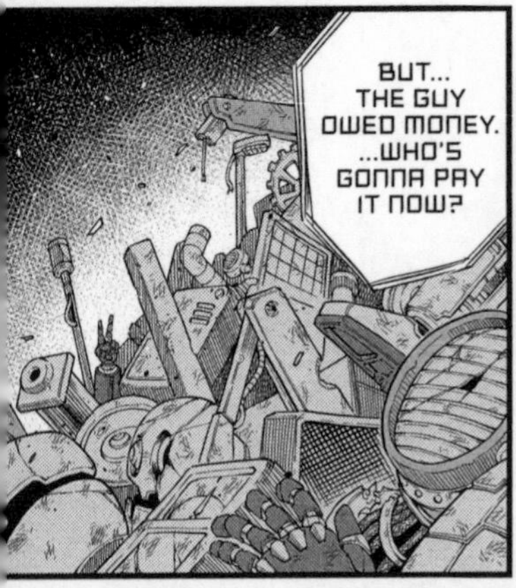
BUT... THE GUY OWED MONEY. ...WHO'S GONNA PAY IT NOW?

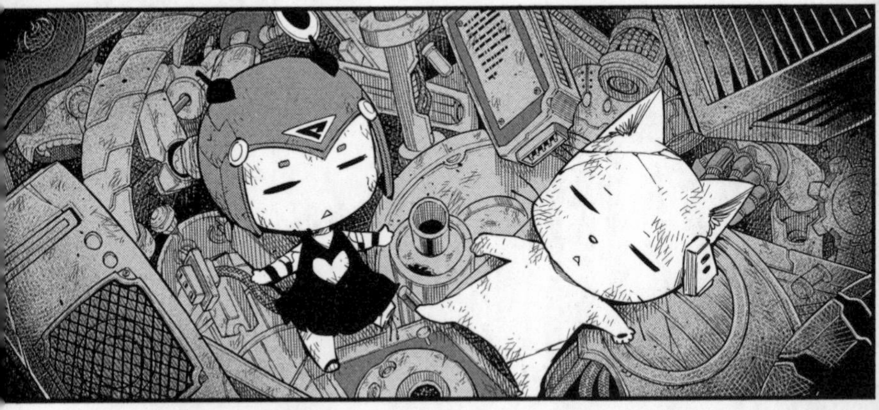

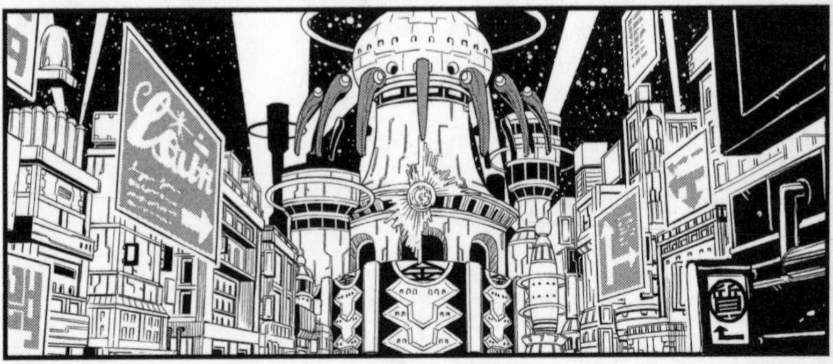

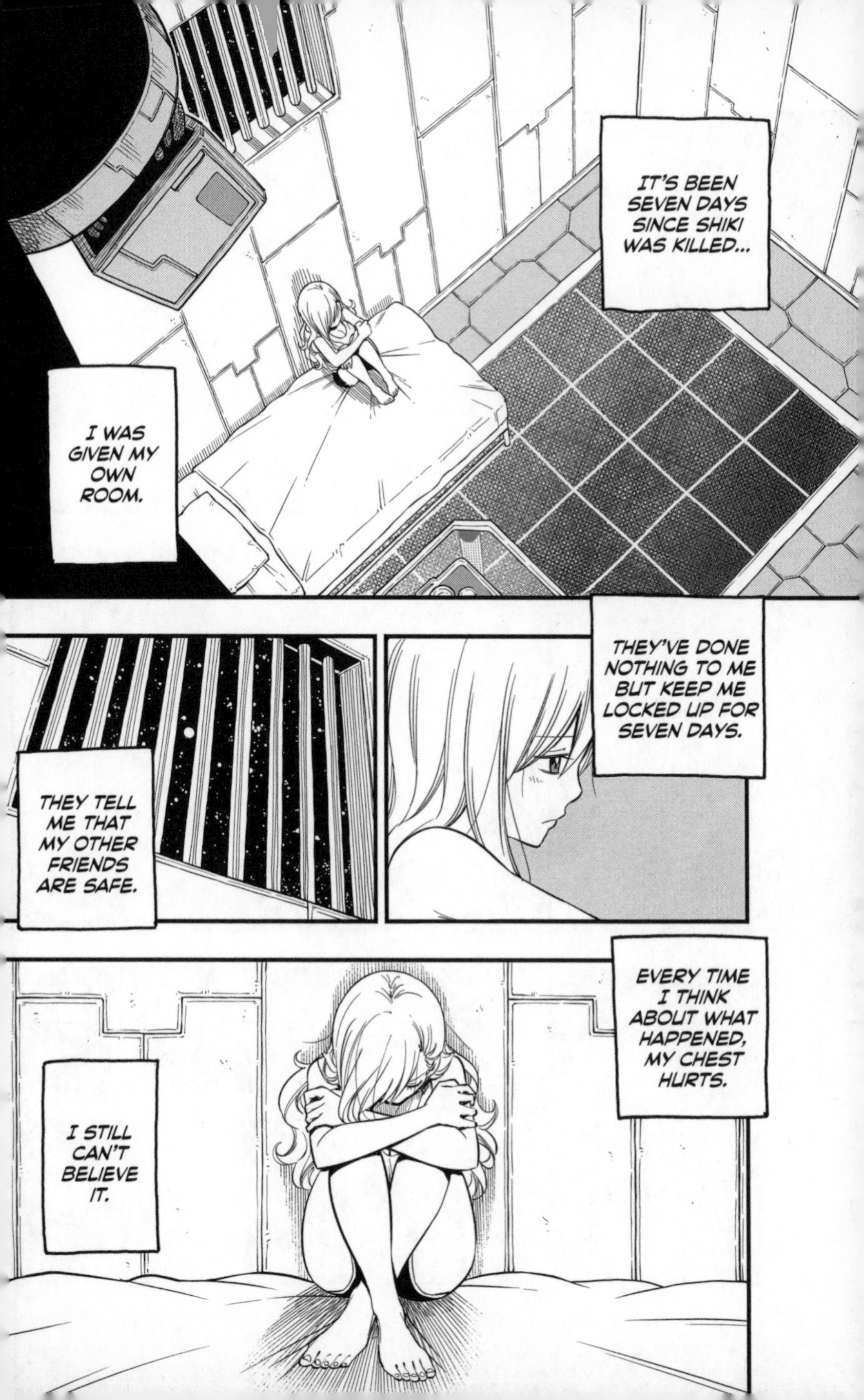
IT'S BEEN SEVEN DAYS SINCE SHIKI WAS KILLED...
I WAS GIVEN MY OWN ROOM.
THEY'VE DONE NOTHING TO ME BUT KEEP ME LOCKED UP FOR SEVEN DAYS.
THEY TELL ME THAT MY OTHER FRIENDS ARE SAFE.
EVERY TIME I THINK ABOUT WHAT HAPPENED, MY CHEST HURTS.
I STILL CAN'T BELIEVE IT.

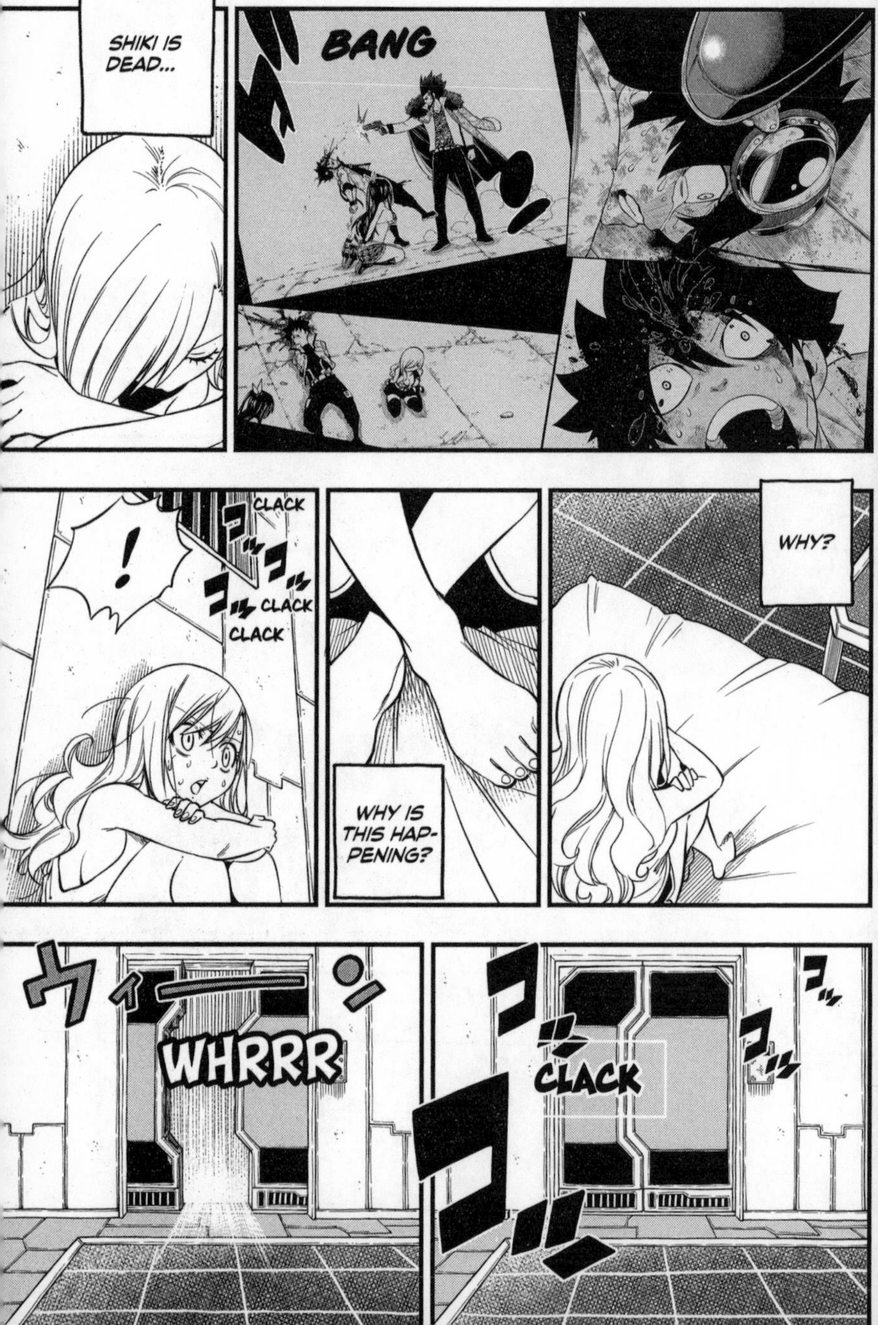
BANG
SHIKI IS DEAD...
WHY?
WHY IS THIS HAPPENING?
CLACK
CLACK
CLACK
!
CLACK
WHRRR

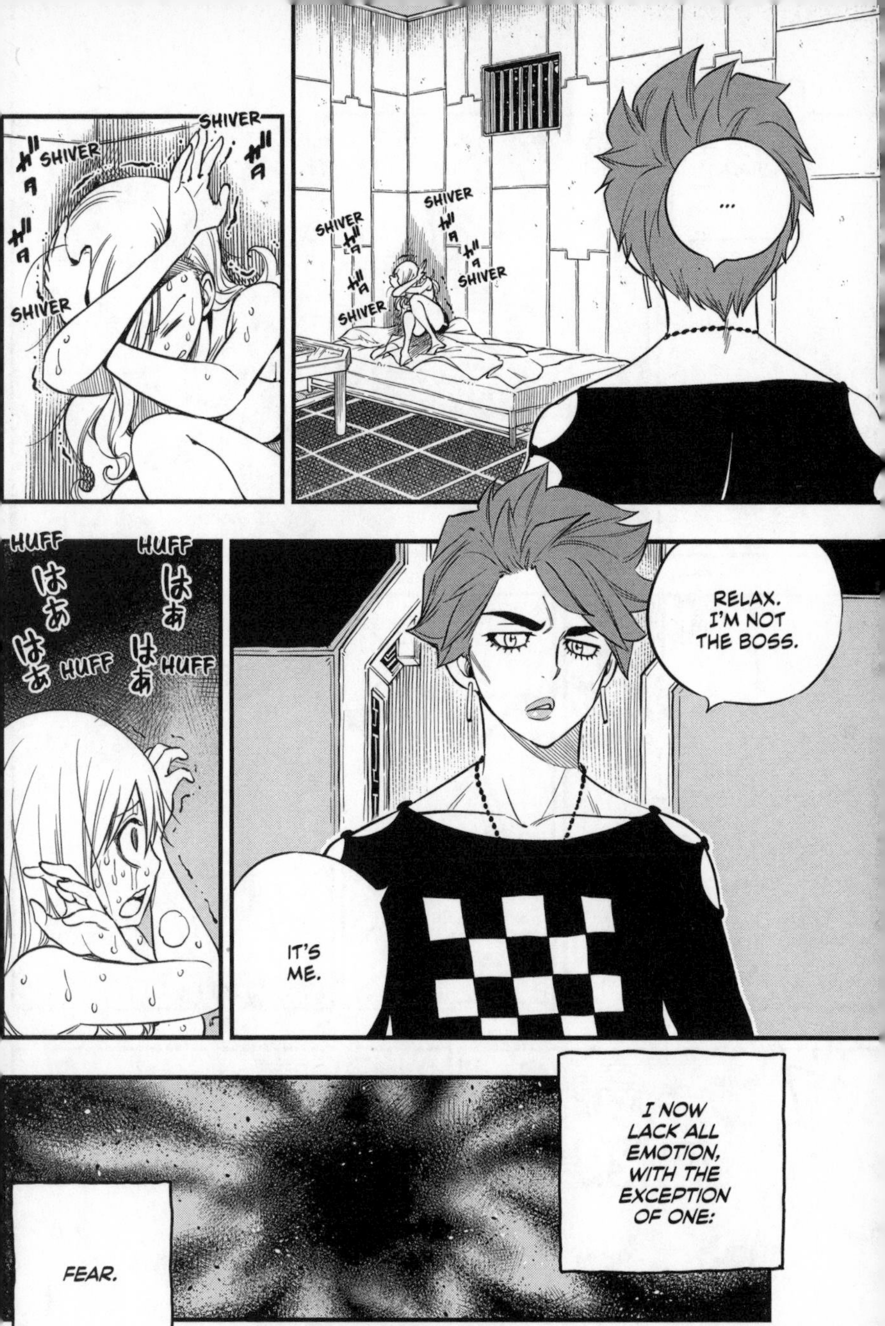

SHIVER
SHIVER
SHIVER
SHIVER
ガタ
ガタ
ガタ
...
SHIVER
SHIVER
SHIVER
ガタ
ガタ
ガタ
RELAX. I'M NOT THE BOSS.
IT'S ME.
HUFF
はあ はあ
HUFF
HUFF
はあ はあ
HUFF
I NOW LACK ALL EMOTION, WITH THE EXCEPTION OF ONE:
FEAR.

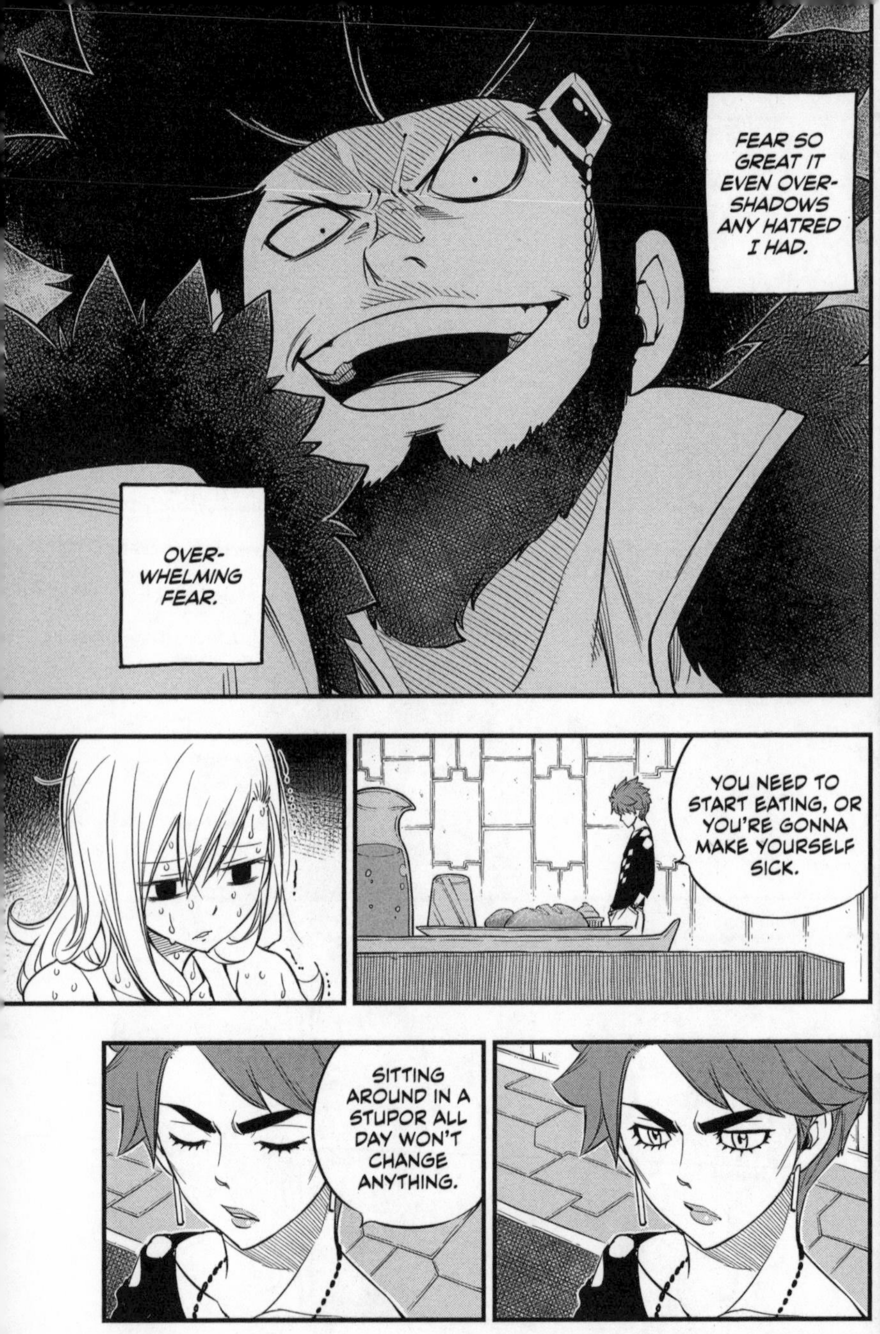
FEAR SO GREAT IT EVEN OVER-SHADOWS ANY HATRED I HAD.
OVER-WHELMING FEAR.
YOU NEED TO START EATING, OR YOU'RE GONNA MAKE YOURSELF SICK.
SITTING AROUND IN A STUPOR ALL DAY WON'T CHANGE ANYTHING.

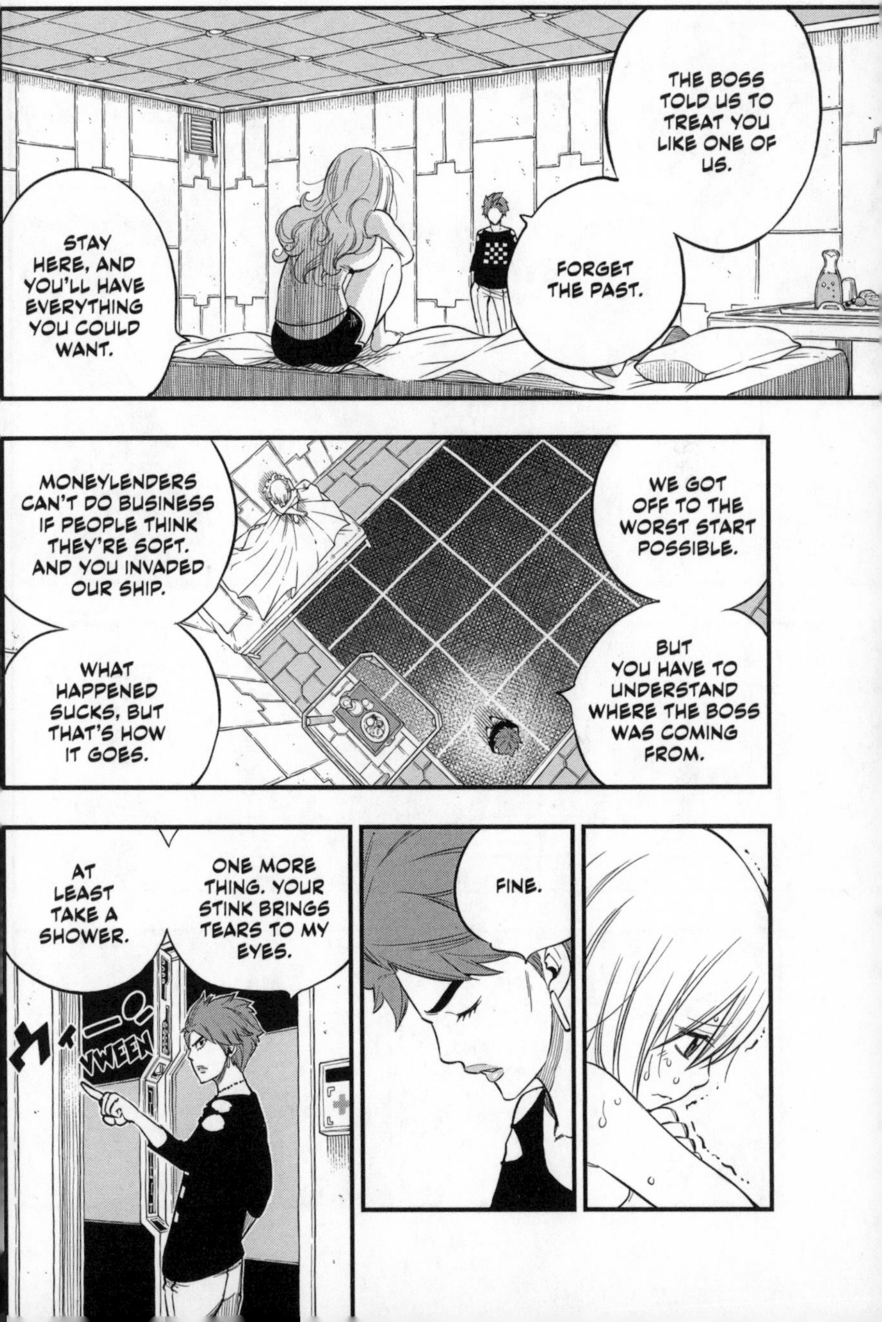
THE BOSS TOLD US TO TREAT YOU LIKE ONE OF US.
FORGET THE PAST.
STAY HERE, AND YOU'LL HAVE EVERYTHING YOU COULD WANT.
WE GOT OFF TO THE WORST START POSSIBLE.
BUT YOU HAVE TO UNDERSTAND WHERE THE BOSS WAS COMING FROM.
MONEYLENDERS CAN'T DO BUSINESS IF PEOPLE THINK THEY'RE SOFT. AND YOU INVADED OUR SHIP.
WHAT HAPPENED SUCKS, BUT THAT'S HOW IT GOES.
FINE.
ONE MORE THING. YOUR STINK BRINGS TEARS TO MY EYES.
AT LEAST TAKE A SHOWER.
VWEEN

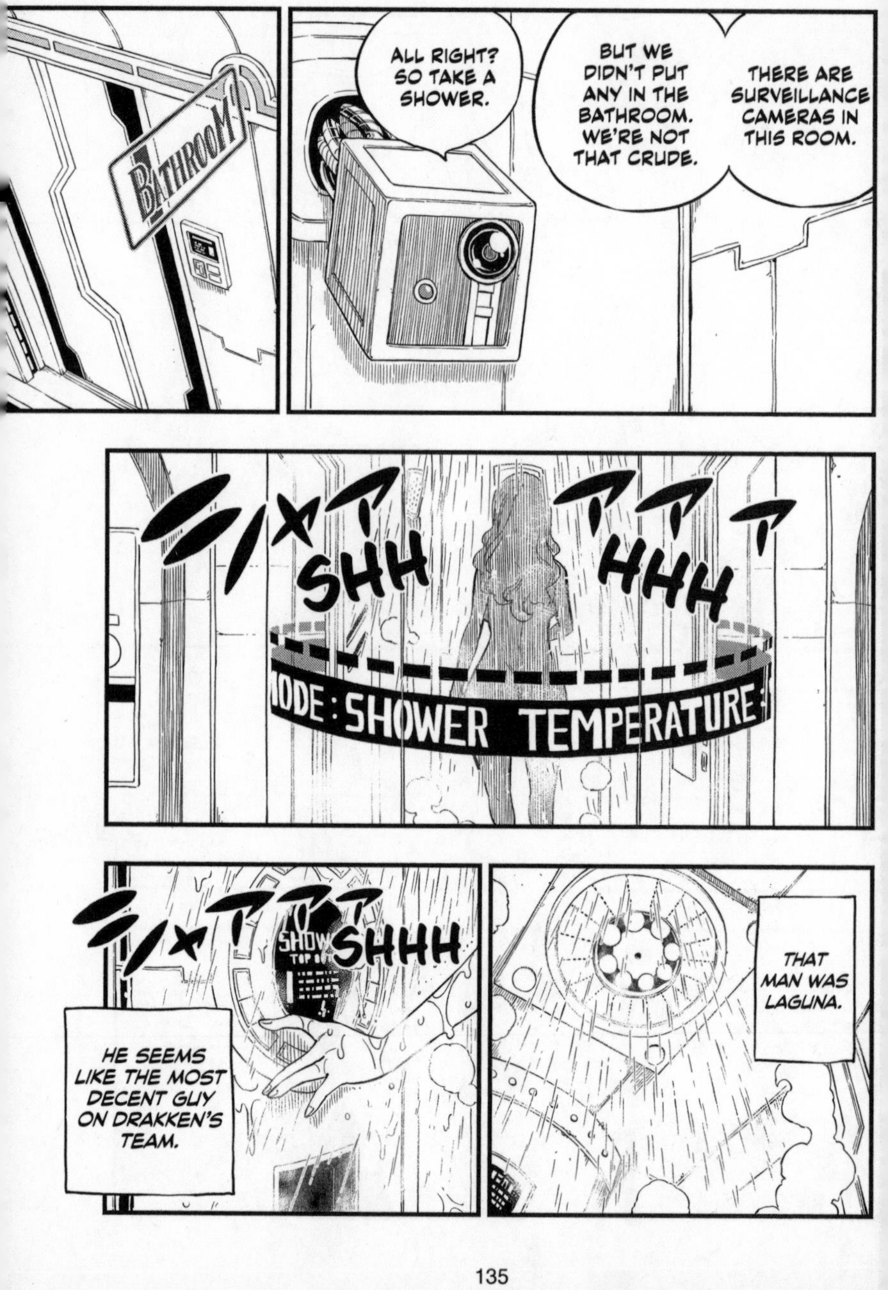
THERE ARE SURVEILLANCE CAMERAS IN THIS ROOM.
BUT WE DIDN'T PUT ANY IN THE BATHROOM. WE'RE NOT THAT CRUDE.
ALL RIGHT? SO TAKE A SHOWER.
BATHROOM
SHH HHH
ODE : SHOWER TEMPERATURE
THAT MAN WAS LAGUNA.
SHHH
HE SEEMS LIKE THE MOST DECENT GUY ON DRAKKEN'S TEAM.

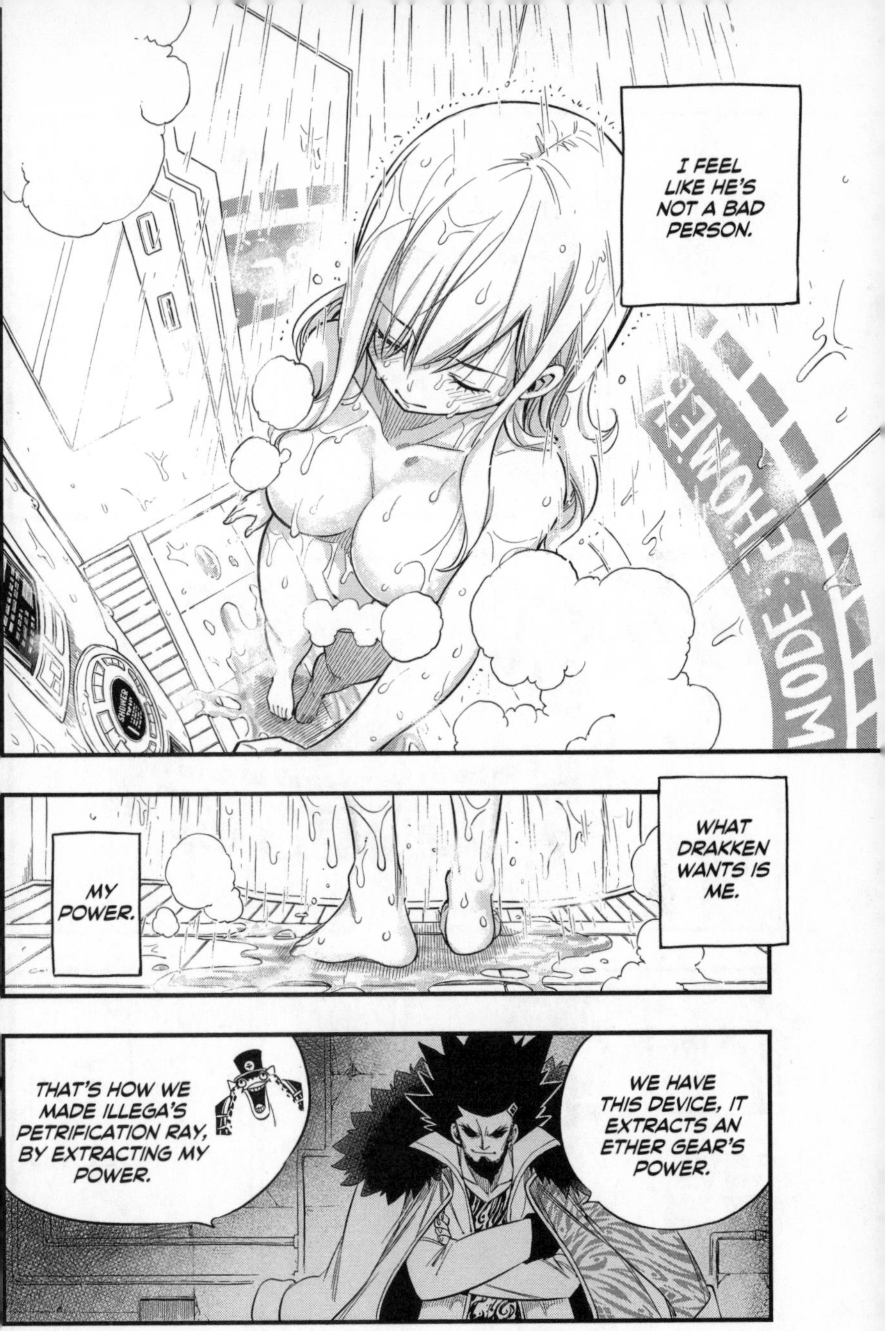
I FEEL LIKE HE'S NOT A BAD PERSON.
WHAT DRAKKEN WANTS IS ME.
MY POWER.
WE HAVE THIS DEVICE, IT EXTRACTS AN ETHER GEAR'S POWER.
THAT'S HOW WE MADE ILLEGA'S PETRIFICATION RAY, BY EXTRACTING MY POWER.

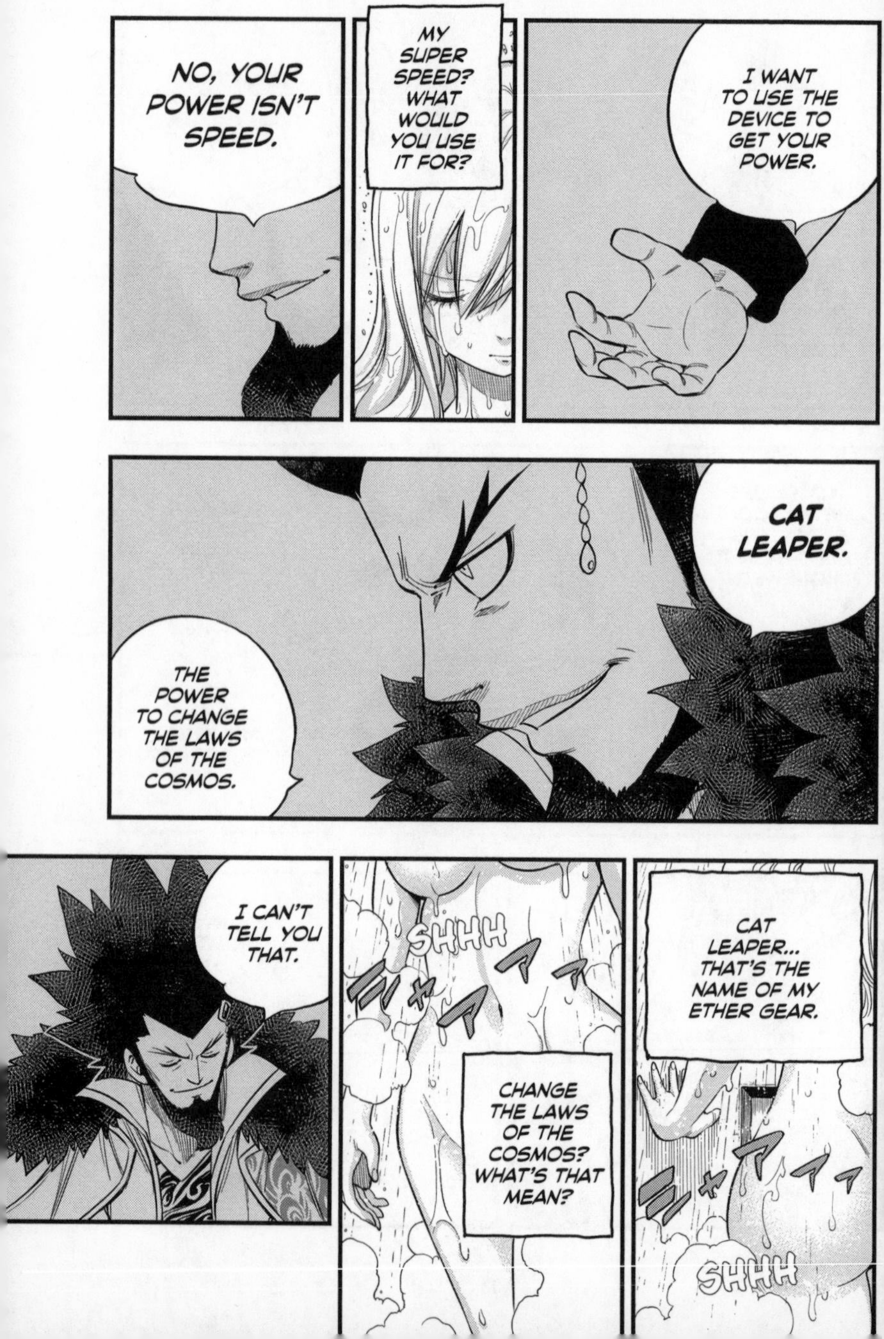
I WANT TO USE THE DEVICE TO GET YOUR POWER.
MY SUPER SPEED? WHAT WOULD YOU USE IT FOR?
NO, YOUR POWER ISN'T SPEED.
CAT LEAPER.
THE POWER TO CHANGE THE LAWS OF THE COSMOS.
CAT LEAPER... THAT'S THE NAME OF MY ETHER GEAR.
SHHH
SHHH
CHANGE THE LAWS OF THE COSMOS? WHAT'S THAT MEAN?
I CAN'T TELL YOU THAT.

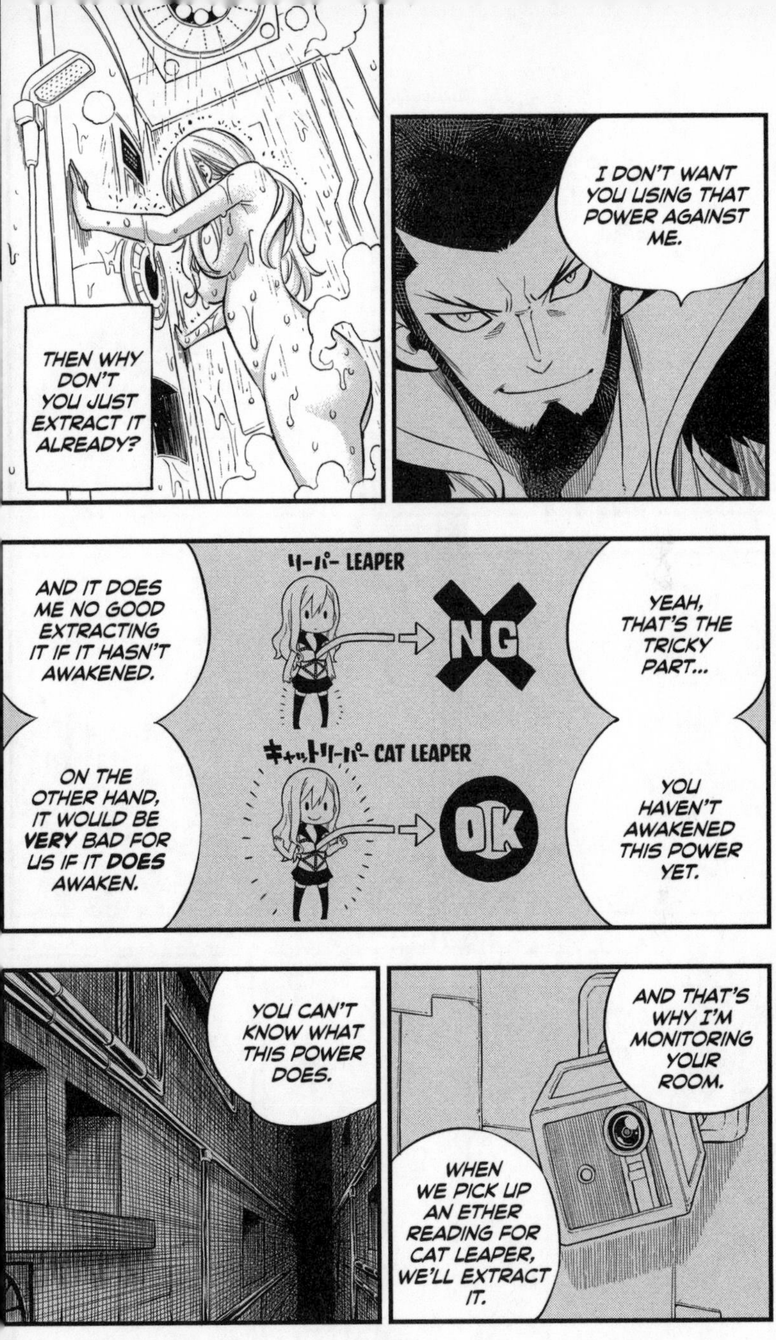
I DON'T WANT YOU USING THAT POWER AGAINST ME.
THEN WHY DON'T YOU JUST EXTRACT IT ALREADY?
YEAH, THAT'S THE TRICKY PART...
リーパー LEAPER
AND IT DOES ME NO GOOD EXTRACTING IT IF IT HASN'T AWAKENED.
NG
YOU HAVEN'T AWAKENED THIS POWER YET.
キャットリーパー CAT LEAPER
OK
ON THE OTHER HAND, IT WOULD BE **VERY** BAD FOR US IF IT **DOES** AWAKEN.
AND THAT'S WHY I'M MONITORING YOUR ROOM.
WHEN WE PICK UP AN ETHER READING FOR CAT LEAPER, WE'LL EXTRACT IT.
YOU CAN'T KNOW WHAT THIS POWER DOES.

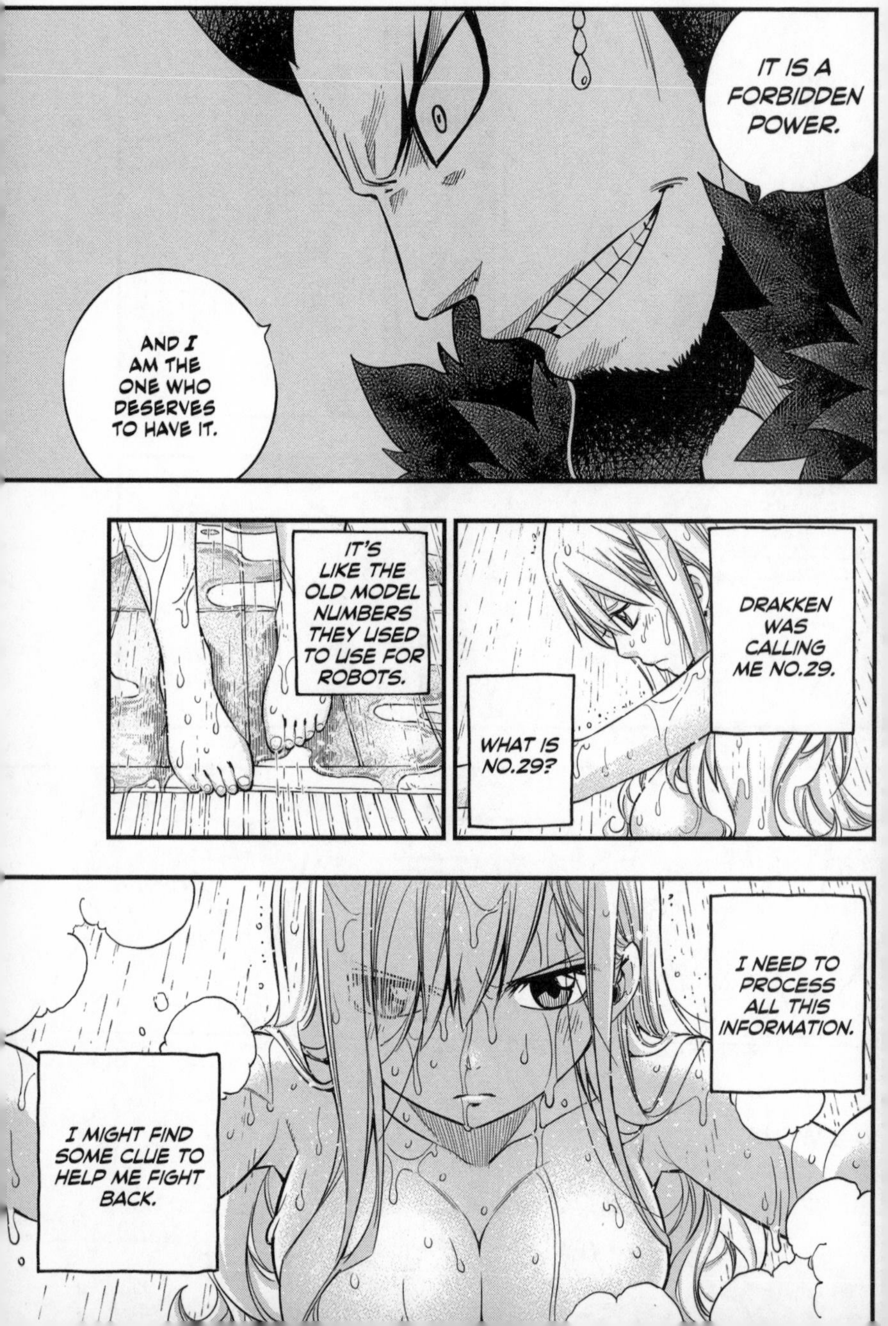
IT IS A FORBIDDEN POWER.
AND I AM THE ONE WHO DESERVES TO HAVE IT.
DRAKKEN WAS CALLING ME NO.29.
WHAT IS NO.29?
IT'S LIKE THE OLD MODEL NUMBERS THEY USED TO USE FOR ROBOTS.
I NEED TO PROCESS ALL THIS INFORMATION.
I MIGHT FIND SOME CLUE TO HELP ME FIGHT BACK.

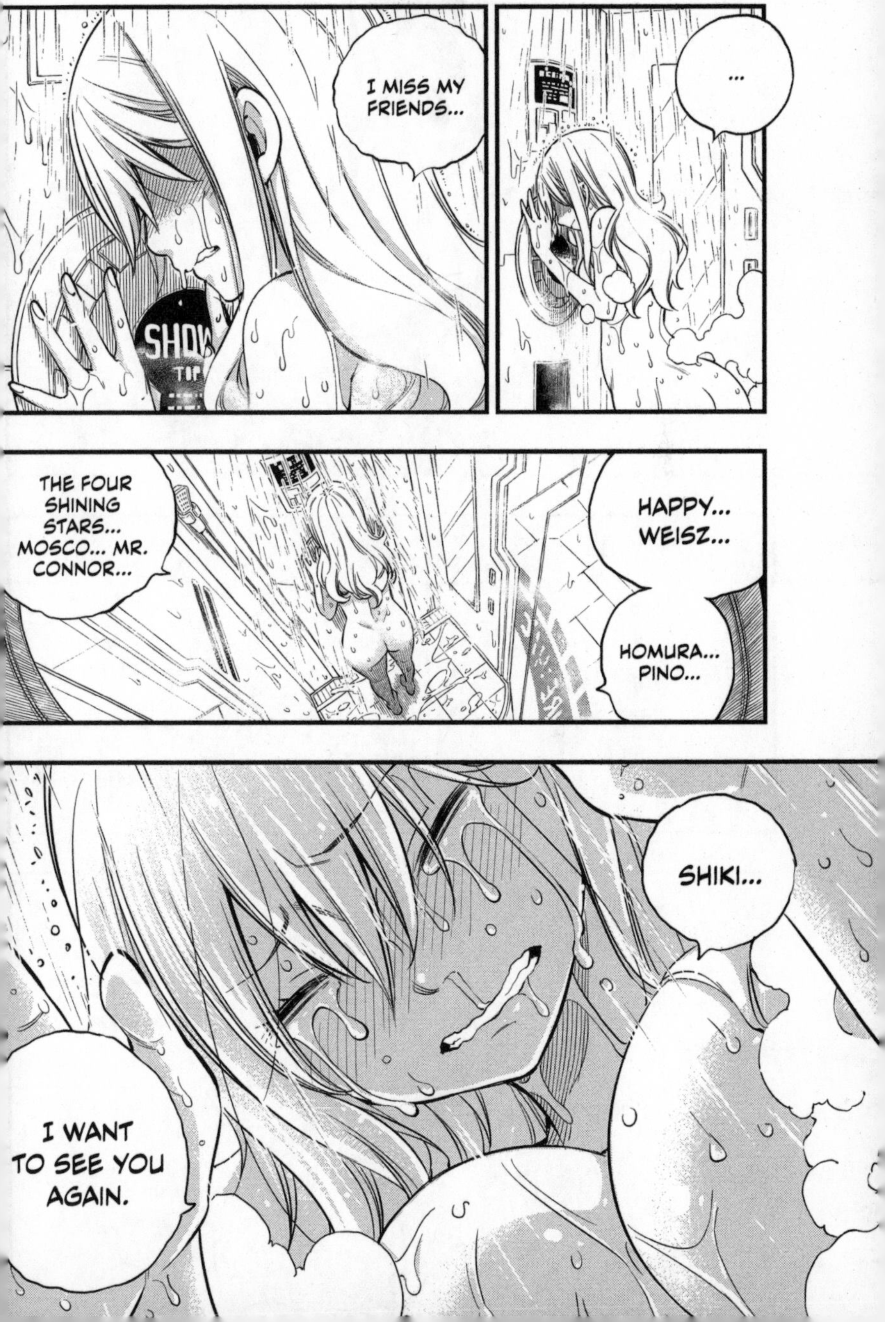
...
I MISS MY FRIENDS...
HAPPY... WEISZ...
HOMURA... PINO...
THE FOUR SHINING STARS... MOSCO... MR. CONNOR...
SHIKI...
I WANT TO SEE YOU AGAIN.

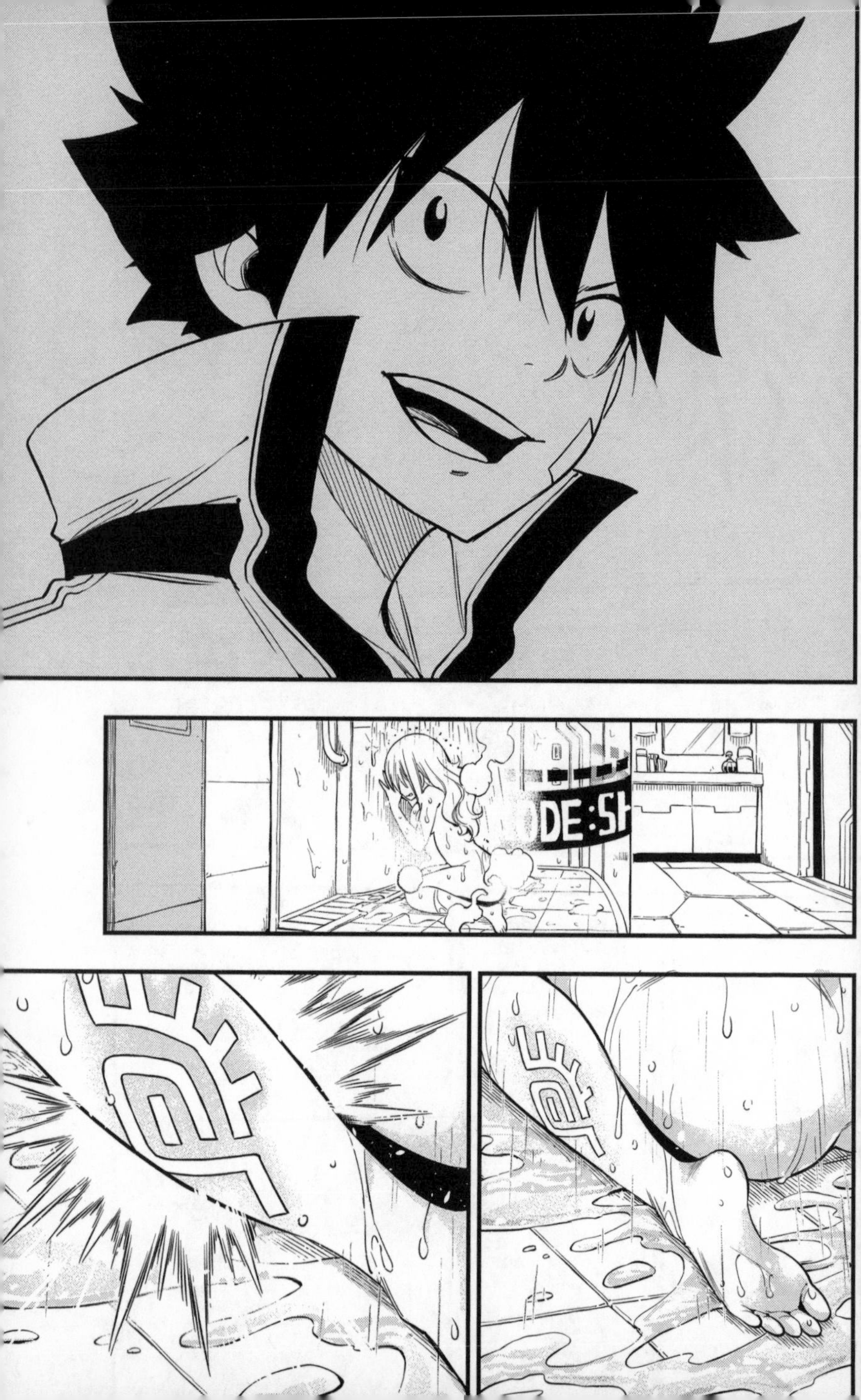
DE:SH

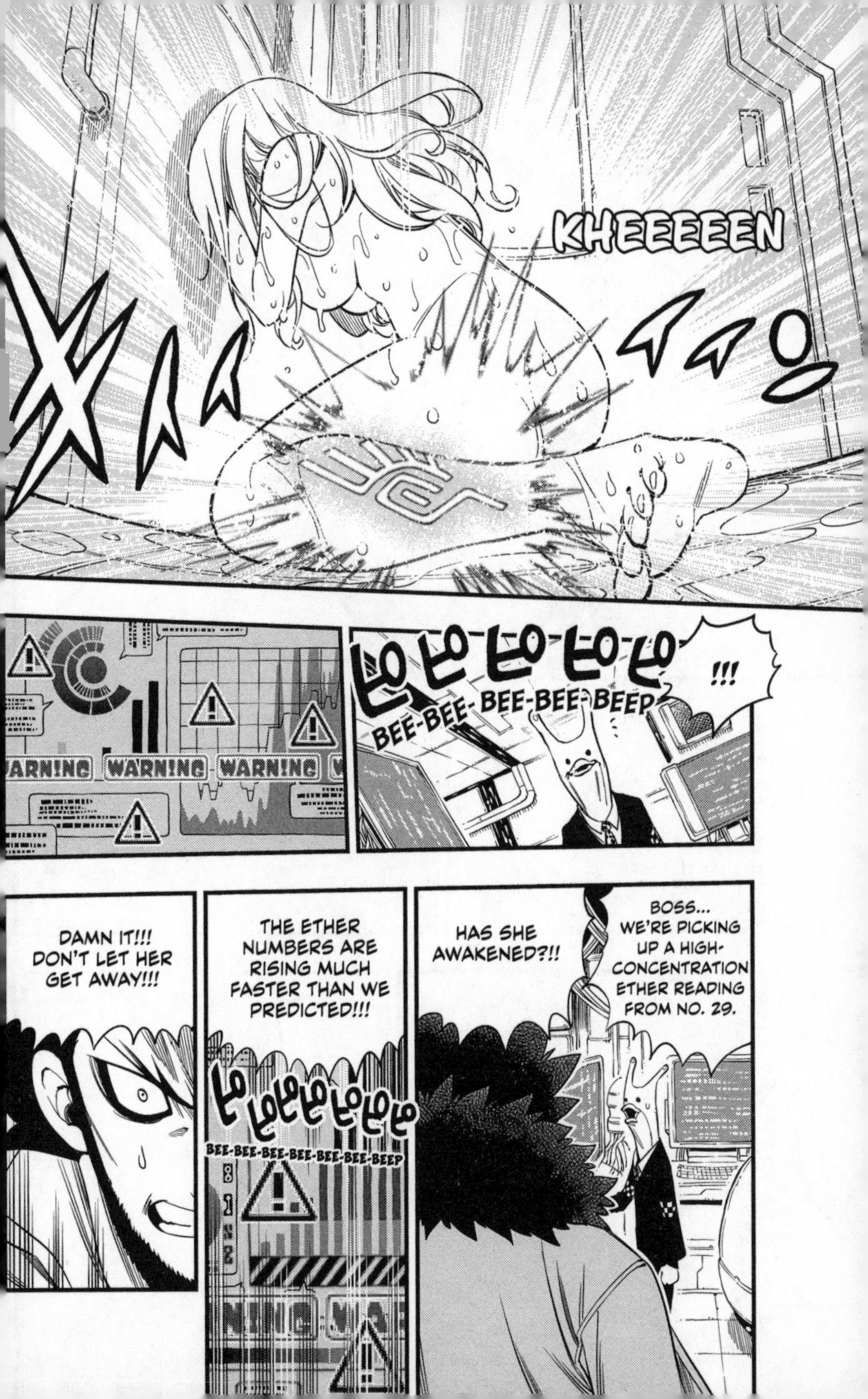
KHEEEEEN
BEE-BEE-BEE-BEE-BEEP
!!!
ARNING WARNING WARNING
BOSS... WE'RE PICKING UP A HIGH-CONCENTRATION ETHER READING FROM NO. 29.
HAS SHE AWAKENED?!!
THE ETHER NUMBERS ARE RISING MUCH FASTER THAN WE PREDICTED!!!
BEE-BEE-BEE-BEE-BEE-BEE-BEEP
DAMN IT!!! DON'T LET HER GET AWAY!!!

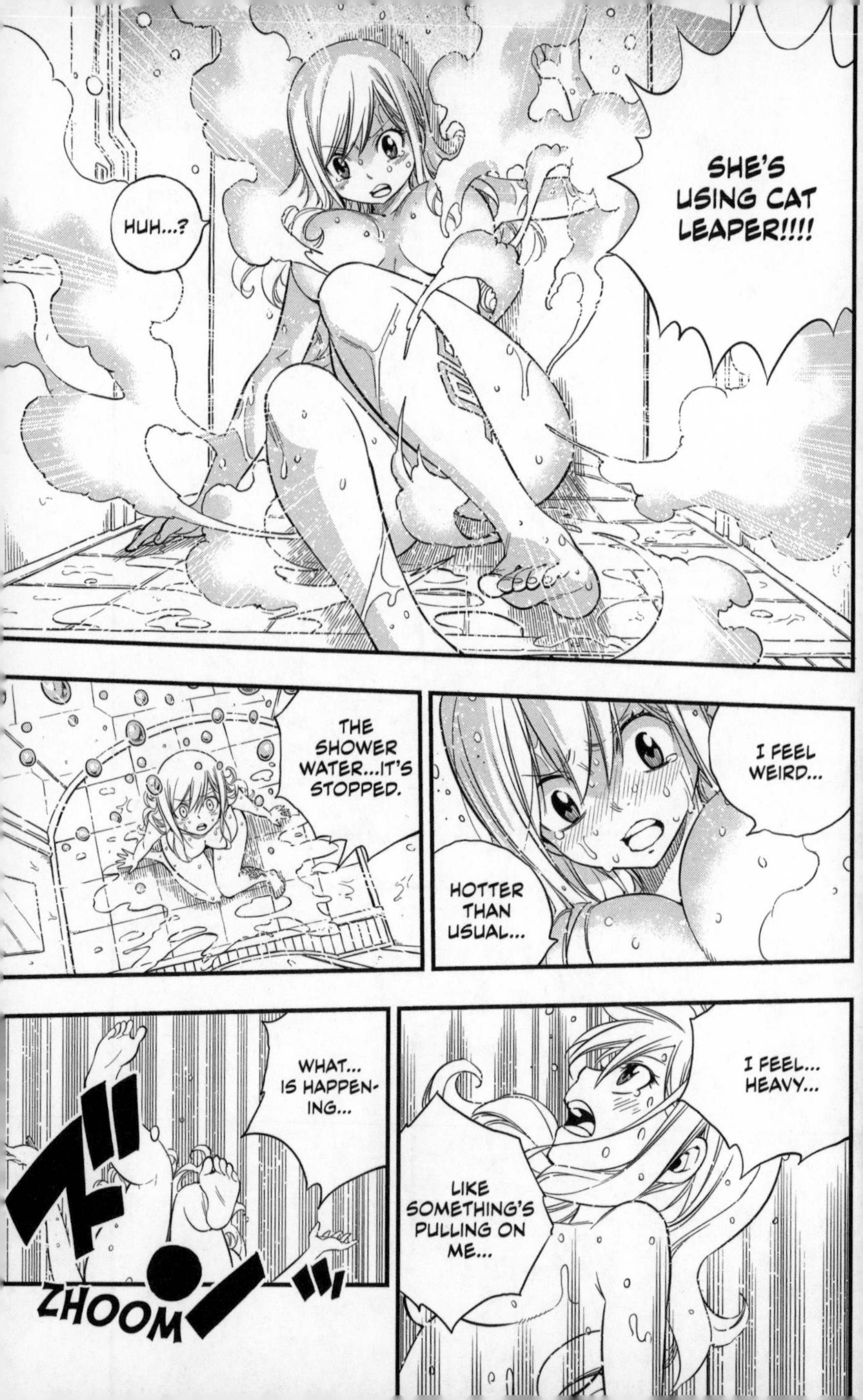
SHE'S USING CAT LEAPER!!!!
HUH...?
I FEEL WEIRD...
HOTTER THAN USUAL...
THE SHOWER WATER...IT'S STOPPED.
I FEEL... HEAVY...
LIKE SOMETHING'S PULLING ON ME...
WHAT... IS HAPPENING...
ZHOOM

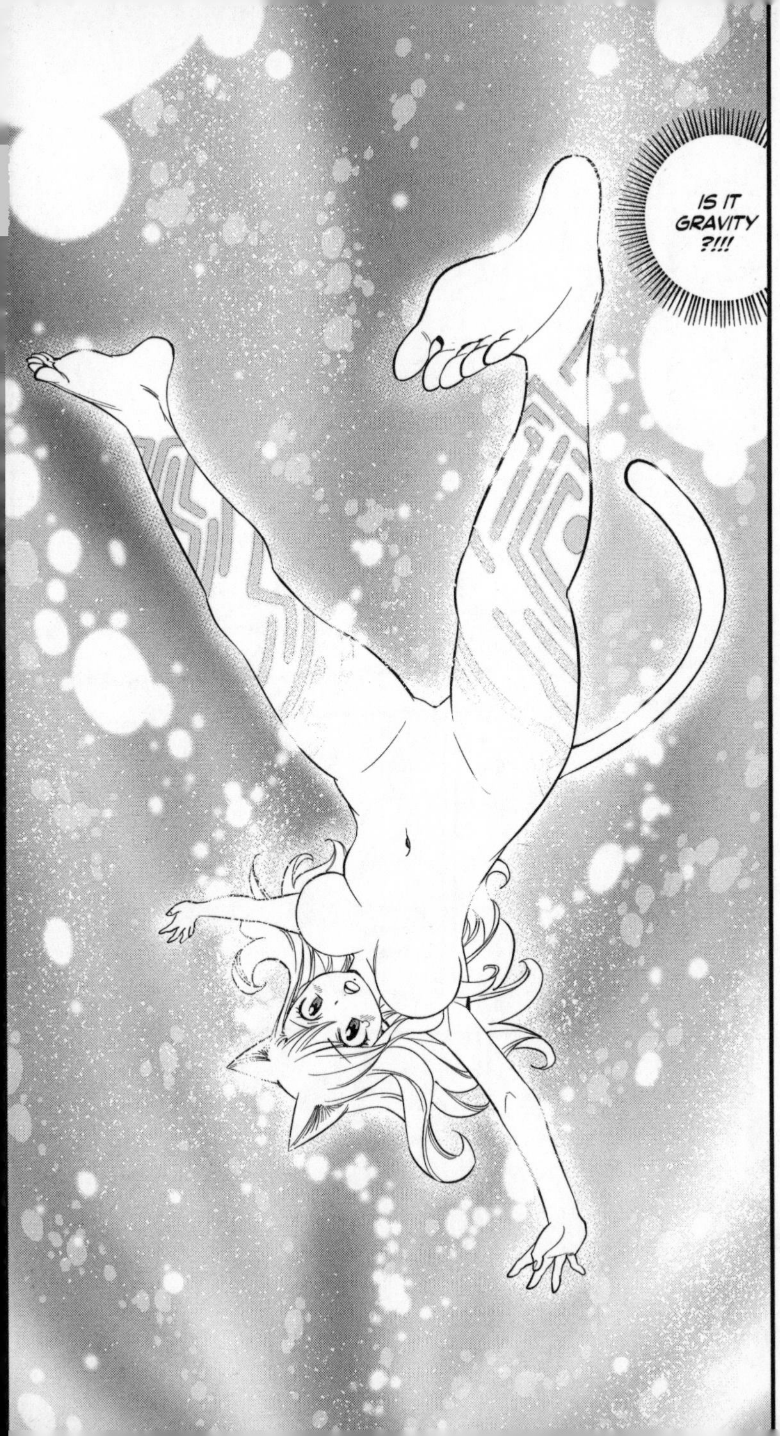
IS IT GRAVITY ?!!!

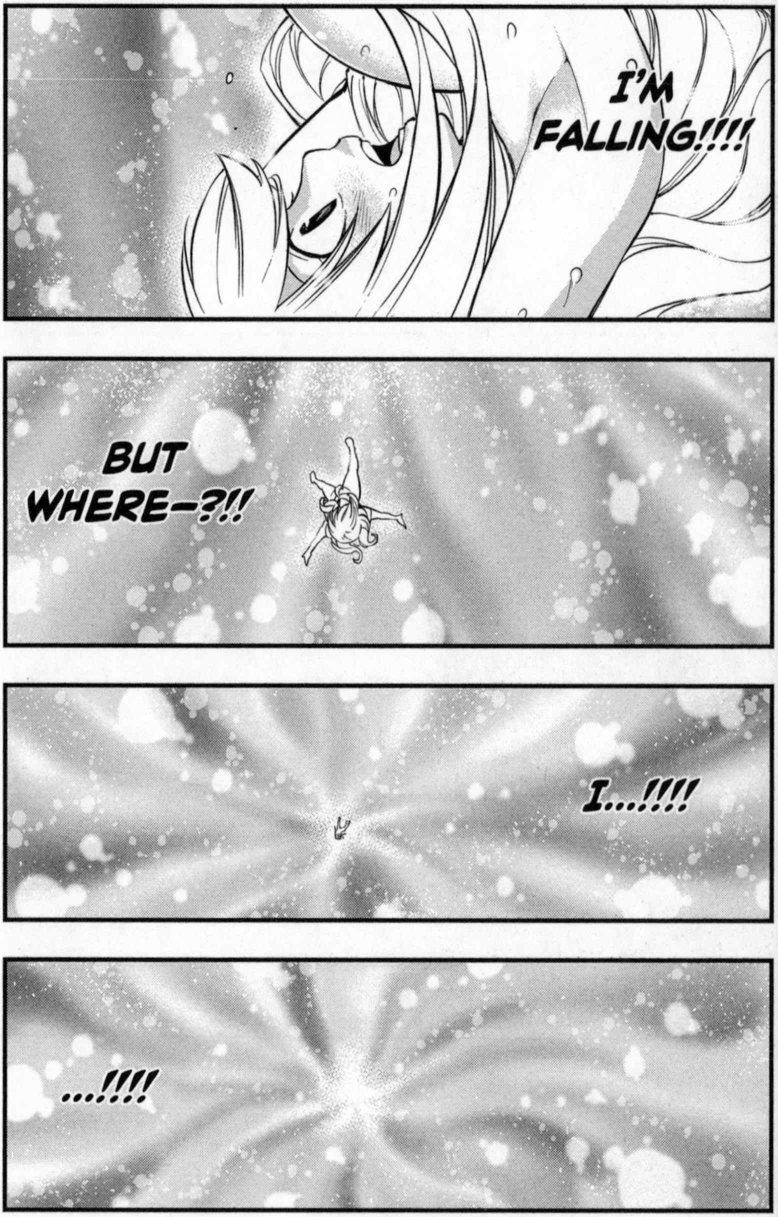
I'M FALLING!!!!
BUT WHERE–?!!
I...!!!!
...!!!!

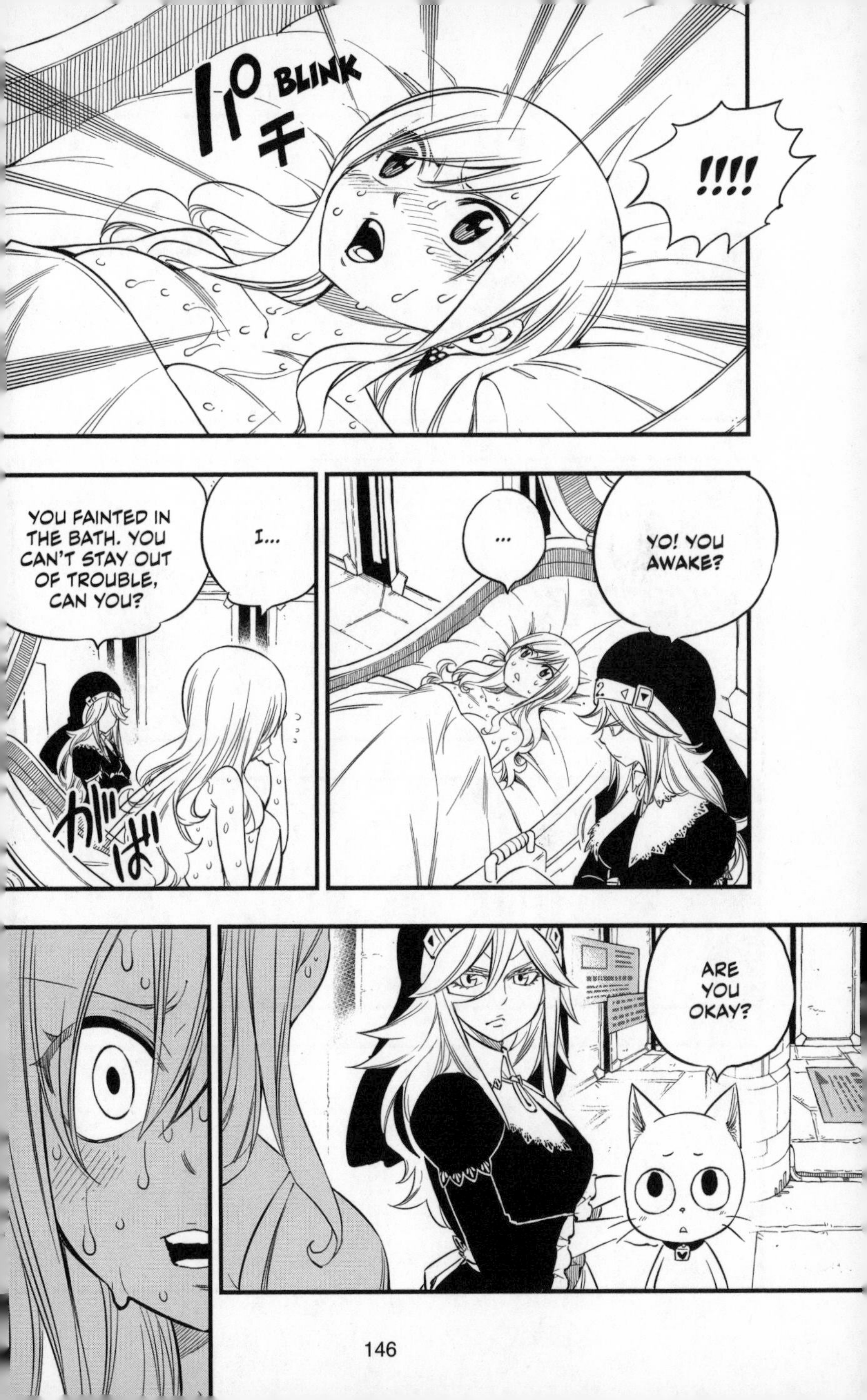
BLINK
!!!!
YO! YOU AWAKE?
...
I...
YOU FAINTED IN THE BATH. YOU CAN'T STAY OUT OF TROUBLE, CAN YOU?
ARE YOU OKAY?

EDENS ZERO

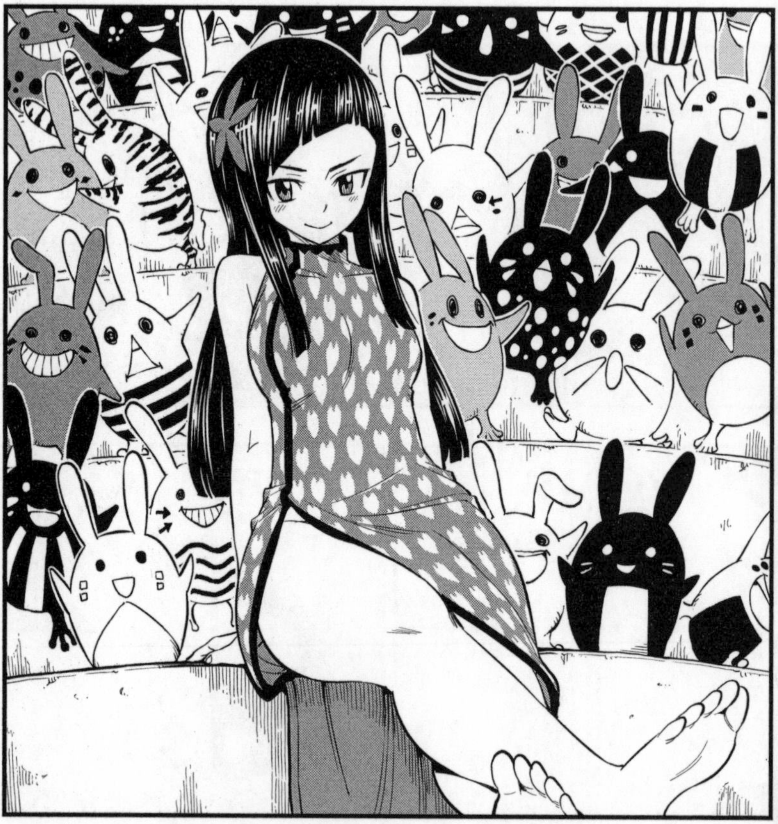

CHAPTER 85: OUR FUTURE

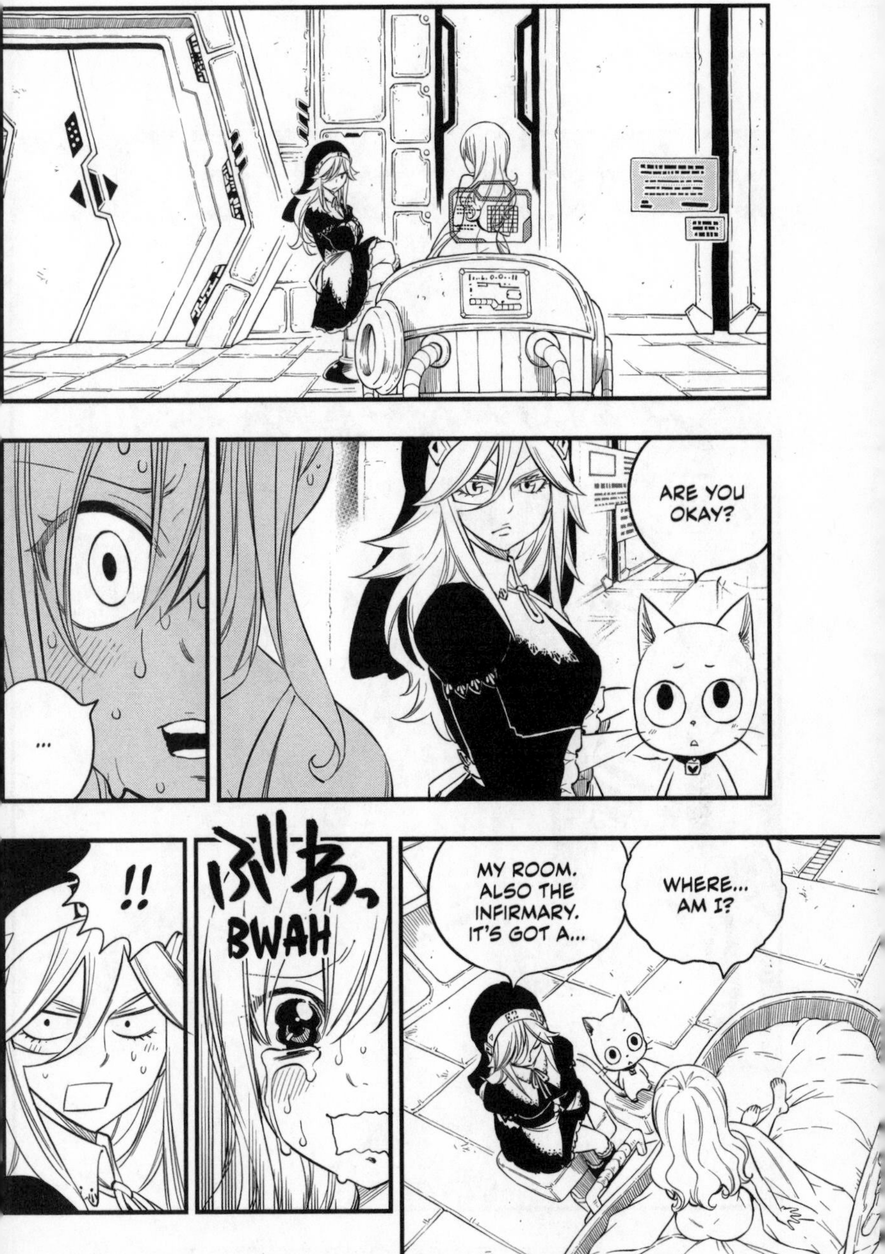
ARE YOU OKAY?
...
WHERE... AM I?
MY ROOM. ALSO THE INFIRMARY. IT'S GOT A...
ぶわっ
BWAH
!!

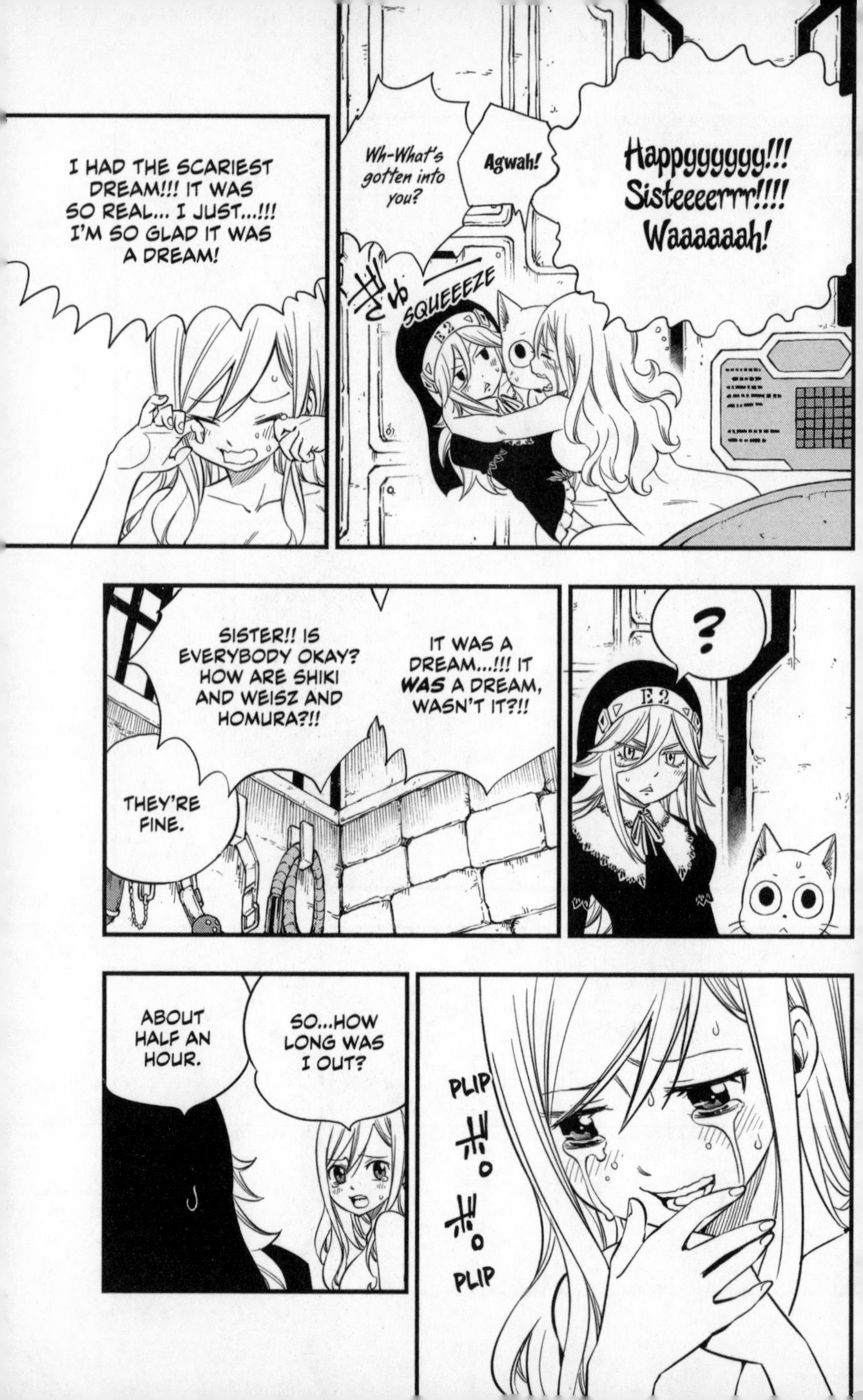

Happyyyyyyy!!! Sisteeeerrrr!!!! Waaaaaah!
Agwah!
Wh-What's gotten into you?
SQUEEEEZE
I HAD THE SCARIEST DREAM!!! IT WAS SO REAL... I JUST...!!! I'M SO GLAD IT WAS A DREAM!
?
IT WAS A DREAM...!!! IT **WAS** A DREAM, WASN'T IT?!!
SISTER!! IS EVERYBODY OKAY? HOW ARE SHIKI AND WEISZ AND HOMURA?!!
THEY'RE FINE.
PLIP
PLIP
SO...HOW LONG WAS I OUT?
ABOUT HALF AN HOUR.

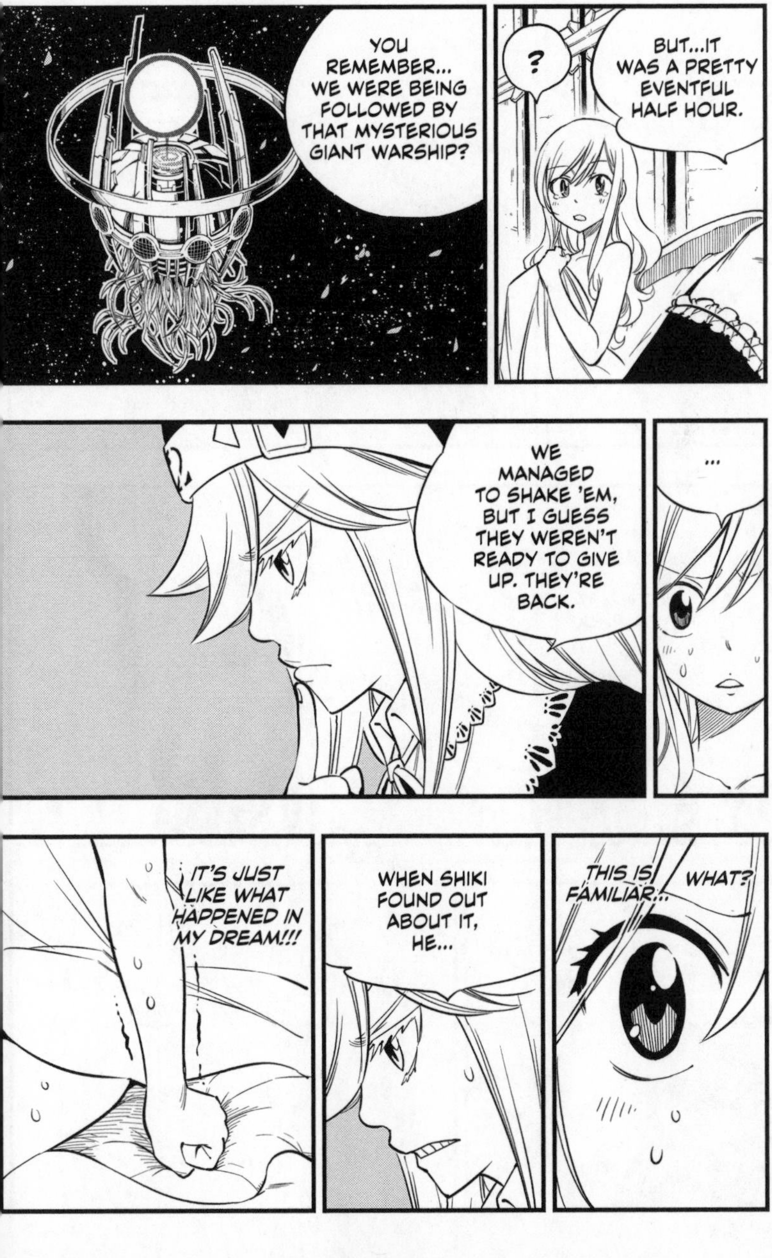
BUT...IT WAS A PRETTY EVENTFUL HALF HOUR.
?
YOU REMEMBER... WE WERE BEING FOLLOWED BY THAT MYSTERIOUS GIANT WARSHIP?
...
WE MANAGED TO SHAKE 'EM, BUT I GUESS THEY WEREN'T READY TO GIVE UP. THEY'RE BACK.
WHAT?
THIS IS FAMILIAR...
WHEN SHIKI FOUND OUT ABOUT IT, HE...
IT'S JUST LIKE WHAT HAPPENED IN MY DREAM!!!

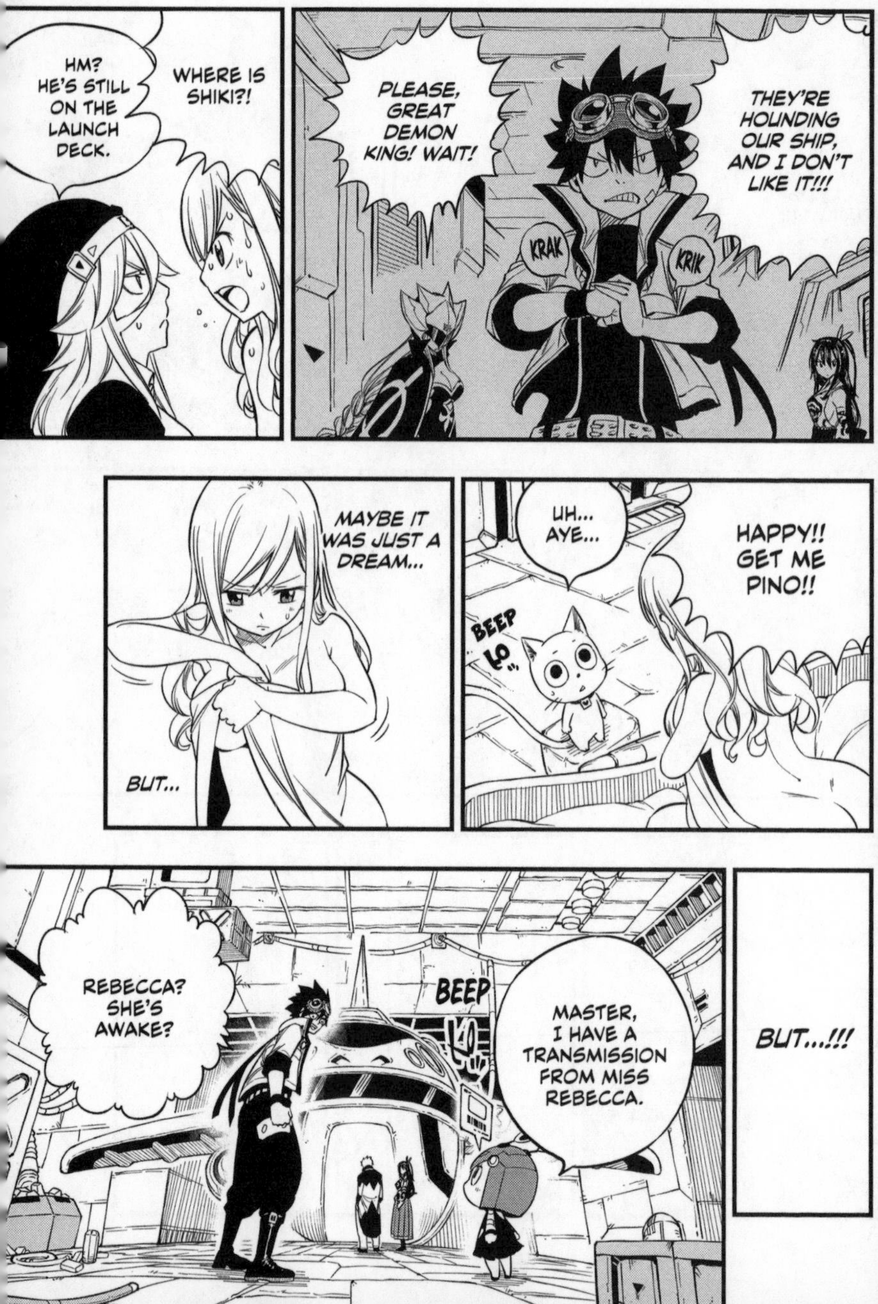
THEY'RE HOUNDING OUR SHIP, AND I DON'T LIKE IT!!!
KRIK
KRAK
PLEASE, GREAT DEMON KING! WAIT!
WHERE IS SHIKI?!
HM? HE'S STILL ON THE LAUNCH DECK.
HAPPY!! GET ME PINO!!
UH... AYE...
BEEP
MAYBE IT WAS JUST A DREAM...
BUT...
BUT...!!!
MASTER, I HAVE A TRANSMISSION FROM MISS REBECCA.
BEEP
REBECCA? SHE'S AWAKE?

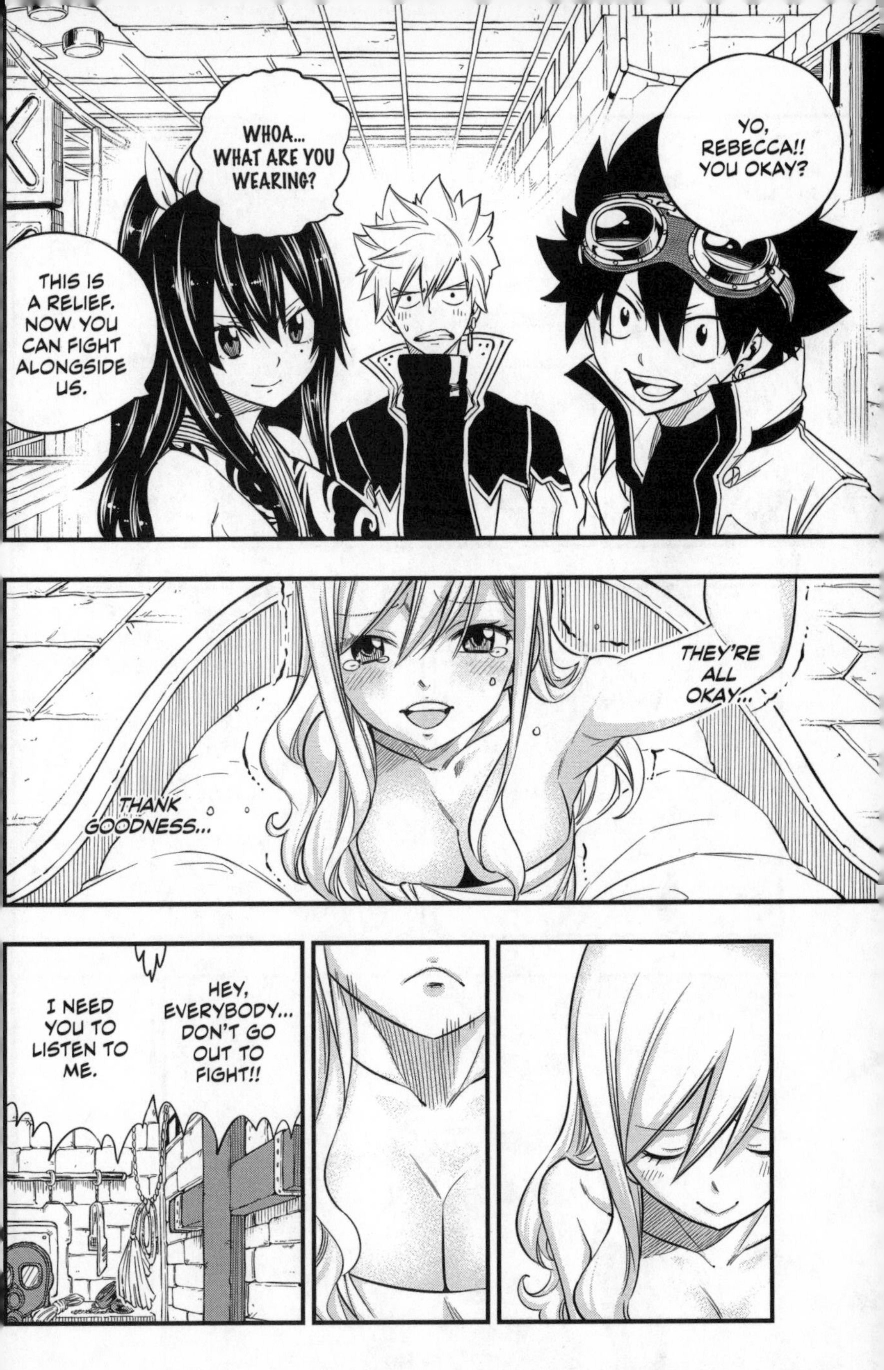
YO, REBECCA!! YOU OKAY?
WHOA... WHAT ARE YOU WEARING?
THIS IS A RELIEF. NOW YOU CAN FIGHT ALONGSIDE US.
THEY'RE ALL OKAY...
THANK GOODNESS...
HEY, EVERYBODY... DON'T GO OUT TO FIGHT!!
I NEED YOU TO LISTEN TO ME.

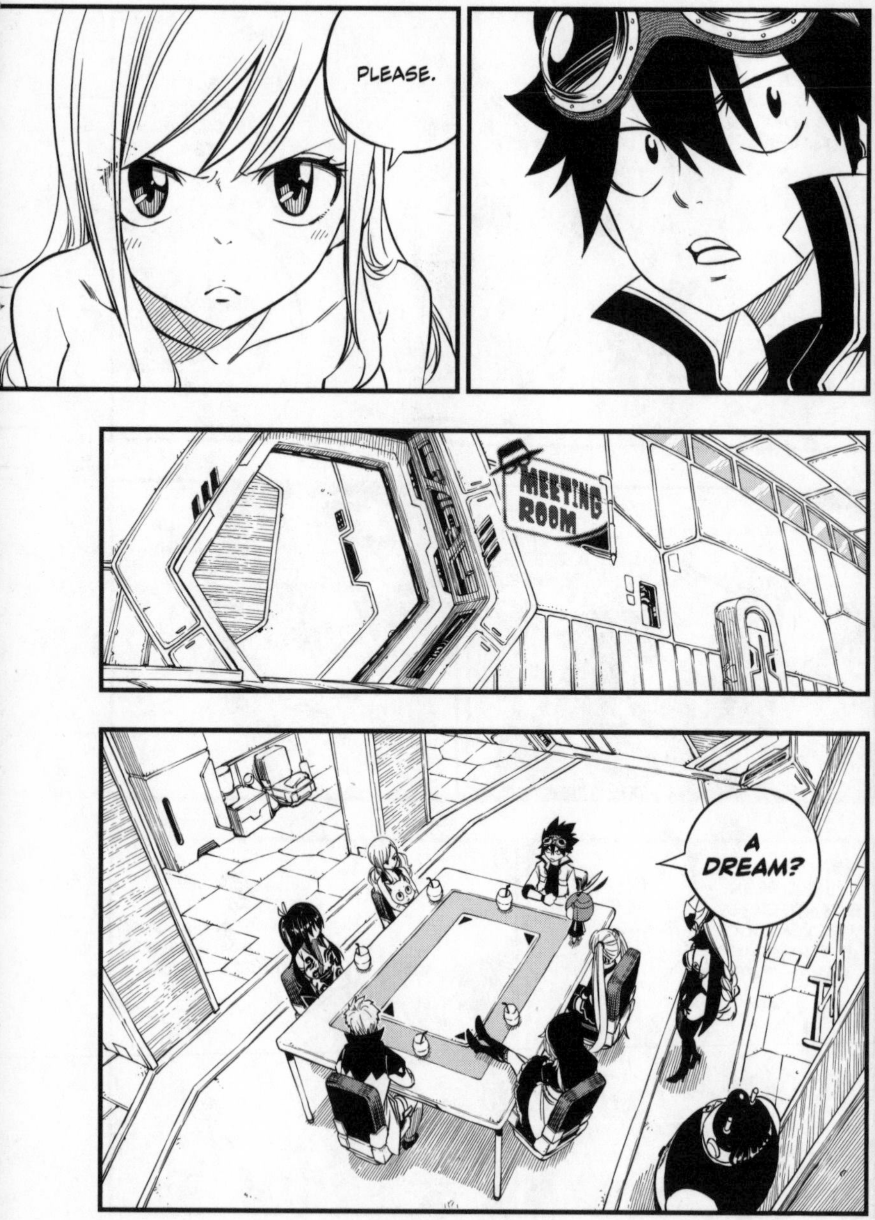
PLEASE.
MEETING ROOM
A DREAM?

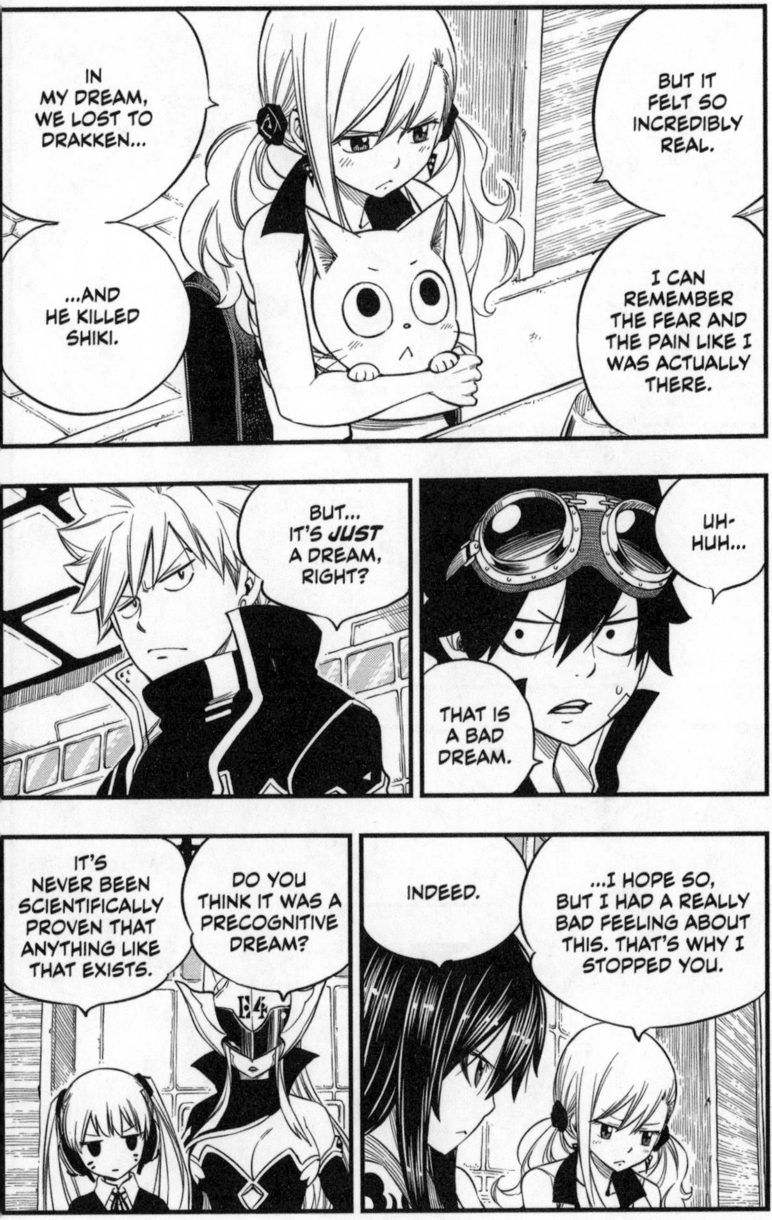
IN MY DREAM, WE LOST TO DRAKKEN...
...AND HE KILLED SHIKI.
BUT IT FELT SO INCREDIBLY REAL.
I CAN REMEMBER THE FEAR AND THE PAIN LIKE I WAS ACTUALLY THERE.
BUT... IT'S *JUST* A DREAM, RIGHT?
UH-HUH...
THAT IS A BAD DREAM.
DO YOU THINK IT WAS A PRECOGNITIVE DREAM?
IT'S NEVER BEEN SCIENTIFICALLY PROVEN THAT ANYTHING LIKE THAT EXISTS.
INDEED.
...I HOPE SO, BUT I HAD A REALLY BAD FEELING ABOUT THIS. THAT'S WHY I STOPPED YOU.

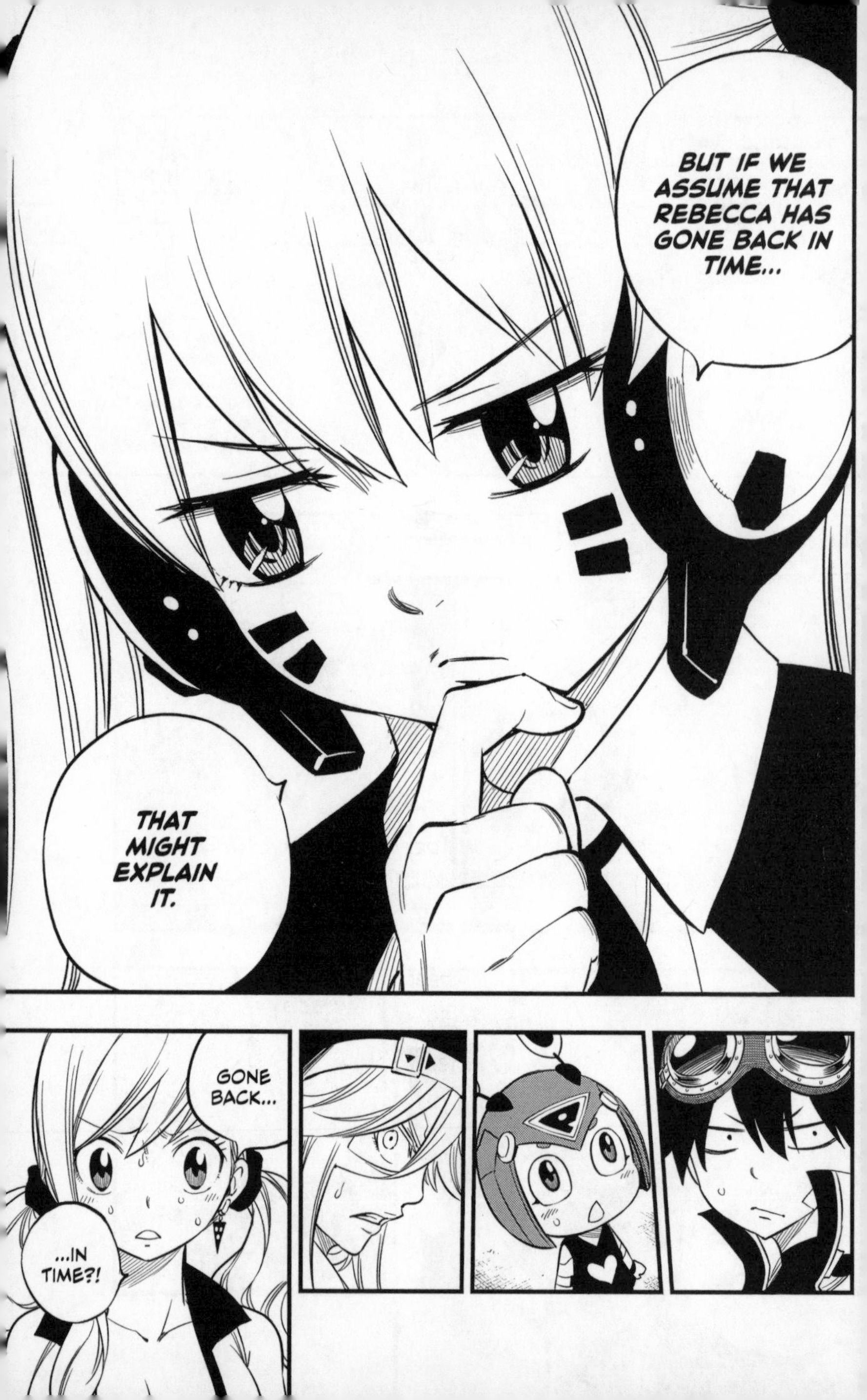
BUT IF WE ASSUME THAT REBECCA HAS GONE BACK IN TIME...
THAT MIGHT EXPLAIN IT.
GONE BACK...
...IN TIME?!

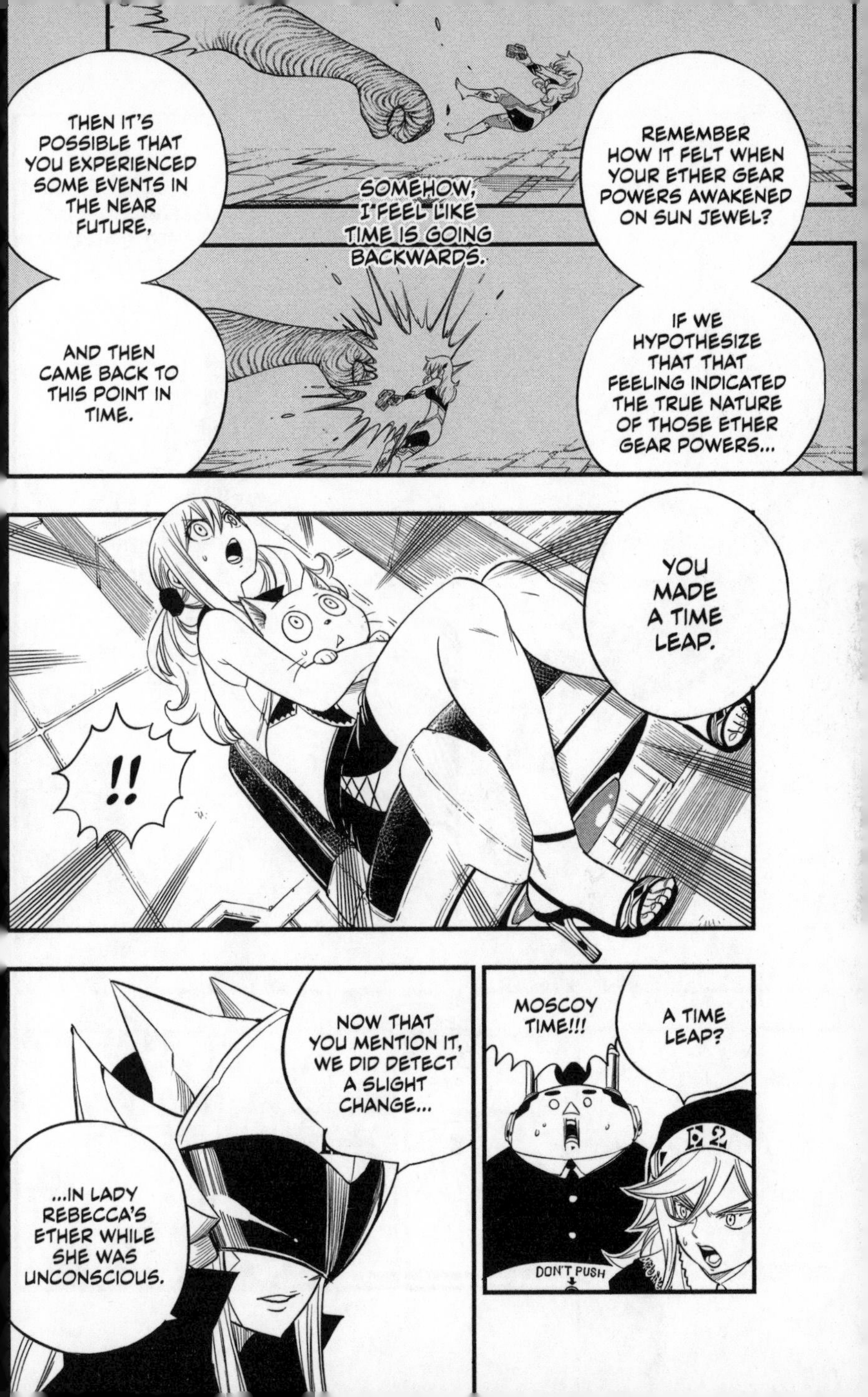
REMEMBER HOW IT FELT WHEN YOUR ETHER GEAR POWERS AWAKENED ON SUN JEWEL?
IF WE HYPOTHESIZE THAT THAT FEELING INDICATED THE TRUE NATURE OF THOSE ETHER GEAR POWERS...
SOMEHOW, I FEEL LIKE TIME IS GOING BACKWARDS.
THEN IT'S POSSIBLE THAT YOU EXPERIENCED SOME EVENTS IN THE NEAR FUTURE,
AND THEN CAME BACK TO THIS POINT IN TIME.
YOU MADE A TIME LEAP.
!!
A TIME LEAP?
MOSCOY TIME!!!
DON'T PUSH
NOW THAT YOU MENTION IT, WE DID DETECT A SLIGHT CHANGE...
...IN LADY REBECCA'S ETHER WHILE SHE WAS UNCONSCIOUS.

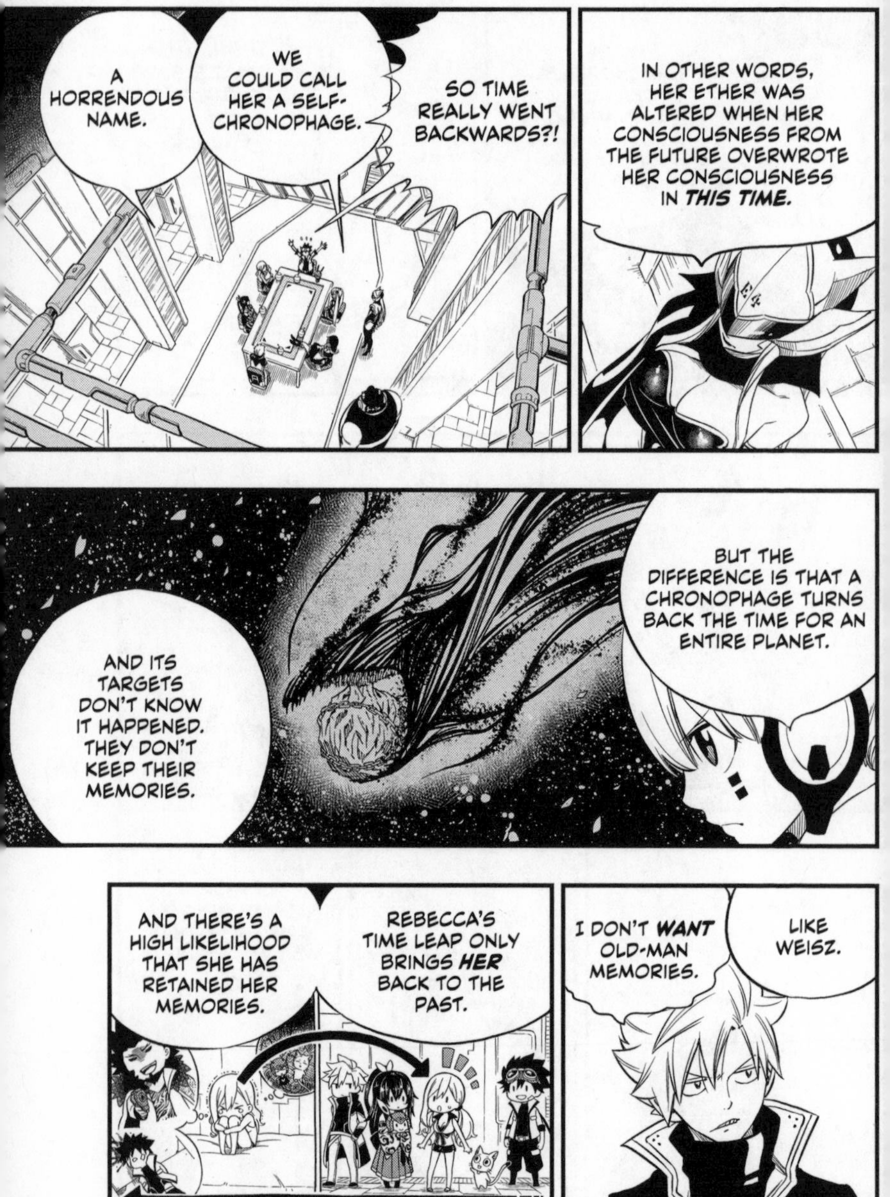
IN OTHER WORDS, HER ETHER WAS ALTERED WHEN HER CONSCIOUSNESS FROM THE FUTURE OVERWROTE HER CONSCIOUSNESS IN *THIS TIME.*
SO TIME REALLY WENT BACKWARDS?!
WE COULD CALL HER A SELF-CHRONOPHAGE.
A HORRENDOUS NAME.
BUT THE DIFFERENCE IS THAT A CHRONOPHAGE TURNS BACK THE TIME FOR AN ENTIRE PLANET.
AND ITS TARGETS DON'T KNOW IT HAPPENED. THEY DON'T KEEP THEIR MEMORIES.
LIKE WEISZ.
I DON'T *WANT* OLD-MAN MEMORIES.
REBECCA'S TIME LEAP ONLY BRINGS *HER* BACK TO THE PAST.
AND THERE'S A HIGH LIKELIHOOD THAT SHE HAS RETAINED HER MEMORIES.

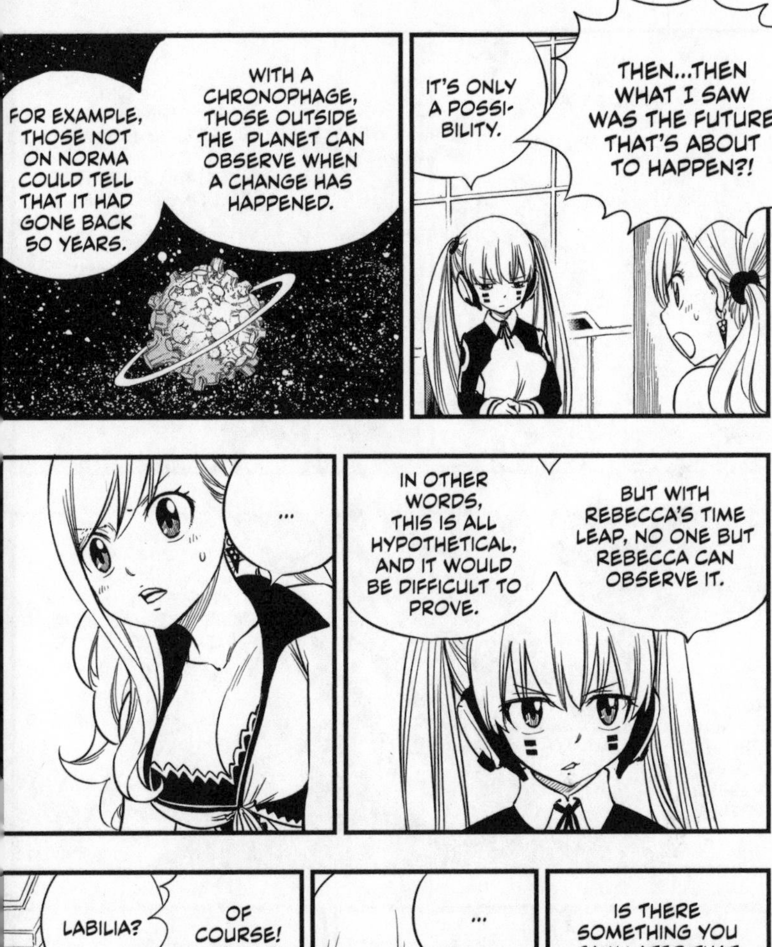
THEN...THEN WHAT I SAW WAS THE FUTURE THAT'S ABOUT TO HAPPEN?!
IT'S ONLY A POSSI-BILITY.
WITH A CHRONOPHAGE, THOSE OUTSIDE THE PLANET CAN OBSERVE WHEN A CHANGE HAS HAPPENED.
FOR EXAMPLE, THOSE NOT ON NORMA COULD TELL THAT IT HAD GONE BACK 50 YEARS.
BUT WITH REBECCA'S TIME LEAP, NO ONE BUT REBECCA CAN OBSERVE IT.
IN OTHER WORDS, THIS IS ALL HYPOTHETICAL, AND IT WOULD BE DIFFICULT TO PROVE.
...
IS THERE SOMETHING YOU SAW LATER THAT WE CAN CHECK ON NOW?
...
OF COURSE! LABILIA!!!
LABILIA?
THAT B-CUBER BULLY?

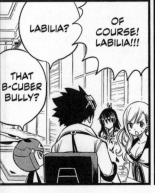

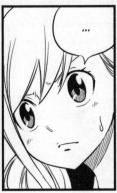

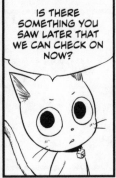

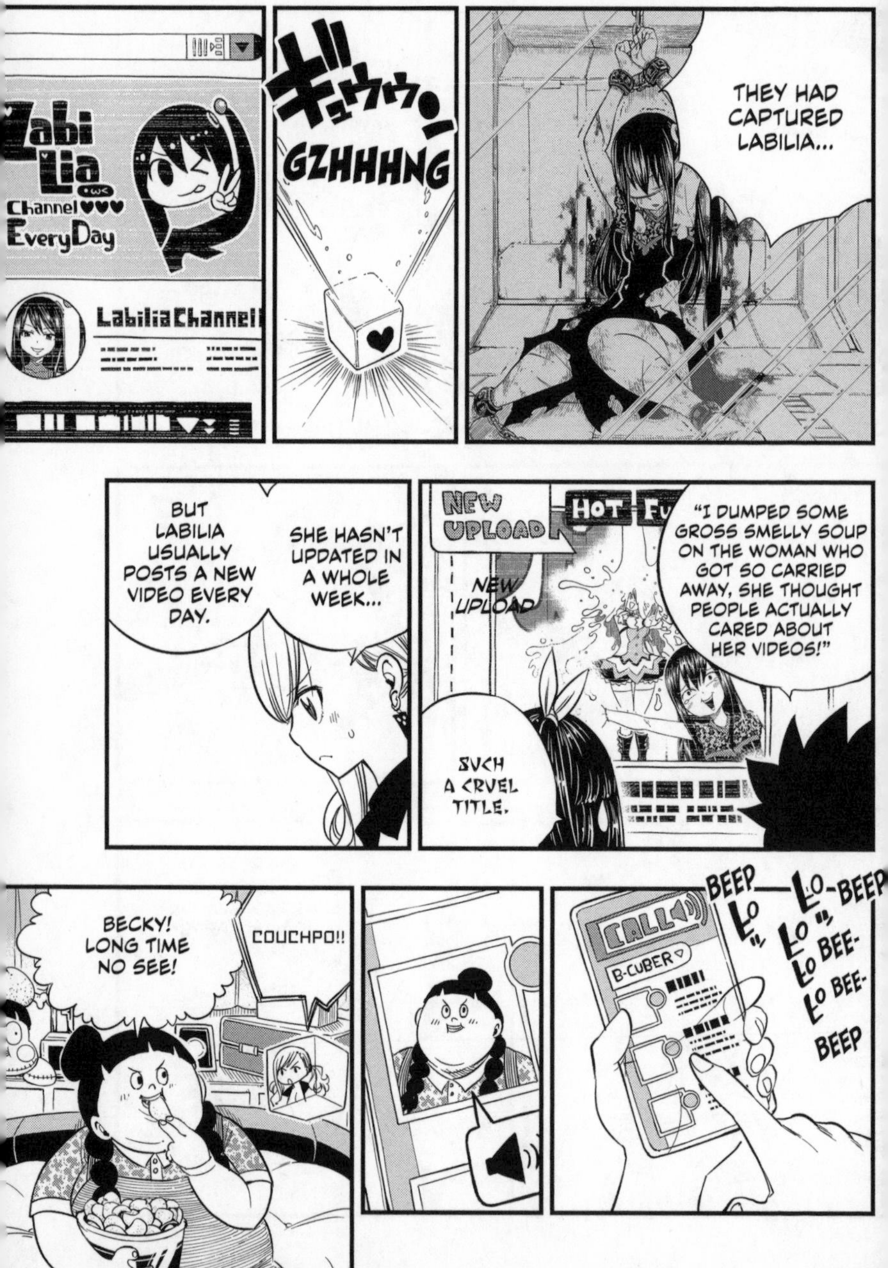
THEY HAD CAPTURED LABILIA...
ギュウウ
GZHHHNG
Labi Lia
Channel♥♥♥
EveryDay
LabiliaChannel
NEW UPLOAD
HOT
"I DUMPED SOME GROSS SMELLY SOUP ON THE WOMAN WHO GOT SO CARRIED AWAY, SHE THOUGHT PEOPLE ACTUALLY CARED ABOUT HER VIDEOS!"
NEW UPLOAD
SUCH A CRUEL TITLE.
SHE HASN'T UPDATED IN A WHOLE WEEK...
BUT LABILIA USUALLY POSTS A NEW VIDEO EVERY DAY.
BEEP—BEEP
BEE-BEE-BEEP
CALL
B-CUBER
COUCHPO!!
BECKY! LONG TIME NO SEE!

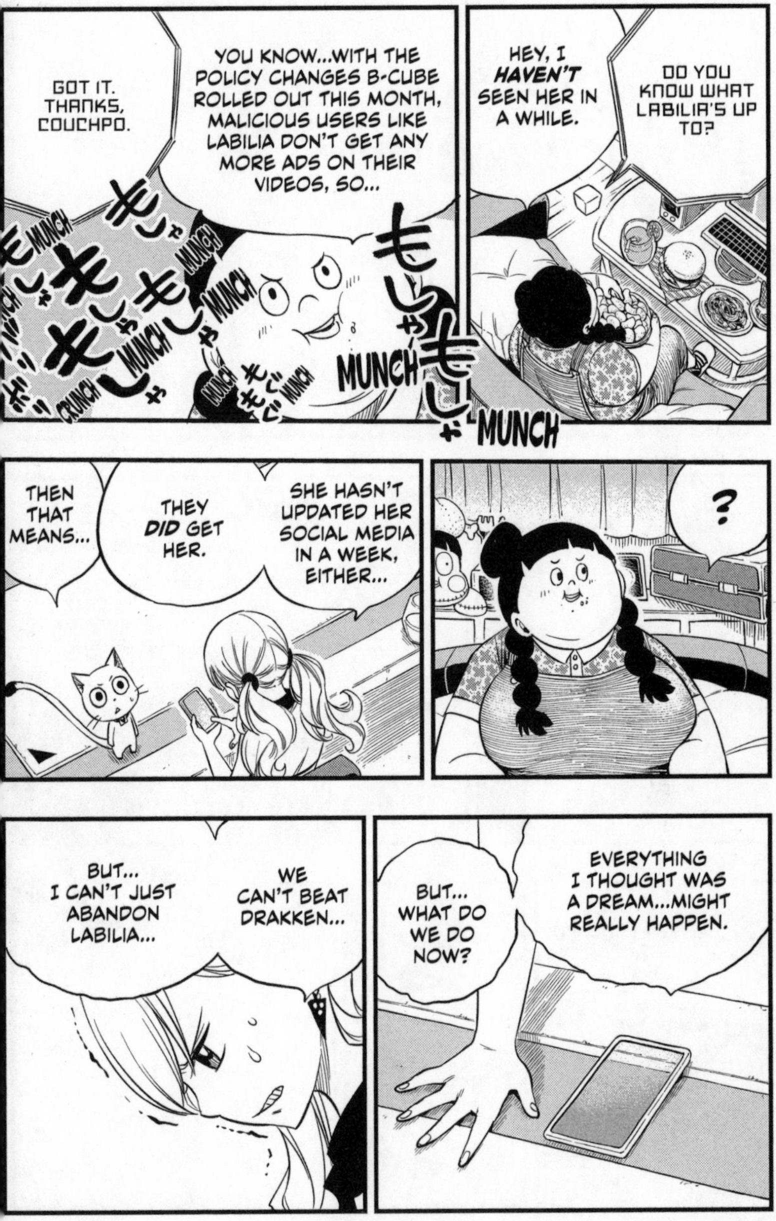
DO YOU KNOW WHAT LABILIA'S UP TO?
HEY, I *HAVEN'T* SEEN HER IN A WHILE.
MUNCH
YOU KNOW...WITH THE POLICY CHANGES B-CUBE ROLLED OUT THIS MONTH, MALICIOUS USERS LIKE LABILIA DON'T GET ANY MORE ADS ON THEIR VIDEOS, SO...
GOT IT. THANKS, COUCHPO.
MUNCH
MUNCH
MUNCH
MUNCH
MUNCH
MUNCH
MUNCH
CRUNCH
?
SHE HASN'T UPDATED HER SOCIAL MEDIA IN A WEEK, EITHER...
THEY *DID* GET HER.
THEN THAT MEANS...
EVERYTHING I THOUGHT WAS A DREAM...MIGHT REALLY HAPPEN.
BUT... WHAT DO WE DO NOW?
WE CAN'T BEAT DRAKKEN...
BUT... I CAN'T JUST ABANDON LABILIA...

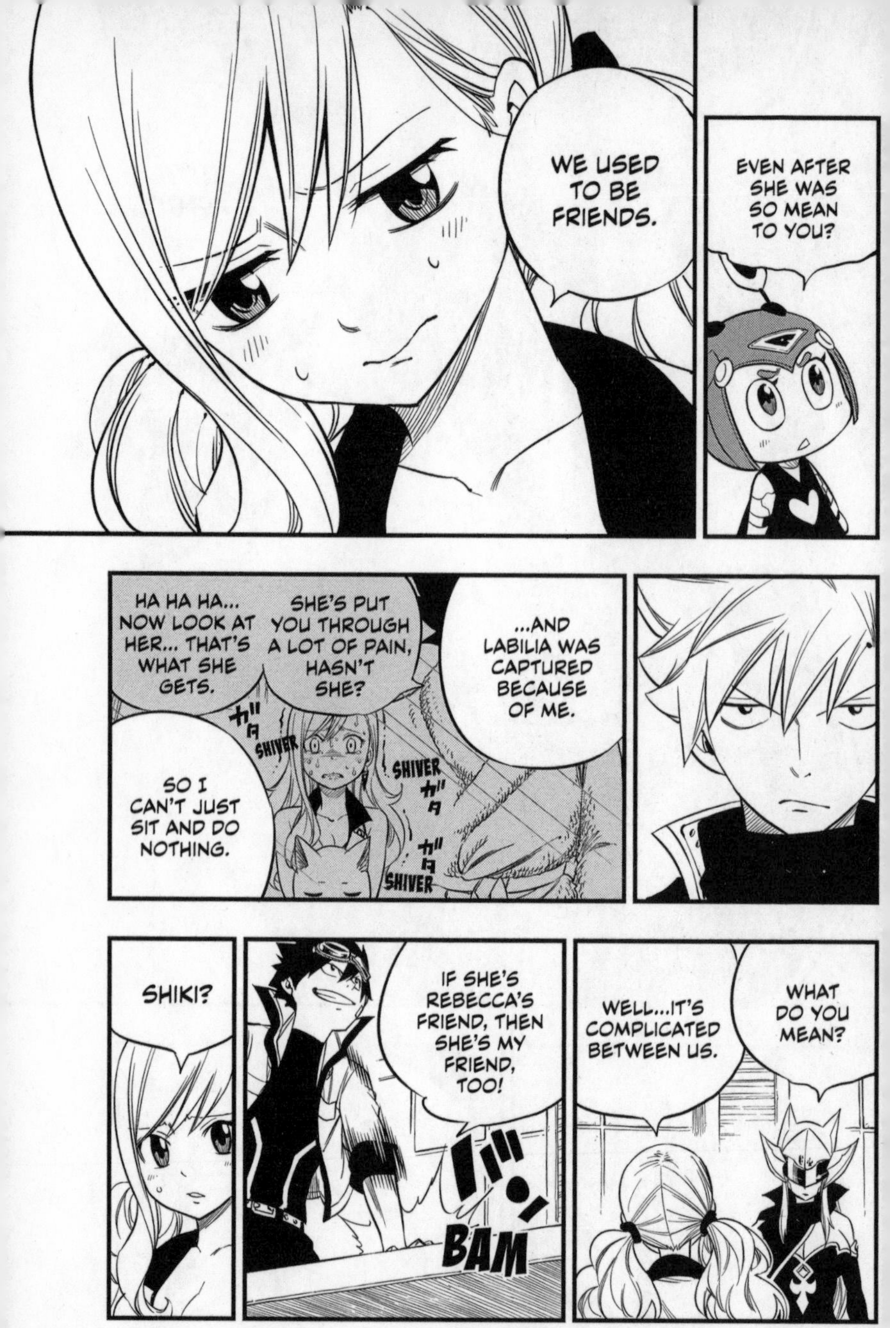
EVEN AFTER SHE WAS SO MEAN TO YOU?
WE USED TO BE FRIENDS.
...AND LABILIA WAS CAPTURED BECAUSE OF ME.
SHE'S PUT YOU THROUGH A LOT OF PAIN, HASN'T SHE?
HA HA HA... NOW LOOK AT HER... THAT'S WHAT SHE GETS.
SHIVER
SHIVER
SHIVER
SO I CAN'T JUST SIT AND DO NOTHING.
WHAT DO YOU MEAN?
WELL...IT'S COMPLICATED BETWEEN US.
IF SHE'S REBECCA'S FRIEND, THEN SHE'S MY FRIEND, TOO!
BAM
SHIKI?

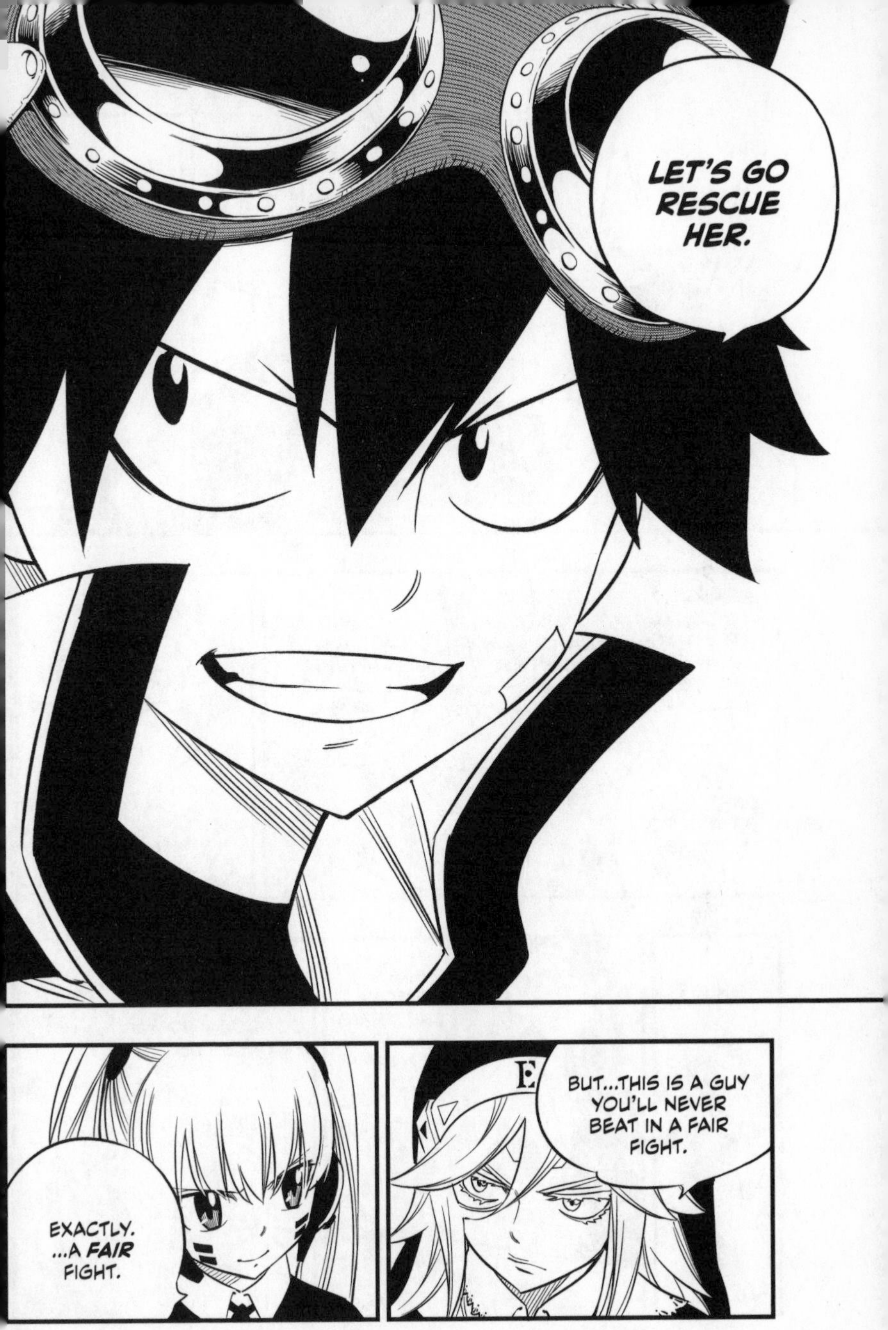
LET'S GO RESCUE HER.
BUT...THIS IS A GUY YOU'LL NEVER BEAT IN A FAIR FIGHT.
EXACTLY. ...A *FAIR* FIGHT.

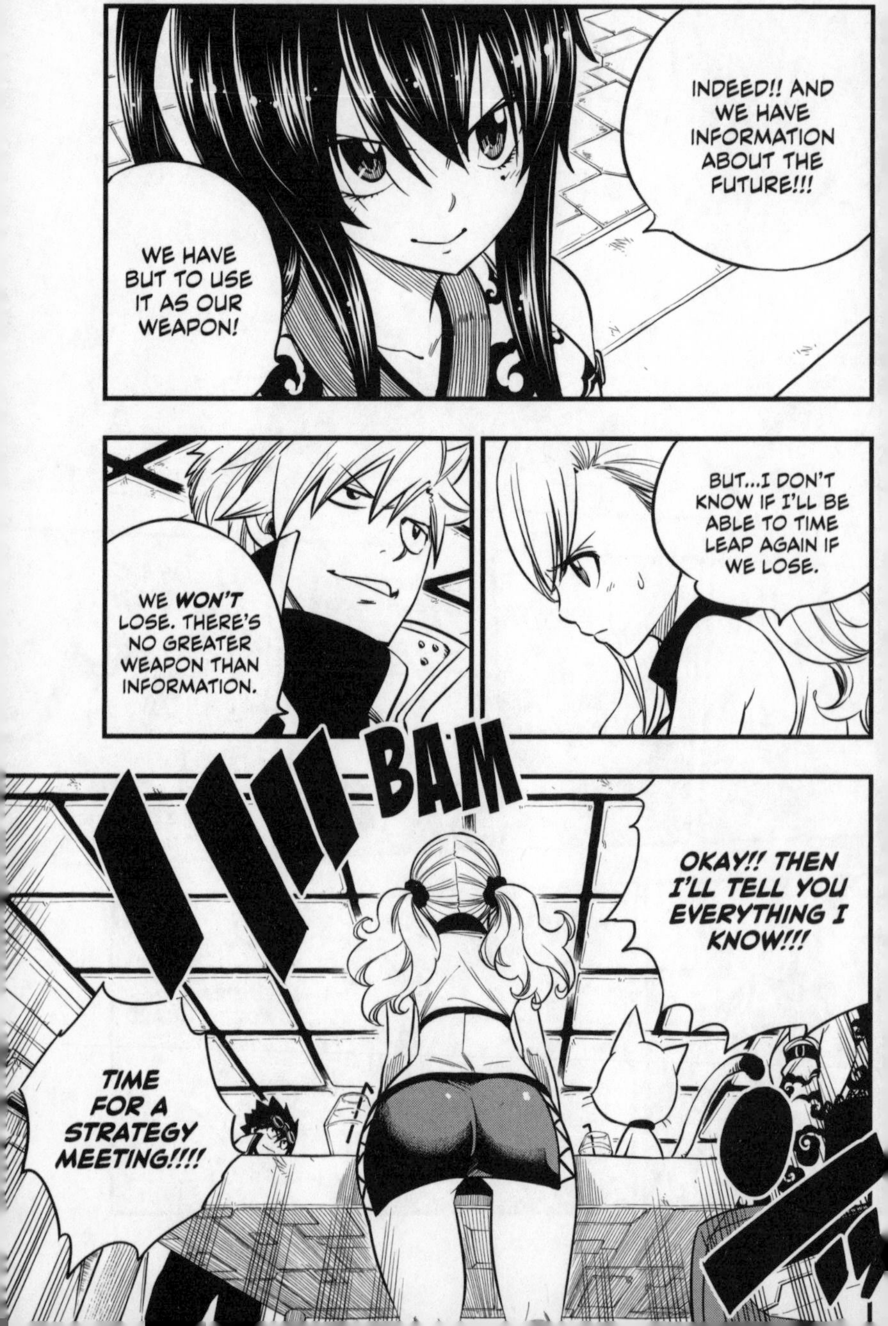
INDEED!! AND WE HAVE INFORMATION ABOUT THE FUTURE!!!
WE HAVE BUT TO USE IT AS OUR WEAPON!
BUT...I DON'T KNOW IF I'LL BE ABLE TO TIME LEAP AGAIN IF WE LOSE.
WE WON'T LOSE. THERE'S NO GREATER WEAPON THAN INFORMATION.
BAM
OKAY!! THEN I'LL TELL YOU EVERYTHING I KNOW!!!
TIME FOR A STRATEGY MEETING!!!!

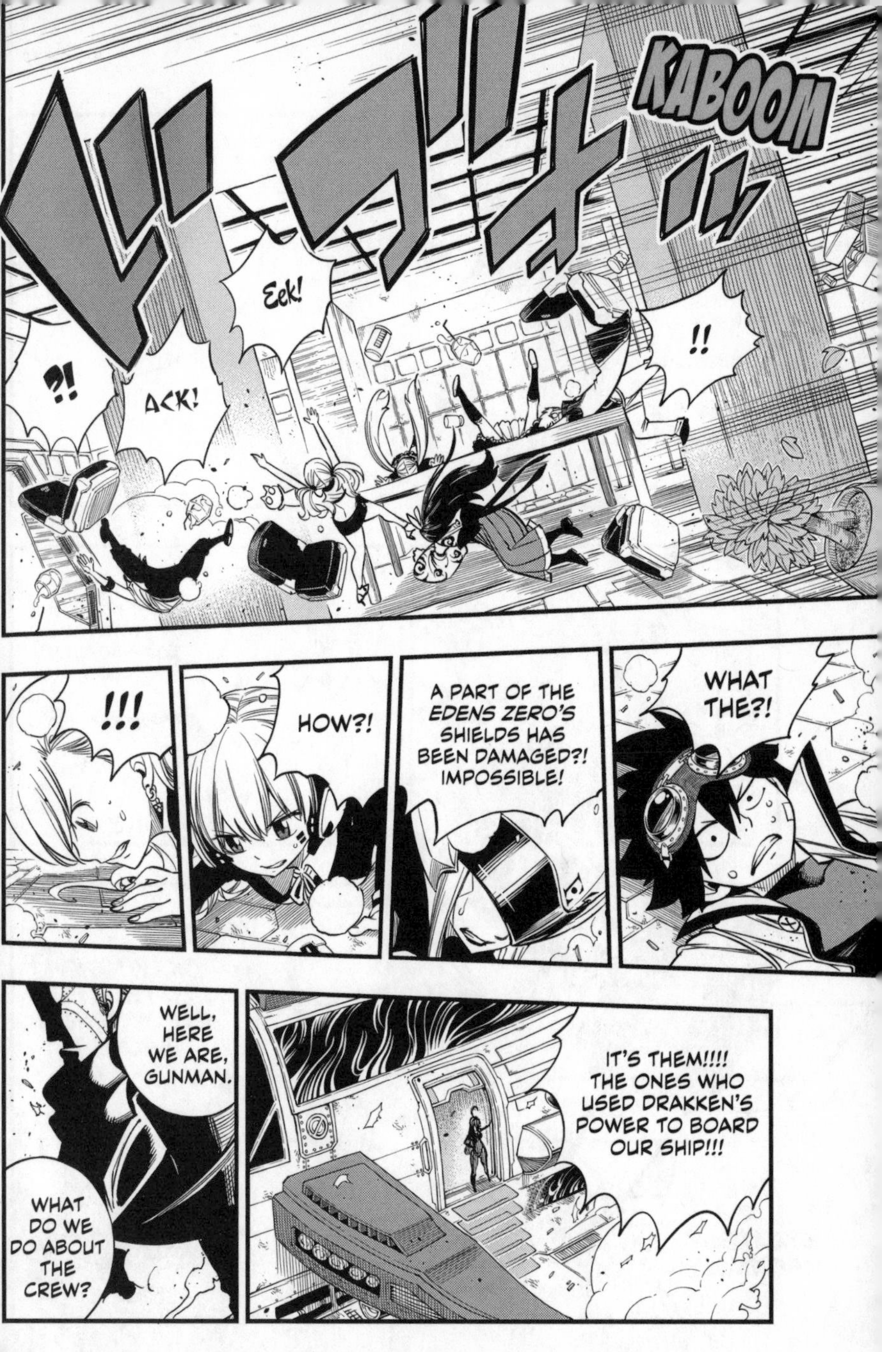
KABOOM
!!
Eek!
ACK!
?!
WHAT THE?!
A PART OF THE EDENS ZERO'S SHIELDS HAS BEEN DAMAGED?! IMPOSSIBLE!
HOW?!
!!!
IT'S THEM!!!! THE ONES WHO USED DRAKKEN'S POWER TO BOARD OUR SHIP!!!
WELL, HERE WE ARE, GUNMAN.
WHAT DO WE DO ABOUT THE CREW?

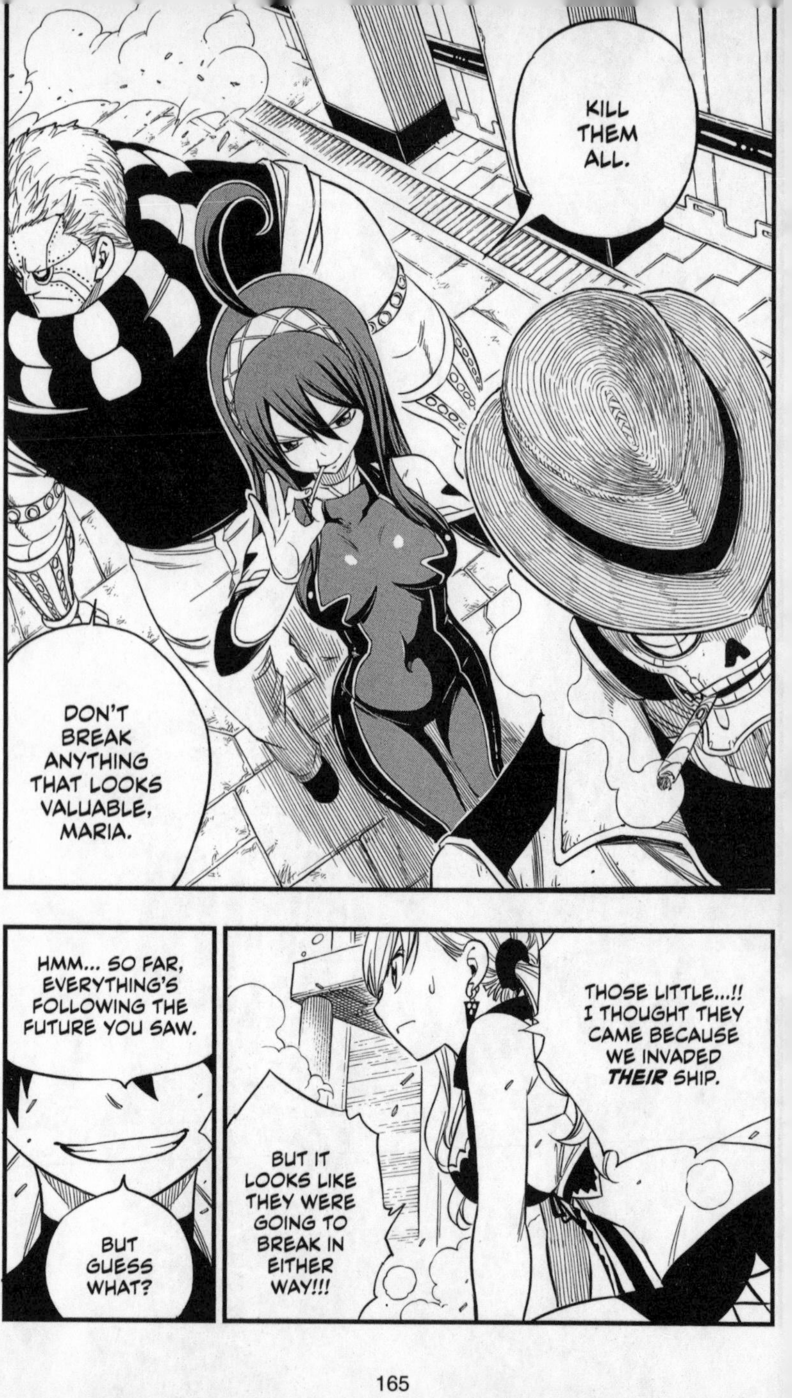
KILL THEM ALL.
DON'T BREAK ANYTHING THAT LOOKS VALUABLE, MARIA.
THOSE LITTLE...!! I THOUGHT THEY CAME BECAUSE WE INVADED *THEIR* SHIP.
BUT IT LOOKS LIKE THEY WERE GOING TO BREAK IN EITHER WAY!!!
HMM... SO FAR, EVERYTHING'S FOLLOWING THE FUTURE YOU SAW.
BUT GUESS WHAT?

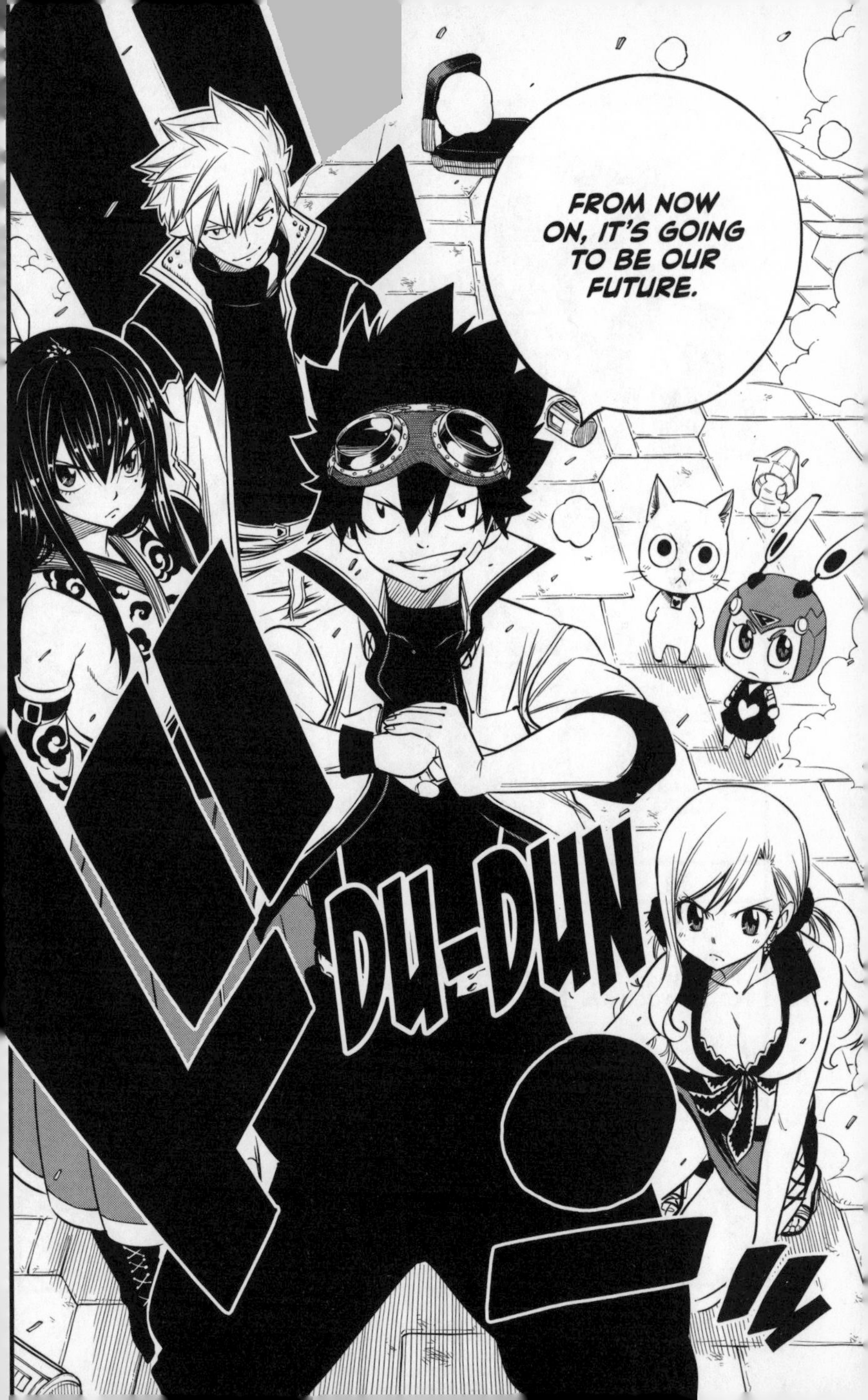
FROM NOW ON, IT'S GOING TO BE OUR FUTURE.
DU-DUN

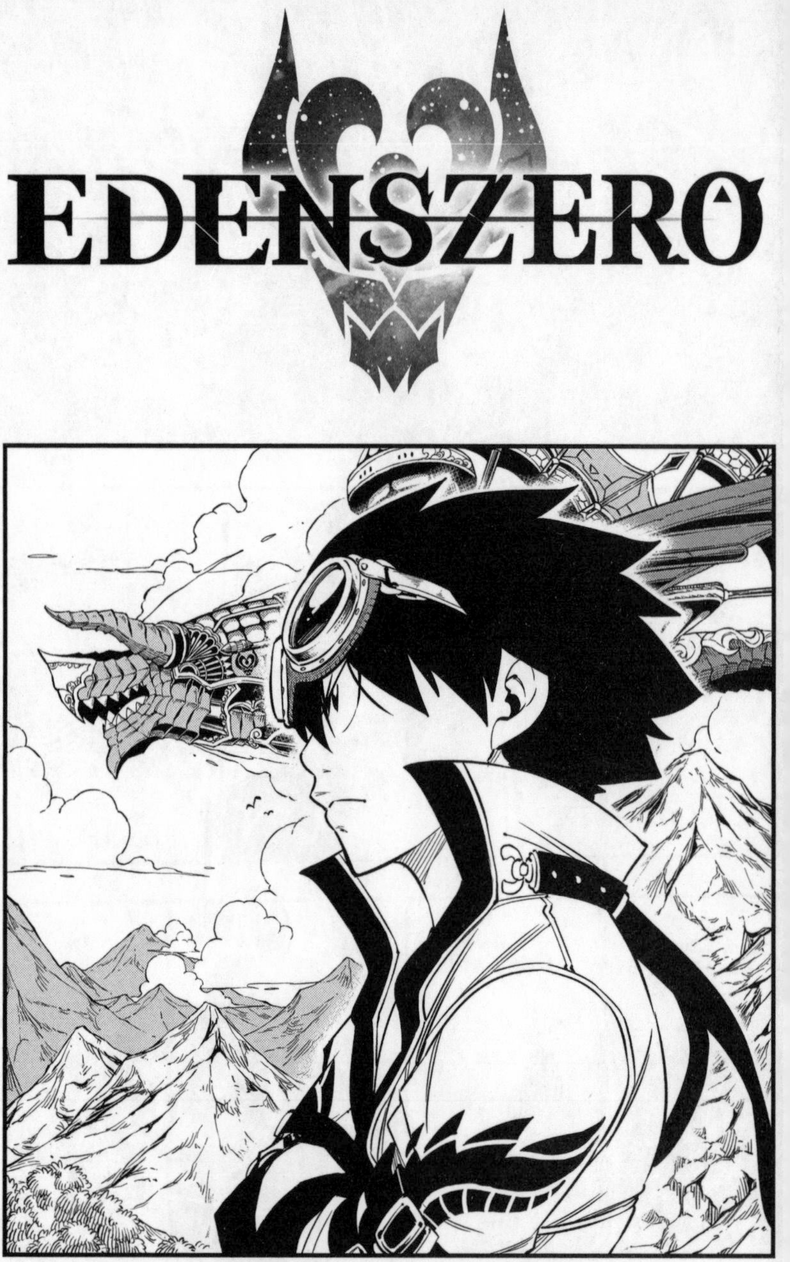

CHAPTER 86: EZ-ATTACK!!

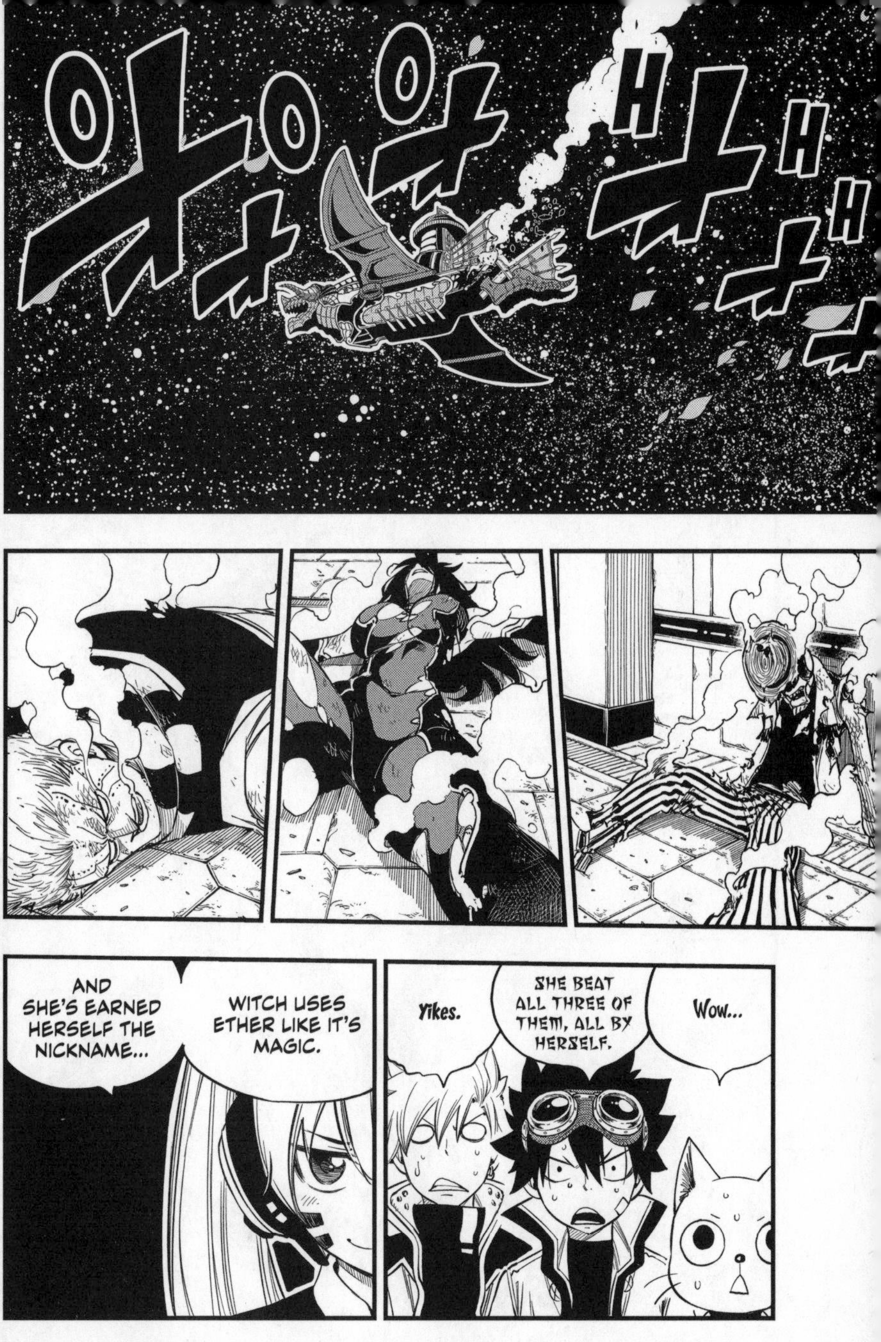
H
H
H
H
Wow...
SHE BEAT ALL THREE OF THEM, ALL BY HERSELF.
Yikes.
WITCH USES ETHER LIKE IT'S MAGIC.
AND SHE'S EARNED HERSELF THE NICKNAME...

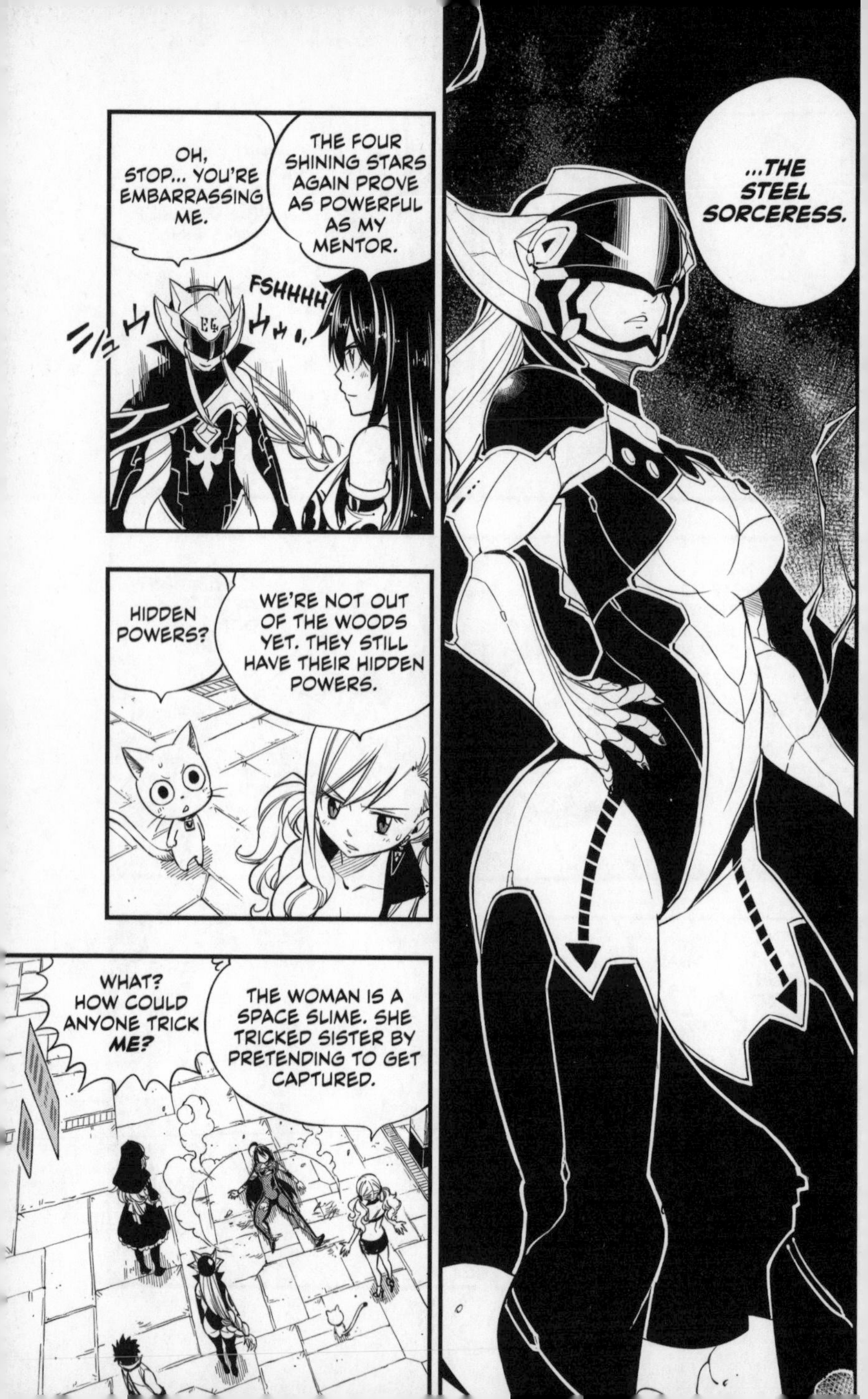
...THE STEEL SORCERESS.
THE FOUR SHINING STARS AGAIN PROVE AS POWERFUL AS MY MENTOR.
OH, STOP... YOU'RE EMBARRASSING ME.
FSHHHH
WE'RE NOT OUT OF THE WOODS YET. THEY STILL HAVE THEIR HIDDEN POWERS.
HIDDEN POWERS?
THE WOMAN IS A SPACE SLIME. SHE TRICKED SISTER BY PRETENDING TO GET CAPTURED.
WHAT? HOW COULD ANYONE TRICK *ME?*

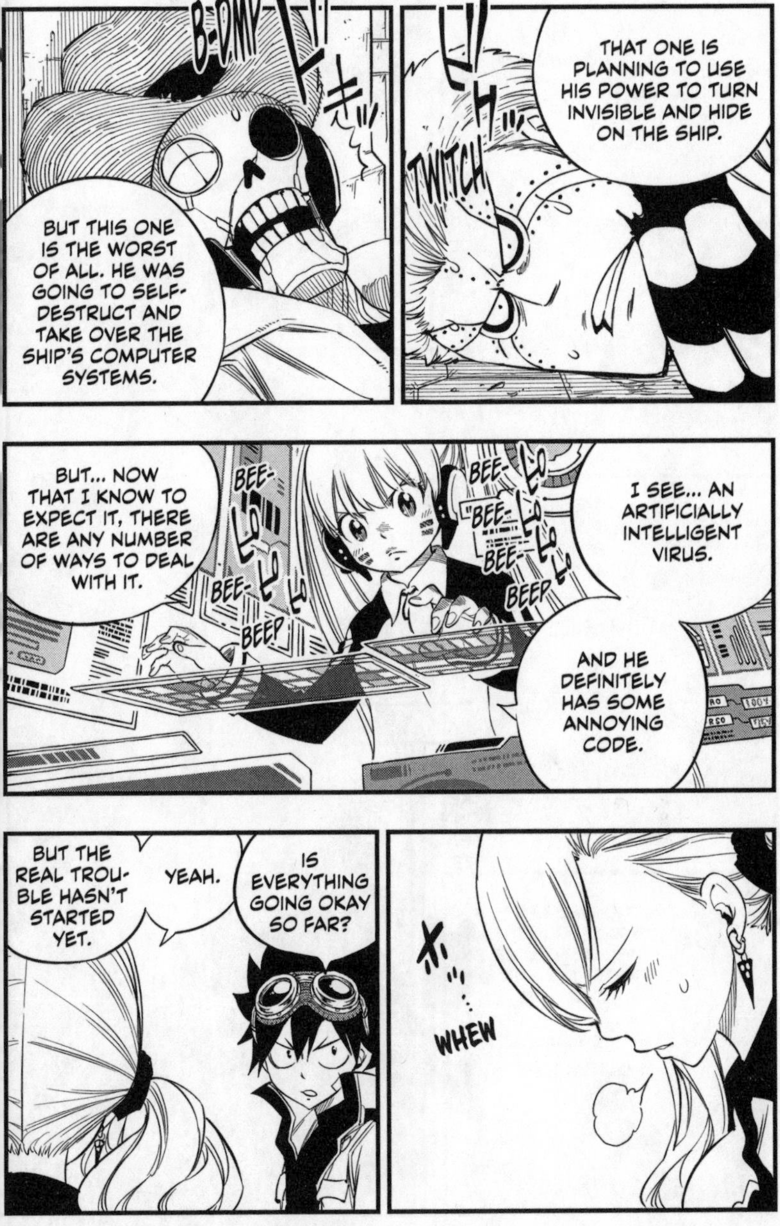
TWITCH
THAT ONE IS PLANNING TO USE HIS POWER TO TURN INVISIBLE AND HIDE ON THE SHIP.
B-DMP
BUT THIS ONE IS THE WORST OF ALL. HE WAS GOING TO SELF-DESTRUCT AND TAKE OVER THE SHIP'S COMPUTER SYSTEMS.
I SEE... AN ARTIFICIALLY INTELLIGENT VIRUS.
AND HE DEFINITELY HAS SOME ANNOYING CODE.
BEE- BEE- BEE- BEEP
BUT... NOW THAT I KNOW TO EXPECT IT, THERE ARE ANY NUMBER OF WAYS TO DEAL WITH IT.
BEE- BEE- BEEP
...WHEW
IS EVERYTHING GOING OKAY SO FAR?
YEAH.
BUT THE REAL TROUBLE HASN'T STARTED YET.

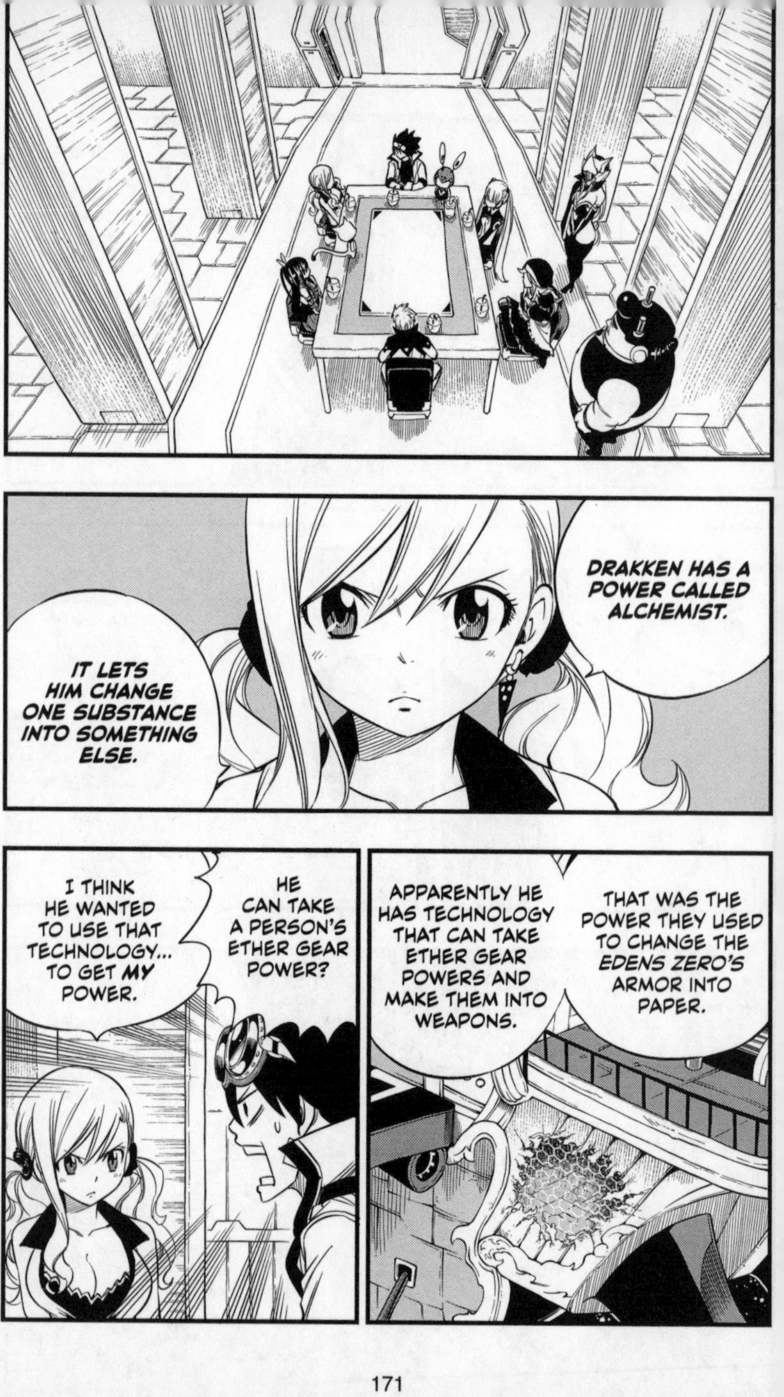
DRAKKEN HAS A POWER CALLED ALCHEMIST.
IT LETS HIM CHANGE ONE SUBSTANCE INTO SOMETHING ELSE.
THAT WAS THE POWER THEY USED TO CHANGE THE EDENS ZERO'S ARMOR INTO PAPER.
APPARENTLY HE HAS TECHNOLOGY THAT CAN TAKE ETHER GEAR POWERS AND MAKE THEM INTO WEAPONS.
HE CAN TAKE A PERSON'S ETHER GEAR POWER?
I THINK HE WANTED TO USE THAT TECHNOLOGY... TO GET MY POWER.

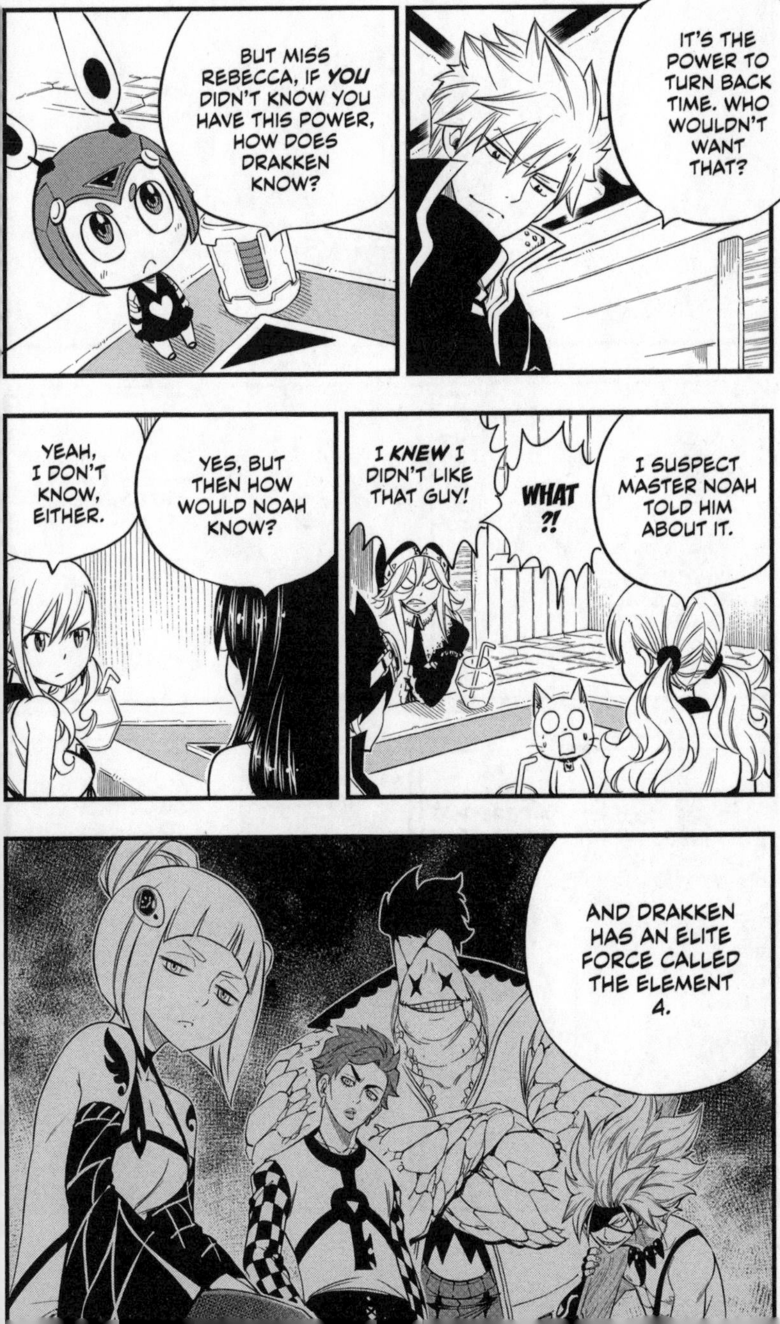
IT'S THE POWER TO TURN BACK TIME. WHO WOULDN'T WANT THAT?
BUT MISS REBECCA, IF *YOU* DIDN'T KNOW YOU HAVE THIS POWER, HOW DOES DRAKKEN KNOW?
I SUSPECT MASTER NOAH TOLD HIM ABOUT IT.
WHAT ?!
I *KNEW* I DIDN'T LIKE THAT GUY!
YES, BUT THEN HOW WOULD NOAH KNOW?
YEAH, I DON'T KNOW, EITHER.
AND DRAKKEN HAS AN ELITE FORCE CALLED THE ELEMENT 4.

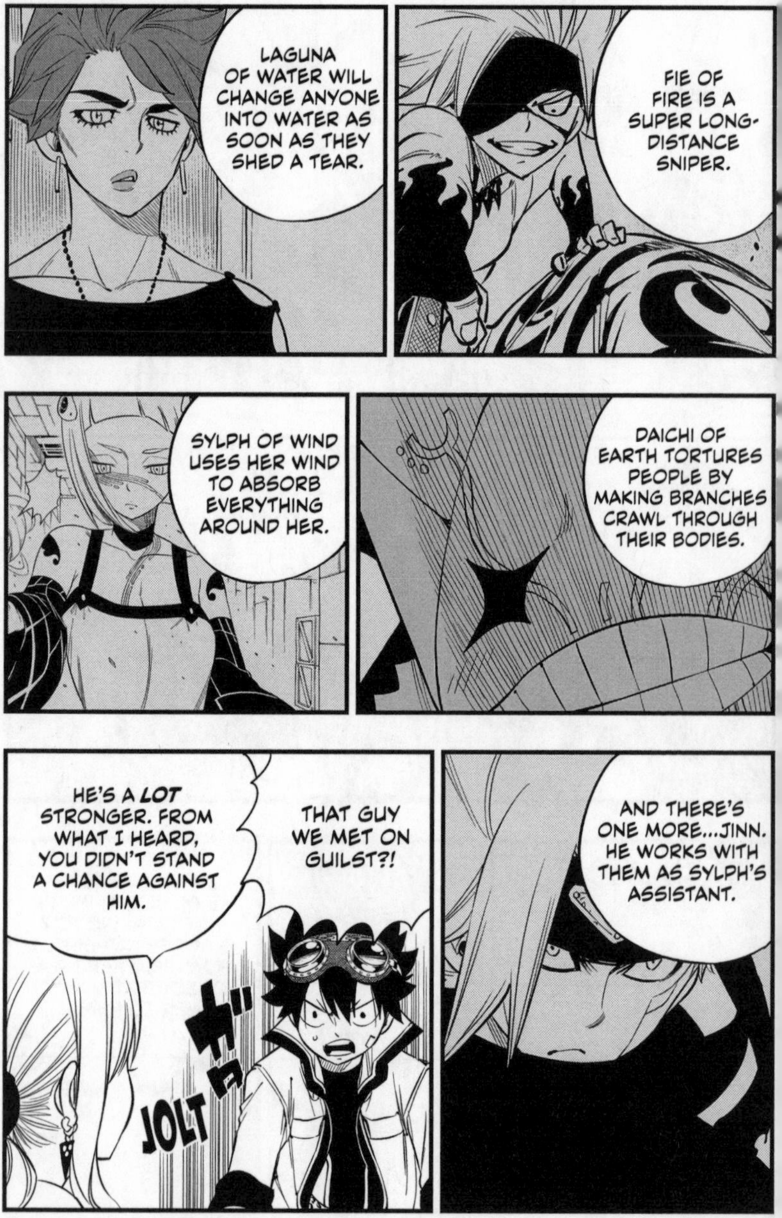
FIE OF FIRE IS A SUPER LONG-DISTANCE SNIPER.
LAGUNA OF WATER WILL CHANGE ANYONE INTO WATER AS SOON AS THEY SHED A TEAR.
DAICHI OF EARTH TORTURES PEOPLE BY MAKING BRANCHES CRAWL THROUGH THEIR BODIES.
SYLPH OF WIND USES HER WIND TO ABSORB EVERYTHING AROUND HER.
AND THERE'S ONE MORE...JINN. HE WORKS WITH THEM AS SYLPH'S ASSISTANT.
THAT GUY WE MET ON GUILST?!
HE'S A LOT STRONGER. FROM WHAT I HEARD, YOU DIDN'T STAND A CHANCE AGAINST HIM.
JOLT

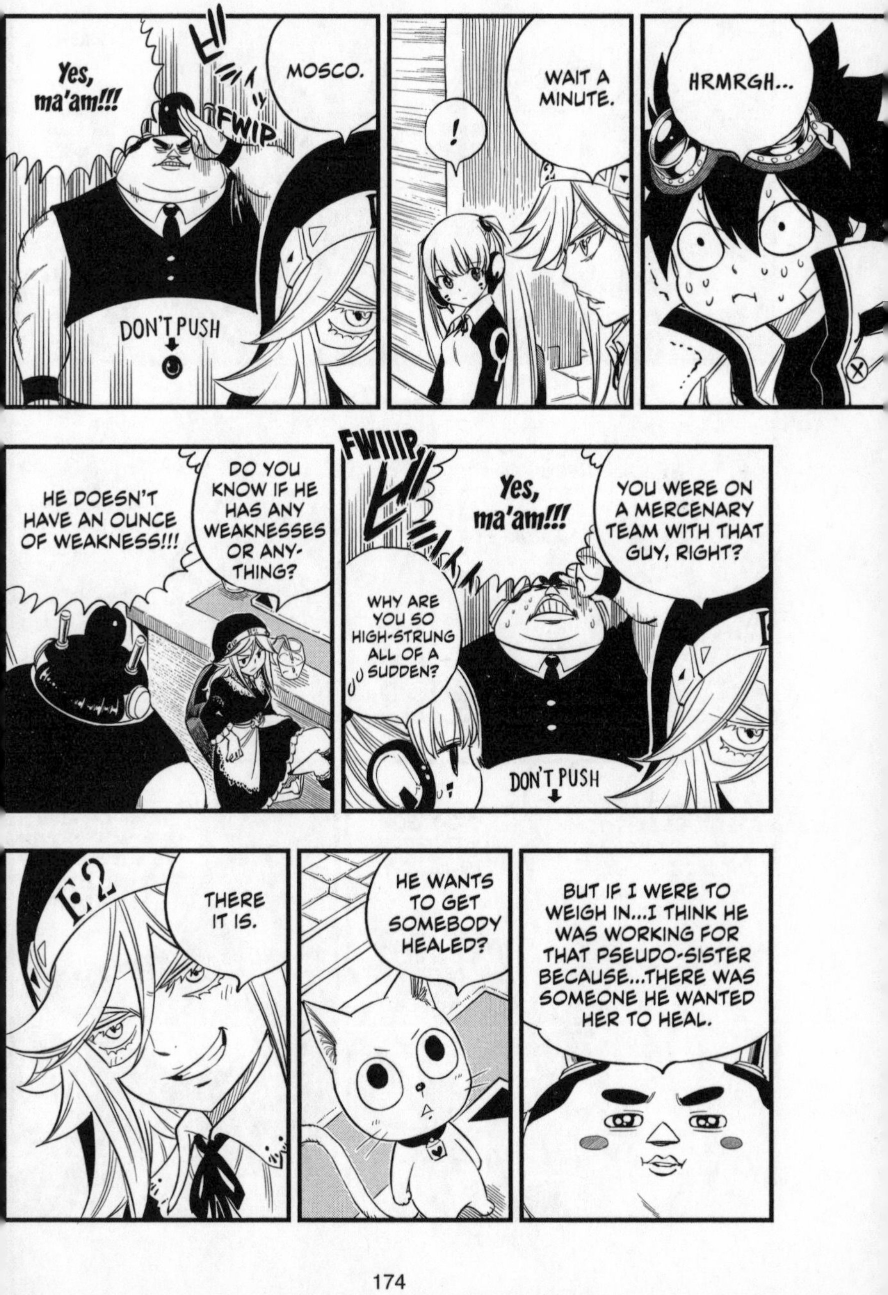
HRMRGH...
WAIT A MINUTE.
!
MOSCO.
FWIP
Yes, ma'am!!!
DON'T PUSH
YOU WERE ON A MERCENARY TEAM WITH THAT GUY, RIGHT?
Yes, ma'am!!!
FWIIIP
WHY ARE YOU SO HIGH-STRUNG ALL OF A SUDDEN?
DON'T PUSH
DO YOU KNOW IF HE HAS ANY WEAKNESSES OR ANY-THING?
HE DOESN'T HAVE AN OUNCE OF WEAKNESS!!!
BUT IF I WERE TO WEIGH IN...I THINK HE WAS WORKING FOR THAT PSEUDO-SISTER BECAUSE...THERE WAS SOMEONE HE WANTED HER TO HEAL.
HE WANTS TO GET SOMEBODY HEALED?
THERE IT IS.
E2

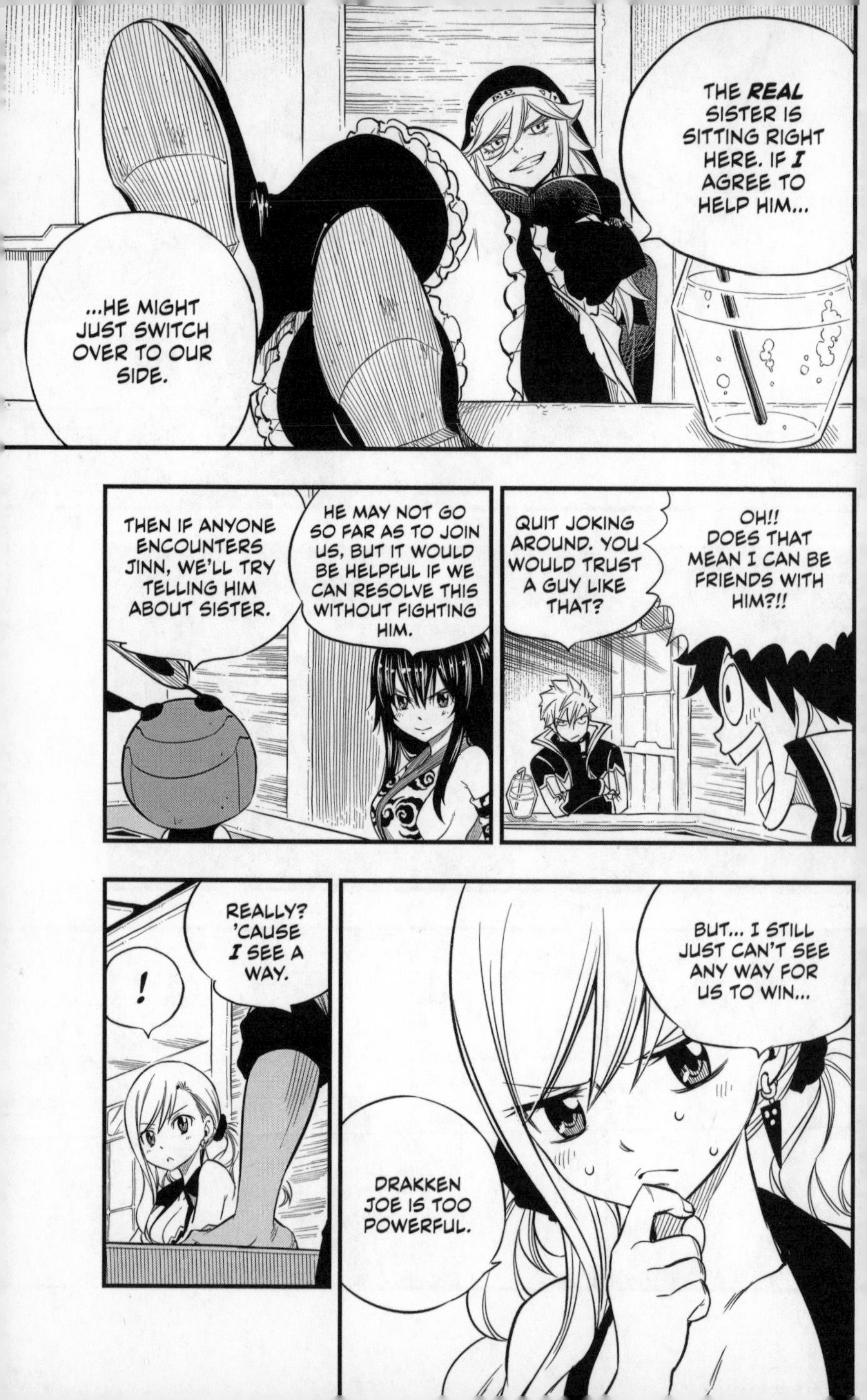
THE REAL SISTER IS SITTING RIGHT HERE. IF I AGREE TO HELP HIM...
...HE MIGHT JUST SWITCH OVER TO OUR SIDE.
OH!! DOES THAT MEAN I CAN BE FRIENDS WITH HIM?!!
QUIT JOKING AROUND. YOU WOULD TRUST A GUY LIKE THAT?
HE MAY NOT GO SO FAR AS TO JOIN US, BUT IT WOULD BE HELPFUL IF WE CAN RESOLVE THIS WITHOUT FIGHTING HIM.
THEN IF ANYONE ENCOUNTERS JINN, WE'LL TRY TELLING HIM ABOUT SISTER.
BUT... I STILL JUST CAN'T SEE ANY WAY FOR US TO WIN...
DRAKKEN JOE IS TOO POWERFUL.
REALLY? 'CAUSE I SEE A WAY.
!

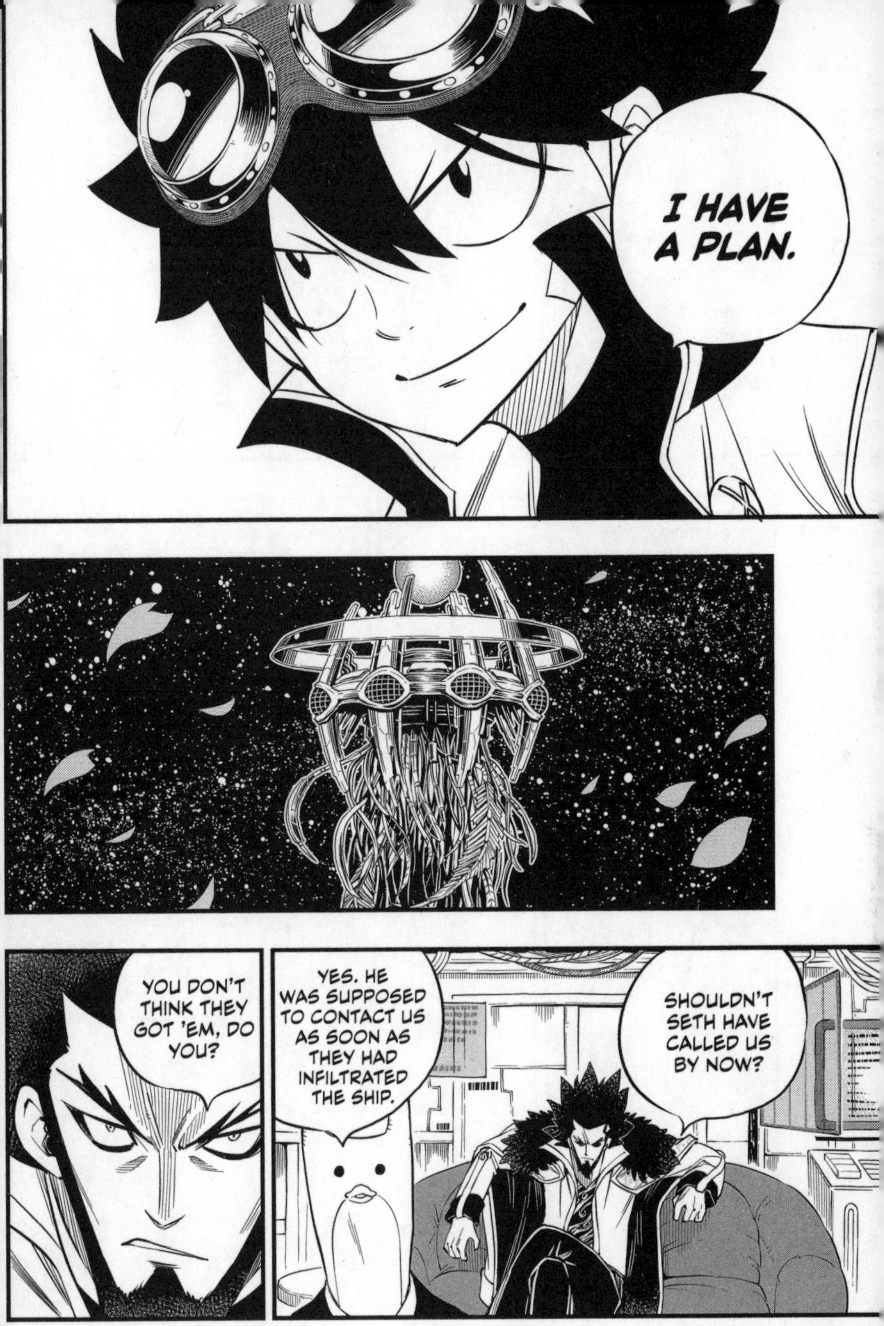
I HAVE A PLAN.
SHOULDN'T SETH HAVE CALLED US BY NOW?
YES. HE WAS SUPPOSED TO CONTACT US AS SOON AS THEY HAD INFILTRATED THE SHIP.
YOU DON'T THINK THEY GOT 'EM, DO YOU?

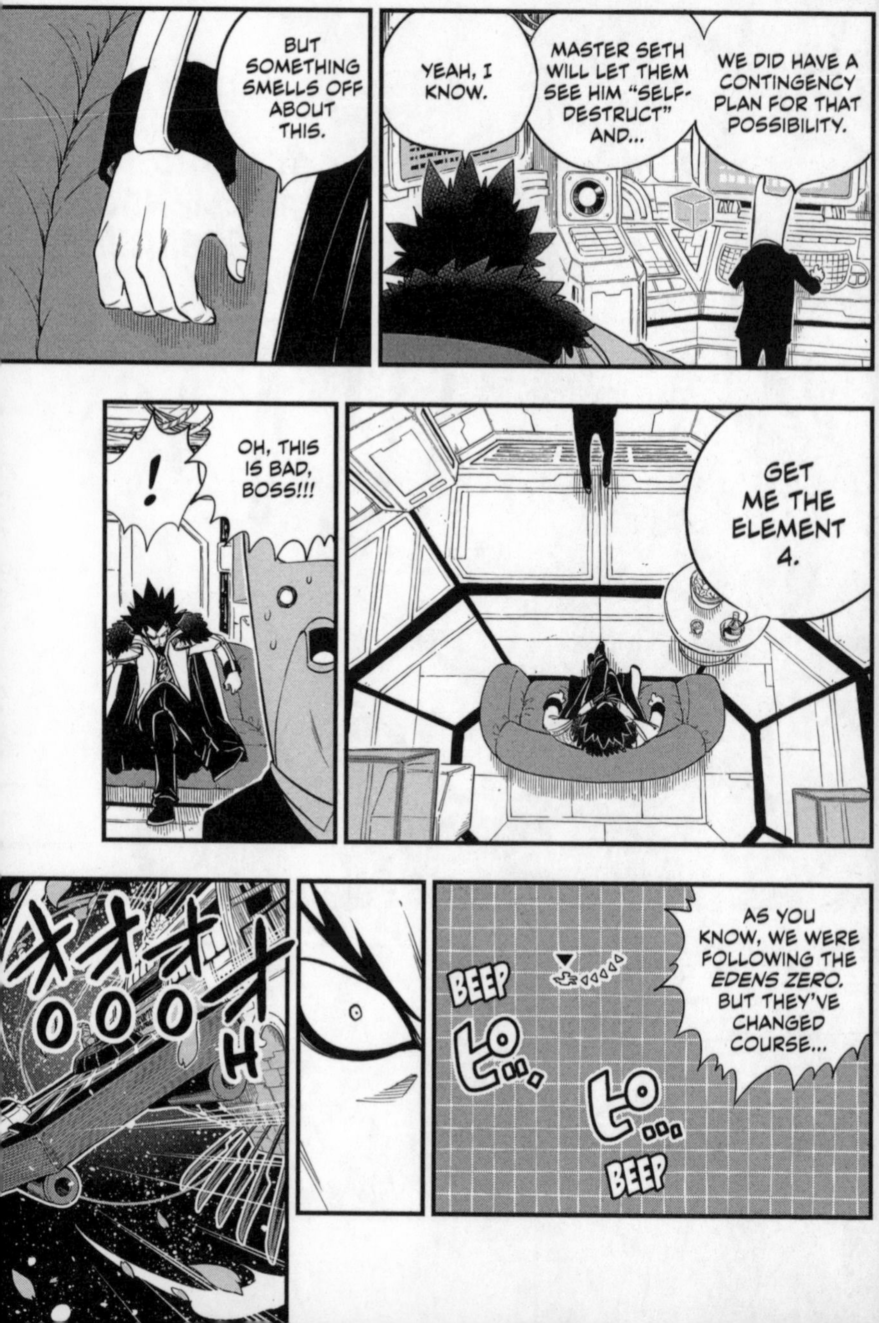
WE DID HAVE A CONTINGENCY PLAN FOR THAT POSSIBILITY.
MASTER SETH WILL LET THEM SEE HIM "SELF-DESTRUCT" AND...
YEAH, I KNOW.
BUT SOMETHING SMELLS OFF ABOUT THIS.
GET ME THE ELEMENT 4.
!
OH, THIS IS BAD, BOSS!!!
AS YOU KNOW, WE WERE FOLLOWING THE *EDENS ZERO.* BUT THEY'VE CHANGED COURSE...
BEEP
ピ
ピ
BEEP
オオオオ
OOOH

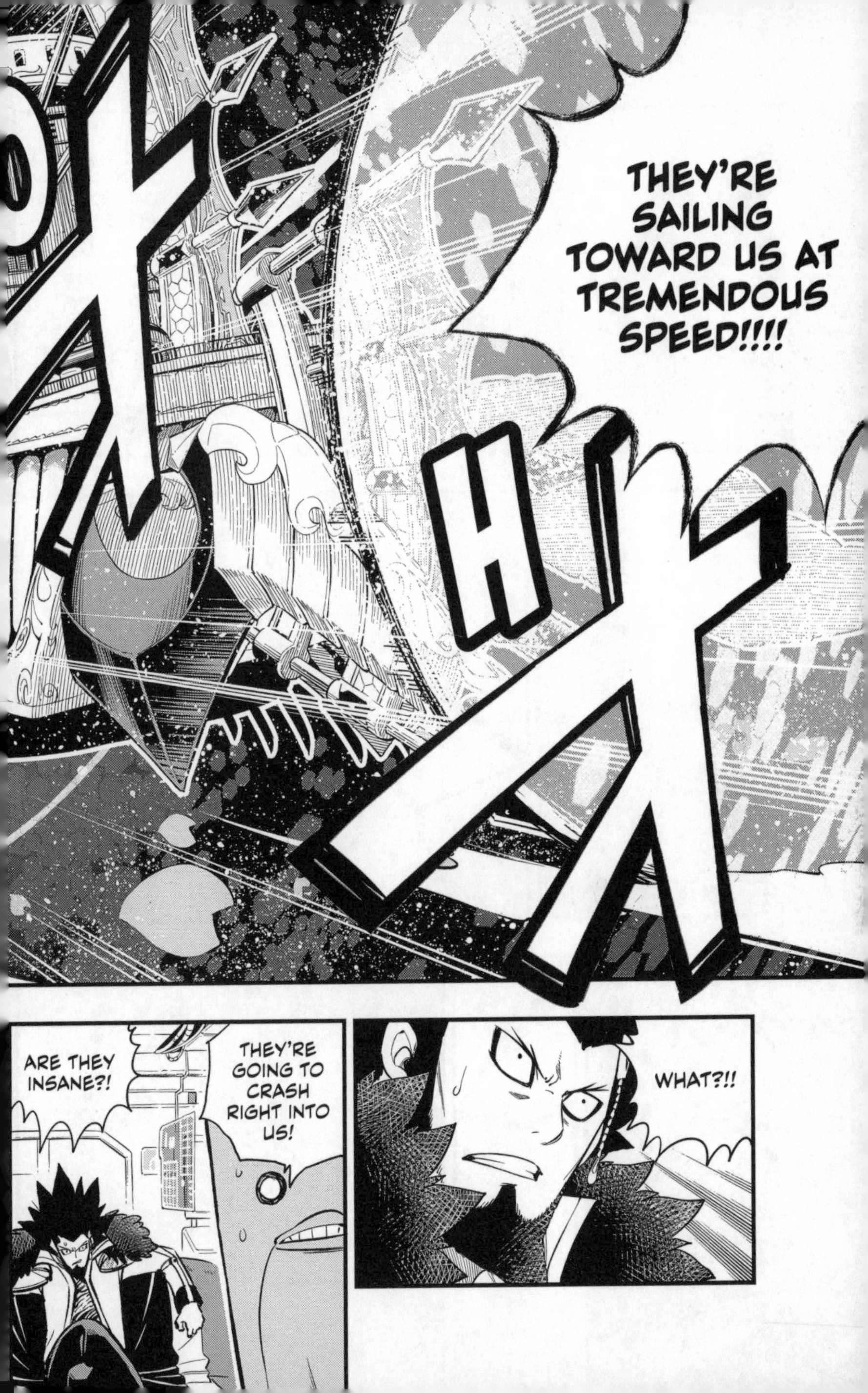
THEY'RE SAILING TOWARD US AT TREMENDOUS SPEED!!!!
WHAT?!!
THEY'RE GOING TO CRASH RIGHT INTO US!
ARE THEY INSANE?!

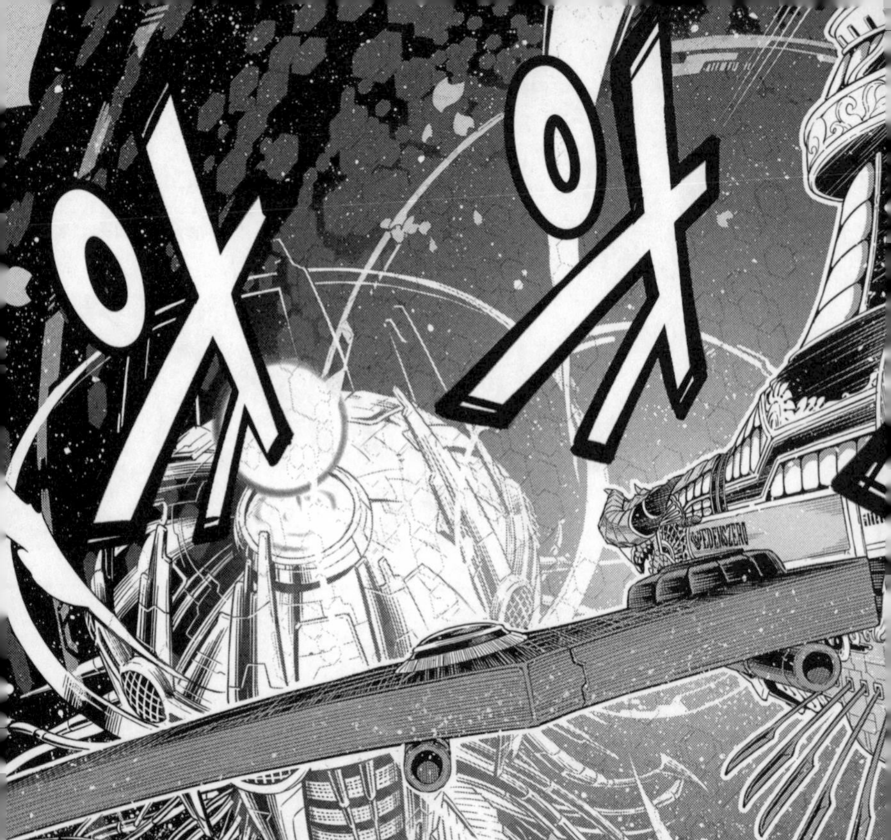

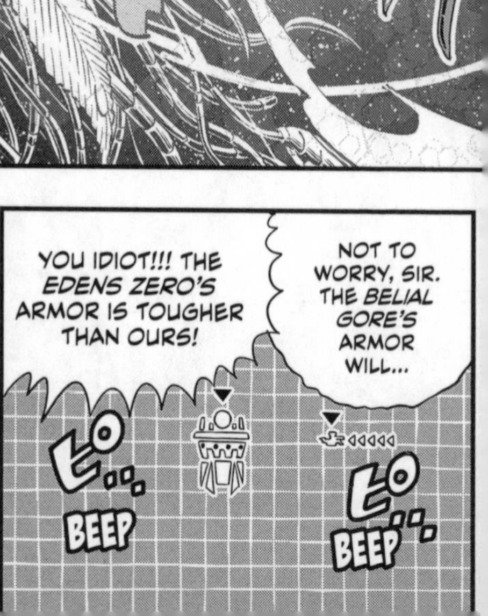
NOT TO WORRY, SIR. THE *BELIAL GORE'S* ARMOR WILL...
YOU IDIOT!!! THE *EDENS ZERO'S* ARMOR IS TOUGHER THAN OURS!
BEEP
BEEP

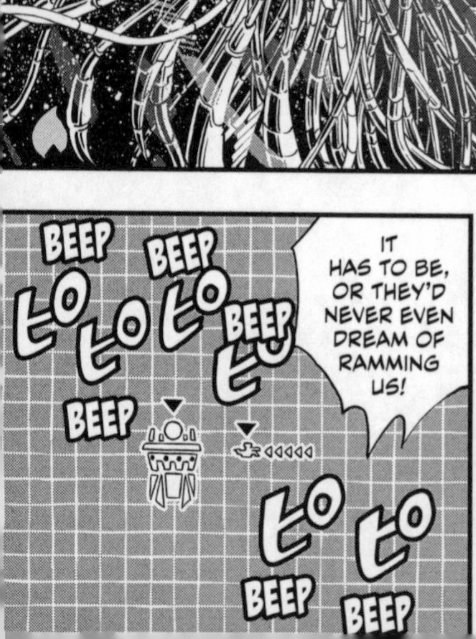
IT HAS TO BE, OR THEY'D NEVER EVEN DREAM OF RAMMING US!
BEEP
BEEP
BEEP
BEEP
BEEP
BEEP

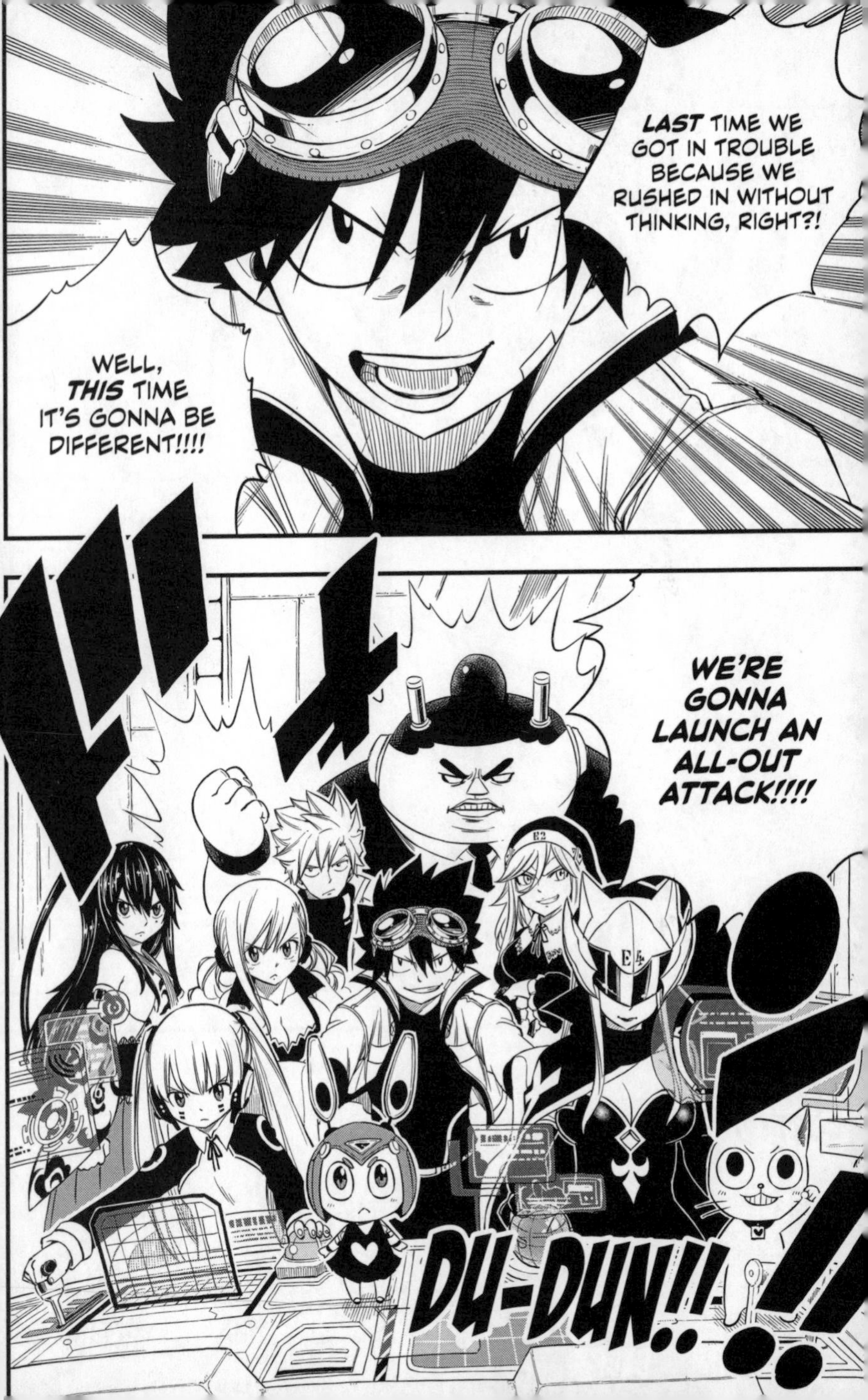
LAST TIME WE GOT IN TROUBLE BECAUSE WE RUSHED IN WITHOUT THINKING, RIGHT?!
WELL, THIS TIME IT'S GONNA BE DIFFERENT!!!!
WE'RE GONNA LAUNCH AN ALL-OUT ATTACK!!!!
DU-DUN!!

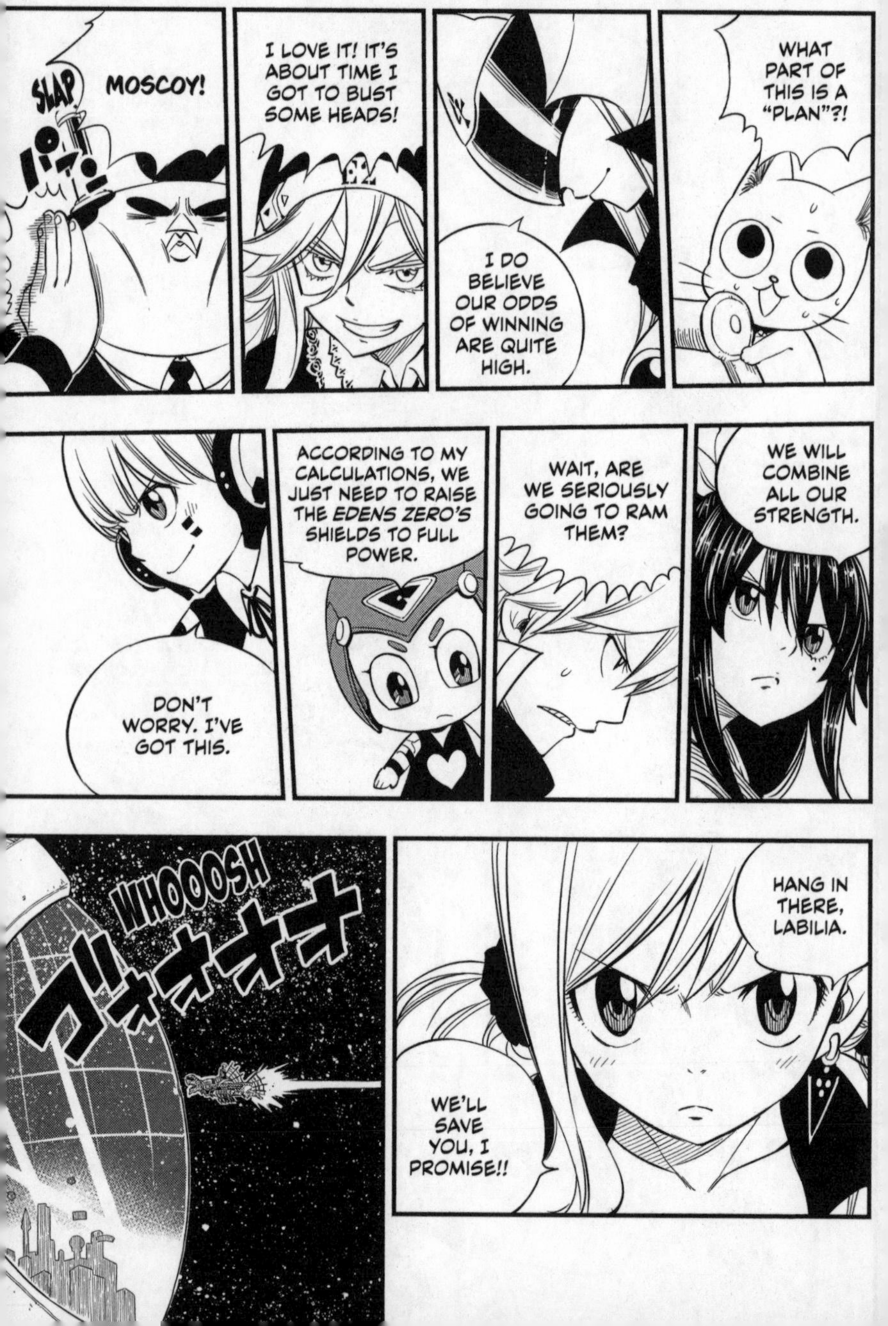
WHAT PART OF THIS IS A "PLAN"?!
I DO BELIEVE OUR ODDS OF WINNING ARE QUITE HIGH.
I LOVE IT! IT'S ABOUT TIME I GOT TO BUST SOME HEADS!
MOSCOY!
SLAP
WE WILL COMBINE ALL OUR STRENGTH.
WAIT, ARE WE SERIOUSLY GOING TO RAM THEM?
ACCORDING TO MY CALCULATIONS, WE JUST NEED TO RAISE THE *EDENS ZERO'S* SHIELDS TO FULL POWER.
DON'T WORRY. I'VE GOT THIS.
HANG IN THERE, LABILIA.
WE'LL SAVE YOU, I PROMISE!!
WHOOOSH
ゴォオオオ

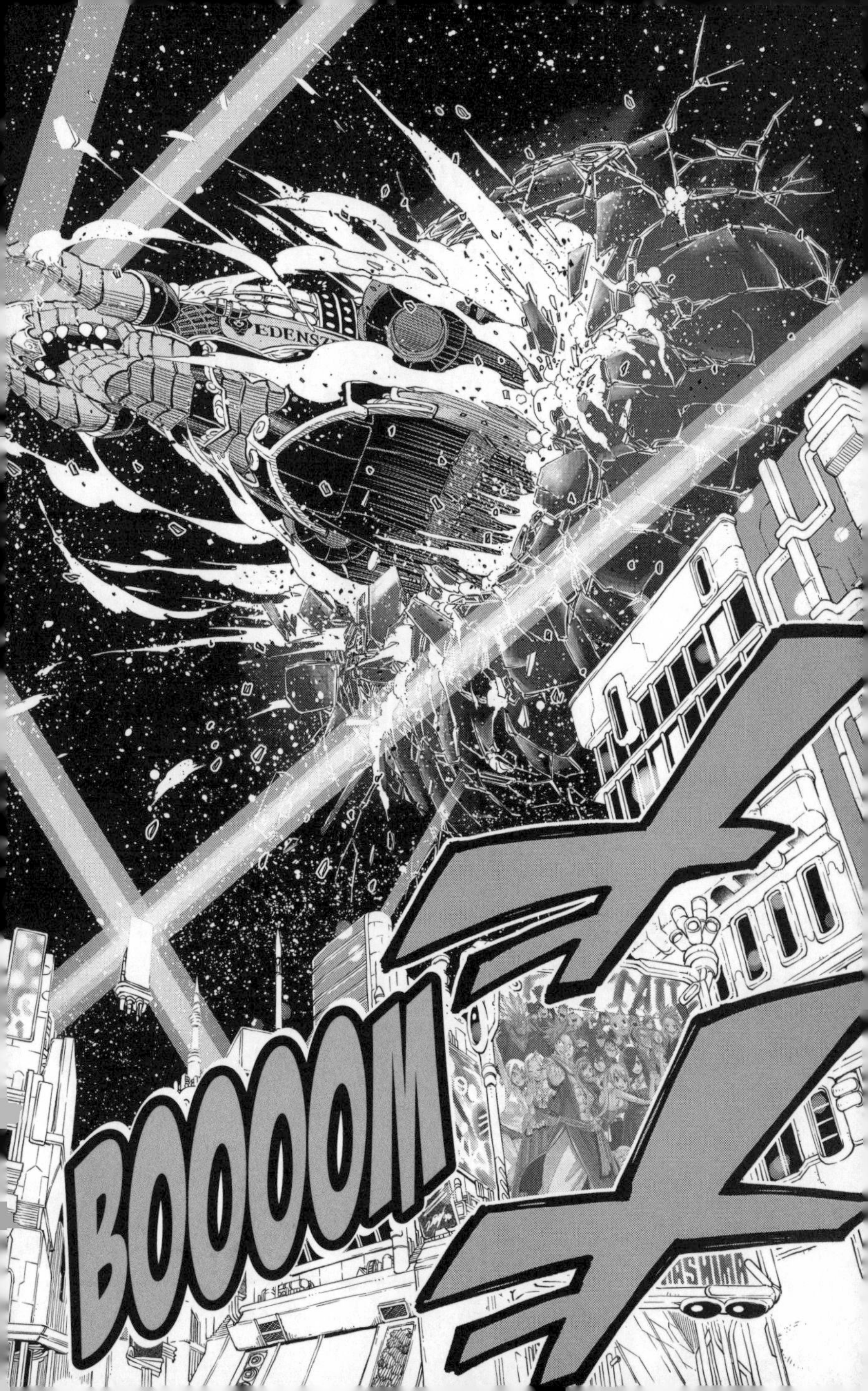
BOOOOM

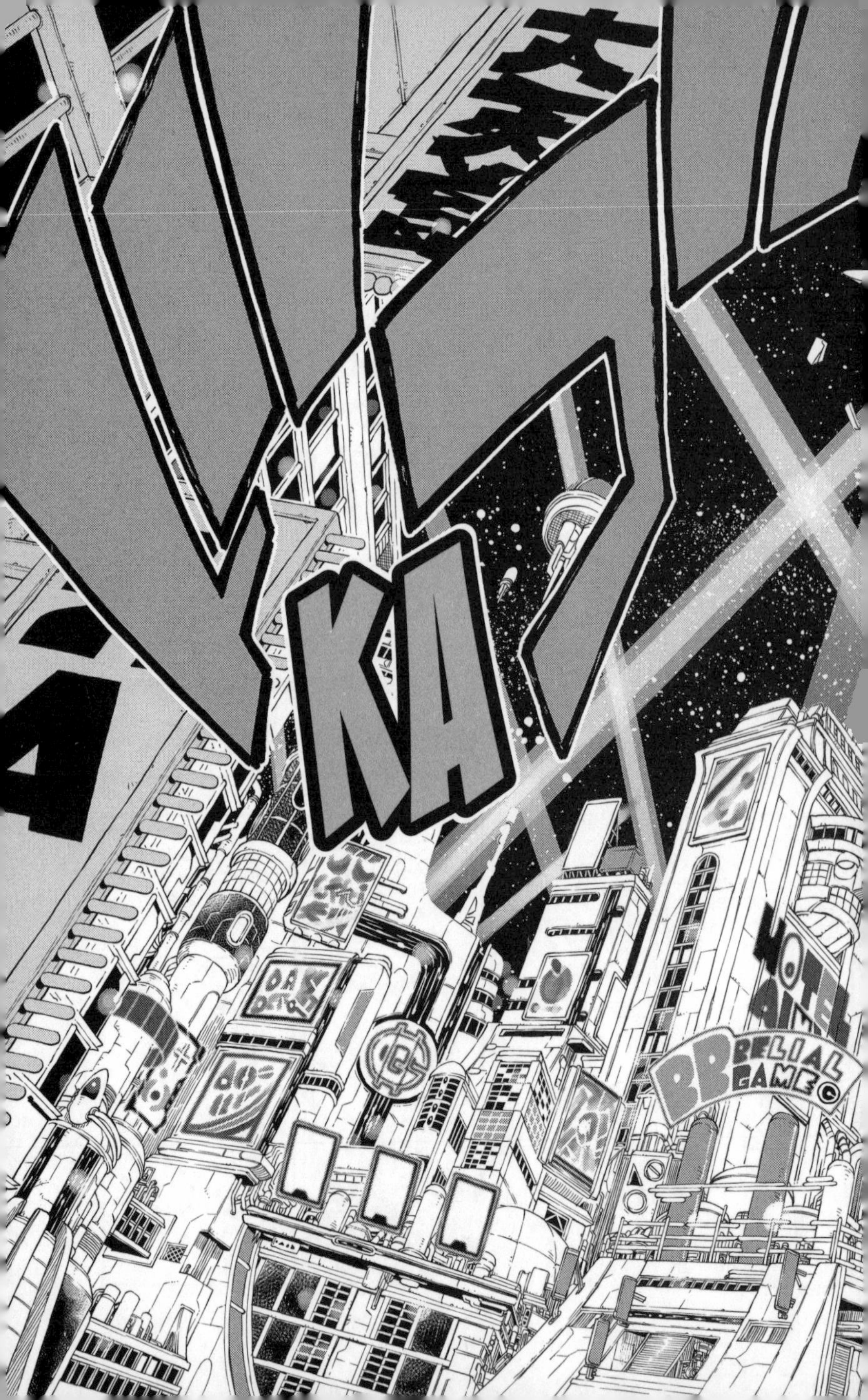
KA
HOTEL
BELIAL GAME

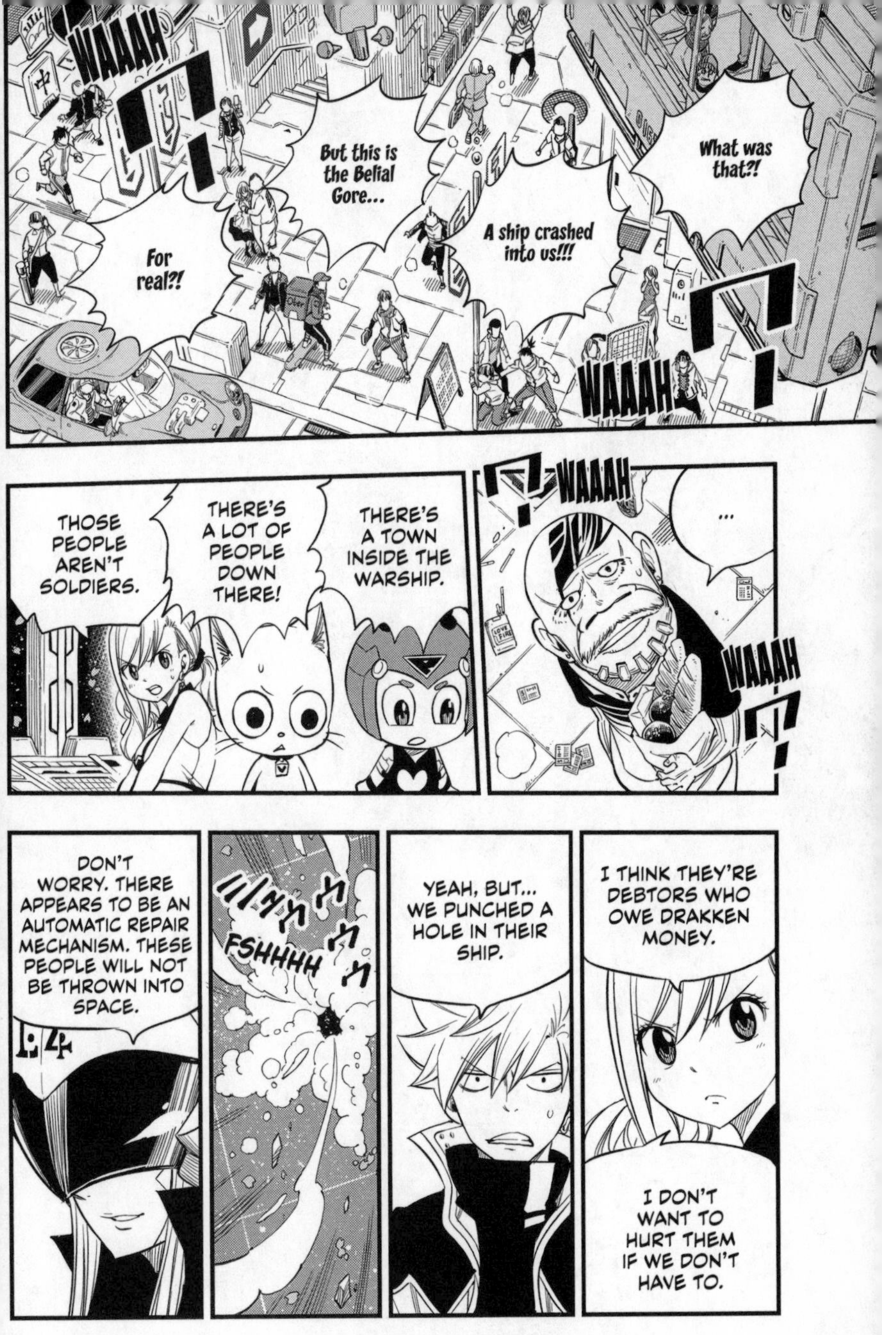
WAAAH
What was that?!
A ship crashed into us!!!
But this is the Belial Gore...
For real?!
WAAAH
WAAAH
...
WAAAH
THERE'S A TOWN INSIDE THE WARSHIP.
THERE'S A LOT OF PEOPLE DOWN THERE!
THOSE PEOPLE AREN'T SOLDIERS.
I THINK THEY'RE DEBTORS WHO OWE DRAKKEN MONEY.
I DON'T WANT TO HURT THEM IF WE DON'T HAVE TO.
YEAH, BUT... WE PUNCHED A HOLE IN THEIR SHIP.
FSHHHH
DON'T WORRY. THERE APPEARS TO BE AN AUTOMATIC REPAIR MECHANISM. THESE PEOPLE WILL NOT BE THROWN INTO SPACE.

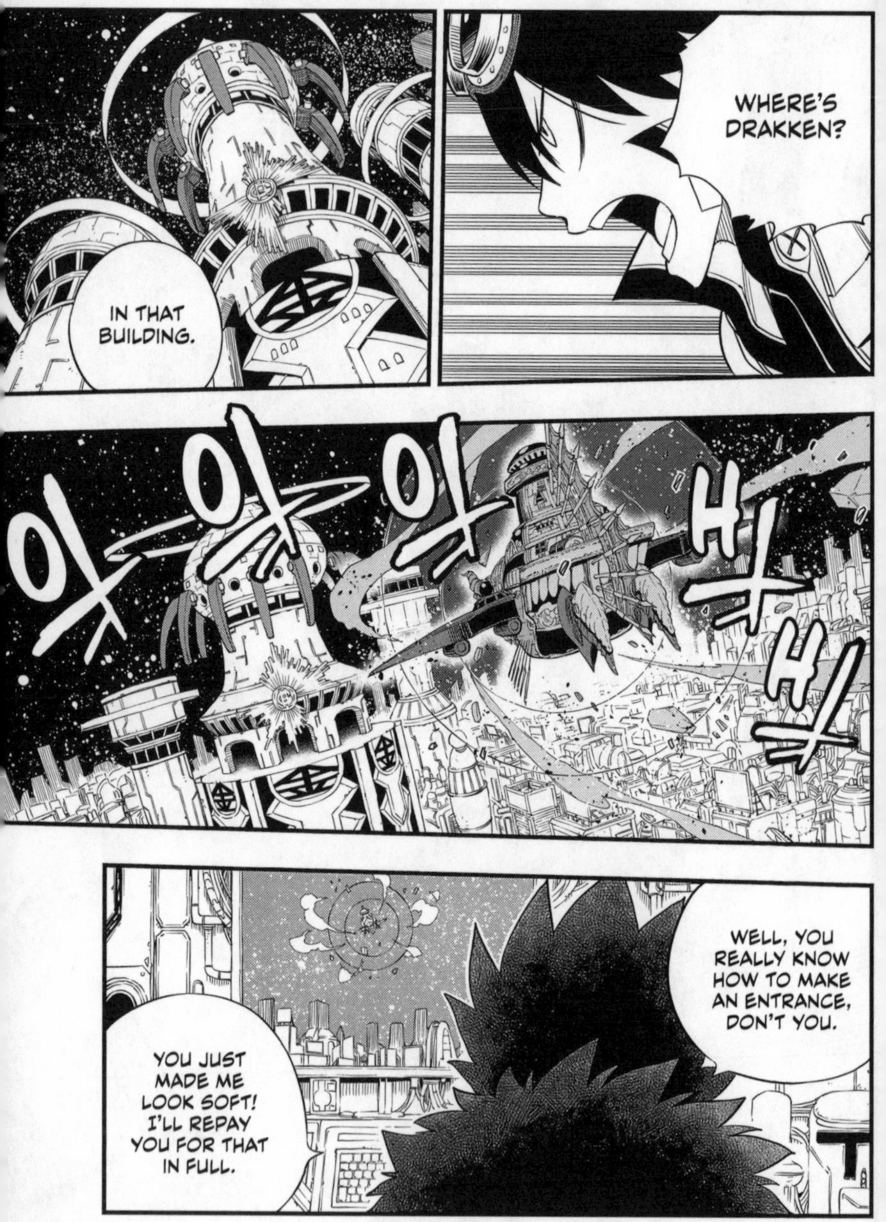
WHERE'S DRAKKEN?
IN THAT BUILDING.
WELL, YOU REALLY KNOW HOW TO MAKE AN ENTRANCE, DON'T YOU.
YOU JUST MADE ME LOOK SOFT! I'LL REPAY YOU FOR THAT IN FULL.

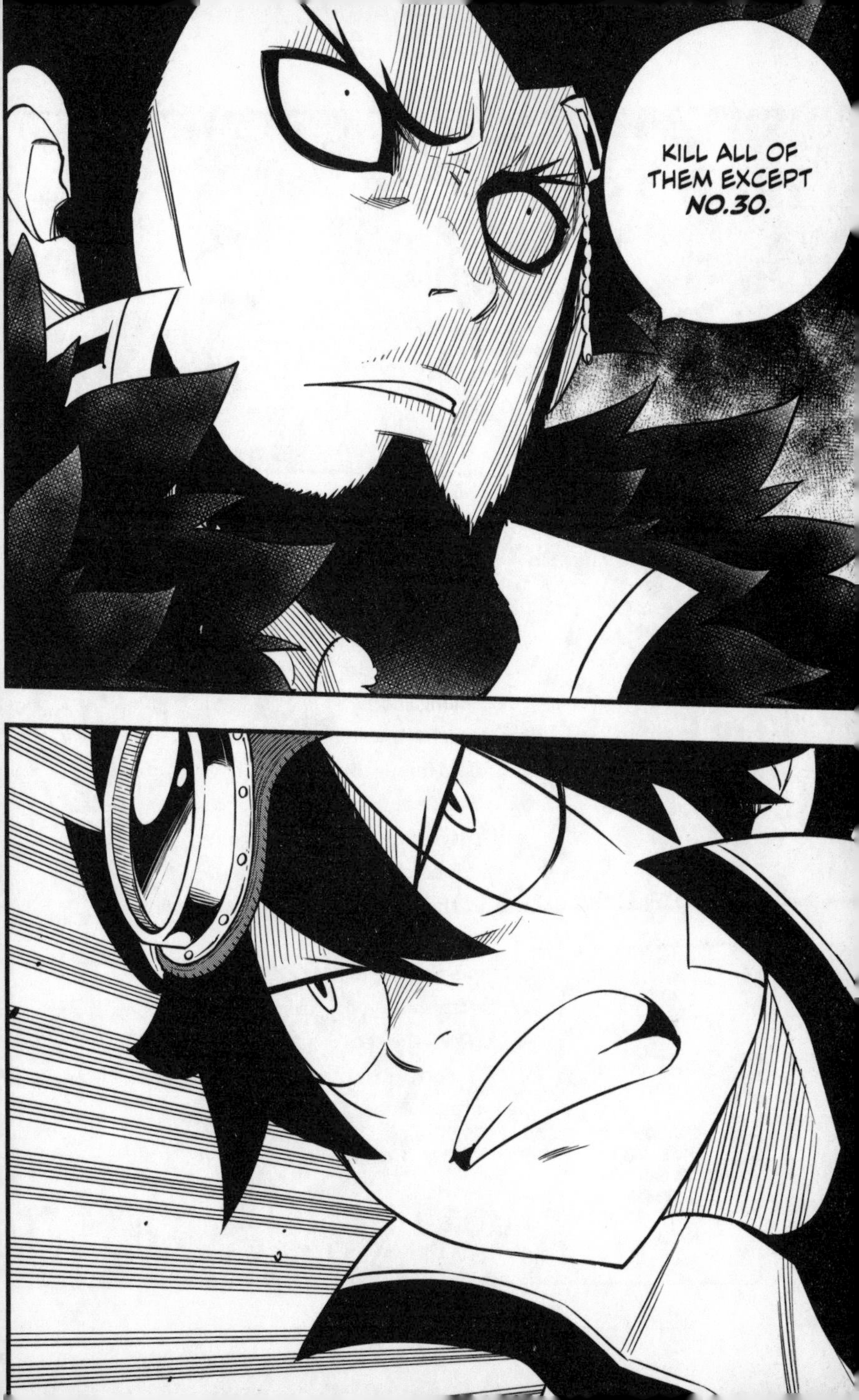
KILL ALL OF THEM EXCEPT NO.30.

AFTERWORD

We're getting an anime! That's great news! And it's thanks to all of your support. Thank you for always cheering us on. And now we can all look forward to the anime together!

I hope that Shiki's gravity fight scenes turn into some really awesome animation. I can't wait to see it!

There are a lot of other elements that could look really good in motion, like when Rebecca is fighting with her blasters, or the special effects in the Sakura Cosmos, so I'm really excited about this.

Personally, this is the third time my work has been animated, so I'm hoping to use my past experience to build a good rapport with the anime staff and participate in the process as a helpful partner.

Now then, as for the manga, some things happen in this volume that are pretty heavy, which is unusual for my series. There are some scenes that were even hard for me to draw. I could have gone on and shown more of those dark developments, but I decided to prioritize the series' inherent pop style and upbeat tempo, and get to the next part of the story relatively quickly. I think this may be one of those times where the taste of the author and the taste of the reader diverge, but this time, I chose story pacing.

There are a lot of series that use time leaps, so I think some of you may have predicted that this was going to happen, but actually, this is not just a time leap. I think the details will be revealed in the story later, but I can be pretty contrary, so I added a few new elements to the time leap trope to create something unique. I hope you have fun analyzing it and going, "Hmmm..." as you read the story.

WELCOME TO THE NEXT INSTALLMENT OF...

◀ 'TIS AWE-INSPIRING. 'TIS AWESOME-LOOKING. 'TIS A VERY PICTURESQUE DRAWING.

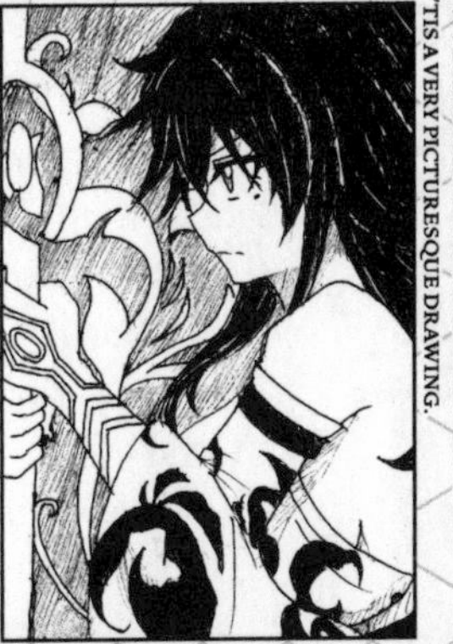

(SOTA SUZUKI-SAN, CHIBA)

◀ MASHIMA'S ONE-HIT KO

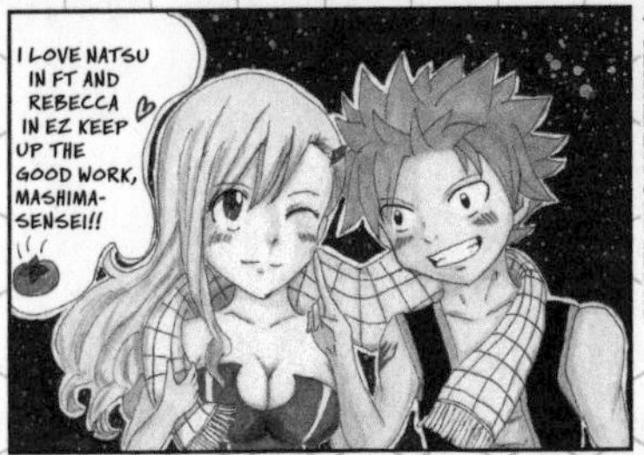
I LOVE NATSU IN FT AND REBECCA IN EZ KEEP UP THE GOOD WORK, MASHIMA-SENSEI!!

(KAMIO-SAN, OITA)

MASHIMA'S ONE-HIT KO

◀ THANKS FOR THE NEW CHARACTER SUGGESTION. MAYBE UNDER HER BANDAGES SHE HAS AN EYE THAT CAN CHARM DEMONS AND PUT THEM UNDER HER CONTROL.

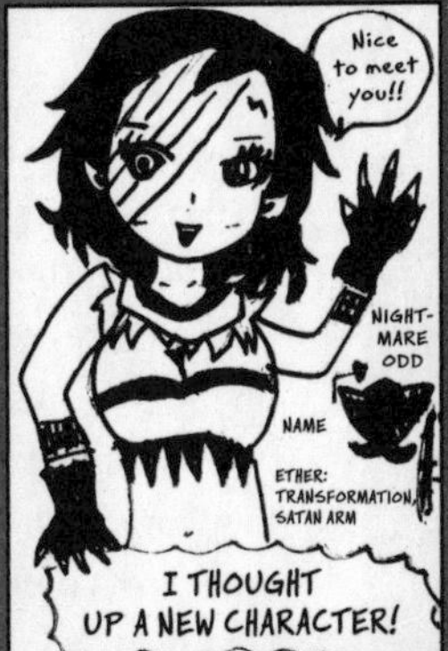
Nice to meet you!!
NIGHT-MARE ODD
NAME
ETHER: TRANSFORMATION, SATAN ARM
I THOUGHT UP A NEW CHARACTER!

(SALLY★-SAN, OITA)

◀ NICE. THEY'RE RIDING DOLPHINS ♪ HAPPY LOOKS VERY INTO SOMETHING... IS IT THE FISH?

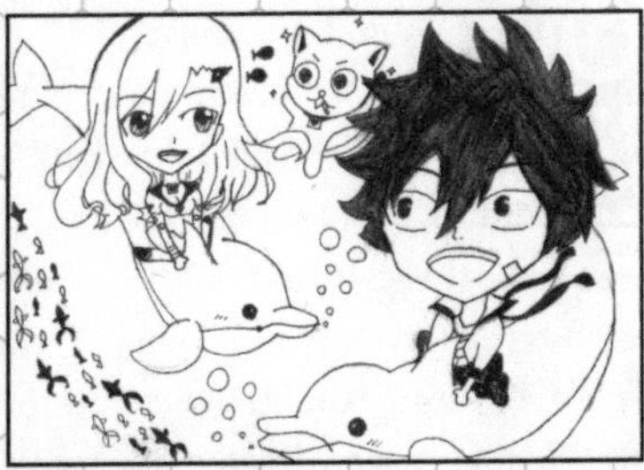

(YUKIYOKONKO-SAN, WAKAYAMA)

◀ I LOVE IT WHEN PEOPLE TELL ME THEIR FAVORITE SCENES. THANKS!

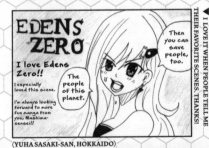

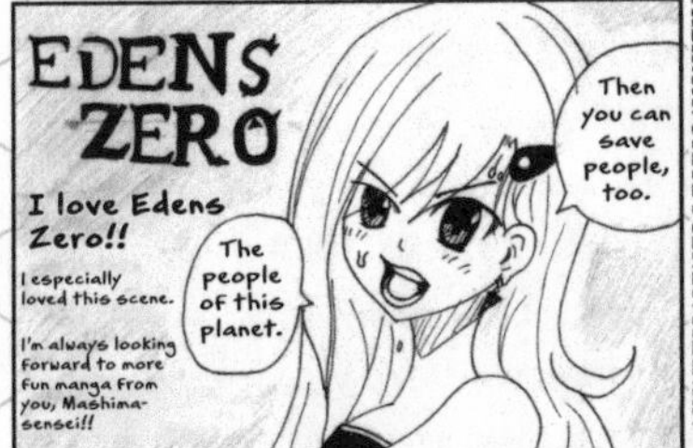
EDENS ZERO
I love Edens Zero!!
I especially loved this scene.
I'm always looking forward to more fun manga from you, Mashima-sensei!!
Then you can save people, too.
The people of this planet.

(YUHA SASAKI-SAN, HOKKAIDO)

EDITOR'S NOTE: DRAWING SUBMISSIONS LIMITED TO JAPAN.

ΞΞ DRAWING

(RYOKI NAKAJIMA-SAN, HOKKAIDO)

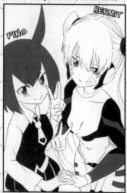

PINO

HERMIT

▲ THESE TWO VALUE THE HEART MORE THAN ANYONE. THEY HAVE A SOOTHING, HEARTWARMING EFFECT.

(HIROFUMI OKAJIMA-SAN, HYOGO)

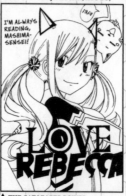

I'M ALWAYS READING, MASHIMA-SENSEI!

YAY!

LOVE REBECCA

▲ THE CAT LEAPER POWER AWAKENED. I HOPE YOU DO KEEP READING!

(SATOMI-SAN, FUKUOKA)

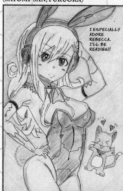

I ESPECIALLY ADORE REBECCA. I'LL BE READING!!

▲ CATS ARE GOOD, BUT SO ARE RABBITS. THE POWER OF A BUNNY IS GREAT ♥

(AYA-SAN, GIFU)

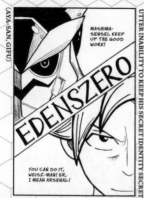

MASHIMA-SENSEI, KEEP UP THE GOOD WORK!

EDENSZERO

YOU CAN DO IT, WEISZ-MAN! ER, I MEAN ARSENAL!

▼ LOOK FORWARD TO MORE OF THIS HERO'S POINTLESSLY OBSESSING OVER HIS ACTION POSES AND UTTER INABILITY TO KEEP HIS SECRET IDENTITY SECRET

(LEONA-SAN, SAITAMA)

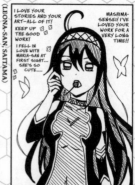

I LOVE YOUR STORIES AND YOUR ART—ALL OF IT! KEEP UP THE GOOD WORK!

I FELL IN LOVE WITH MARIA-SAN AT FIRST SIGHT... SHE'S SO CUTE....

MASHIMA-SENSEI! I'VE LOVED YOUR WORK FOR A VERY LONG TIME!!

▼ DID YOU LIKE HER IN SPACE SLIME FORM, TOO! HER STRETCHY LEGS WERE THE HINT.

Young characters and steampunk setting, like *Howl's Moving Castle* and *Battle Angel Alita*

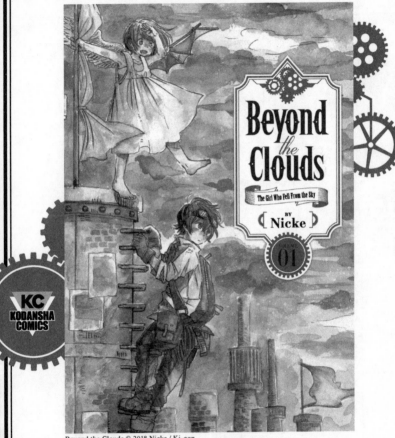

Beyond the Clouds
The Girl Who Fell From the Sky
BY Nicke
VOLUME 01

KC KODANSHA COMICS

A boy with a talent for machines and a mysterious girl whose wings he's fixed will take you beyond the clouds! In the tradition of the high-flying, resonant adventure stories of Studio Ghibli comes a gorgeous tale about the longing of young hearts for adventure and friendship!

The boys are back, in 400-page hardcovers that are as pretty and badass as they are!

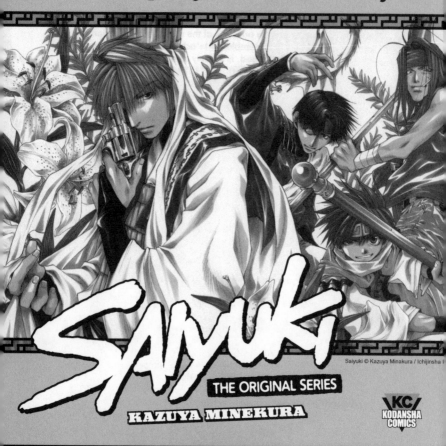

Saiyuki
THE ORIGINAL SERIES
KAZUYA MINEKURA

KC/
KODANSHA
COMICS

"AN EDGY COMIC LOOK AT AN ANCIENT CHINESE TALE." —YALSA

Genjo Sanzo is a Buddhist priest in the city of Togenkyo, which is being ravaged by yokai spirits that have fallen out of balance with the natural order. His superiors send him on a journey far to the west to discover why this is happening and how to stop it. His companions are three yokai with human souls. But this is no day trip — the four will encounter many discoveries and horrors on the way.

FEATURES NEW TRANSLATION, COLOR PAGES, AND BEAUTIFUL WRAPAROUND COVER ART!

EDENS ZERO 10 is a w...
places, and incidents are th...
or are used fictitiously. Any...
persons, living or...

A Kodansha Comics Trade Paperback Original
EDENS ZERO 10 copyright © 2020 Hiro Mashima
English translation copyright © 2020 Hiro Mashima

Published in the United States by Kodansha Comics, an imprint of
Kodansha USA Publishing, LLC, New York.

Publication rights for this English edition arranged through
Kodansha Ltd., Tokyo.

First published in Japan in 2020 by Kodansha Ltd., Tokyo.

ISBN 978-1-64651-037-5

Original cover design by Narumi Miura (G x complex).

Printed in the United States of America.

www.kodanshacomics.com

9 8 7 6 5 4 3 2 1
Translation: Alethea Nibley & Athena Nibley
Lettering: AndWorld Design
Editing: David Yoo
Kodansha Comics edition cover design by Phil Balsman

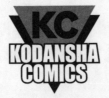

Publisher: Kiichiro Sugawara

Director of publishing services: Ben Applegate
Associate director of operations: Stephen Pakula
Publishing services managing editor: Noelle Webster
Assistant production manager: Emi Lotto, Angela Zurlo